U NU OF BURMA

U Nu of Burma

RICHARD BUTWELL

✻

STANFORD UNIVERSITY PRESS

STANFORD, CALIFORNIA

To

RENA, MARIE, *and* MARGARET,

three devoted aunts

Stanford University Press
Stanford, California
© 1963, 1969, by the Board of Trustees of the
Leland Stanford Junior University
Printed in the United States of America
First published 1963
Second printing, with a new concluding chapter, 1969
SBN 8047-0155-5
L C 76-97911

PREFACE

This is an account of a man in political life—a living man and one on whom history's pages have yet to close. This study was started when U Nu was out of office in 1959, and the research on it largely completed by the time he returned to power in 1960. U Nu left office again, involuntarily, in March 1962, literally days before the completion of the first draft of this book. When I visited Burma again in mid-1962 Nu was under detention, and it was said that he might be held prisoner until his legal parliamentary mandate expired in 1964. This sequence of events surely suggests caution in anticipating the future direction of Burma's political movement.

U Nu himself met with me in 1959–60, but this is by no means an authorized study. Nu was very helpful—as were other Burmese political figures, whose names are listed at the end of this book. Gratitude is expressed also to the U.S. Educational Foundation in Burma (Fulbright Program), the School of Advanced International Studies of the Johns Hopkins University, the University of Illinois Research Board, and St. Antony's College, Oxford, for financial and other assistance. The Defense Services Historical Research Institute, Rangoon, generously made its facilities available. Professor Fred von der Mehden of the University of Wisconsin offered much helpful advice during the year we were both involved in research in Burma. I am particularly grateful to those who read all or part of this book in manuscript form: Dr. Hugh Tinker of the School of Oriental and African Studies of the University of London, and Professors John Cady of Ohio University, Josef Silverstein of Wesleyan University, Frank Trager of New York University, Lucian W. Pye of the Massachusetts Institute of Technology, William C. Johnstone of the School of Advanced International Studies of the Johns Hopkins University, and Rupert Emerson of Harvard University. Dr. Hla Pe of the School of Oriental and African

Studies, U Thaw Kaung, Mr. Stanford Chain, and Daw Khin Khin Kha of the University of Rangoon, Daw Mya Thein, formerly of the U.S. Educational Foundation (Burma), Daw Khin Than Yin, U Wan Nyunt, and Mr. John Okell provided valuable translation assistance. U Htun Myaing, who headed the U.S. Educational Foundation (Burma) during 1959–60, rendered countless services then and subsequently. Daw Khin May Yi of the Foundation was also very helpful. I also received valuable assistance from numerous librarians in and outside Burma and from the staff and students of the Graduate Program of International Relations and the Department of History and Political Science at the University of Rangoon. Professor Tai Hung-chao, formerly my graduate assistant at the University of Illinois and now a member of the Department of Political Science at Wayne State University, helped me considerably, too. Miss Elaine Lasky of Stanford University Press should be thanked for her editorial work on the text of this book. Mrs. Catherine VonRiesen typed the manuscript with great patience. I remain, however, responsible for all errors of fact or judgment.

I should also like to thank Macmillan and Company Ltd., London, and St Martin's Press, New York, for permission to quote from Thakin Nu, *Burma under the Japanese,* and The Guardian Ltd., Rangoon, for permission to quote from Nu's *Man, the Wolf of Man.* I am indebted to Gordon N. Converse for the frontispiece, and to Wide World Photos, Inc., for various photographs as indicated in the insert.

PREFACE TO REVISED SECOND PRINTING

The release of U Nu from detention in 1966 and his subsequent service on the National Unity Advisory Board in 1968–69 (when he proposed a return to democratic political institutions in Burma) prompted me to add an additional chapter to the original text of this book. Except for half a dozen changes in Chapter 19, the text is unchanged from the original. Supplementary bibliographical material has also been added, covering both the years since 1962 and new studies of the earlier period. Since this book first appeared in 1963, I have twice revisited Burma—in 1964 and again in 1966.

R.B.

July 1969

CONTENTS

PART FOUR

End of an Era

Four pages of photographs follow p. 160.

PART ONE

❋

PRELUDE TO PROMINENCE

ONE

SATURDAY'S CHILD

FOR TWENTY YEARS after the completion of the British conquest in 1886, Burma was politically quiescent. But nationalism was stirring below the surface. In 1906, a year after Japan's victory over Russia showed Asia that the European powers were not invincible, a group of Burmese university students founded the Young Men's Buddhist Association (YMBA). The days of colonialism were numbered.

Economically, the years after 1886 were dynamic years in Burma. The delta region of lower Burma was rapidly transformed in appearance and importance by the extension of wet rice farming. Cultivators and moneylenders alike rushed to what had formerly been wastelands. The Burmese economy, previously self-sufficient, became dependent on exports—various minerals and timber as well as rice.

The delta district of Myaungmya, where the Irrawaddy River splits into many mouths, was mainly jungle until the early 1890's. Its population, which was only 85,000 in 1881, jumped to more than 185,000 by 1891 and to over 278,000 a decade later. The village of Wakema, situated on the Irrawaddy about fifty miles from the provincial capital of Rangoon, was not officially a town according to the 1901 census, but it grew enough in the next decade to be recorded as a "new town," with a population of 7,031, in 1911. It was in this community of some twelve hundred bamboo dwellings that a first son was born on May 25, 1907, to U San Htun and his wife, Daw Saw Khin, Burmans* both, whose occupation was selling supplies to *pongyis* (Buddhist monks).

Saturday-born first children are supposed to be quarrelsome, and

* Burmans, the predominant ethnic group in Burma, comprise nearly 75 per cent of the total population. Other important ethnic groups are Karens (7 per cent), Shans (6 per cent), Indians, Hindu and Muslim (4 per cent), Kachins (2 per cent), Chins (2 per cent), and Chinese (2 per cent).

hence, after consultation with local astrologers, U San Htun and Daw Saw Khin chose the antidotal name of Nu, meaning "gentle" or "soft," in order to propitiate the *nats,* or spirits.

Since a Saturday first-born might bring about the separation or even the death of its parents, Maung* Nu's grandmother prevailed upon an aunt, Daw Gyi, to buy the boy from his mother for a small sum and make him her own son in order to confuse the *nats,* who might otherwise perpetrate trouble.[1] This was in some ways a token arrangement only, since Daw Gyi, her husband, and Maung Nu's real parents lived together in the same household.

The town of Wakema in which Maung Nu grew up was the administrative center of Wakema township and the largest town in Myaung-mya district. Located in rich rice country, it was independent of the outside world for its requirements during much of the year. With the harvest, however, came the broker, the shipper, and the peddler, and contact was re-established with the world beyond Wakema. At this time of year traveling Burmese folk-opera troupes visited the town, and Maung Nu's father, a fine singer, was sometimes asked to perform with them.

Wet rice farming was the chief occupation in Wakema. Of the 139,000 acres of land under cultivation in the township, over 132,000 were devoted to rice. Tenancy was widespread in Myaungmya district, and Nu's uncle, U Shwe Gon, a major landowner, let a large portion of his land. Nu's aunt was also quite wealthy in her own right, having won a large sum of money in a British sweepstakes lottery.[2]

The first decade of Nu's life appears to have been normal, happy, and seemingly richer as a consequence of the birth of a second son to his parents, their only other child. Born a year after Nu, the brother, whom Nu found a most enjoyable companion, was called Oo.

Although Nu's parents were pious, he did not have a notably religious upbringing. He and Oo entered a monastery as novitiates before they were ten;[3] they also took lessons in Buddhism from *pongyis* and visited famous pagodas with their parents. But these activities were expected of all Buddhist boys in Burma, and seem to have been perfunctory for Nu. Indeed, contrary to the strict injunctions of Burmese

---

* The first element of all Burmese names, both male and female, is a prefix indicating age or status. A boy is "Maung," a young man "Ko," and an older or important man "U." "Ma" is the prefix for a young woman's name, and "Daw" for that of an older woman or one of distinct accomplishment or social status. The boundaries between these prefixes are not firm.

Buddhism, the boy developed a taste for alcohol at the age of nine, and by the age of twelve was a confirmed drunkard.[4] He has described this phase of his life in a third-person autobiographical preface to his novel titled *Man, the Wolf of Man.*

> In his native town the nickname of "Tate Sanetha," "Saturday-born street Arab," was well known to everybody. The owner of this unsavory appellation was a nine-year-old boy, bad beyond his years. Already he was a boon companion of drunkards. By the age of twelve he was a heavy drinker. Often, as a sequel to his drinking bouts, his stupefied little body might be seen carried home on somebody's shoulder. His father, deeply ashamed and hopeless of reclaiming him, could only banish him to live as he would in a paddy godown outside the town. The boy brewed his own liquor there.[5]

His fellow drunkards were mostly men many years his senior, who impressed him with their swaggering manner. He took pride in doing things other boys his age did not dare to do. The fact that his uncle and adopted mother—and his real mother, too—tended to spoil him also probably contributed to the youth's shortcomings;[6] Nu himself has said that he was "a pampered boy."[7] His father and other members of the household tried to win Nu from his drinking, but to no avail.

At last, however, he came to his senses.

> At the age of eighteen something deep down inside him suddenly changed. . . . Beauty in things claimed his heart. A cool moonlight night, a verdant prospect, pretty women, sweet music began to move him profoundly. Whenever he was so moved by things of beauty he wanted to be alone with his joy. Such joy is known only to those who have experienced it. Disturbed from such a state the unfortunate devotee of beauty was distraught. That was why he could not suffer anyone to disturb him.[8]

The youthful Nu had a "secret talisman"—a photograph of a Burmese bride-to-be cut from an English-language newspaper. By his own admission, it had an extraordinary influence on him. "It inspired him with thoughts, he wanted to do good deeds, champion the weak, subdue the oppressors, like a knight of chivalry."[9] Resolved to reform, he set himself tasks like forgoing a meal or two and sitting in the sun for an hour. His shortcomings diminished within the year, "and the scorn of others lessened."[10] He later credited his reform in part to the growing influence of Buddhism. Buddhism gave him "a new sense of values," stemming from "an urge for the fulfillment of *paramis*," or Buddhist ideals.[11]

Moved by such influences, Maung Nu stopped his drinking in his eighteenth year after taking a vow of abstinence for a period of five years. He kept this vow for seven years, but resumed drinking at the age of twenty-five before finally giving it up altogether when he was twenty-seven. Subsequently, he avoided even medicines containing alcohol.

Nu was by no means altogether irresponsible in his early teens, however. Even at that time he was strongly moved by the inequity of British rule, and he took responsibility for instructing younger students in the "national school" established in Wakema as a result of the nation-wide student boycott of 1920.

His political sentiments had their roots in the influence of his father. Limited in formal education, U San Htun was an intelligent local politician, an early member of the YMBA, and later a Wakema leader of the General Council of Burmese Associations (GCBA), the first avowedly political nationalist organization in the country.[12] He was, by all accounts, an impressive man—physically handsome and a capable public speaker. Although he was only a small-town trader and not wealthy, his personality seems to have qualified him for membership in the local elite, no small accomplishment in comparatively well-off Wakema.[13] Moreover, he was a man of some vision. His intense patriotism did not prevent him from admiring the high standards of a British education, and he had come to regret his own inability to read English (though he could read and write Burmese). Anti-British though he was, he sent Nu to a government school.[14]

Nu's mother, Daw Saw Khin, was a simple, pious woman. She was illiterate but appreciated, too, the value of education, and sacrificed in many ways to aid the schooling of both Nu and Oo. She was not stern, and influenced her sons "more by example than by precept."[15]

Nu was a somewhat sickly child but grew into a physically fit young man and a good athlete. He was fond of singing and dancing and remained so in his adult years despite the austerity of other aspects of his life. Like most children, he had his share of accidents, including one in which he nearly drowned in the river near his home. He grew up, in short, like many another Burmese boy—except for his drinking and, more important, his early introduction to politics and nationalism.

This early world of Maung Nu was to leave its indelible imprint on a boy whose name meant "gentleness," but who was not destined to live in gentle times.

The Young Men's Buddhist Association, with which U San Htun was associated, played an important role in the development of Burmese nationalism, but until 1917 its activities were only indirectly political. In that year Britain's announcement of a policy of gradual development of self-governing institutions for India was greeted with joy by Burmese nationalists, who interpreted the policy as applicable to Burma as a province of India. But their hopes were dashed when the Government of India Act, ultimately introduced in the British Parliament in 1919, applied only to India proper. This sequence of events jolted Burma politically, and in 1920 the YMBA resolved to convert itself into the decidedly political GCBA.[16]

The British subsequently capitulated to Burmese demands, and governmental reforms comparable to those introduced in India were inaugurated in Burma in 1923. The flames of nationalism had been vigorously fanned, however, and the first nationwide expression of Burmese nationalist sentiment, the student boycott of 1920, had already taken place. Nu has said of it, "The most important early influence shaping my life in a political sense was the 1920 boycott. . . . I became politically conscious, as it were, overnight. I was then thirteen years old. The cries for freedom—freedom from [the] British yoke—thrilled me."[17]

The spark that touched off the school strike of 1920 was Britain's University Act of 1920, which elevated Rangoon College to university status. Burmese nationalists objected that the proposed higher (and more restrictive) standards would adversely affect their drive for self-government by limiting the number of University students and thus the size of the emerging nationalist elite, and that Britain sought to keep Burma a colony by controlling the educational system. The result was a nationwide anti-British protest of unparalleled dimensions, which led to the establishment of "national schools," schools designed to provide an education that was Burmese in orientation and to demonstrate the competence of the Burmese to educate their children.

At the time the strike broke out Maung Nu was a student in the Fifth Standard* of the Wakema Anglo-Vernacular Government School. Like the other students at the school, and thousands more throughout the country, he joined the boycott. When the year-long strike ended, Nu enrolled at the new national school in Wakema, where "the political spark ignited in my breast by the boycott movement gradually developed into a flame."[18]

The Wakema national school, which was housed in a monastery,

* Before the Second World War there were three levels of schools in Burma: primary (ages 6–10), middle (11–14), and high (15–18). The Fifth Standard is the first year of middle school.

lacked adequate financial support, and U San Htun and others had to work hard to keep it going. San Htun felt he had to enroll Nu in the school,[19] even though this inevitably meant an inferior education for the boy. Nu's favorite subjects were history and Burmese, and he read widely on his own during the vacations. His teachers, ill-paid but enthusiastic young men in their late teens and early twenties, lectured their students mainly about the glories of the Burmese past and the contrasting humiliations of imperial domination. The students were encouraged to feel that they were playing a part in the nationalist struggle by their very attendance at a national school. Some, like Nu, were drafted to teach the younger boys.[20]

Nu's nationalist education coincided with the introduction of new governing arrangements in Burma. A British parliamentary act of 1921, which came into effect on January 2, 1923, provided for a partly elected legislature, but supreme authority still lay with the government in India, which retained control over "central subjects." Under the new system for governing the province of Burma, called dyarchy (two-part division of executive authority), most powers were "reserved" to the British Governor and only minor powers were to be exercised by ministers responsible to the legislature. This was unacceptable to some Burmese leaders, and at a conference in 1921 of certain leading nationalist figures the words "within the empire" were deleted from a resolution proclaiming the desirability of early fulfillment of the objective of home rule. The independence movement was under way.

The Burmese nationalists, however, were plagued with a phenomenon that was to characterize the politics of their country for decades to come: internal differences that seem almost inevitably in Burma to lead to party splintering. The GCBA, divided in its response to the British change of policy, split into several factions—one of which, the Twenty-One Party, put up candidates for the elections of 1922, which the GCBA boycotted. Representatives of both points of view came to Wakema and were quartered in the resting houses of the pagodas, with the result that Maung Nu had an opportunity to view the politicians at close range. Nu himself raised several questions at a meeting held by the Twenty-One Party and addressed by the politician U Ba Si.[21] These were young Nu's first public political remarks.

Nu's initial act of agitation in the protest phase of Burmese nationalist politics had taken place a year earlier during the visit to Wakema of the Burma Reforms Investigatory Committee headed by Sir A. Frederick Whyte. The GCBA boycotted the Whyte committee, and only a few politicians participated in its hearings. The police tried to protect the launch carrying the members of the committee when it docked at Wakema, but a crowd of national-school teachers and students broke through the cordon, surrounded the launch, shouted anti-British slogans, and threw a few stones. The committee hastily departed. Nu "was among the most vociferous youngsters who shouted political slogans . . . [and] discharged their youthful exuberance upon the Whyte committee, members of which we regarded as agents and stooges of British imperialism."[22]

Maung Nu was to learn more about British imperialism, mostly its shortcomings, before he finished his national-school education. After completing the Seventh Standard (with honors), he left the Wakema school to become a student at the best-known of the national schools established in the wake of the 1920 student boycott, the Myoma National High School in Rangoon. The first boy from Wakema to go to Myoma, he left for Rangoon in the spring of 1922, dressed in jacket and *longyi* (skirt) of coarse homespun cloth and wearing his long hair in the traditional top knot.

The Myoma National High School in Rangoon was one of the few national schools to survive beyond the early 1920's. Financial difficulties closed most of the others by the end of 1922;[23] most of the rest held classes in the poorly equipped *pongyi kyaungs,* or monasteries. The Myoma National School amounted to no more than several makeshift wooden structures, but even this was far better than most of the national schools. The main building, where classes were held and where some of the boarders lived, was "a big hut," according to those who taught and studied there at the time. There were about four hundred boys enrolled, most of them day students.

"While at Myoma National High School," Nu has said, "I was still a devil-may-care fellow. I was seized by a burning desire to champion the cause of the weak and the maltreated. I continued to carry out the self-imposed duty of fighting, both in verbal and physical senses, anyone guilty of highhandedness and injustice, be he an insider or an outsider, be he of comparable strength or of a stronger frame. Probably that was my main interest."[24] One of his classmates, a husky fellow, took to eating the scraps left on the other boys' plates at the end of the evening meal, thus usurping the prerogative of the underfed tableboys. Nu intervened for the tableboys, and a vigorous exchange of blows ensued. The two boys were called before the headmaster and whipped.[25]

Maung Nu was also a good student, although not one of the best.

He studied Burmese and English history, the Burmese and English languages, and geography. He was best in history, but he improved his English considerably—he even took to writing plays in English. He was a member of the students' union, the boarders' union, the debating society, and a few other groups, but took little interest in their activities. He was a good boxer and played some football (soccer).

Nu's thoughts during these years were not especially political. Classmates[26] agree that Nu was not yet "really politically conscious," though his close friend U Thein Han recalls that "we were at least sufficiently alert politically to want to do errands for the nationalist politicians—and that sort of thing." Nor was Nu more than ordinarily concerned with events beyond Burma's borders. He has said that he was "aware of events outside Burma, and of men like Gandhi and Sun Yat-sen, but not to the extent of falling under the influence of any country or any man."[27]

Nu describes his career aspirations as he completed his studies at Myoma National High School in these words: "Up to the age of eighteen years the present writer had no particular ambition in life. His boyish fancies sometimes dwelt on the glories of becoming a township officer or sub-divisional officer with enviable powers. Sometimes he fancied it was more independent to be a lawyer. But they were mere fancies tickled by his immediate environment. They had no permanent place in his breast."[28]

According to U Myint Thein,[29] who became superintendent of Myoma shortly after Nu's departure in 1925 for the University of Rangoon, Nu "left an unusual memory behind him. At various meetings, like the debating society, I would hear it said: 'If only Maung Nu were still here.' I had the impression that he was well-liked but on the quiet side. He was referred to as being 'philosophic,' though I am quite sure that he was not really that. He was intelligent and a good student but not an outstanding one. There was nothing especially conspicuous about him, and yet he was remembered."

A glimmering of the future Nu is revealed in this description. It was to become a hallmark of the man in later years that he impressed without seeming impressive.

❀

TWO

NATIONALIST EMERGENT

THAKIN BA THAUNG was the leader of a small group of youthful nationalist dissenters at the University of Rangoon in the late 1920's who felt that the older political leaders were not doing enough to gain Burma back for the Burmese.[1] The students who met with Ba Thaung—Ba Sein, Thein Maung, Lay Maung, Tun Swe, and Ohn Khin—were later to play roles of varying importance in the anti-colonial struggle. At the University they talked among themselves about the injustices of British rule, turning to political agitation only after their graduation, as members of the Dobama Asiayone ("We Burmans Association").

Although Ko Nu* did not belong to the Ba Thaung group, he knew all its members. According to Ba Thaung, Nu was "not politically conscious at this time," a view echoed by three other contemporaries, Ohn Khin, Win, and Ba Sein.[2] He was anti-colonial, but his concerns at the moment were apparently more personal than political. Nu himself does not remember any intense religious feeling at that time.[3] According to Myanaung U Tin,[4] however, "he was more of a real Buddhist than the rest of us, who were not especially devout in those days." Nu would rise early every Sunday morning to go to the Shwedagon Pagoda, best known of Burma's religious shrines, to take part in the holy labor of washing down its large platform.[5]

To many of his fellow students Nu was known as "philosopher Nu." Professor U Ba Nyunt, an undergraduate contemporary and later head of the department of history and political science, has explained that "we called him 'philosopher' Nu, not because he was philosophical, but because he was so serious about everything."[6] U Tin adds, "Nu was

---

* Nu was now known as Ko (rather than Maung) Nu because of the enhanced status of being a student at the University.

eccentric as a student, also being called 'Don' after Don Quixote. He supported causes. One day he interfered in a fight between a big dog and a little dog, hitting the big dog on the head with a brick because it was superior to the little one, and he did not want the latter hurt. People laughed at him. One cannot say that Nu as an undergraduate was particularly respected—he certainly was popular."[7] He dressed oddly too, having little money for clothing. One classmate has recalled that he "always wore a scarf around his neck, even in the hot season."

A prominent contemporary and later Ambassador to the United States, U Win, has stated that Nu "did not have any particularly close friends as an undergraduate."[8] He seemed to hold himself at some distance from others. Usually quiet and withdrawn, he was not active socially or in extracurricular activities. Moreover he was subject to fits of temper. His friend U Tin recalls that "Nu was handy in those days with his left fist—and also with his left arm to extend about a person in asking forgiveness. 'Ko Nu,' I heard a friend once say, 'it seems that every week you are putting your left arm around me.' "[9]

Ordinarily "freshers" spoke only at "fresher" debates, but Nu was not to be so contained: he spoke frequently from the floor in University-wide debates. He was sometimes heckled, partly because he presumed to speak as a "fresher" and partly also because of the quality of his English. On one occasion a senior student rose and instructed him to sit down. Nu challenged him to try to make him do so, raising his fists defiantly. Seniors were given extraordinary deference at the University of Rangoon in those days, and Nu's action was much talked about.[10]

Nu's first four or five attempts at public speaking were dismal failures. After each failure he punished himself by abstaining from a meal, but to no avail. Each time he rose to speak, "he only found himself out of breath and soaked with sweat." Finally, he did bring himself to speak at a women students' debate: "After the lady speakers had done, as soon as the chairman permitted floor discussion, up he jumped and the words came tumbling out. At last he had spoken in public. And since then he has had no more difficulty about speaking in public."[11]

Nu became a good public speaker in both English and Burmese during his undergraduate years. He was also a fair student, regarded as able and reasonably diligent by most of his teachers. He had to work his way through the University,[12] which probably was one of the reasons for his not doing better as a student. Owing partly to financial difficulties, he took only the general pass degree, and did not remain to do additional honors work.

Professor D. G. E. Hall, who taught both Nu and his friend Ko

Thant in a European history class, has recalled that "they were good boys and good students, though not good enough to take honors degrees in history,"[13] owing to their inadequate national-school training. "If Nu could have done honors work in any subject," according to Professor Hall, "it would have been English." Nu loved English literature. His "real ambition," born in "his deepest heart" in his eighteenth year, was to become a great writer in English.[14]

The drive to write dominated him. His friend U Thein Han, himself later a distinguished literary figure, has said that Nu was "almost mad with the urge to write."[15] "Like a crowd jostling at the entrance of a cinema," Nu later wrote, "subjects for his pen had been seething in his mind."[16] Once he became so preoccupied with a play he was writing that he could not bring himself to study for an examination. An impatient friend snatched away the play and tore it up. During one vacation Nu built himself a hut outside of town in which he lived alone and spent his time writing. He wanted to write at least a hundred books.[17] Playwriting to Nu

> was like a disease that I could not shake off. I thought so well of myself that in the competition for the Prince of Wales Prize I submitted five plays and sent off English translations to England. Now when I read them in cold blood I find them ridiculous. But at the . . . time I simply had to write them and submit them and send them off to England. It was a mental and physical obsession and, if prevented from doing so, I probably would have been seriously ill.[18]

When he was graduated from the University in 1929, it was his "firm intention to become an English playwright."[19] He sent one of his plays to George Bernard Shaw for critical evaluation, but Shaw neither acknowledged nor returned it.[20] Shaw (whose *Caesar and Cleopatra* and *Candida* Nu read as a college student) greatly impressed him, and he "began to toy with the idea of becoming the Bernard Shaw of Burma." His English was still imperfect, but he reflected that Joseph Conrad had learned English only at the age of twenty. Unhappily, however, Nu was overcome by the mere itch to write. As a result, "he wrote far more than he ever read and thus missed the substance of mastering English for the shadow of writing English and only just managed to pass his B.A. examination."[21] Nu could not find a publisher for his plays, and finally gave a couple to a friend who needed copy for a "dying" magazine.[22]

By this time his friends were urging him to take a more active role in politics. "His comrades, knowing his affliction, feared lest he should abandon politics for authorship and conspired together to run down his efforts at writing." Nu was more and more inclined to agree with them. British imperialism increasingly seemed to him "a danger as urgent as a fire next door"; like such a fire, it had to be fought immediately. Writing could wait. "For the present," Nu wrote, "Mr. Bernard Shaw of Burma had to be content with beckoning from a distance while politics claimed the immediate attention."[23]

Nu remained in Rangoon seeking employment for several months after his graduation from the University. It was about the end of this period, in 1930, that the Dobama Asiayone was formed. Nu did not join the movement, being still politically uncommitted and moreover on the point of leaving Rangoon; but several of his undergraduate friends became leading members. Like Ba Thaung's small group at the University, the Dobama was not at first an agitational body, nor did it have many members. "We were comparatively few at the start," Ba Thaung, the Dobama's chief founder, has recalled. "There weren't many who were willing to put their neck on the block in those days." Almost from the beginning the Criminal Investigation Department of the colonial government kept a close watch on the Dobama Asiayone, and the fear that this produced among some young Burmese (or their parents), coupled with political apathy, kept the members of the movement to a few.

The members of the Dobama Asiayone called themselves *Thakins*. *Thakin* was a term meaning "sir" used to address Britishers. Thakin Ba Thaung claims to have first employed the title politically, influenced by the "slave" and "master" societies of Shaw's *Man and Superman*.[24] The editor-politician U Tun Pe, however, has stated that Nietzsche and his "Gospel of Superman" provided the model. He quoted Ba Thaung as saying, "The goal is not the creation of a national unit built upon military power or wealth but the production of an elite from whom geniuses will arise who will show mankind new values."[25]

Many of those who were attracted to the Dobama movement also joined the All-Burma Youth League, formed in 1931, also under the leadership of Thakin Ba Thaung. Nu did become a member of this organization, which sought to encourage the national-school movement and to influence students in other schools as well. Nu, in fact, became a leading figure in the Youth League, possibly its most active member outside Rangoon. The Dobama and the Youth League grew steadily closer in the early 1930's, and Nu's participation in the League stimulated his interest in politics. But Nu did not join the Dobama Asiayone itself until after he had left the University again following the 1936 students' strike.

Pantanaw, to which Nu went from Rangoon in 1930, was a small town in the delta district of Maubin, situated next to his native Myaungmya district. He had accepted the post of superintendent of the national high school there, an assignment that he tackled with vigor and competence. According to Thakin Ba Sein, "Nu took the teaching position in Pantanaw because this was the only job he could get." This may be so, but there is evidence that Nu expected to like the work. Moreover, his friend Thant was there and urging him to come.[26] It was at Pantanaw that their association, formed at the University, grew into a close friendship that was to endure through the years. Thant, who was one day to be Secretary-General of the United Nations, was headmaster of the national school of which Nu was superintendent.

Nu taught English, and Burmese and English history, in addition to performing his administrative duties. A popular teacher, he was fiery in his condemnation of colonial domination and moving in his accounts of the glories of the Burmese past. He maintained contact with the young nationalist politicians of the Dobama Asiayone and worked vigorously on behalf of the All-Burma Youth League.

Nu's duties as superintendent of the Pantanaw national high school frequently brought him into contact with the president of the school committee, a wealthy rice-miller. The president had a daughter, Daw Mya Yee, with whom Nu fell in love and to whom he dedicated sonnets "aflame with emotion."[27] Daw Mya Yee was a quiet person, limited in her formal education. She was a devout Buddhist, however, and she and Nu found great enjoyment in their visits together to pagodas. During these years at Pantanaw Nu seemed to become more attached to his country's traditional faith, although he was still not a man of outstanding religious dedication. Commenting on this change in his outlook, Nu has said, "Previously, if I broke a resolution, I went without dinner or sat in the sun. But after twenty-five I resolved to refrain from serious evil doings all my life and, if I should fail to do so, my self-punishment would be death."[28]

Daw Mya Yee* and Nu were married in 1931, but not without difficulties. Daw Mya Yee's father insisted on a more suitable match for his daughter, and so Daw Mya Yee, in love with Nu, fled her family household. She rushed to Nu's residence only to discover that he had

* Burmese women retain their names after marriage.

gone home to visit his parents. Her father, meanwhile, had gone to the police, charging that she had absconded with some of his possessions, the almost ritualistic response of a Burmese father in what was not an uncommon situation. Daw Mya Yee was hidden in a local fishery while a motor-boat was dispatched to Wakema to bring back Nu. The returning school superintendent and his beloved then eloped across the Irrawaddy and went off to Rangoon for their honeymoon.[29]

Nu and his bride subsequently settled down in Thongwa, where Nu continued to teach in the national-school system. They did not return to Pantanaw because of the hostility of Daw Mya Yee's parents. Nu's parents-in-law ultimately became reconciled to their daughter's marriage, but not to her husband's profession. They brought pressure on Nu to enter the civil service and even sent him to Rangoon to inquire about a position.[30] Nu himself, meanwhile, was becoming dissatisfied with teaching in a national school. In 1934 he resigned his post and returned to Rangoon, where he worked for a while for a Burmese-language newspaper, the *White Owl*.[31]

On his return to Rangoon, Nu astonished his friends and former University classmates with the strength of his interest in the nationalist cause. Although his parents-in-law wanted him to become a civil servant, he chose instead to return to Rangoon University to study law. In an open letter to Principal D. J. Sloss of University College at the time of the students' strike of 1936, Nu stated his reasons for choosing this course of study:

> The fault of my coming back to the College lies, not in me, but in my countrymen. They will not have any man to be their leader who has no Bar-at-Law or B.L. degree after his name, although those who cut their throats are mostly these lawyers. And as one of my chief ambitions is to become the leader of my countrymen, not for the sake of satisfying my vanity but to lead them out of their misfortune, I feel that I should try to satisfy their requirements of leadership by becoming a Bachelor of Law.[32]

Nu returned to the University of Rangoon in 1934. Both Burma and the University had changed since his undergraduate years. By 1934, although the Dobama Asiayone was not yet a force of major significance in national politics, it was rapidly becoming one. The Thakins (and some of the older politicians) were beginning to perceive the importance of mobilizing the masses behind their programs, and the depression and the Indo-Burmese riots of 1931 had caused resentment throughout Burma. The University was still comparatively quiescent politically, but militant nationalism was growing in the student body. A Students' Union, established in 1931, provided the mechanism for fostering and mobilizing student discontent. It was in the early 1930's, too, that Marxism made its first inroads at the University.

By 1934, Nu, too, had changed. One of his former teachers has described him as "much more intense and emotional in his nationalist feelings."[33] His close associates during this period, who were to be his friends and political colleagues for many years to come, felt the same way. The most important of them were Ko Aung San, Ko Kyaw Nyein, Ko Thein Pe, Ko Ohn, and M. A. Raschid. Nu and the other Burmese were soon working as a team in University politics. They were joined subsequently by Raschid, the son of Indian parents domiciled in Burma.

Nu and his friends decided to capture control of the Students' Union in the 1935–36 academic year. Ko Tha Hla, who was elected to the Union's executive committee as a member of the group, has stated that the "real powers" drafted Nu to run for the presidency, the "powers" being Kyaw Nyein, Aung San, Raschid, Thein Pe, and Thi Han. According to Tha Hla, "Nu was a very modest young man, too modest to have sought the presidency himself."[34] Raschid, by contrast, recalls that Nu definitely sought the job and "was not co-opted."[35]

Raschid was selected to run for Vice President and Ohn for Treasurer, and other members of the faction for the other seats on the executive committee. No opposition candidates presented themselves, and the Nu slate was declared elected.[36]

The Students' Union was never again the same. Its leaders continued to sponsor cultural activities, social affairs, and sporting events, but increasing attention was given to political affairs. There were lively debates, and leading politicians of the day were invited to debate before the Union members on subjects of national interest. Although identification with any particular party, including the Dobama Asiayone, was scrupulously avoided, the increasingly political character of the Union came as a disappointment to the University administration. "We realized, of course, that the students would be swept up in the nationalist movement," Principal Sloss stated many years later, "but we hoped that it would be a more gradual thing."[37]

The new student leaders formed a remarkably congenial working team. Aung San later remarked that the Union executive committee was "the most harmonious I have ever worked with," and Nu has described it as the "most successful" in his experience.[38] There was hardly an occasion on which a vote had to be taken on any important issue.[39]

Nu, by now one of the best public speakers in the country, was chief spokesman for the group. But he by no means dominated the Union's executive committee. Some of his contemporaries, in fact, subsequently asserted that Nu was only a figurehead in the Students' Union. Kyaw Nyein, some claimed, was the most important person in the executive committee; others have stated that Raschid was the real leader. Actually, each of the student nationalists was a leader in his own right.

Kyaw Nyein, described in later years as a very good scholar and a sort of student intellectual, was actually neither but was a superb organizer. Raschid, probably the most intellectually competent of the group, was also an able organizer and an accomplished speaker. The first Secretary of the Students' Union at the time of its formation in 1931, he probably would have been its second President if he had not been an Indian. Raschid was generally regarded as a pleasant person; Kyaw Nyein had a caustic streak and was less well-liked. Thein Pe, like Nu as an undergraduate, was considered somewhat eccentric; he was, however, a shrewd plotter, an outstanding writer and orator, and personally popular. Ohn, regarded as "neurotic" by Principal Sloss and as "mixed up" by Professor Hall, was extremely skillful as a manipulator.[40] Aung San was probably the most personally disciplined of the group, but he was shy and had yet to develop the charismatic quality that was to characterize his leadership only a few years later. Nu by no means determined the actions of these men and their able colleagues Thi Han, Tha Hla, and Tun Ohn. But, at the same time, they accorded him deference, partly because he was six years older than most of them (he was called "Ko Gyi," or Elder Brother, Nu).

In his second period as a student, Nu was generally considered a very faithful Buddhist. Tha Hla heard him say that he was "going to be a Buddha,"[41] but such a remark is not necessarily significant, since all Theravada Buddhists believe, or are supposed to believe, that they will ultimately become Buddhas. Yet he did spend many hours in meditation, and proclaimed that he would aid the attainment of independence by saying rosaries. Some of his colleagues, who nonetheless accepted him as a leader because of his ability and sincerity, resented the time he spent in religious activity.

As might be expected, the student nationalists had their political heroes, some of whom reflected ideological positions quite at variance with Buddhism. Gandhi, Nehru, and Subhas Chandra Bose they respected, but they reserved their chief admiration for England's more spectacular enemies: Hitler, Mussolini, and Ireland's revolutionary leaders.[42] Nu and his friends were also much impressed by Japan's successful defiance of the Western imperialist nations, but were critical of Japanese aggression in China, an Asian land.

Nu has often been described as inclined toward democracy in this period, but he was not. In his inaugural speech as President of the Students' Union, he declared, "I dislike democracy, where much time is wasted in persuading the majority and in trying to get the consent of the majority. Democracy is good in name only. . . . It cannot work in the period of dictatorship of Hitler and Mussolini."[43] Principal Sloss, who regarded him then and later as a friend, has called the young nationalist "neurotic as a political leader. He could switch so very quickly from a quiet, calm person to a very emotionally aroused one. He would speak very rapidly when aroused and used strong but not bad language."

That nationalism emerged as a major force at the University of Rangoon during the student years of Nu and his friends is in a way surprising. The University in 1935 was a pleasant place, and the quality of the education offered was high. The teachers, generally, were able men and sympathetic to Burmese aspirations. The costs of a University education were comparatively low, and students usually spent their college years in a relatively carefree manner. On the national scene, the new constitution of 1935, which was to take effect in 1937, provided for the separation of Burma from India and for more self-government.

But jobs were scarce and wages low, and world events were increasingly sinister. There was, in addition, an ill-defined feeling of disturbance among the students at the University. This feeling lacked any origins in specific grievances, did not seem to be politically rooted, and probably was not related to any dissatisfaction with the educational system as such. Quite the opposite, in fact, may have been the case. To many students the transition from village bamboo huts to a modern university was a difficult experience—as was the transition from traditionalist thinking to the ideas of the Western heritage. Change was in the air, and as always, it was accompanied by a feeling of insecurity.

❀

THREE

THE 1936 STUDENTS' STRIKE

FEW SIGNS of student dissatisfaction were evident at Rangoon University in the dry season of 1935–36. "Few students in Burma," *New Burma* wrote on February 2, 1936, "seem to have grasped the immense significance of the fact that students in Egypt and China have made dramatic moves in the political affairs of their respective countries and are . . . responsible for keeping alive legitimate agitation for wrongs to be righted, injustice removed and self-respect [restored]."[1]

This and other inflammatory articles in *New Burma* were actually written by students themselves, however, notably Aung San, the restive editor of the University students' magazine, and Nyo Mya, a member of the magazine's staff. Nu himself was "itching for a strike."[2] In an open letter to Principal Sloss, Nu wrote: "My idea of desiring the students to go on strike is this—until and unless students show their organized force, by going on strike, the authorities will never be brought to their senses, they will never give up their high-handed attitude, and they will never realize the fact that students can feel hurt when they are pricked."[3]

So concerned had University authorities become with Nu's behavior that Principal Sloss went so far as to recommend Nu for a scholarship to Britain—"as a means of getting him out of the country," according to his close friend, U Thant. His father wanted Nu to accept the scholarship, but Nu refused and wrote Thant (still in Pantanaw) that he would not be bribed by the colonial authorities.[4]

The series of events that culminated in the students' strike of 1936 began with several provocative speeches by Nu denouncing a University lecturer as immoral and criticizing Principal Sloss and his subordinates. Fearing that the administration might take over full control of the Union, Nu prayed that "the Almighty may visit condign punishment on the head of the authority which orders the transference of the control of the Union from the students to the University authorities."[5] Subsequently, with the concurrence of the University's governing board, Sloss expelled Nu from the University. Two days later Nu's friend Aung San, the editor of *Oway,* the student magazine, was expelled for printing an assault on a University official. The piece, written by Nyo Mya, appeared under the title "A Hell Hound at Large":

> Escaped from Awizi a devil in the form of a black dog.
>
> Had been during its brief span on earth a base object of universal odium and execration, sentenced to eternal damnation for churlishness, treachery, ruffianism, pettifogging, etc. A pimping knave with avuncular pretensions to some cheap wiggling wenches from a well-known hostel, he was also a hectic popularity hunter, shamming interest in sports, concerts and other extracurricular student activities. His only distinguishing marks are buboes and ulcers due to errant whoring.
>
> Will finder please kick him back to hell.[6]

Aung San's expulsion caused greater indignation among the students than Nu's. The question was what to do. Nu, Raschid, and Aung San did not want the executive committee to call a strike without a discussion of the matter by the whole Union.* Kyaw Nyein and some of the others, however, wanted dramatic action.[7] Finally, with Nu and Aung San abstaining because of their personal involvement, the remaining members of the executive committee voted a compromise plan. As a protest, they would not sit for the annual examinations due to be given in March, and they would inform the student body of their decision at a meeting on February 25.[8]

At the February 25 meeting Kyaw Nyein and others delivered fiery speeches in favor of a strike. Nu spoke last. While cautioning the students not to be swayed by affection for him, he reminded them at length of the heroic anticolonial struggles of students in India.[9] When Vice President Raschid, who was presiding because of Nu's expulsion and who had spoken in favor of moderation, rose to inquire the decision

---

* Tha Hla, "1936 Strike," V. Nu's reaction to his own expulsion seems to have been mild at first. According to Tha Hla, a member of the executive committee, "He did not wish to bring it to the notice of the RUSU at all, as he did not feel justified to have the entire RUSU involved on account of him alone" (*ibid.,* I). His open letter to Principal Sloss, which was published in *New Burma* on February 26, the day after the strike began, but seems to have been written several days earlier, is bitterly critical of the University but specifies that he will make no protest and will not seek readmission.

of the students, his voice was drowned out by shouts of "Let's go out, go out!" and "Down with the Principal!"[10] "Somebody shouted [to] get in the buses for a demonstration ride," and Raschid was picked up off his feet and carried out of the hall. Within minutes some seven hundred students had evacuated the hall and crowded into waiting buses.[11] The buses made their noisy way to the historic Shwedagon Pagoda, where a strikers' camp was established. For the next three months, all eyes in Burma were turned toward the Shwedagon.

Newspaper reporters hastened to the Shwedagon Pagoda to interview the strike leaders, who, having acted more on impulse than on principle, at first found themselves hard pressed to justify their behavior, let alone set forth their objectives. After one futile press conference, they decided to come out for modification of the University Act.[12] Since they knew nothing about the Act, Raschid (who had been reluctant to go on strike in the first place) was assigned the task of reading it and finding objections to it. He worked through the night while Ko Nu slept peacefully—an augury of things to come. Ultimately Raschid became one of the three workhorses of the movement, along with Kyaw Nyein and Aung San. Nu was the speechmaker, but not the organizer or the negotiator.

The student leaders quickly set about organizing for the struggle ahead. They set up as their "supreme authority" a Boycotters Council, composed of nine members of the Students' Union executive committee and twenty-four hostel representatives; there was also an Inner Council, made up of the executive committee and two or three other members. Nu, Raschid, and Aung San were the President, Vice President, and Secretary, respectively, of the Boycotters Council. Nu's friend of undergraduate days, Thakin Ba Sein of the Dobama Asiayone, tried unsuccessfully to capture control of the strike for his party. U Saw, leader of the Patriotic Party, made a similar attempt, but was no more successful. The Dobama, however, was probably the most influential of the outside groups advising the young nationalists. Others gave advice, too, and many gave generously of money, food, and bedding. So well cared for were the boycotters, in fact, that many gained weight.

After a brief debate, the boycott leaders moved quickly to expand the scope of the strike. Nu, Raschid, and Ohn feared at first that the responsibility of directing a multisided boycott might prove more than the young leaders could handle. But Aung San, as President of the All-Burma Student Movement, and Kyaw Nyein did not share this view, and in the end it was unanimously agreed to encourage strikes in as many other schools as possible. Cadres were sent to high schools in all the urban centers, and their success was overwhelming: students at some forty-seven schools in addition to those in Rangoon joined in the strike. Annual examinations were postponed throughout Burma.

Ten demands were made by the strikers following Raschid's reading of the University Act, and the student leaders insisted that all of them be accepted. These included the right of student representation on the University Council, abolition of the Principal's power of expulsion, the reinstatement of expelled students, the reduction of certain fees, assurance that strikers would not be punished, and the holding of examinations one month after the boycott's end.[13] At Nu's urging, the Boycotters Council omitted the names of the students whose reinstatement was demanded. The authorities might justifiably refuse to readmit him, Nu argued, and the strikers might then be forced to accept less than unconditional surrender.[14]

The first reaction of the University authorities to the strike was to demand that the students return to their classes by February 28. The demand was ignored. After the failure of several attempts by proboycotter Burmese nationalist politicians in the legislature to have an investigatory committee established which would include students or their known supporters, the University Council voted to request that the Chancellor of the University, the Governor, appoint a commission to investigate the causes of the boycott.

During this time, Nu toured the country criticizing "slave education" and calling for the establishment of a national college. This "crusade," as Tha Hla has called it, was his own idea and won only the grudging acceptance of his associates. Speaking rapidly in a voice shrill with emotion, he was applauded wherever he went, and undoubtedly played a major role in whipping up anticolonial sentiment among his countrymen.

For Nu, education was the means of ending Burma's subjection. In this respect, he admired the Nazi example. "National Socialism, which has had the education of German youth at the forefront of its program, has raised Germany from the position of a vanquished and downtrodden nation into that of a first-class power."[15] In a speech at Prome on March 13, he declared, "At the present time, a Burman automatically raises his hand to his forehead when he sees the body of a fellow human being caged in a pair of trousers and when that trousered person speaks a smattering of English. You will see from this . . . to what depths of degradation we have fallen, and we have been led to these depths by the educational policy of the University."[16]

In general, Nu's speeches were longer on emotion than they were on fact. On one occasion, he and Raschid were in Henzada on a speaking tour and Raschid had gone to bed, leaving Nu to harangue the audience. Nu assailed the University Act in his speech, but on being asked precisely what was wrong with the Act and what should be done about it, found himself unable to reply. He finally said that he did not know but would get Raschid, "who knew everything." Raschid was astonished at the degree of his frankness, but Nu told him sternly, "We must be honest."[17]

On another occasion Nu embarrassed his colleagues by declaring publicly that the strike was successful because by writing auspicious numbers on a wall of the University convocation hall he had gained the strikers the support of the *devas* (spirits). "When I approached Nu on the subject," Kyaw Nyein has related, "he said in effect, 'Yes, yes, I appreciate Raschid's and your organizational work, but, despite such work, we would not be as successful as we are without the *devas*.'"

"Even then Nu used to count his beads," Kyaw Nyein recalls. "There are one hundred and eight of them in the Buddhist rosary, and Nu tried to count these one thousand times. Many times we wanted to see him in connection with important matters, but he was busy counting his beads, particularly in the evening or late at night."[18] Yet, for all their criticism, his associates regarded Nu as an inspiring leader. "He never lost faith in the cause," Raschid has said, "even in the darker moments."

In the end, speeches were not enough. Maintaining morale was difficult, and the number of strikers at headquarters steadily declined. Eager to see their families and weary of what had become a monotonous routine, many students went home to celebrate the Water Festival in April and never came back. Negotiations to end the strike were clearly in order, and were entrusted to Vice President Raschid. He received policy guidance from the Inner Council, in which Nu played a significant role, but Nu himself refused to meet with the officials.

Ultimately, it was Raschid who got the Boycotters Council to agree to end the strike. Aung San and Ohn—and Nu, too (although less actively because of his frequent absences from Rangoon)—supported him in this.[19] But Raschid maintained that all the major demands of the students had been met. Thein Pe has charged that Raschid and Ohn compromised student objectives and that Nu did not realize the degree to which Raschid was doing so, since Nu was off "making speeches and saying rosaries and prayers for the success of the strike."[20] "I took my stand on the basis of numbers," Raschid asserted. "When we permitted the students to go home for the holidays, we had them sign pledges that they would come back. Only about half did so."[21]

The strike ended officially on May 10. By June, everybody except Nu was back at the University, sitting for the examinations. Nu, who did not want to return, was to continue his activities in a larger arena.

Even during the time he was President of the Students' Union, Nu continued his writing. Indeed, in 1934, his first year as a law student, he had written the play *U Kalain* (*Mr. Crooked*), the story of a corrupt monk. The play was published in 1938 as part of a volume of plays by Nu[22] and received wide recognition in connection with Thein Pe's popular novel *Tetpongyi*, which is also about corrupt monks. It was not as the Bernard Shaw of Burma that Nu found a publisher, however, but rather as a nationally known political figure, a nationalist leader to be reckoned with. It was in 1936 that he acquired the nickname *Natha Kyopyat*, "The Bull Let Loose," a Burmese colloquialism for a man who will go to any extent to accomplish his goal.[23]

Although Nu was unquestionably in favor of a University strike as a protest against British colonial rule, he did not intentionally encourage the one that took place. When it came, he served it to the best of his ability. Nu's part in the strike is probably best described by Raschid: "[Nu was] a good man in mobilizing public opinion behind us, making speeches, and that sort of thing. He avoided details altogether, however. This was why the burden of negotiating and operational leadership fell to Aung San, Kyaw Nyein and myself. Nu had no interest in, and quite frankly no talent for, this type of activity."[24]

Although the strike was precipitated by the petty grievances of a small minority of student leaders, it was in a larger sense "a manifestation of the nation's latent feelings and resentment against foreign domination."[25] The strike served as a rallying point for Burmese nationalist sentiment. Its psychological effect was to carry Burma through the remaining years of British and Japanese rule to independence in half the time "Ko Gyi" Nu had predicted in his speeches. In terms of protest behavior, the strike marked the beginning of the abandonment of constitutional methods for more forceful techniques.

For the young men who played the chief roles in the strike, this was the first major political trial, both individually and as a team. For Ko Nu it was more: the beginning of a nationwide reputation in protest politics and of a national following.

❄

FOUR

POLITICAL APPRENTICE

AFTER THE 1936 strike, Nu joined the staff of the *White Owl,* a pro-nationalist Burmese-language newspaper edited by U Ba Cho,* a grad-ualist socialist and the leader of the Fabian Party. Attracted by Ba Cho's ideas and personality, Nu became an active member of the Party. Ba Cho encouraged Nu in his belief in *nats,* but he was also a dedicated Buddhist and a vigorous opponent of Communism.

Besides articles for the *White Owl,* Nu also wrote plays and did some translating, including a rendering of Shakespeare's *Julius Caesar* into Burmese.[1] But Fabian socialism and playwriting were not enough, and in 1937 Nu yielded to the arguments of his friends in the Thakin movement and joined the Dobama Asiayone. It was at this time that he became Thakin Nu, as he was to be known for more than a decade.

By 1937, the Dobama was no longer composed exclusively of young intellectuals. The editor and politician U Tun Pe has divided the mem-bers into four groups: the largely Westernized, "intellectually supe-rior" Marxists, who had been "converted to Thakinism with a venge-ance"; the "hybrids," who sought to reconcile Marxism and Buddhism; a large number of ex-policemen, former *pongyis,* and onetime govern-ment servants who were "weak on ideology, but active as field work-ers"; and finally, those "who knew on which side their bread was but-tered."[2]

The one consistent aspect of Thakin ideology was its strongly na-tionalist character; it was otherwise an odd and shifting mixture of largely borrowed political and economic concepts. The young nation-alists read Marx, Nietzsche, Upton Sinclair, Sun Yat-Sen, Hitler, Mus-

---

* Ba Cho was called "Deedok," or "White Owl," U Ba Cho to distinguish him from many other Ba Cho's.

solini, Nehru, and various writers of Ireland's Sinn Fein movement. Thein Pe, one of Burma's first Communists, has called the interest in Hitler and Mussolini "strictly surface,"[3] but Thakin thought was not devoid of racism, and Aung San in particular was strongly attracted by Nazi methods of building a nation that was respected for its power.

During this period Thakin Nu flirted with Communism: "You'll be the Lenin of Burma, and I'll be your Maxim Gorki," he once told Thakin Than Tun.[4] Thakin Thein Maung, leader of the faction within the Dobama Asiayone with which Nu came to be associated, had met a number of Communists in 1931 in London, where he had gone as a representative of the All-Burma Youth League. He had joined Palme Dutt's "League Against Imperialism," and had brought back to Burma many leftist books. Nu himself read widely during these years, perhaps more so than during any period in his life.

Probably the most important Communist influences on Nu were his friends Than Tun, Thein Pe, and Soe, Communists all. Than Tun had been prevented by poverty from attending the university; he worked closely with Nu and Aung San in various Dobama assignments. Thein Pe collaborated with Nu in translating and in other literary work in the Red Dragon Book Club; he also worked with Nu, and with Aung San and Hla Pe (Bo Let Ya), in maintaining liaison with the student movement in the country. Soe was an intellectual leader of the Thakins and the most assertive of Burma's young Communists.

During this period Nu wrote an article, "I Am a Marxist,"[5] in the form of a conversation between himself and "my old friend U Sein." In this conversation Nu at first insisted to Sein that Communism was antireligious, but was persuaded that Communism and Buddhism were reconcilable when Sein asked: "How can people who starve and have to struggle from day to day for their very existence practice religion?" Ultimately, Nu agreed that "to help work for Marxism would be to repay our gratitude to Buddha for his suffering in all his aeons of existences for the benefit of mankind."

Nu's brief Communist leanings probably did not have their roots in his own living conditions, poor though these may have been. "Before World War II," Nu recalled years later, "I lived in . . . a little rented room, for which I paid a monthly rent of twenty rupees. As for clothes, I had no change of dress. On most days I filled myself with fried Indian crushed peas and dhall, liberally washed down with water. On some days I could not even afford that."[6]

Two decades later, Nu explained his views of this time to a congress of his ruling political party, the Anti-Fascist People's Freedom League

(AFPFL): "When we were younger, we had not yet studied Marxism in detail and in all its aspects. Neither did we know Buddhism in detail or with any exactness. At that time, more or less on hearsay and cursory reading, we impetuously loudly claimed that Marxism was the same as Buddhism. We are very remorseful for having made, at one time, such ill-considered and unfounded claims."[7]

Nu's flirtation was with Marxism rather than with Bolshevism. J. S. Furnivall, perhaps the most knowledgeable and sympathetic of all those who have written of contemporary Burma, has said of Nu and his non-Communist Dobama associates: "They could not reconcile Marxian materialism with Buddhism and, rejecting the Communist doctrine of the inevitability of violence, preferred to call themselves Socialists."[8]

The primary aim of the Dobama Asiayone was early and unconditional independence for Burma. One of the group's targets was the Government of Burma Act of 1935, which separated Burma from the Indian Empire and gave the Burmese a larger measure of self-government. The nationalists saw the Act as a device for divorcing Burma from India's progress toward independence, and for perpetuating political institutions that allowed Europeans and others to thwart Burmese aspirations within the framework of parliamentary structure. On April 1, 1937, the day the Act went into effect, Nu led a small group of Dobama agitators who burned the Union Jack and a copy of the Act in front of the High Court in Rangoon.

The Dobama participated in the new system through a subsidiary organization, the Komin Kochin, which had three members elected to the Legislative Council in 1937. (They did not, however, participate in any of the four governments formed between 1937 and 1942.) One of the three was Thakin Mya, later a founder of the Burmese Socialist Party and probably the most important Dobama leader of the late 1930's.

Nu was asked by the elders of Wakema to stand for election to the legislature, but declined; nor was he ever a Komin Kochin candidate.[9] He also refused to serve as President of the Dobama Asiayone. "I did not want power," he later explained.[10] He did become the Dobama's treasurer, however—"a treasurer without treasure," as he called himself.[11]

The Dobama remained primarily an extra-parliamentary political movement whose chief activity was seditious speechmaking. As seen by the British, it "assiduously spread among the people, and particularly among the youth, of Burma a poisonous and anti-social creed of domestic and industrial unrest and individual indiscipline."[12] The anti-Indian riots of the summer of 1938, in which 220 persons were killed and another 936 injured, were officially alleged to have had roots in the "spirit of excitement and indiscipline" encouraged by the Thakins.

The late 1930's were generally tempestuous years in Burmese politics. The young agitators Ba Swe and Ba Hein were arrested while leading a march of oilfield workers from Yenangyaung to Rangoon; demonstrations in Mandalay resulted in the creation of fourteen new martyrs (seven of them monks); and Aung Gyaw, who died in a student riot in Rangoon (to whose leaders Nu served as adviser), became a new symbol of resistance to British rule.

The strength of the Dobama Asiayone continued to increase in part because of its efficient political organization and enthusiastic, able leaders, but chiefly because of its growing appeal to the masses. Dr. Ba Maw's Sinyetha (Poor Man's) Party was the first to appeal to the economic interests of the masses, but only sixteen Sinyetha candidates were elected to the 132-seat lower house in the 1936 voting—and Ba Maw suffered an eclipse in popularity following a two-year Premiership (1937–39) far less radical than his promises. The Thakins, meanwhile, continued to organize. Thakin Mya founded the All-Burma Peasants Organization in 1938, and Ba Swe was a main moving force behind the inauguration of the All-Burma Trade Union Congress in 1940.

Jockeying for power within the Dobama, however, probably lessened its effectiveness somewhat. In 1937, Thakin Kodaw Hmaing had recruited Nu, Aung San, and others, hoping that the introduction of new blood would heal the breach between the competing Ba Sein and Thein Maung factions. But most of the young nationalists, including Nu and Aung San, joined the more radical Thein Maung wing—partly because of a belief that Ba Sein and some of his supporters were too close to the British, but also because they saw in it a greater chance to take over the organization.[13] This they soon accomplished, with Aung San becoming the party's General Secretary, and Nu and Hla Pe gaining seats on the Executive Committee. Together with Mya, Than Tun, and Kodaw Hmaing, these men became the moving force of an increasingly aggressive Thakin movement.

Relations among the young nationalist leaders were complicated in 1939 by the establishment of two new conspiratorial groups: the first Communist cell to be formed in the country, and the Burma Revolutionary Party (BRP). Thein Pe was chiefly responsible for the found-

ing of the Communist body; the BRP, a counter-organization to the
Communists, was founded by Thakins Mya and Chit (himself later a
Communist), and Kyaw Nyein.

Describing the BRP, Kyaw Nyein has said,

> Nu, Aung San, Bo Let Ya [Hla Pe] and their associates were the
> second wave of University graduates to associate themselves with
> the Dobama Asiayone. The first wave were largely talkers. They
> had the courage to take defiant stands publicly, but they did not
> think in terms of seizing power. The BRP represented some ele-
> ments of the second wave of student nationalists and the beginning
> of a third wave—Ba Swe and Hla Maung in particular. It was
> time, we felt, to commence the revolutionary struggle. This was
> the political struggle to seize power; it was not basically a class
> struggle in the economic sense, for we were not really socialists yet.
> Frankly, we did not think we would succeed; some of us thought
> we might die in the process. Others, however, would come after
> us.

Thakin Nu was not a member of the BRP because he could not
bring himself to be a party to violence. According to Kyaw Nyein,
however, "We regarded him as one of us spiritually."[14]

The Thakins sought to end British control not only in the political
realm but in the area of education as well. In 1937, Nu almost singlehandedly established a "national college" (located at the Myoma National High School) to compete with the "colonial" University of Rangoon. U Ba Thwin was its Rector, Nu the Registrar, and Hla Pe one
of the Assistant Registrars. The college attracted some sixty students,
who studied mainly the Burmese language and Burmese history, but
financial difficulties forced it to close after only a year.[15]

In December 1937, Nu helped organize the Red Dragon Book Club,
which issued over seventy books before World War II.[16] Thakins Than
Tun and Ohn Khin were fellow founders of the club. Nu, the first President, was succeeded by Ohn Khin—under whose management, toward
the end of its existence, the club (which had some five or six thousand
members) actually showed a profit.[17]

The books issued by the club dealt primarily with contemporary
politics. Two of the more popular titles were John Strachey's *Theory
and Practice of Socialism* and Palme Dutt's *World Politics.* Saya Hein
translated Batt O'Connor's *With Michael Collins in the Fight for Irish
Independence* and Dan Breen's *My Fight for Irish Freedom,* and Thein
Pe edited Sun Yat-Sen's *San Min Chu I* (Three People's Principles).
A translation of Hendrik Van Loon's *The Story of Mankind* and a

number of original works by Burmese writers were also issued. Among the latter were Thein Pe's biography of Thakin Kodaw Hmaing, the club's first issue, and his two-volume novel *Student Boycotter*; a book by Thakin Soe on socialism; and studies of Hitler, Marx, the Paris Commune, "Soviet democracy," and Burmese problems.

Thakin Nu translated several books for the club, notably Dale Carnegie's *How to Win Friends and Influence People* (which became a Burmese bestseller), Edgar Snow's *Red Star Over China,* and portions of *Das Kapital.*[18] He also contributed to several anthologies, wrote a small book on the Russian Revolution, and popularized Communist ideas through his articles in the Red Dragon journal.[19]

Two of the plays Nu wrote at this time dealt symbolically with contemporary political problems.[20] *Thuraka,* an Orwellian piece in which the leaders of a community of pigs basely ally themselves with a predatory tiger, was directed at political adversaries of the Thakins, who allegedly cooperated with the colonial British. *Converting the Elder Brother* is about a soldier who has an affair with a married woman. Written to ridicule certain Burmese politicians who were allegedly steeped in adultery, it asks a rhetorical question: if a man cannot be trusted with another man's wife, how can he be entrusted with the affairs of the nation?

In 1939 Nu made a good-will trip to Chiang Kai-shek's China and returned to write a glowing account of what he had seen (and much that he did not see) called *Ganda-layit.** The book indicated that Nu was familiar not only with Sun Yat-sen's "Three People's Principles," but also with the rising Chinese Communists (although his discussion of Mao Tse-tung, whom he did not meet, bears a striking similarity to John Gunther's treatment in *Inside Asia*).[21] Nu was highly critical of the Japanese: after World War I, "instead of combining the strength which they possessed and the favorable opinion which the Asians had of them and providing leadership for freeing Asia from European domination, they followed in Western imperialist footsteps and destroyed that favorable opinion."[22]

An earlier essay by Nu on the problem of imperialism, "Do It Now or Don't Do It at All,"[23] appeared about a year before his trip to China. The essay began with a description of cattle being driven to the slaughterhouse by a cowherd who had only a small cane. The cattle were obviously the Burmese people, the cowherd the colonial ruler—weak because of the challenge posed by the Germans and Italians in Europe and by Japan in the Far East.

* Ganda-layit is a classical Burmese name for China.

Despite the popularity of his writings and the impact of his speeches, Nu was not one of the leaders of the Dobama Asiayone. He was out-ranked by at least three younger men: Aung San, Than Tun, and Thakin Soe. Nu, who willingly assumed a secondary position, was highly respected, however, owing in good part to his leadership in the 1936 strike, his piety, and his attractive personality. "The ordinary people in the country liked Nu much better than any other young Tha-kin," Kodaw Hmaing has said.[24]

The Government of Burma Act of 1935 provided for limited cabinet government and a two-house national legislature, the lower of which was wholly elected (though from communal and commercial as well as territorial constituencies). The United GCBA held the largest num-ber of seats (46) in the 132-seat House of Representatives but U Ba Pe, its leader, was unable to form a government, and it fell to Dr. Ba Maw, whose Sinyetha Party numbered only 16 legislators, to patch together a coalition government with himself as Prime Minister, Bur-ma's first under the new arrangements of expanded self-rule. In gen-eral, Ba Maw governed wisely, but he was opposed at every turn by U Ba Pe and by U Saw, the head of the Patriotic Party, a "jovial but sinister scoundrel,"[25] who had his own pocket army. In early 1939, after violent nationalist demonstrations, Ba Maw's government fell, and one of his ministers, U Pu, became the new Premier. The new cabinet included both U Ba Pe and U Saw, who was its strongest mem-ber until he suddenly shifted to the opposition in September 1940, as a prelude to his own assumption of the Premiership. U Saw remained as Prime Minister until January 1942, when, en route home from talks in London, he was arrested for conspiring with Japan and detained in Africa. He was succeeded by Sir Paw Tun, who served until the British abandoned Rangoon to the invading Japanese.

Both Ba Maw and U Saw were self-seeking and unscrupulous when out of office, and were by no means perfect when office was theirs (though both addressed themselves earnestly, and with some effect, to Burma's more pressing social and economic problems). The Thakins, by contrast, were relatively unselfish and incorruptible—in part, admit-tedly, because of the minor role they played in the formal parliamentary arena, where the main questions of public policy were determined.

The Thakins were willing to accept any ally against the hated British rule, however, including Japan and Ba Maw. Thus it was that the Thakins joined with Ba Maw in the "Freedom Bloc," which was de-signed to take advantage of Britain's involvement in a broadening war to advance the cause of Burmese independence. For Ba Maw it was also a way back from the "political wilderness."[26]

Although Thakin Nu was a relatively minor figure in the Dobama hierarchy, he and Than Tun were the two Thakins best known to Ba Maw at that time, and their support of the Freedom Bloc proposal seems to have helped bring Ba Maw into the alliance. The actual approach to Ba Maw was made by Aung San, on behalf of a Dobama faction favoring "armed struggle" against the British. The Thakins apparently thought that Ba Maw had contacts with the Japanese which could be exploited in any fighting with Britain.[27]

The Freedom Bloc denounced Britain's policy of involving the Burmese in the war without their consent. The Bloc called upon "the British Government through the Burma Government to implement in Burma their declared aims in the present war by immediately recognizing Burma as an independent nation with the right to frame her own constitution and giving effect to this recognition as far as practicable in the present governance of Burma."[28] The Thakins, Dr. Ba Maw and his followers, and the other members of the Freedom Bloc carried their protest into the bazaars, among the industrial workers, and throughout the country. At the Tharrawaddy conference of the Dobama Asiayone on May 12, 1940, Thakin Nu termed Burma's declaration as a belligerent by Britain "an affront which no self-respecting and freedom-loving people can accept or tolerate." The declaration called for nothing short of complete independence: "Dominion status, or any other status within the imperial structure, is wholly inapplicable to Burma, as it would bind Burma in many ways to British policies and economic structure."[29]

The Freedom Bloc's position was that the Burmese nationalists would support Britain and fight her foes if Britain would guarantee Burma's independence after the war; otherwise the Thakins and their allies would fight the British. "For that I was sent to jail for two years," Nu told a youth conference in Rangoon nearly two decades later.[30] Some of the nationalist agitators escaped arrest, including Aung San, who went to Amoy to "seek international contacts to aid his country."[31] He made contact there with the Japanese, possibly accidentally, and was sent to Japan for military training. He and twenty-nine other nationalists, called the "Thirty Comrades," returned to Burma in 1942 with the Japanese.

From the jail at Insein (just north of Rangoon), where he was first placed, Nu was moved—as the British retreated before the Japanese in

1942—to the cholera-infested jail at Mandalay. It was at Insein that he wrote one of the saddest of his novels, *Man, the Wolf of Man,* the title a Burmese translation of Thomas Hobbes's bitter phrase "Man is to man a wolf."[32] In its preface he wrote:

> One dull day in jail his thoughts suddenly lighted on the fact that the ambition of his eighteenth year was still to be realized. Here he was in his thirty-fourth year and the sixteen years he had lost would never be recalled. He felt so bereft that he had to console himself with the thought that although he had not realized his personal ambition he had at any rate had a hand in subduing the fire that was consuming his country.[33]

Nu wrote another novel in Insein jail and was allowed to produce one of the plays he wrote there, with fellow prisoners as members of the cast. Two of the plays that he translated into English at Insein were subsequently published and sold during the Japanese occupation. Later, in Mandalay jail, Nu wrote seven more plays.

FIVE

UNDER THE JAPANESE

THE INVASION of Burma began on December 9, 1941, but despite heavy bombing Mandalay did not fall to the Japanese until May 3, 1942. Rangoon had fallen two months before, on March 7. Mandalay jail, where Thakin Nu had been imprisoned by the British, ordinarily held no more than 1,500 convicts, but 3,000 were crowded into the filthy, cholera-ridden prison at the time of the Japanese attack.

In April 1942, more than a month after the fall of Rangoon, visitors arrived at the jail to see Nu: a Chinese Nationalist General whom Nu had known in Rangoon before the war and in Chungking on his good-will mission, and Nu's nationalist friend, the editor "Deedok" U Ba Cho. The Chinese and the British wanted Nu to go to China to supply Thakin support in their fight against the Japanese. But since China and Britain were allied against Japan, Burma could not aid China without at the same time helping Britain. Hence, despite the wretched conditions in the jail, Nu agreed to go only if Britain would promise Burma independence after the war. Nu suggested that the Chinese convince the Governor, Sir Reginald Dorman-Smith, to cable London recommending independence for Burma. Nu also demanded that his Communist colleagues be allowed to accompany him to China. They were his teachers and friends, he said, who had made him aware of the threat posed by the "fascists." Nu specified not only Thakins Soe, Ba Hein, and Kyaw Sein, who were with him in the Mandalay jail, but also Thakin Than Tun, a prisoner in Monywa jail.[1]

A few days later U Ba Cho returned with the report that Nu's demands had been met. So it was that Nu and the other young nationalists set out by "Black Maria"—door bolted—for Maymyo and thence to Lashio, at the western end of the Burma Road, for the flight to Chungking. But the Japanese had closed the Burma Road, and the car had to turn back at Maymyo. The next day, all but the political prisoners were released from Mandalay jail. On May 1, 1942, two days before the fall of Mandalay to the Japanese, the remaining prisoners were able to bribe the chief jailer and gain their freedom.[2]

Kyaw Nyein and Thein Pe, political and personal friends from the days of the University strike, met Nu in Kanbaing village with the news that although Aung San and the other Thirty Comrades, who had entered the country in January, had aided the invading Japanese, the Communists and the Burma Revolutionary Party had begun resistance activities against the Japanese almost immediately. The "Burma Independence Army," as the force led by Aung San was called, became the "Defense Army" in late 1942 and the "National Army" in 1943. Although both Nu and Aung San subsequently became members of the Japanese-sponsored wartime government, they also simultaneously supported the work of the resistance movement. Aung San, Ne Win, and other Army leaders informed Dr. Ba Maw, who headed the government set up by the Japanese, that they realized Japan had "cheated" them.

Once again Nu attempted to forsake politics for writing. This time, however, to the familiar pressures from longtime nationalist associates was added a new one: Japanese suspicion. The outspoken Nu, who had written harshly of Japan's imperialist activities in his 1940 book on China, was being watched by the *kempetai*, or military police. His colleagues finally convinced him to protect himself by associating with the Japanese-sponsored regime.

Shortly after he arrived in Rangoon following his release from Mandalay jail Nu was summoned to a meeting to discuss governing arrangements under the Japanese. Thakin Mya, wisest and most experienced of the leaders of the prewar Dobama Asiayone, subsequently introduced Nu to the Japanese Colonel Suzuki, who took Nu with him to see Dr. Ba Maw. At his second meeting with Ba Maw, Nu learned that he was to participate in a "Preparatory Committee" to frame a constitution; he immediately refused. Ba Maw, however, insisted that Nu, Aung San, and Than Tun permit him to "train" them to govern the country. Finally, Nu reluctantly agreed to serve on the committee if Dr. Ba Maw would not press him to participate in the government subsequently formed.[3]

The patriotic and courageous if highly vain Ba Maw sought Thakin aid and endorsement as a means of limiting the extent of Japanese domination and exploitation of occupied Burma—his royal pretensions and other shortcomings notwithstanding. "Ba Maw did not make major decisions during the war years without consulting the Thakins," U Ohn Khin has stated, "which meant consulting Thakin Nu, who was both influential among the Thakins and the main link between Dr. Ba Maw and the Dobama nationalists."[4] "Dr. Ba Maw trusted Nu alone of the Thakins," according to Thakin Tin,[5] and Nu, for his part, aware of Ba Maw's real power under the Japanese, used his influence to aid members of the anti-Japanese resistance movement.

During these years Nu was "closer to Dr. Ba Maw than most of Dr. Ba Maw's own group."[6] As the war progressed, many of the young men around Ba Maw gradually lost confidence in him, but Nu remained loyal. According to Ba Maw, "Nu's most important service during these years was bringing the younger and more radical elements into our political coalition. Aung San and Than Tun played a part in doing this, too, but Nu was most important in this respect."[7] Although Thakin Mya was primarily responsible for organizing the only political party permitted in the country, the Dobama Sinyetha Asiayone, formed by the merger in 1942 of Dr. Ba Maw's Sinyetha Party and the Dobama Asiayone, Nu served as its first Secretary-General. Indeed, it was Nu who suggested that the party be formed.[8] Although this official party was created primarily as a means of uniting Burma's highly individualistic politicians and thus limiting opportunities for Japanese exploitation of differences among them, "it was also an excellent device to keep a hand on the pulse of the people," according to a veteran Burmese newsman.[9]

Thakin Tin, who worked closely with Nu in the Dobama Sinyetha Asiayone, has said that his friend accepted the post of Secretary of the party "in order to avoid participation in the formal apparatus of government at this time."[10] But according to Dr. Ba Maw, Nu was not in his initial "pre-independence" government "because he was not nominated by the Thakins." Thakins Than Tun and Mya, and Aung San, were the ablest of the Dobama politicians who cooperated with him during the period of Japanese occupation, Dr. Ba Maw has said— Thakin Mya suave and perceptive and Than Tun possibly the most intelligent of the younger nationalists, with seemingly boundless vitality. "Aung San," according to Ba Maw, "had common sense, more of it than any of the others. He was erratic and intolerant and hard to get along with, but he saw things as they really were, divorced himself from all this ideological nonsense, and rolled up his sleeves and got to work." As for Thakin Nu, "he was a dreamer—not a worker."[11]

Only about half a dozen of the 120 appointments in Dr. Ba Maw's first government, established on August 1, 1942, were made from the ranks of Thakins or Aung San's Burma Independence Army. Dr. Ba Maw's own political cronies predominated, and hence the Thakins were

suspicious of Ba Maw. Thakins Mya and Than Tun thought of resigning, but Nu helped to deter them. "That would have been just what
the Japanese wanted," he later wrote, "as they were always doing their
best to find a weak joint and split the parties."[12]

According to Ba Maw, the Japanese adviser to the Preparatory
Commission actually drew up the basic documents governing Burmese
independence and Burma's relations with Japan.[13] Nu did not play a
major role in this; "framing rules and so on makes my head ache; it
does not interest me and I don't understand it," he has said. But, Nu
wrote, "four of us, Kodaw Hmaing, Thakin Mya, Thakin Than Tun
and I, held the scales, and the side to which we gave our votes could
win." These Thakins did not use their influence for fear of undermin-
ing Dr. Ba Maw and thus playing into Japan's hands.[14]

In *Burma under the Japanese,* Nu tells of an incident that occurred
shortly before independence was obtained:

> While Dr. Ba Maw was pressing forward against the Japanese
> on the main front, he also had to settle accounts with us in the rear.
> Shortly before he was due for election as *Adipati* the three of us,
> Thakin Mya, Thakin Than Tun and I, went to see him in his office.*
>
> "Now, *Ahnashin,*" we said, "we have fulfilled our pledge to
> support you to the best of our ability, how about the other matter
> that we mentioned?"
>
> "What is that?" he asked.
>
> "Group dictatorship, of course."
>
> "Well, what about it?"
>
> "We want to be certain of our position while there is still time.
> If you don't agree we shall be unable to support you in the election
> for *Adipati.*"
>
> When Dr. Ba Maw heard this he took up the watch that was
> lying on the table and was so shocked that he stared straight ahead
> for a couple of minutes without saying a word. Then he went on,
> "But isn't that just what I've been saying? For ages I've been urg-
> ing the appointment of an Inner Circle. Wasn't it I who first had
> the idea? Very well, then form your Inner Circle. It ought to have
> been formed long ago."

"Our only object," according to Nu, "was to let Dr. Ba Maw understand how far we would go in supporting him."[15] An "Inner Circle"
was formed—including, besides Nu, Thakins Mya, Than Tun, Aung

---

* *Adipati* is a Burmese term for leader or head of state. *Ahnashin,* in the next
line, is from the Burmese term *Ahnashin Mingyi,* literally dictator-king, a title
Ba Maw assumed.

San, and Chit[16]—which functioned throughout the war as a largely autonomous (and informal) political body. Although it had no official status, its members frequently brought collective pressure to bear on Ba Maw, and the "Inner Circle," subsequently expanded, played a major role near the war's end in launching the anti-Japanese "Anti-Fascist Organization."

Despite his increasingly important role in Burmese politics these were still learning years for Nu. About the way leaders and secretaries were appointed (Ba Maw supporters were usually named leaders and Thakins secretaries), he wrote:

> A Thakin would say, "I can't possibly agree to this man being appointed a leader. During all the trouble, he remained in hiding and now he turns up for the first time at this tea-party wearing a Dama* head-dress for the elections." And a Dama would reply, "Do you call that man a Thakin? During the Burma Independence Army time all he did was confiscate a gun and use it to attack Damas." And then suddenly they would recollect themselves and burst out laughing. And I thought to myself, "So this is the way to become a public man," and noted it as Lesson No. 1 in the Politician's A B C.[17]

Dr. Ba Maw clearly was not popular with the Japanese. Though an opportunist, he was also a dedicated nationalist and no puppet of Japan. He enjoyed the pomp and prestige of office, but resented the Japanese as he had the British. Even before independence, at a meeting in Singapore with Japanese Prime Minister Tojo (and the Indian nationalist Subhas Chandra Bose), he complained about the activities of the Japanese Army in Burma.[18] Nu accompanied Ba Maw to the meeting, although he held no formal office at the time.

While the constitution for independence was being drawn up, the Japanese tried to tempt Nu, with the promise that he would succeed to Ba Maw's office, into aligning himself against Ba Maw. Nu, however, proclaimed his loyalty to Ba Maw, stating unequivocally that he did not want the job.

Thakin Nu was soon to have the opportunity to deal officially with Japan: he became Foreign Minister in the reorganized government that assumed office on August 1, 1943. Dr. Ba Maw was *Adipati,* or Premier, and among Nu's Cabinet colleagues were Thakin Mya, Deputy Prime Minister; Dr. Thein Maung, Ba Maw's longtime right-hand

* Dr. Ba Maw's political supporters were known as Damas.

man, Minister of Finance; Thakin Than Tun, Minister of Land and Agriculture; Aung San, a Major General in the National Army, Minister of War; Thakin Lay Maung, Minister of Transport; and Bandoola U Sein, Minister of Propaganda and Prosperity.

Nu had refused to accept the post of Foreign Minister, despite Ba Maw's urging. Finally, on July 30, the night before the reorganization, members of the Thakin Inner Circle called on Nu and persuaded him to take the post. In 1956, Nu described this visit to Members of Parliament from his party: "Bogyoke Aung San, Thakin Mya, U Ba Swe, U Kyaw Nyein and other colleagues insisted on my acceptance of office and even held out a threat that they would quit politics if I refused to join up."[19]

The prerogatives of office could not compensate for the humiliation of Japanese domination. "As a Minister, I was given for my residence a big brick house, a motor car and a good salary which enabled me to buy good clothes," Nu has stated. "I not only had regular meals but good food." Yet he was not happy: "Every day was miserable for me, and every day I longed for my old life of poverty, because although I was a Minister, I had no power at all, and had to look on without daring to protest at the tyrannies and atrocities perpetrated by the fascist Japanese all over the country. Every day and every hour, I lived in expectancy and dread of the Japanese *kempetai* coming to get me."[20]

Incidents like the following hurt Nu's nationalist pride. After much coaxing from his driver, he had finally agreed to fly the Burmese flag on his official car. His reluctance had stemmed from the fact that it would call attention to any discourtesy tendered him. A Japanese military policeman halted the car to permit the passage of a Japanese General, and when Nu returned home he "tore the flag off, and I would not take the car again that day, but went to my office by taking a boat across the lake." According to Nu, "This kind of thing happened so often that in the end I went down with dysentery and was confined to my house."[21]

The most serious strain on relations with the Japanese with which Nu had to deal as Foreign Minister was an attempt by a follower of Major General Isamura (military head of the Burmese-Japanese Relations Department) to assassinate Dr. Ba Maw. Isamura was transferred to Singapore and his henchmen were given fifteen-year prison sentences. "But as a matter of fact," Nu has written, "they were kept in a house where, as many people could see quite plainly, they were plentifully supplied with food and women." The Burmese government, moreover, was not allowed to prosecute a Burmese aide of one of the henchmen, who was involved in the assassination attempt.

According to Nu, he had only three tasks of any importance during his year as Foreign Minister: apologizing for a Burmese soldier who had bayoneted a Japanese (which he never did), attempting to arrest the Burmese who had participated in the attempt on Ba Maw's life (which was unsuccessful), and arranging precedence at the wedding of the *Adipati*'s daughter, Tinsa Maw. For the rest, the Foreign Office had charge of sending telegrams to the Axis powers—on national holidays, birthdays, and such. The wires were so numerous that the Foreign Office became known as the Telegraph Office.[22] At first Nu looked at these telegrams personally, but soon got bored and stopped. Neither Foreign Minister Nu nor *Adipati* Ba Maw had any significant influence on such an important foreign policy matter as the use of Burmese soil for Japan's attempt to invade India in 1944.

Nu, who early in the war had turned down a chance to go to China, later had another opportunity to leave Burma. His friend Than Tun, though a minister in the Ba Maw government, was active in the resistance movement. Than Tun promised that the next plane out would carry Nu and his family to India, if Nu wanted to go. "But it was merely on the spur of the moment that I agreed to go," Nu later wrote, "and, when I came to think over the matter, I could not make up my mind."[23] Yet the insults Nu endured as Foreign Minister wearied him. Hence on December 9, 1944, after slightly more than a year as Minister of Foreign Affairs, he moved to the Information Department.

At an early press conference for Japanese editors Nu was typically outspoken, attacking "the habit of slapping people which is indulged in by the Japanese."[24] The Japanese press, understandably, carried no word of the conference. Nu also created some controversy by publicly attacking *pongyis* for interfering in politics. "As our Lord the Buddha said," he later wrote, "to lead the life of a monk is as delicate a task as to balance a grain of mustard seed on the point of a needle. So how can a *pongyi,* who must walk so delicately, do the work of a politician, the roughest of all worldly pursuits?" Elders among the *pongyis* complained of Nu's attitude and activities to the Minister for Religious Affairs, and the matter came before Dr. Ba Maw. Because of the stir Nu had created, Ba Maw decided that he was not suited for the Information Department. According to Nu, Ba Maw "thought it far more serious to hurt the feelings of the *pongyis* in whom he trusted than to annoy the Japanese editors. So he urged me to go back to the Foreign Office, but as I objected very strongly the matter was dropped."[25]

Usually, however, Nu's speeches were politically useful to Ba Maw. Indeed, Ba Maw once asked Nu, "Deedok" U Ba Cho, and Henzada U Mya to stump the country "to preach about Greater Burma." The three main points of their talks were to be "Our Government," "Our Property," and "Our War." Ba Maw asked Nu to speak out vigorously on the first two; the purpose of the third was to make the Japanese "less suspicious." Nu and Aung San also traveled to Karen villages in the delta region, attempting to ally this important ethnic group with the Burmese regime. Both men (and Than Tun, who also tried to conciliate the Karens) believed that the unity of its minority peoples was essential to the development and strength of the "new Burma."

In a public address of appreciation to the *Adipati,* as reported in a Japanese-controlled newspaper, Nu thanked Ba Maw "for introducing into the country the principle of leadership based on the slogan 'one blood, one voice, one leader.' "[26] The slogan actually was closer to the nationalist battle cry of the Dobama Asiayone of the late 1930's than to the political philosophy of Ba Maw. "One blood" (restrictive nationalism) was hardly the sort of thinking the Japanese would intentionally foster among Burmese politicians, "one voice" seemed in essence Nu's "group leadership," and "one leader" hardly differed in spirit from the young Thakins' glorification of Hitler and Mussolini or Thakin Ba Thaung's inspiration from Nietzsche. Nu probably meant what he said.

Nu was highly critical of the way many of his countrymen behaved during the Japanese occupation. During these years, he later declared, "political power meant wealth to many selfish people."[27] He understood, however, that when people "have been enslaved very few can retain any self-respect or sense of personal shame. They place little value on the strength they might derive from social unity with their own folk, or of using this common social unity to promote the national welfare; they value more highly the strength they derive from making common cause with foreigners, and instead of using their position to help their people they use it to cut their throats."[28]

Yet, however much Nu, Aung San, Than Tun, and the others might be seeking to prepare their people for ultimate independence and self-reliance, they did not see how close they were to their goal. "Five years ago," Nu said when independence came in 1948, "few of us alive today, however hard we fought for freedom, imagined it was so near at hand."[29] "When the AFPFL was first formed," Nu declared in 1956, "independence and political power were more or less a distant mirage. Before us lay untold misery, extreme sacrifices and insuperable obstacles."[30]

From the start, the younger nationalists had borne the burden of Burmese underground resistance to the Japanese. Thein Pe the Communist and Kyaw Nyein of the Burma Revolutionary Party were among the first resistance leaders. Thakin Soe, also a Communist, joined the resistance movement after his release from Mandalay jail. Kyaw Nyein subsequently participated as well in Dr. Ba Maw's government, while the Communist Than Tun, an early member of Ba Maw's Japanese-sponsored administration, simultaneously and increasingly assumed a role of leadership in the underground. Thein Pe fled to India with Thakin Tin Shwe in 1942 and established liaison between the resistance movement and the British. Tin Shwe returned to Burma by British aircraft in early 1944 and made contact with the growing underground, and later the same year Thein Pe obtained "formal recognition" by the Commander of Britain's "Force 136" (created to aid resistance movements in enemy countries) of the main anti-Japanese organization in occupied Burma. This recognition meant that the British would supply arms to the Burmese resistance forces, a point that caused intense disagreement among British officials and was to have a major effect on post-war Burmese political development.[31]

The Anti-Fascist People's Freedom League, the nationalist organization that played the primary role in obtaining Burmese independence from the British after Japan's surrender in 1945, was first called simply the Anti-Fascist Organization ("People's Freedom" being subsequently added to indicate the aims of the post-Japanese period). The AFO, the resistance organization for which Thein Pe obtained "Force 136" recognition, was formally founded at a meeting at Thakin Nu's house in Rangoon on August 1, 1944.[32] Although there had been a resistance movement against the Japanese from the start of the occupation period, it had been made up of separate uncoordinated groups—Thakin Soe, for example, led a virtually autonomous wing of anti-Japanese Burmese Communists. Several members of the Ba Maw government did virtually everything in their power to facilitate resistance activity and to rescue its perpetrators when they were caught. Thakin Nu's was probably the most important role in this regard. Nu himself, however, did not actively participate in resistance activity, although he usually knew what was going on. As he has described it, "In all our discussions we were like brothers discussing family affairs that concerned the whole family, including those who took no active part in them."[33]

The August 1944 founding meeting of the AFO was not the first session of its type among the groups that joined ranks at this time. Army leaders, including Aung San, and various "partisans" had met from time to time at Kyaw Nyein's and Ne Win's houses. (Ne Win, known before the war as Thakin Shu Maung, was second to Aung San in command of the National Army.) The August 1944 meeting was convened by General Aung San, War Minister in the Ba Maw government, because he felt that a successful revolt against the Japanese would soon be possible. He was strongly supported in establishing the AFO by the intelligent and vigorous Communist, Thakin Than Tun.

The main groups joining to form the AFO were the Army, the Burma Revolutionary Party, and the Communists. Other groups that associated themselves with the AFO soon after its founding were the East Asia Youth League, Dr. Ba Maw's Mahabama (Greater Burma) Party (which displaced the Dobama Sinyetha as the official political organization), the Sanghas' Asiayone (a political organization of Buddhist clergy), and several of the major ethnic groups, the Karens, Shans, Kachins, Chins, and Arakanese.[34] Present at the founding meeting of the AFO, besides Nu, were "the members of the Inner Circle, Thakin Mya, General Aung San, Thakin Than Tun and Thakin Chit."[35] Although in *Burma under the Japanese,* written only a year after the conference, Nu did not list Kyaw Nyein and Ba Swe as members of the Inner Circle, they too were clearly important in founding the AFO. The leaders of the new organization during the remaining war years were Aung San, Ne Win, and Bo Let Ya of the Army; Kyaw Nyein, Ba Swe, and Thakins Mya and Chit of the BRP (which shortly after the war became the Socialist Party), and Thakins Than Tun, Soe, and Ba Hein of the Communists. Aung San headed the AFO's "Supreme Council."

Thakin Nu was not formally a member of the AFO because of his abhorrence of violence. However, he approved the document "Rise and Attack the Fascist Dacoits!" that was read to those who gathered at his house the night of the founding meeting. The Army was given responsibility for printing this proclamation and distributing it to revolutionaries throughout the country for further circulation. Dr. Ba Maw was aware of the activities of the AFO, having been informed of its formation and intentions by Nu, Thakin Than Tun, and later Aung San himself. He refused to join the young revolutionaries, but neither did he oppose them. Without his cooperation, in large measure the result of Nu's liaison work, the AFO might have been at least partly checked. The Communists, one of the three major groups in the AFO, made a definite ideological contribution and their leaders participated in the shaping of resistance strategy, but they supplied only 26 cadre leaders for district organizing in contrast to some 800 from the Army and the BRP.[36]

The revolt against the Japanese began on March 27, 1945, after General Aung San and most of the 10,000-man Burma National Army had marched out of Rangoon to fight the "enemy." The next Burma's Japanese rulers heard of the Army it was attacking their garrison at Pegu. Although the BNA played a secondary role in ousting the Japanese, its support of the returning British facilitated the British advance considerably. Two months later, in May 1945, when the British had reoccupied Rangoon and established the headquarters of their military administration there, Aung San brought the resistance movement out into the open as the Anti-Fascist People's Freedom League. The following month the BNA changed its name to the "Patriotic Burmese Forces" (whose veterans were later known as the "People's Volunteer Organization"). Having sided with the British against the Japanese, Aung San, Than Tun, and the other AFPFL leaders now sought to pry Burma loose from British control.

Nu accompanied Dr. Ba Maw in the disorderly Japanese retreat from Rangoon. It had been decided previously that Nu and Aung San would go into hiding when Than Tun left on a mission to contact the British, since Than Tun's absence would arouse the suspicions of the Japanese. But, as the time of departure approached, Nu hesitated. He "began to think that if I disappeared without warning him [Dr. Ba Maw] it would be a nasty jar." He felt that "from my first appointment as Minister, I had pledged my loyalty to him and I could not lightly break this pledge."[37] Equally important were the pleas of Kyaw Nyein and Hla Maung that Nu stay to prevent the Japanese from harming their Burmese political prisoners. Nu told Bo Let Ya that "there would be complete chaos if he did not accompany Dr. Ba Maw."[38] There are others, however, who say that Ba Maw talked Nu into departing with him.

The retreat began on April 22, 1945. Ba Maw, who had given Nu only one day's warning, advised Nu not to accompany him, Nu has said, because of the disfavor in which Nu was still held by the Japanese. "However, I rejected this advice," Nu has written, "as there would certainly be many Thakin leaders on the Moulmein side whom the Japanese had caught before they managed to get away, and I had undertaken to protect them. But I would not follow him outside Burma."[39] Nevertheless, however voluntary his determination to make the retreat, Nu was clearly a hostage.[40]

Nu, Ba Maw, Thakin Mya, and other government officials—and their families—started out on the journey that began in automobiles Nu has described as "worn-out contraptions" and continued in a variety of dilapidated conveyances. Nu's wife, Daw Mya Yee, and his five-year-old son and baby daughter were with him, and at one point Nu carried Daw Mya Yee on his back and his tiny daughter on one arm. The dangerous and difficult journey ended at Mudon, near Moulmein in peninsular Burma. There Nu spent his time reading books borrowed from the Moulmein Library.

It was at Mudon on August 14, 1945, that Dr. Ba Maw told Nu and his other ministers of the dropping of the atomic bomb, the Soviet Union's entry into the war, and Japan's intention to surrender. Thus ended Ba Maw's career as a major participant in Burmese politics; though often a valuable critic in the politics of independent Burma, he was never again a serious contender for top leadership.

The war years were important ones for Thakin Nu. He had been tested frequently, had behaved remarkably well for a man of limited political experience, and had learned much. Moreover, his was a role of crucial importance in Burma's wartime politics. As the war progressed, it became increasingly apparent that Burma had two chief leaders: Dr. Ba Maw, tragic in his role as the spirited leader of a pseudo-independent land, and Aung San, powerful commander of the Burma National Army and chief founder of the AFO. Than Tun, Thakin Mya, Kyaw Nyein, Ba Swe, Thakin Soe, Bo Let Ya, and Bo Ne Win played lesser roles but played them well. Nu, however, was the link that enabled them to work together and ultimately to achieve their goal.

SIX

❀

A NEW LEADER

TOWARD THE END of the Second World War the leaders of the various factions that made up the Anti-Fascist Organization forgot their rivalries and disagreements in their common bid for Burma's freedom. Although both military and civilian officials subordinate to Admiral Lord Louis Mountbatten (Supreme Allied Commander for Southeast Asia) were opposed to Force 136's supplying arms, in early 1945, to the resistance movement led by the AFO, Mountbatten decided not to reverse the policy.[1] Mountbatten also disagreed with Governor Sir Reginald Dorman-Smith (who spent the war years at Simla, in India) on the policy to be pursued toward the AFO. Mountbatten, aware of the increasing unity among the AFO leaders, favored "leniency and conciliation," describing the AFO as a "coalition of political parties commanding the largest following in the territory," but Sir Reginald would not agree to AFO participation in his Executive Council before his return to Burma. In the eyes of the Governor, the AFO leaders were traitors and hardly the spokesmen of the Burmese nation. Some of Mountbatten's own officers were opposed to his treatment of those Burmese who had aided Japan, and urged him to arrest Aung San immediately as a war criminal. But the Supreme Commander's views prevailed in London, and Aung San's Patriotic Burmese Forces were accepted by Britain as a temporary ally and were given financial and other support. Mountbatten encouraged the leaders of the AFO by such actions as his private audience with Aung San and Than Tun in Rangoon in June 1945, after the victory parade of British and Burmese forces, and his subsequent meetings with Aung San (which were followed by the disbanding of the Patriotic Burmese Forces and the enlistment of many PBF fighting men in the regular Army).

Thus Mountbatten acted against the judgment of most of his associates, and certainly against Sir Reginald Dorman-Smith's Simla government, in his relations with Aung San, leader of the Anti-Fascist People's Freedom League (as the AFO was known after the return of the British to Burma). At first there were military reasons for acting as he did, but ultimately political considerations seemed to weigh equally heavily in the Admiral's decisions. The AFPFL was a growing force, and it unquestionably would have been of major importance in the political development of postwar Burma in any case—but Mountbatten's backing clearly strengthened its position, both politically and militarily. Mountbatten, for his part, recognized the AFPFL for what it was: a unified Burmese assault on continued British rule that could not in the end be denied with the resources at Britain's disposal, concerned as Britain was with the simultaneous thrust for independence on the Indian sub-continent. By early May 1945, when the British returned to Rangoon, the AFPFL included virtually every political opinion group in the country, including most of the minority peoples. The Patriotic Burmese Forces, moreover, were ready to fight, if necessary, for their country's freedom. The strong-willed Aung San was the head of this military arm of the nationalist movement as well as the leader of the AFPFL proper.

Admiral Mountbatten's Southeast Asia Command was not the British Government, however, and Prime Minister Winston Churchill and his Conservative Party were of no immediate mind to succumb to the demands made by the AFPFL at Japan's defeat and Ba Maw's fall. British plans for post-war Burma were revealed in the White Paper of May 10, 1945, which proclaimed Britain's ultimate aim to accord self-government to the Burmese.[2] But "the re-establishment of stable conditions, the restoration of buildings, communications, and public utilities, and the rehabilitation of agriculture and other essential industries" made it necessary to continue to suspend the 1935 Constitution. The Governor would rule the country, nominally independent under the Japanese, with the help of a "small and mainly official" Executive Council, which would subsequently be expanded. Representative government would not be re-established for at least three years.

The AFPFL denounced the White Paper on the grounds that it was regressive; it seemed, moreover, to contain no concessions whatever to Burmese nationalist demands. The League was unwilling even to return to the political condition of Burma on the eve of the war with Japan. The nationalists also took exception to the policy of rehabilitating the Burmese economy by means of so-called "projects" utilizing prewar British firms and to the recognition of abandoned Indian Chettyar land holdings. Aung San offered Britain the cooperation of Burma as an independent nation, but Governor Dorman-Smith, who had taken over responsibility for most of the country from Admiral Mountbatten's military administration in mid-October, refused his offer. Instead, on November 1, the Governor appointed an Executive Council made up of three Britons and nine Burmese, none of whom were members of the AFPFL. Relations between Dorman-Smith and the AFPFL deteriorated steadily during the next six months, and a new Governor, Sir Hubert Rance, took office in late August 1946. Faced with a general strike which developed from a police strike that was exploited by the AFPFL, Rance sought and obtained from London permission to negotiate with Aung San. On September 26, a new Executive Council was formed that included six members of the AFPFL and three politically independent Burmese. Aung San was Deputy to the Governor, who headed the Council, and he was also Minister of Defense.

The AFPFL had entered the postwar period united in its demand for independence, but other serious differences divided the movement, which was led by several strong-willed political figures. The most important of the AFPFL leaders was unquestionably Aung San, who led the veterans of the disbanded Patriotic Burmese Forces (the People's Volunteer Organization) as well as the AFPFL itself. The steady and perceptive Thakin Mya, one of the older AFPFL leaders, directed the mass All-Burma Peasants Organization, although Thakin Tin was its nominal leader, while Thakin Than Tun, the leader of the Communists, was generally regarded as number two man in the League (second only to Aung San and probably ahead of Thakin Mya). The first split within the AFPFL occurred among the Communists—or, more accurately, between Thakin Soe, on the one hand, and Than Tun and Thein Pe, on the other. Thakin Soe formed his own Communist Party, the Communist Party of Burma (as distinct from the Burmese Communist Party) in March 1946; it was proscribed four months later. A showdown between Aung San, President of the AFPFL, and Than Tun and the other Communists followed shortly afterward. The politically shifty Aung San, in an effort to increase his control of the party, proposed Kyaw Nyein as General Secretary of the AFPFL, the post that Than Tun had held since the League's inception. The outraged Than Tun countered with the nomination of fellow Communist Thein Pe and forced the issue to a vote but lost by the narrow margin of 53 to 52. The Communists subsequently vehemently denounced Aung San and the AFPFL, even though they remained within the party. When Governor Sir Hubert Rance invited Aung San to form an interim government in September 1946, Than Tun demanded two portfolios for the Communists; however, they were given only one (which went to Thein Pe). The attacks on Aung San and the party became ruthless to the point of obscenity, and the following month the Communist representatives were expelled from the Executive Council of the AFPFL.[3] The motion for their expulsion was made by Thakin Nu.

After the split with Thakin Soe the unity within the AFPFL among the Communists led by Than Tun had caused the non-Communist leftists to draw closer together. These came to form the Socialist Party, which, originally established in September 1945 from the nucleus of the prewar Burma Revolutionary Party, later developed a strong and formal enough organization to become a counterpoise to the Communists. Ba Swe, one of its chief founders (with Kyaw Nyein), was its first President, and became its Secretary-General when the older Thakin Mya returned to Rangoon and became head of the party. The Communists were "probably the single best organized force within the AFPFL in the immediate postwar period," according to U Win, who was elected President of the Trade Union Congress (Burma) at this time by forces concerned to prevent the Communist takeover of labor which was in progress.[4]

Despite these developing divisions, Aung San, like Dr. Ba Maw and Thakin Nu in the war years, was convinced of the need for unity among Burma's nationalists against the common foe, British colonialism. The result was that the AFPFL came to be more a party in its own right than the coalition or alliance it had really started out to be. For all but the Communists, accordingly, the AFPFL came first, the component organizations second. Yet there were still hints of divided loyalties.

Thakin Nu's role within the AFPFL in the struggle against the British was an important one, although Nu was not, on the surface, a major participant in the jockeying for power. He had taken no active part in politics in the immediate postwar period, having retired to Moulmeingyun to write and meditate, but he clearly supported Aung San and the AFPFL. Besides *Burma Under the Japanese,* which he started in Moulmeingyun and completed in Rangoon, Nu wrote articles for the Burmese-language newspaper *The New Light of Burma,* and another tract on Marxism. Nu's retirement in Moulmeingyun was extremely short-lived, however. Well-liked and regarded as an uncompromising advocate of Burmese independence, he was also known for his desire and ability, demonstrated during the period of Japanese occupation, to hold together the diverse and frequently warring factions of the Burmese nationalist movement. Largely for this reason, practically everybody wanted him to return to politics.

It was not surprising that the Communists were among those who wanted Nu back in the political arena in view of his ideological orientation in the late 1930's, his close wartime links with Thakin Than Tun (and the high regard in which he held him), and his postwar writings favorable to Marxism. Of the Communists, Thein Pe Myint was the most active in soliciting Nu's return to politics; he and the other Communists, including Than Tun, were "increasingly annoyed" that Aung San was "not as socialist-oriented" as they. According to the editor U Ohn Khin, "Thein Pe had the idea of getting Nu active and on his side so as to stack the cards against Aung San." Ohn Khin remembers telling Thein Pe that he was playing with fire: "If he goes along with you, you're a winner. But, if somehow he ends up on the other side, you'll have different thoughts about your wisdom."[5] The Socialists too, increasingly alarmed by the aims and organizational strength of the Communists, actively urged that Nu give up his retirement.

Aung San also clearly felt the need for a reliable and strong lieutenant in the final drive for independence, and regarded Nu as the most suitable person for the job.[6] Nu himself stated in 1956 that "Aung San and other members of the AFPFL Executive Council sent for me several times and asked me to accept the Vice Presidentship of that great organization and assured me that I could carry on my literary pursuits and that I need not devote more than two hours a week to AFPFL matters."[7] "I felt it impossible to refuse anymore," Nu said in another speech.[8]

Upon his return to political life, Nu did not immediately become a major influence within the AFPFL. A former colleague has recalled that he sat quietly in a corner at meetings of the leaders of the League and took no active part in the discussions.[9] "In terms of his ranking among the leaders," U Ba Swe has recalled of the early months following Nu's return to politics, "Thakin Nu was well behind Thakin Mya, and Thakin Mya was not even a close second to Aung San."[10] Yet his importance among the AFPFL leaders increased rapidly—and the British, among others, took note. Sir Hubert Rance, the British Governor who replaced Dorman-Smith, termed Nu the "unseen power behind the AFPFL Executive Councilors."[11] Aung San usually took Nu with him when he consulted with the Governor. According to Sir Hubert, "There is no question that Aung San relied heavily upon him, that he was competent and respected, and that he was a power in his own right."[12]

There were several reasons for Nu's increasing importance. Foremost was his close association with Aung San, dating back to their days together at the University of Rangoon and in the Dobama Asiayone in the 1930's. Nu also helped Aung San explain the aims and role of the AFPFL to the nation, and he helped to defend his close friend from the attacks of others, including the Communists. Nu sought to keep the Communists in the AFPFL, however, and to woo them back when they left, because of the high value he placed on national unity in the last hours of the struggle for independence and the first years of freedom. Indeed, in November 1946 he declared: "May the real Communist movement in Burma be successful and may the leadership by unscrupulous people, who are misusing the name of Communism . . . be quickly destroyed."[13] He finally sanctioned the expulsion of the Communists because their continued presence in the League weakened it more than their ouster. Because of the threat posed by the Communists, Nu earlier "gave his blessing"[14] to the organization of the Socialist Party within the AFPFL by Ba Swe, Kyaw Nyein, and others.[15]

Like Aung San, Thakin Nu demanded that primary political loyalty be to the League itself, and he never became a member of the inner group of Socialist leaders. Nonetheless, the Socialists trusted Nu, and this trust plus Aung San's backing and need of him largely underlay Nu's rapidly increasing importance within the AFPFL. He was trusted by everybody: the conservative old-line nationalists, the Socialists, the leaders of the minorities, Aung San, the British, and even the Communists. He was a sort of political broker, as he had been under Dr. Ba Maw. Yet he was honest, dedicated to the nationalist cause, single-minded in his desire for emancipation from colonial rule, and free from personal ambition. When the AFPFL joined the revised Governor's Executive Council under Sir Hubert Rance, Nu has said, "I stayed out in spite of repeated requests from my colleagues to change my mind."[16]

Although the AFPFL cooperated with Governor Sir Hubert Rance, its leaders still had their doubts about the sincerity of British intentions. Though he was opposed to mass political protest action as an initial tactical move, as proposed by the Communist Than Tun, Thakin Nu clearly backed the idea of a "national movement of defiance, led by the AFPFL," if by the end of January 1947 the British would not promise that they would withdraw completely within a year. Nu had come to the conclusion, he later said, that the time was ripe "to strike for independence." Aung San, sympathetic to Nu's view, called a meeting of the Executive Council to discuss it, but Kyaw Nyein was the only person to support Nu. However, Aung San moved a resolution that in effect adopted Nu's proposal, and it was carried unanimously.[17]

Nu's position was that before any negotiations began the British should issue a statement declaring that the talks would deal with independence and that Burma would be free to leave the Commonwealth. At Aung San's instruction, Nu presented the resolution to the Governor, and it was this action that was presumably chiefly responsible for Prime Minister Clement Attlee's offer, on December 20, 1946, of independence to Burma on the same terms as India and his accompanying invitation to send a Burmese delegation to London for negotiations.

Although the British had done what Nu wanted, he remained suspicious of their intentions. In "a kind of ultimatum"[18] to Aung San, Nu insisted that the AFPFL demand that the Constituent Assembly elections be held outside the framework of the Government of Burma Act of 1935, the colonial constitution of British Burma, in order to remove the country's misgivings as to whether "real independence" was to be forthcoming. At the request of the Executive Council, Nu spoke to the Governor on the subject, but without success. Nu felt so strongly, however, that he proposed that the senior nationalist politician Thakin Mya resign his Home Affairs portfolio temporarily in order to permit Nu, not a member of the government, to take his place on the independence delegation to London. Although Thakin Mya and the Socialists endorsed Nu's proposal, testifying to his growing political strength, Aung San told Nu that it was necessary for him "to remain behind to organize public demonstrations in support of the London discussions." Aung San, for his part, "undertook to try to obtain the concessions relating to the elections, and if he failed to do that, to stop the discussions and come home."[19]

The Aung San–Attlee Agreement, signed on January 27, 1947, promised elections on Burma's terms in April, convocation of the Constituent Assembly the following month, and transformation of the Executive Council into an interim government for Burma until authority was formally transferred. The Frontier Areas, inhabited by non-Burmans, would themselves choose whether to join independent Burma proper. The wily U Saw, who replaced Dr. Ba Maw as Premier before the war, and who was one of the non-AFPFL members of the Burmese delegation, refused to sign the agreement—for reasons of personal political advantage. However, on February 16, 1947, the Supreme Council of the AFPFL, of which Thakin Nu was a member, unanimously endorsed the London agreement.

Leaders of the Frontier Areas, Aung San, and other top AFPFL figures met at Panglong in the southern Shan States in February to discuss the problem of union. Representatives of the Shans, Kachins, and Chins agreed to enter into "immediate cooperation" with Aung San's "interim government." Thakin Nu did not attend the Panglong meeting, but he did visit a conference of the Supreme Council of the United Hill Peoples to urge union with Burma proper, and was an outspoken supporter of racial unity among the various Burmese peoples. He was also a member (for Burma proper) of the Frontier Areas Enquiry Committee,[20] created by the British Parliament and headed by M.P. David Rees-Williams, which held hearings in March and April 1947 and recommended "autonomous states" for the Shans and Kachins but reached no definite decisions regarding the other indigenous minority peoples.

The position of the hill peoples in the new Burma was not the only constitutional question that had to be resolved after Aung San's return from London: there was also the decision whether or not to remain in the Commonwealth. Governor Sir Hubert Rance has stated that Aung San "was satisfied that he could persuade the people to accept independence within the Empire";[21] Attlee has written that during the London negotiations Aung San "began to realize the desirability of remaining in the Commonwealth."[22] Thakin Nu, however, vigorously urged that Burma withdraw completely from the Commonwealth. Nu argued with Aung San and other members of the Executive Council that anything short of a full severance of the constitutional ties with the United Kingdom would split the AFPFL and would be exploited by the Communists. Burma's young leaders, moreover, expected that "India would not accept Dominion Status and Burma did not want to be any whit inferior to India."[23] Thus was the important decision taken for Burma to leave the Commonwealth.

As Vice President of the AFPFL, Nu played an important part in directing the campaign for the Constituent Assembly elections of April 9, 1947. But he did not stand for election to the Assembly despite Aung San's urging that he do so.[24] With independence definitely promised by the British and with preparations under way for the transfer of authority, Nu sought once more to return to his writing. He hoped that this time it would be "a permanent divorce from politics."[25]

The AFPFL swept the board in the April elections, winning 170 of the non-communal seats, compared to 10 for the combined opposition. The Communists, who in opposing negotiated independence denounced the Aung San–Attlee Agreement, won seven of the 10 seats, mostly in the Pyinmana and Akyab constituencies (they had put up 29 candidates). None of the Communist leaders were candidates, however, a situation that amounted to a partial boycott of the voting, since Than Tun neither trusted British intentions nor wished power transferred to a non-Communist government. The "Independence-First Alliance" of Dr. Ba Maw, U Saw, and Thakin Ba Sein also boycotted the elections, as did the Karen National Union, indicating that some leaders of a key minority did not support the AFPFL independence policy.

When the AFPFL Assembly member for Mergui died by drowning, Aung San resumed his efforts to get Thakin Nu to stand for election. This time he succeeded, but only after the usual struggle. According to Nu, "When I was adamant, Bogyoke burst out 'The country is doomed.' He was so upset that his voice turned hoarse. I had to comply with the request to stand for election from Mergui Constituency but I insisted on one condition: to permit me to leave office when the Constituent Assembly completed its functions."[26] Nu ran unopposed.

The Constituent Assembly began its deliberations in Rangoon on June 9, and two days later unanimously elected Nu its President. On June 16, Aung San moved a resolution in the Assembly proclaiming Burma's intention to establish itself as an independent and sovereign republic. A week later, a Burmese mission headed by Nu arrived by air in London to report to the British Government Burma's intention to leave the Commonwealth, and to discuss details of the transfer of power. The warmth of British friendship for Burma pleased Nu, and he became convinced of the sincerity of the retreating British. On July 8, when the talks ended, the British Government announced that a large measure of agreement had been reached.[27]

On Saturday, July 19, 1947, the AFPFL leaders were occupied with their usual tasks in the preparations for independence. Although it was still the monsoon season, the day was a fine one "with a bright sun playing in a blue sky." Busy officials moved about the main Secretariat building in downtown Rangoon, Burmese and English with business to transact came and went, and in a conference room on the second floor Aung San, Deputy Chairman of the interim government, met with his fellow Executive Councilors. U Kyaw Nyein and U Tin Tut were the only Council members absent from the meeting. There was only routine business on the agenda.

At 10:40 "an ugly unearthly noise" was heard from the chamber in which the Council was meeting. Those who went to investigate found that "chairs had tumbled down, tables had been upset and on the floor there was blood trickling in little sad streams from the wounds of the Councilors who were lying in different positions dead or dying."[28] Aung San (only 32), Thakin Mya (leader of the Socialist Party), "Deedok" U Ba Cho, the Karen leader Mahn Ba Khaing, the Sawbwa (hereditary ruler) of Mongpawn (state), the capable Indian Muslim A. Razak, U Ba Win, and others had been murdered. It was a hideous crime: the assassination of the top leaders of a politically inexperienced and backward land struggling toward a new era of freedom. Burma had had few enough leaders as it was; now some of the best of these few were gone.

The crime had been perpetrated by henchmen of U Saw—prewar Premier and dissenting member of the mission headed by Aung San that had gone to London in January—out of personal ambition and desire for revenge. U Saw, who wanted to lead independent Burma, believed that Aung San had instructed his supporters to shoot him. It cannot be said in U Saw's defense that he was motivated by cause or principle. He rarely was.

The crime had been well planned. Rather than meeting at Government House (just outside Rangoon proper), the Executive Council was meeting at the Secretariat, a less formidable and protective structure. Moreover, relatively inexperienced Burmese guards had only recently replaced British ones at the Secretariat. The four youths responsible for the actual slaying, dressed in Army uniforms and carrying Sten and Tommy guns, just brushed by the downstairs guards, but they had to kill the one upstairs.[29]

Fleeing from the Secretariat, the slayers hastened to the home of Thakin Nu to remove one more man who stood between the crazed U Saw and the leadership of independent Burma, but Nu was not there.[30]

U Saw expected that the Governor would have no choice but to name him Deputy Chairman (Premier-designate of independent Burma); if he did not do so, the ambitious veteran politician would use force. But U Saw had sorely miscalculated: nothing could have been farther from the minds of Sir Hubert Rance and his superiors in London.

Aung San's assassination was not a surprise to top Burmese and British leaders. Aung San himself knew that an attempt might be made on his life, Nu (among others) has said.[31] The Governor, too, has said that he knew of a plan to murder the Bogyoke. According to Sir Hubert Rance, "Men disguised as police had stolen some 200 guns, and this meant that something was up. I saw Aung San on Wednesday, July 16, and warned him. We both knew that U Saw was at the bottom of it all. Aung San said that 250 men would be rounded up on *Sunday, July 20, including U Saw* [italics mine]. He said that he couldn't move before then because the police could not manage it."[32]

By noon there were few in the capital who had not heard the news of Aung San's martyrdom. The streets were almost free of movement. The nation was stunned. Diehards among the English cited the assassinations as proof that the Burmese were not ready for self-government. But the crisis passed without further disaster, largely as a result of the swift and decisive response of Governor Sir Hubert Rance and the courage of Thakin Nu in an hour of great personal loss and trial. As Thakin Tin (later Deputy Premier of an independent Burma) has put it, Nu had the courage "alone among us all to take the chair of leadership on which the blood that had flowed from the heart of Aung San was still wet."[33]

The surviving members of the AFPFL Executive Council met the same afternoon; it was not a formal meeting, although all had been asked to attend. Nu, as AFPFL Vice President, was, of course, there. No decision had been made regarding a successor to Aung San when Governor Sir Hubert Rance called Nu to Government House. Sir Hubert pressed upon Nu the responsibility of immediately forming a new AFPFL government, and the leadership of that government. Nu accepted, but returned to the Executive Council meeting to get the approval of the remaining AFPFL leaders. Nu clearly was his colleagues' choice to succeed Aung San, but the initiative had come from the Governor.

Thakin Nu and the other members of the new Executive Council were sworn in by the Governor on the same night. They assumed their duties the next day. On the night of July 19, Nu broadcast a message to the nation. U Saw and his henchmen, meanwhile, were rounded up by the police, as the Governor moved swiftly to head off any further violence. Sir Hubert Rance had served Burma well in a time of great need.

Nu, too, had responded in a courageous fashion. He did not want to be Premier and told the Governor so; the Governor had to press him to accept the responsibility. "He probably had never thought of the possibility of being 'premier,'" U Ohn Khin has said, "and the loss of Aung San and his other beloved friends, as well as his sorrow in seeing Burmese slaying Burmese in such an hour, represented a real shock."[34] Nu himself spoke on the subject in 1954: "When Bogyoke Aung San and other leaders were assassinated on the 19th of July 1947, it fell to my lot to form the government. You will no doubt remember that I refused to take on the responsibility, partly because I did not feel inclined to accept it and partly because my knowledge of administration was nil."[35] But the Governor pressed him, and as he had done several times before, Nu, conscientious and dedicated, acceded.

PART TWO

❀

THE MAN AND HIS BELIEFS

SEVEN

❋

A REMARKABLE BUDDHIST

U Nu* lived very simply even after 1947, when the sudden deaths of Aung San and other ranking nationalist politicians elevated him to a leading position in the government of Burma. Nu's residence, whether he was in or out of office, was always modestly furnished and displayed only a handful of mementos of his nationalist and international political activity—one, a picture of his family with Yugoslav President Tito's family. Nu dressed tastefully, but not lavishly, in the traditional short-waisted, long-sleeved jacket; skirt-like *longyi*; split-toe sandals; and close-fitting headdress with flowing bow. He usually ate lightly, avoiding rich food. Physically vigorous and healthy, Nu slept only five hours nightly while in office, rising about 4:30 for two hours of Buddhist meditation before starting the day's work. By breakfast, he had given alms-food to visiting monks and, weather permitting, had taken a brisk walk.

The living arrangements of Nu's household were unusual. When he was Premier, he spent the nights in a small hut in the garden of his official residence.[1] His aged mother, who had tuberculosis, also lived there until her death. In 1948, Nu took a vow of sexual abstinence, although this is by no means required by Buddhism of its lay adherents, and he and his wife have lived in different buildings since then. Previously, however, they had had five children, the youngest of whom was 16 in 1962. Nu's oldest child has lived with his aunt, Daw Mya Yee's sister, and her husband since infancy.[2] A busy man, Nu has spent little time with his family and speaks of them only occasionally, although he has always appeared affectionate to them. His wife, however, has traveled widely with him through the years. Nu's remoteness from both

* Nu dropped the prefix "Thakin" in 1951.

his wife and his children is consistent with his Buddhist belief that suffering results from "attachment," which includes attachment to one's family.[3] Nu's relations with his brother, the fairly well-off U Oo, have frequently bordered on the hostile. In 1951, Oo, a breeder and owner of race horses, supported the People's Peace Front, led by the leftist U Aung Than, brother of Aung San, against Nu and the AFPFL.[4] Their mother on her deathbed effected a degree of reconciliation between the two men so opposite in so many ways.

His vow of celibacy was typical of Nu. In 1938 at the Shwedagon Pagoda he took a similar pledge to abstain from "spiritous liquor," and the same year he also vowed that "I would not be unfaithful to my wife." He took the vow of celibacy at the age of 41, half a year after independence. "On July 20, 1948, when the insurrection was causing anxiety," Nu has said, "I went into my prayer room and before the Holy Image took the vow of absolute purity, making a wish at that time that if I kept that vow the insurgents might be confounded."[5]

As Premier, Nu both transacted business and entertained at his official residence, but he spent much of his time there in his little hut, which was connected to the main building by a causeway. He took lunch with his family in the main building, however, usually around eleven. Nu used to be a total vegetarian, eating meat only in unavoidable circumstances in keeping with the Buddhist prohibition against the taking of life. But doctors persuaded him to "take a little fish"[6] for health reasons (including failing eyesight).

The working day began in earnest for Premier Nu after lunch. When the Parliament was not in session, he received a steady stream of visitors at his official residence, but his political lieutenants came only when called for—or when the matter at hand was extremely pressing.[7] Even during his frequent tours of the country, Nu maintained his strict dietary habits as well as his practice of spending about four or five hours a day in meditation.

Official activities, particularly entertaining, took up many of Nu's evenings between 1948 and 1958 (and again in 1960–62). On the rare occasions when he did have a free evening, he would do a little reading. The late hours of his evening were spent counting the beads of the Buddhist rosary. Nu went to sleep a little before midnight.

When he left office in late 1958, Nu disposed of all his personal belongings, except for a few pieces of clothing. He stated that he had been poor when he became Premier and would leave office the same way. His critics charged that he was being theatrical and that his behavior was irrelevant, since his wife was well-to-do in her own right. But the fact is that material things have always meant little to Nu, and he actually had to borrow money to meet his household expenses when he was out of office between October 1958 and April 1960.[8]

U Nu's apparent selflessness has always been accompanied by a warm and endearing manner. "The most immediately impressive thing about Nu," Jawaharlal Nehru has said, "is his radiant personality—it wins him friends wherever he goes."[9] But a close friend of many years has stated that Nu is "at one and the same time a spontaneously personable fellow and one who has to push a little."[10]

A handsome man with swarthy brown skin and gentle, searching eyes, Nu seemed to fascinate all who met him. His charming half-smile often became roaring laughter, and the seemingly permanent puckering of his eyebrows suggested a perplexity that usually did not exist. His round face lent itself to easy caricature by political cartoonists, and in photographs he appears deceptively squat. The *guang baung,* or traditional Burmese headdress, which Nu invariably wore in public, hid his closely cropped hair. When he again became Premier in 1960 (at 52) he appeared remarkably youthful.

Nu's sense of humor and merriment was clearly revealed in his frolicking with visiting Chinese Premier Chou En-lai during the 1960 Water Festival and 1961 Independence Day celebration. During one Water Festival, at what was expected to be a routinely dull tea-party, Nu's wife, in keeping with the spirit of the Festival, suddenly poured a large pail of water over the Yugoslav Ambassador, a strapping man of six-foot three. Nu did the same to the American Ambassador, and the fun began. Most of the well-attired foreigners soon entered the spirit of the Festival, and everybody appeared to be having the best of times. Nu was by then much more relaxed than the small, frightened man who in 1947, at the time of his negotiations with Prime Minister Attlee, did not seem to know what to do at his own reception in London.[11]

Through the years Nu became unquestionably Burma's number one raconteur, delighting in both private conversation and public speeches —often rather long ones. But Nu also listened and he usually learned quickly. Moreover, he seemed interested in everything and everybody he encountered, asking questions and jotting down ideas that came to him.

During the campaign for the 1960 parliamentary elections, Nu confessed, as *The Nation* of Rangoon reported it, that "an intensely holy life had made him unconsciously proud." "But when I read the teachings contained in my lectures I realized that I myself must practice what I preach," he said.[12] U Law Yone, *The Nation*'s editor, literally translating "U Nu" into English as "Mr. Tender," has written that the name belies the character of the man. As Law Yone has put it, "He will never be a Stalin, but there is a good deal of granite in his make-up."[13]

Thakin Kodaw Hmaing, the "grand old man" of Burmese nationalism, has remarked on Nu's "basic simplicity,"[14] but not many men who have worked with or against him would agree. U Law Yone has noted of Nu that "naïveté and shrewdness are so unevenly blended that one never knows which will be uppermost at any given moment."[15] Law Yone has also said: "U Nu is a complicated fellow. I know the animal that lies so near the surface in him, and it is a wonder the way he keeps it in check. He is handsome, personable, smart, and emotional; he loves pleasure and is easily moved. Yet he keeps himself in check. This is in large measure a reflection of his Buddhist discipline."[16]

According to Dr. Ba Maw, "there are two U Nu's: Nu the man and Nu the politician. Nu the man is beyond question possessed of outstanding integrity; Nu the politician is cunning and scheming. The man I would trust with my money; I would go tiger-hunting alone with him. The man I love more than any other Burmese political figure, but I am very suspicious of Nu as a politician." Ba Maw, whom many respect and regard as Burma's most perceptive political critic, feels that Nu and his political contemporaries are "products of their times. They came into their own as political figures in an era when there was a premium on the devious. Nu, like the others, will not take the straight way to an objective—but the indirect and the tricky. But, as an individual, he is honest."[17]

Seven times in his life* Nu has donned the yellow robes of a Buddhist priest and, head shaven, has entered a monastery.[18] He has spoken and written much on the subject of Buddhism.[19] Nu also eats only one meal about half the days of the year, in the spirit of Buddhist self-denial. "What I do now is not a patch on what I did in the past," he stated in 1960.

Nu has said that he became strongly religious as a result of World War II,[20] and that the most important single influence in shaping his religious outlook was "the insight I acquired as a consequence of the growing realization of the knowledge I had acquired in previous ex-

---

* Including a period of 45 days prior to the last two months of the campaign for the 1960 parliamentary elections.

istences."[21] Nu has developed from a "hereditary Buddhist," as he has put it, to one who has thought his own way to his philosophic conclusions and has realized not only his own need of religion but also his country's.[22]

Nu believed that the creation of a public image of himself as a religious man was necessary for national salvation. "I believe that the Buddha teaches more by example than precept," he has said. "Hence, it behooves his disciples to do the same. I don't see how we can improve ourselves and others without strong devotion to our beliefs. By 'we' I mean not only individuals but also parties, nations, etc."[23] Nu also has stated: "In the matter of religion, as in the realm of politics, leadership . . . is necessary to guide the people in order that they may not fall into error."[24]

His role of "promoter of the faith" is one way in which U Nu seemed to his own people to resemble the Burmese kings of the past.[25] Characteristic of his official support of Buddhism was his government's sponsorship of the Sixth Great Theravada Buddhist Synod of 1954–56, for which a "peace pagoda" and a man-made cave, among other buildings, were constructed at a cost of $6 million. The goal of this international meeting of clergy and laymen, according to Nu, was to "purify" Buddhism.[26] This was Nu's chief goal, too, in sponsoring the 1950 Pali University Act and legislation setting up a Buddha *Sasana* Council to promote the study and propagation of Buddhism and to supervise the monks. Nu also created the cabinet post of Minister of Religious Affairs, ordered government departments to dismiss civil servants 30 minutes early if they wished to meditate, commuted prison sentences of convicts who passed examinations on Buddhism, brought sacred relics of the Buddha from Ceylon and sent them on tour of the nation, and encouraged the restoration of ancient pagodas as well as the teaching of Buddhism to non-Buddhists. For these actions Nu has been accused of living in "a past in which the King, in exercise of his personal right and will, spent most of the people's money and labor in building religious edifices, holding festivals without end, going on costly pilgrimages and doing things like that."[27] And former Cabinet colleague U Tun Pe has compared him to a spendthrift "oriental monarch."[28]

Equally zealous as an individual in seeking to spread the Buddhist faith, "Nu has even tried to convert me to Buddhism," Indian Prime Minister Nehru has said, adding, "It is not that Nu is religious that is so eye-catching but the earnestness of his convictions."[29] He also has sought to convert non-Buddhists who have served in his household, saying to one to whom he gave Buddhist books and religious objects, "we obviously knew each other in a previous existence—otherwise we would not have been thrown together in this one." According to another former employee, Nu discouraged his oldest daughter as a biology student because he did not approve of dissecting animals; "he made her do this in the official guest house on Inya Road—not at home!" "Nu has lots of spirit to back up his convictions," Premier Nehru has said, "—like lecturing the Americans on Buddhism. I really was surprised when I heard that." According to a reporter accompanying U Nu on his 1955 visit to the United States, Nu felt that one of the most important reasons for this visit was the propagation of Buddhism.[30]

But Nu also supported other religions. His government paid the expenses of Roman Catholic priests who went on a pilgrimage to the Vatican, for example, and provided funds for translating the Koran into Burmese. During the fighting against Karen insurgents he allowed the Anglican Bishop of Rangoon, the Right Reverend George West, safe-conduct across the lines to administer communion. From his 1955 tour abroad he brought home 98 bottles of water from the Jordan River and 1,112 crucifixes for Burmese Catholics; he had personally filled the bottles of Jordan River water.

U Nu's tolerance was tested in 1953 when there was considerable public clamor among the Buddhists, a majority in Burma, against Muslim slaughter of cattle on the religious holiday of Idd. Nu declared in a radio broadcast:

> I abhor killing of any living creature. This abhorrence makes me to avoid taking meat in any form and that is why I have become a vegetarian. Since I abhor killing and have become a vegetarian, will it be expedient to prohibit slaughter of any creature in the Union and order that the peoples of the Union must turn vegetarians? By no means. . . . It will not do in this modern world to adopt a rash attitude like, "We form the majority. We will do what we like irrespective of what others like or dislike." . . . If a majority community imposes its will by force on a minority in any country, then this country will go to the dogs sooner or later.[31]

"Freedom of worship is important at all times," Nu said in a message on the Burmese New Year in 1954, "but it assumes the utmost importance in a new country."[32] Religious differences must not be allowed to weaken the nation. "The Roman Catholic community in Burma," he told the National Eucharistic Congress in 1956, "is a model community, whose loyalty to the country remained constant and unimpaired even in the dark days of the insurrection when the fate of the Union hung in the balance."[33]

Nu has suggested that he may be a Buddha-in-the-process-of-be-coming,[34] and many in Burma, particularly among the peasant masses, believe him. Others, however, have accused U Nu of using religion for personal political advantage, particularly in the 1960 parliamentary election campaign. "U Nu will sit in a pagoda for ten hours, if necessary, if he thinks it will help him politically," onetime Cabinet colleague and subsequent political opponent U Ba Swe stated after Nu's victory over Ba Swe's party in that election.[35] According to another longtime close friend, U Raschid, Nu wanted "very much to go down in history as the leader who made Burma a Buddhist state again—a twentieth century Alaungpaya."[36]

Outstanding in U Nu's view of the universe is his concept of the "mind of man":

It may be likened to an electric light which is kept on for one hour. I would say that the light shines steadily for one hour but in point of fact, with the click of the switch, a spark is made and it dies but is followed immediately by another spark and yet another. However, the process being so fast, the eye sees only a steady brilliant glow, and not the individual sparks that go to make the light.

So it is with the mind that "may traverse a million subjects in the twinkling of an eye." This ever-changing mind does not die with the body "but takes root in some other body, be it that of man or spirit or animal or insect."

The cause of suffering, according to Nu, is desire, in turn the result of man's being "blinded by his conception of his ego." But this consciousness of self can be extinguished and desire overcome by meditation. The central task of Buddhism, Nu has told audiences in the United States, Communist China, and India, as well as in his native Burma, is to seek "complete awareness." When man has become "aware of the futility of it all, then the desire will be stilled."[37] According to Nu:

What is . . . required is the sense of awareness at the first impact of sight, sound, scent, taste, touch and thought. If you open the door, all visitors waiting outside the door will enter the room. But if you close the door after the entry of the first person the rest of the visitors will be kept outside. In the same way, if you apply a sense of awareness every time you see, or hear, or eat, or smell, or touch, or think, mental states of attachment or revulsion will not occur in you so long as that awareness lasts.[38]

The development of "awareness" as a result of meditation is the
first step in the attainment of true wisdom; the last stage "is reached
when the Mind is shed of all desire, repulsion, fear and attachment,
and when all these passions have been spent, the Mind reaches that
state of equilibrium and tranquillity, which ensures that the chain of
existence and rebirths has been broken forever, and the escape from the
thirty-one planes of existence is now achieved."[39] Then, only, can man
begin to seek the Truth. "Without getting rid of the mind-defilement,
to try to seek the Truth through mere reasoning or through mere intellectual power will lead to failure," Nu has said.[40]

To attain *nirvana,* or enlightenment, man must observe certain
moral precepts[41] without deviation, he must develop mental concen-
tration, and he must strive to attain "intuitive knowledge."[42] And man
must do all this himself. "The Buddha cannot by his power bring good
or evil to anyone," Nu has said. "The Buddha can only show the way
to living things, pointing to different paths that would lead to good or
evil."[43]

Even to be reborn as a human being, man must observe the basic
Five Precepts, and he must observe them sincerely—unlike the leopard
in a story Nu tells:

> Once upon a time, a black leopard, which lived on an island near
> the shore of a river, found that he was cut off from all possibility
> of hunting for food, because of a sudden flood during the night.
> Then the black leopard said to himself that as he was not going to
> get any food that day, he might as well keep the Sabbath, and so
> he resolved to keep the Precepts. The Spirit of the Forest wanted
> to test the sincerity of the black leopard, and taking the form of a
> goat, let the leopard hear its bleating. When the leopard saw the
> goat, he decided that it would not do as yet to keep the Sabbath that
> day, and so he postponed his observance of the Precepts. The leop-
> ard chased after the goat, but the goat disappeared. Then the leop-
> ard said to himself that his observance of the Precepts was quite
> intact, and decided to continue keeping the Sabbath.[44]

Although good deeds do not fully determine man's lot at any particular moment, and *viriya,* or effort, "alone cannot produce good results," according to Nu, "past karma" is "unforeseeable," and "we
cannot depend entirely upon it." Effort, which includes the exercise
of one's intelligence, is important.[45] "Just as it is not possible for a
vehicle to run on one wheel, no God or karma can give a man . . .
benefits without his own efforts," Nu has said.

Nu has come a long way since the late 1930's, when he argued that Buddhism and Communism were compatible. In 1958 he stated that "anyone who professes a religious belief must abandon Marxism,"[46] and even earlier, in 1950, he said that any wisdom that might be attributed to Karl Marx was "less than one-tenth of a particle of dust that lies at the feet of our great Lord Buddha."[47]

The Buddhist revival in Burma that has been credited to Nu was calculated in part to strengthen the country against the Communists. But Nu also believes that "the Buddha teaches us how to conduct ourselves for worldly gains." During the campaign for the 1960 parliamentary elections he urged members of his political party to practice *myitta,* or love, for its practical consequences. The politician with *myitta* does not anger others. He shows his love by helping and paying homage to his parents, his wife and children, and the *nats.* For if a politician does not show gratitude to his parents, Nu asked, how can he be expected to see to the welfare of a public which is not related to him?[48]

Buddhism for U Nu has clearly been a creed with a practical relevance, and he has sought to embody its principles in his government policies. He imposed a ban on the slaughter of cattle, for example, a prohibition that was lifted by Premier General Ne Win during the eighteen months Nu was out of office in 1958 to 1960. A few days before he resumed the Premiership in April 1960 Nu asked Ne Win to reimpose the ban in order that Ne Win might acquire merit to bolster his own karma. Ne Win did not do so, however, and Nu himself reinstated the prohibition on April 4, 1960, two hours after having been sworn in again as Prime Minister.

The prohibitions of U Nu's Buddhism are many, and often the demands of political leadership in a new country beset with insurrections and problems of modernization and economic development make it impossible for Nu to observe them. For example, Nu clearly could not honor the prohibition against killing in a civil war against Communist and other insurgents—nor could he carry out a program of land nationalization in harmony with the stricture not to take what is not given.

U Nu's view of man's virtue contains elements of both pessimism and optimism. Nu has said that "persons who are born wicked" are "exceptions rather than the rule,"[49] but that "man relishes evil more than good." The basic difference between good men and bad ones, for Nu, is not in their thoughts, which are evil in both cases, but in the fact that "good men can control the urging of their evil thoughts."[50]

The need for moral reform in Burma is an urgent one, Nu has often stated. The people of Burma have "no sense of shame or fear, the worst of our evil characteristics,"[51] according to Nu, who believes that "the enjoyment of pleasures in this existence" may well result in "endless misery in *samsara* [rebirth]."[52] But "mere warnings will not reduce immorality; only a "sustained and systematic program of reform, pursued with sincerity, zeal and determination, can uproot it."[53]

"The standards of personal, national and international morality are absolute," Nu told an entering class at the University of Rangoon in 1956, "and if you lower them but an inch, failure and disappointment and sorrow will result."[54] In India the same year he stated, "With colors, there are various shades between black and white, and in merchandise, there can be 'second,' 'third' and 'fourth' qualities. But with conduct, there can be no intermediate stage, no second quality, and the dividing line between bad and good conduct is always clear and distinct. . . . Therefore, practice self-discipline and follow the moral rules of conduct, so that you can repeat, with pride and full confidence, the words of Tennyson's Sir Galahad:

> 'My strength is as the strength of ten,
> Because my heart is pure.' "[55]

According to Dr. Ba Maw, however, "U Nu's speeches . . . remind you of the wrong kind of revivalist preacher trying to sublimate his repressed sex with a lot of very edifying words which hide more than they reveal."[56]

According to Nu, no matter how good its policies or ideologies, a country's development is dependent, in the last analysis, on "good" leaders.[57] "However perfect a plan may be," U Nu has said, "it will be of no avail if the right type of man is not obtainable to implement it."[58] Moreover, if the political leaders do not behave virtuously, the masses will awaken to the "depredations" of those who are "corrupt and dishonest," and will shout, "Down with them!"[59] Nu's moral position does not permit a double standard. As he has expressed it, "If you find me turn[ed] into a termite, please do not withhold your hand." "There is a Burmese saying," Nu has said, " 'Pound the main rice harder.' "[60]

But Nu can forgive others. His old friend the Communist Thein Pe Myint spent the evening with Bo Ye Htut and some of the 3rd Burma Rifles the day before they mutinied, and was jailed, but Nu could not bear the thought of an old nationalist comrade behind bars and had him released shortly afterward. Nu can also be firm in deal-

ing with those of a less compassionate nature than he. Visiting the
Civil Hospital in Moulmein in 1958, he was so moved by the acute
shortage of space that he ordered an immediate meeting of the municipal councilors and told them to vacate their building and make it into
a hospital annex.[61]

U Nu's religious beliefs include more than Buddhism alone. Nu
apparently also believes in *nats,* the spirits propitiated by the Burmese
from earliest known times. When the location of a new Students' Union
building on the campus of the University of Rangoon was being decided
upon, Nu opposed construction near adjacent Inya Lake because this
would necessitate the chopping down of trees housing *nats.* The final
site was selected only after an airplane flight over the campus to survey the tree situation. A conservationist, Nu also, in 1956, broadcast
an appeal to the nation to grow more trees and preserve the nation's
forests, the home of the *nats.*[62]

During the decade following independence, when he was Burma's
Premier, Nu made the *balinatsa* ceremony, "feast of the spirits," virtually an official event. General Ne Win, Prime Minister in 1958–60,
discontinued the practice, but Nu renewed it upon his return to office
in 1960. During Nu's observance of the ceremony in 1959, while he
was out of office, his political party issued a statement indicating that
Nu credited past performance of the ritual with contributing to the
defeat of the various insurgents in the civil war that particularly en-
dangered the country in the late 1940's and early 1950's.[63] There are
those who say that Nu is only using the *nats* to play upon a Burmese
folk belief for political purposes, but they are in a minority.

Nu would not make important decisions as Premier without consulting an astrologer. According to U Kyaw Nyein, longtime political associate, "there is not an astrologer of reputation in Rangoon that
Nu has not consulted at least once."[64] The date of the start of Burmese independence (4:20 A.M.) was astrologically chosen, as was the
hour the Sixth Great Buddhist Synod began (12:12 P.M.). When Nu
temporarily resigned the Premiership in 1956, he moved out of the
Prime Minister's official residence at the auspicious hour of 9:00 A.M.
Nu is also superstitious in other ways. Once when he was Premier,
the car in which he was riding to a public gathering ran over a dog.
Nu interpreted this as an evil omen and immediately returned home,
canceling his program.[65] This, however, does not make him any less
devoted to Buddhism. He remains a remarkable Buddhist and a remarkable politician.

✻

EIGHT

A POLITICAL MIND

In a speech to the Constituent Assembly on September 24, 1947, in which he advocated adopting the new Burmese constitution, U Nu called Burma "leftist," explaining that "a leftist country is one in which the people working together to the best of their power and ability strive to convert the natural resources and produce of the land . . . into consumer commodities to which everybody will be entitled each to his need."[1] Such a socialist system, he said many times afterward, would help man realize the Buddhist ideal of escape from desire. But with the years, Nu's ideas changed, and by the late 1950's he seemed to think rather that Buddhism would make socialism possible. "You can't change economic systems without first changing the human heart," he said in 1957.[2] Nu believed that greed and exploitation stemmed mainly from failure to realize that material things were impermanent. Yet, by late 1959, he seemed to turn once again to his old view. "The reason why an average Buddhist concerns himself not with the final release from *samsara* but with the acquisition of property is to be found in the economic system that prevails in the world," he said at that time.[3]

In mid-1948, Nu spoke of "the age of the magic tree," when "all the peoples of the world had their needs satisfied [and] were prosperous and happy." Nu blamed greed for the disappearance of this "tree of fulfillment."[4] The idea of private property developed, society was split into two classes, and "the evil system of exploitation of one class by another emerged."[5] The use of force by the exploited class resulted in repression at the hands of their exploiters—the origin of government. The concept of private property also resulted in disease, retardation of cultural development, and the emergence of capitalism (which "leads to imperialism").[6]

During the years of anti-colonial agitation, Nu told the Burma Chamber of Commerce in 1950, capitalism and imperialism were intimately associated in the minds of the revolutionaries, "and it has been impossible to view the two in isolation."[7] In his novel *Man, the Wolf of Man,* Nu described "production" in colonial Burma as "abundant," but "the masses starved in the midst of plenty while wealth became more and more concentrated among a handful of capitalists."[8] Of the peasants, he wrote: "The land that their ancestors had wrested from the jungle, the land that had been handed down from generation to generation, the land generations of cultivators had worked happily in knee-deep mud in rain and sun, with buffaloes and bullocks as companions, that land had been taken away from them by legal and economic processes which they did not understand."[9] The "contemptuous" capitalists regarded the farmers as "their legitimate prey,"[10] while the poor farmers thought, "Our karma is not good."[11]

From his earliest days in politics, Nu has professed socialist goals. He alludes in his speeches to such Western socialist literature as More's *Utopia,* Tommaso Campanella's *The City of the Sun,* and works by James Harrington, Robert Owen, Saint-Simon, Fourier, Proudhon, and Considerant, as well as Hegel, Marx, and Engels.[12] His addresses often end with passages from the Buddhist scriptures which show that "the views of these socialist leaders are identical at least in spirit" with some of the goals of Buddhism.[13] He refers to the achievements of the Industrial Revolution, the Paris Commune, the British Fabian Society and Labor Party, and the Bolsheviks, and admires the socialist accomplishments of Great Britain, Israel, New Zealand, and Norway. "The establishment of the socialist order," he proclaimed at the height of the campaign for the 1960 parliamentary elections in Burma, "will remain our chief political objective."[14]

Since Nu credits such works as the *Information Please Almanac,* the Penguin *Dictionary of Politics,* H. G. Wells's *Outline of History,* Norman MacKenzie's *Socialism, a Short History,* and the *Encyclopedia of the Social Sciences* with being sources of his socialist ideas,[15] some foreign observers and many of his political opponents have openly doubted Nu's understanding of socialism and his sincerity in espousing it. The truth of the matter is that Nu is not really a great reader; most of his socialist ideas are the result of his personal experience, observations, and discussions with others. What may be difficult for some observers to understand is that although some of the component ideas of Nu's socialism derive from Western thought, others do not, and that his particular brand of socialism clearly has its roots in Burma's Buddhist past. In fact, many of his countrymen identify him with the "Sedja Min," the ideal ruler of Burmese Buddhist folklore and the "bearer of a social utopia."[16]

Although it has been anti-capitalist, especially in the first years of independence, U Nu's socialism has clearly rejected the Soviet example. In 1947, Nu pointed out that Burma was "at least 3,000 miles away from the U.S.S.R." and hence could not think in such imitative terms as the countries of eastern Europe.[17] In a speech to a national congress of the AFPFL in 1958, he declared: "We must take particular care not to allow the exploitation, the tyranny and the oppression that are inherent evils in Communism and state capitalism to become any part of the socialist state we wish to create."[18] And in 1959 Nu asserted, "There is no industry or productive enterprise in any Communist country where *all* the profits are distributed amongst the workers. They get their share only in the form of wages, bonuses and other concessions in exactly the same way as workers do in a capitalist economy, and there is no evidence that this share is larger than in capitalist countries. The only difference is that whereas in the latter a share of the profits goes to the capitalist owners—or the shareholders—in a Communist country a similar or even larger share goes to the state."[19]

U Nu has also objected to the deterministic ideology of Communism, since, as he understands it, this determinism is clearly antagonistic to the creation of karma (good or bad), which can change history.[20] He "cannot accept the view that there is development in nature in a determined manner without any possibility of deviation."[21] Equally strong is his objection to the materialistic character of Marxism. For Nu, who believes in *dhat* or behavior, there is no such thing as matter, the absolutely necessary ingredient of all materialist thought; "all things [are] but aggregates of different kinds of behavior or *dhats*"— which are "never permanent, never indestructible, and never stable."[22]

The "ideal" of democracy, U Nu stated in 1959, derived from "two basic concepts: that man is born free and freedom is his most valuable heritage and asset" and "that man's freedom can be preserved and exercised only if he has a legitimate share in the framing of the laws which regulate his life in society and only if he has the right to participate in the machinery that is set up for the administration of these laws and for otherwise regulating the working of the community as a unit." There is no doubt, Nu declared, that "in what are called the liberal democracies of the world" the freedom of the individual is "both guaranteed and respected in practice."[23]

The two major characteristics of a democratic state, in Nu's opinion, are the enforcement of authority "through the rule of law and not the bayonet" and the free submission of the individual himself to the rule of law. "The objective element in the democratic way of life," he has said, "requires that, while enjoying and asserting your own rights and freedom to the fullest extent, you must also respect the rights and freedom of your neighbor."[24]

The goal of democratic government, according to Nu, is the implementation of "the people's will as far as possible." "Power is not entrusted entirely with anybody"; there are "checks" and "counterchecks." The power of the government is held in check by the parliament, which in turn is "watched and molded by the people."[25]

At the ninth General Assembly of the International Press Institute in Tokyo in 1960, Nu stated his conviction "that democracy cannot be achieved without securing the active participation of the masses." According to Nu, the "first essential condition for democracy to work is complete identification between the leaders and the masses and complete obliteration of all barriers between the two." This identification could be achieved, he felt, "through party organization, specific measures of consultation between members of the party and the masses, the spread of the ideals of democracy through mass educational media, a code of personal behavior, [and close communication with] members of the opposition both in and out of parliament."[26]

Nu rejects the view that some nations are not ready for democracy. He has said that "democracy is man's inherent right, and there is no person or community in the world who can be said to be not ready for it. A principal cause of democracy not working effectively in some countries is the failure to adapt the institutional forms of democracy to local conditions, and this is the real threat that presents itself and which we must try to avert. Democracy . . . is one of the noblest ideas created by man, and there can be no compromise in its application to human society anywhere in the world."[27]

In a talk in late 1959 Nu made use of a fable to show the folly of blind imitation of the habits of others:

There was a man in a village who never observed the sabbath or visited the *pongyi kyaung* [monastery]. His wife was ashamed of his behavior and urged him to obey the sabbath. He replied that he did not know how to, and his wife then said, "Oh, it is easy. You just go to the *pongyi kyaung* and do as the *pongyi* does." The man accordingly visited the *pongyi kyaung*. The *pongyi* on seeing him asked, "What do you want?" The man, remembering his wife's advice, said to the *pongyi* in return, "What do you want?" The *pongyi* then said, "This man must be mad," and the man also replied in exactly the same words. At this the *pongyi* became angry and took off his robe to fight. The man also took off his jacket and the two struggled until they were worn out. When he returned home, his wife asked, "How was the sabbath?" The man replied, "Your sabbath is too tough. If I observe it once a week I shall be dead. Can't I do it twice a year?"[28]

A country and its leaders, Nu has cautioned, must be careful that in maintaining the forms of democratic government, "mostly imported from the West," they "do not at the same time destroy or negate its basic principles."[29]

Great effort may be necessary to make democracy work in a country like Burma in Nu's view, but effort is "one of the three basic principles that all Buddhists believe in." In a 1959 speech, he recounted "what Alaungdaw Zanaka Mintha said about *viriya* [effort]":

Once he was shipwrecked with others. The seamen who [did] not have *"viriya"* made no effort to save themselves and became food for the fishes. But Zanaka Mintha did not give up and kept swimming in the sea. Seeing his perseverance, a *nat* called Manimekhala came down from the heavens and asked the prince: "What good will it do if you keep swimming in this wide sea?" The prince replied, "All the seamen are dead because they have made no effort whereas I am still alive. Not only that, my effort has brought me the good fortune of seeing you. Moreover, all wise men have praised effort and industry and I must therefore continue to exert effort. An effortless person is lost even before he has begun."

According to Nu, "a certain standard of discipline and moral conduct" is also "essential" in a democratic society—for both "the ruler and the ruled."[30] "The democratic way of life," he has said, "is really an unwritten code of personal behavior."[31]

The parliamentary system is the best form of government as Nu sees it, since it offers "the best chance of preserving the essentials of democracy."[32] Political democracy, however, does not exist in a vacuum; if it "is to remain secure and strengthen and deepen its roots" in Burma, then Burma must "make haste to catch up with the twentieth century economically and technologically."[33] The economic well-being of the people must be secured and they must be made free from want; otherwise, the appeal of the democratic approach for them will lessen.[34] Moreover, the masses must not feel that there is a gap between themselves and the civil servants[35] or the politicians. "If we allow the party in a democracy to become a New Class as in Communist countries," Nu has stated, "then there will be no difference between that democracy and Communism."[36]

Communism, Nu observed in July 1959, started from the same basic ideals of freedom and equality as liberal democracy, but its subsequent institutionalization led to a system quite at odds with those ideals. In Communist countries, Nu has stated, there are no real elections, no unauthorized criticism of the government, no free labor unions, no "worthwhile job or employment" for "one who professes a religion and practices it," and no larger share of the profits for the workers than they get in a capitalist country.[37]

The principal difference between the democratic and Communist systems, as Nu sees it, is that in a democracy "the individual is put above the state—a government exists, and justifies its existence, purely so that the individual may live in freedom and security and rise to his full stature in accordance with his abilities and efforts—in a totalitarian state (whether it be of the left or the right) the state is placed above the individual; an individual exists, and justifies his existence, merely for the power and the glory of the state."

According to Nu, "the main danger to democracy from state ownership of the means of production and distribution arises not from the fact of ownership itself, but from the creation of conditions under which state ownership leads to the entrenchment of the party in power, to special and substantial privileges and advantages for the party adherents, to the creation of a new special class—in Djilas' words, to a 'special stratum of bureaucrats,' 'a party or political bureaucracy.' "[38] And a "one-party dictatorship," Nu asserted shortly after independence, would be particularly intolerable in view of the fact that Burma had just emerged from an "evil system in which political power [was] derived from the top few."[39]

In his short story "The Scourge," written before World War II, U Nu used the effort to inoculate the peasantry against cholera to illustrate the clash between traditional and modern values. Opposing inoculation, the headman U Aung Ba states that his belief is in "the Buddha's law of karma," to which the health officer replies:

> Always the law of karma. *That's* your faith. The karma of "Kanhla" village is in a sad state. To tempt providence with faith in karma is not Buddha's teaching. Buddha didn't say that your karma is the only deciding factor. He said there were three deciding factors, your karma, your intelligence, and your industry. Be intelligent, for Buddha's sake, and have this inoculation.[40]

Nu's use of this story also illustrates the role he has sought to play as a bridge between the old and the new world in Burma. The role has been less difficult for him than it might have been, since he does not recognize any conflict between Buddhism and science. In a 1955 speech celebrating the enshrinement of the relics of two of the Buddha's disciples, Saripatta and Magallana, Nu said, "Nowadays, when a person discovers a formula for penicillin, jet planes and atom-bombs, and announces them to the world, scientists make experiments with them. People should not fail to make similar tests with the discoveries of the Buddha which invite personal investigation."[41] "It is the conviction of our leaders," Nu said in New York in 1955, "that Burma can and will retain its spiritual heritage and at the same time share increasingly in the fuller material life which modern methods and techniques make possible."[42]

Until there is sufficient literature available in the vernacular in both the arts and the sciences, however, according to U Nu, Burma's citizens will be "divided into those who are modern [and] those who are medieval and narrow in their outlook."[43] As President of the Burma Translation Society, Nu has been tireless in encouraging dissemination of modern knowledge in his land. And, as Chancellor of the University of Rangoon, he endeavored to persuade the faculty to adopt Burmese as the main language of instruction. Such a policy was necessary, he said, in order to bridge the gap between the "Eastern- and Western-oriented sectors of society" by at least having them communicate in the same language.

But Nu also argued that Burmese should be adopted at the University because it was the main and traditional language of Burma. "Nu is a spiritual and emotional Burmese," a friend[44] has explained, "who is attached to the language of his land just because it is the language of his land. He is not one who sticks to the outdated and old-fashioned, however. But he does do a number of the old things because they are part of the heritage of being Burmese—without actually believing in them. *Nat* worship, for example—a practice of the ancient Burmese and their kings." Daw Mya Yee, Nu's wife, wanted their children to go to English Methodist or St. Paul's School in Rangoon "because of earlier and better English instruction, but Nu insisted on Myoma National School." Nu won; all the children but one, who was sent to school in Darjeeling, India, went to Myoma.

Nu's speeches have always abounded with traditional references and colorful anecdotes drawn from Burmese folklore. Stories about Ananthathuriya, who grappled alone with a crocodile; Paukhla, the son of Razathingyan, who speared an entire Kanyin tree; and Thameinbaran, who killed a large gorilla in mortal conflict, enabled Nu to communicate with many who might not otherwise understand the message of a new Burma.[45]

In some respects Nu has been a dreamer, "not unlike Dr. Ba Maw."[46] In 1947 he predicted that Burma would become "a land of plenty" within five years (despite its war-ravaged condition), and in 1949 he stated that "many branches of modern knowledge such as Relativity, Quantum Theory, Geo-politics, Laissez-faire, Eugenics, Surplus Value, Utilitarianism and so on which are at present accessible only to the privileged few will be within the easy reach of our cowherds, cultivators, hewers of wood and drawers of water."[47]

Yet, if occasionally Nu seemed to feel that changes would occur overnight, he was soon realistically suggesting patience: "Once the fruit has ripened, it is yours for the asking," he told a meeting of dock workers at Dawbon in December 1957. "But keep plucking the small shoots and sprouts too early and the tree must wither before it has time to mature."[48]

On the whole, Nu has shown a remarkably keen comprehension of both the facts and the influence of history. Although he blamed Burma's postwar insurrections on the fact that "we have been under foreign domination and have only just emerged therefrom," and was slashing in his denunciation of the British colonial record in his country, he was no more merciful in treating the pre-British experiences of the Burmese in governing themselves. Only three Burmese kings were ever able to consolidate the country, he pointed out, and when they died their kingdoms "crumbled like a house of cards."[49] The reason for the limited accomplishments and endurance of past Burmese governments, according to Nu, was that they were personal regimes, based on force, which failed to develop the country.

Nu's realism is revealed particularly in his description of the ways of practical politics. "Sometimes you will get support and commendations from the people," he said in 1959 (when he was out of power), "sometimes you don't: sometimes you will feel happy and sometimes you will be faced with arrest, torture and killing."[50] But if a "politician dares not speak or do what he wants to speak or do because of fear, then he dies politically."[51]

U Nu is not an intellectual person. His is not a creative mind, nor is it an especially disciplined one. According to the writer U Thein Han, "There are two kinds of intellectuals in Burma: those with a Western education and those with a traditional education, the latter having little if any knowledge of European ideas and only limited contact with the outside world. Nu stands between them. He has much in common with the second group, but he clearly is much closer to those of a Western education. He is a product of a Western-style education, for the most part, and, unlike members of the second group, he can meet Burmese Western-type intellectuals about on equal terms. He can also meet the second group on a level of mutual understanding, which only a few of the Western-educated people can do."[52]

In an intellectual sense, however, Nu is unfamiliar with Western thought. His speeches on the evolution of democracy, for example, sound like schoolboys' essays with wholesale borrowings from various encyclopedias. "He is less Western as a thinking man certainly than Nehru, and less so than the Vietnamese Communist Ho Chi Minh," a foreign diplomat who has served in India and Vietnam as well as in Burma has said.[53] There are also the most surprising gaps in Nu's knowledge of the West. At a concert at Alma Ata on his 1955 tour of the Soviet Union, for example, he made a brief speech in which he quoted at length from *Twelfth Night* and spoke intelligently on the functions of music—and then asked a member of his party the role of the man with the stick in front of the orchestra.

Premier Nehru, who has said that Nu is "not a speculative thinker," explains, "He tends rather to accept an existent belief system like Buddhism and act within it. However, Buddhism permits intellectual experimentation within its particular framework, and this Nu engages in." Nehru has also stated that he and Nu have not talked much about ideas through the years; "we have talked about democracy's prospects in this or that country but not about the idea of democracy."[54]

Despite Nu's continuing literary ambitions, he does not consider himself "a man of books." He explains, "I have learned very little about either Buddhism or democracy from books."[55] Although he does not read newspapers regularly, he seems to know what is in them and will criticize particular editors and writers from time to time. As Premier, he frequently expressed his desire to devote his full time to writing, and jotted down synopses of the books he intended to write when time permitted.

Most other Burmese authors regard Nu as a good writer who would have been well known for his writings even if he had not been Prime Minister. His style and usual themes are typical of the modern school of Burmese writing. He suffers, however, from his tendency to be pedantic and to lecture his reader. The style of his writing is simple, which makes it, in terms of language at least, understandable to persons of limited education. At the same time Nu appeals to the more educated; his Burmese cultural identity is important in this respect, as is his modernity. A major criticism of Nu's writing is that his style, which is sometimes outstanding, can also degenerate into "something less than commonplace conversational Burmese," as one critic has put it.[56]

The themes of Nu's writings vary. In his writings of the 1930's the influence of Marx and Freud is evident. In most of his work, however—including his only real novel, *Man, the Wolf of Man*—Nu has been primarily concerned with the personal problems of individuals (who may, however, be swept up by the great social forces of their times) and with the tragic nature of life itself.[57] In recent years Nu's themes have been primarily political, as the play *The People Win Through* indicates.

The People Win Through, the best known outside Burma of Nu's dramas, is a morality play more than anything else. Somewhat weak in both plot and characterization, the play deals with the gradual disillusionment of the idealist revolutionary Aung Min, who had joined the Communist insurrection. The play's message is that good democratic methods are superior to the evil totalitarian ways of the Communists. The Buddhist theme that man is the arbiter of his own fate and can conquer evil and do good runs through the work. Made into a film, *The People Win Through* was a box-office disappointment in Burma, probably because it was not strictly entertainment, which the Burmese (including Nu) demand when they go to the movies.

Nu has been a critic as well as a writer, a self-appointed literary guardian of the nation, who has attacked Burma's novelists for writing on the "puerile" theme of "Boy-Meets-Girl"—a criticism he publicly advanced as early as 1937 in his foreword to a book of short stories by his close friend Thein Pe.* Of the novels written in Burma in the 1930's, he wrote: "There are plenty of women but few wives," adding that he was "ashamed to have other people judge Burmese literature by these trashy works, especially as we have had such a fine literature in the past." A high level of literary achievement, he later declared, will bring with it an uplift in the "intellectual and moral values of the people." He has also advised Burmese novelists to draw on the "highly developed technique" of the novel "in other lands," arguing that "it certainly does not require one hundred years to perfect the technique. Fifty years' development is considered sufficient for the purpose."[58]

Nu's efforts to encourage Burmese cultural development have been

* *Everything's All Right, Sir, and Other Short Stories* (Rangoon, 1952).

extraordinary. He appointed a Minister of Union Culture to his cabinet in 1952 and established a state orchestra (of traditional Burmese instruments), a State School of Music and Drama, a School of Fine Arts, a National Library, a National Historical Commission, and a Department of Ancient Literature and Culture at the University of Rangoon. The semi-official Burma Translation Society whose purpose is to make modern knowledge available in Burmese to the Burmese people, was founded largely as a result of Nu's efforts. One of his main accomplishments as Chairman of the Society has been the massive *Encyclopedia Burmanica*. When the first volume of the *Encyclopedia,* which is published in England, arrived in 1954, Nu and most of the Cabinet were at the dock to greet the boat. A large-scale model was placed in an attractively decorated truck and driven through the streets of Rangoon.

Nu's love of Burma is revealed in this encouragement of culture. In 1956, he told the first graduates of the Burma Translation Society's School of Journalism that their accomplishment was "nothing less than an act of high patriotism."[59] In his enthusiasm for Burma he has even wanted to rename M. A. Raschid, his old Indian friend and political colleague, "U Yanshin" (Mr. Immune-from-Harm).[60] He likes to state publicly, especially to foreign groups, that Burma had a "great and flourishing civilization . . . when William the Conqueror was crossing the English Channel,"[61] and in 1956 he told a cultural conference that Burma's civilization was once world-famous.[62] In a speech to the National Press Club in Washington on his trip to the United States in 1955, Nu remarked of Burma's way of doing things:

> It is our way of life. We prefer it to any other way of life on this earth. We do not say that it cannot be improved, or that it cannot be adapted to suit modern conditions, but we do not wish to change its basis. . . . This is not a matter of conceit. . . . We merely say that it is different, that it suits us better, and that we cannot therefore be induced to give it up in exchange for some other way of life, be that the Communist way, the West European way, the American way, or any other way.[63]

Nationalist though he is, Nu is also a citizen of the world, a universalist, a man who knows fully that there is much of great value beyond Burma. Burmese who do not understand the world beyond their shores, he once said, "will be narrow in outlook . . . like the frog of the fable which thought that the swamp it lived in was a vast ocean."[64]

Among Nu's other outstanding characteristics is his integrity. In 1956, Nu wrote in a letter to U Kyaw Nyein, "I have given notice to my wife" that if she ever engages in any dishonest activity "I shall divorce her." He also noted that he had had the BSI (Burma's FBI) investigate the visit of a man they had arrested to his brother, U Oo, an action that hurt his brother very much.[65] Nu has also stated publicly, "Although I will not claim to be wiser or more intelligent than the rest of us—in fact there are many wiser and more intelligent men in the Union—I claim that in the matter of integrity I am not below anyone in the country, with the exception of the holy and devout whose one aim in life is the utter disregard of worldly things."[66] On the eve of independence Nu pledged: "if by chance I misuse my powers as Premier for personal gain in any respect, may I go head first to the lowest hell of Maha Avici."[67]

Nu's conduct bears out his claim to paramount integrity. Once because of his suspicions of American support of Chinese Nationalist guerrillas in Burma, Nu deliberately snubbed former United States Senate Majority Leader William L. Knowland, who was in Rangoon. Nu's letter of apology for this action revealed both his honesty and his humility. (On Nu's subsequent visit to the United States, Senator Knowland received him and introduced him to fellow Senators as though he were a long-lost friend. Nu was much moved.)[68] Nu also refused to accept any honorary degrees in the United States "as a matter of principle"; he had no bachelor's degree, he claimed, having returned it to the University of Rangoon at the time of the students' strike of 1936.

Hugh Tinker, the author of the best survey of present-day Burma, has compared Nu with the English Liberal Gladstone, who was "moved by the very highest ideals but also knew all the tricks in the game politically and was willing to use them when the situation required."[69] That Nu is conscious of the political appeal of his integrity is beyond doubt. In late January 1960, on the eve of the parliamentary elections, he observed, "The Burman . . . has great respect for the leader who is true to himself. . . . Knowledge of this fact is . . . a great help in political organization work."[70]

The strain of trying to lead the good life has often taken its toll on Nu, and on such occasions he has shown himself capable of anger with only limited provocation. In a letter to U Kyaw Nyein in 1956, Nu observed that his health had been affected by his not having had a chance to rest in nine years. "It is perhaps for these reasons that I have become very short-tempered," he said.[71]

In October 1958, Nu told the annual Commanding Officers' Conference at Meiktila of his efforts to control his anger: "When I first became Prime Minister, I too was over-sensitive. Whenever criticisms were leveled against me either in the newspapers or from the political platforms I wanted to crush my critics. But from the day that I realized that grave dangers could arise if a man who wields the immense powers of a Prime Minister were to be over-sensitive and to react violently, I underwent a mental change and learnt to exercise self-restraint."[72]

But this over-sensitivity has been a problem. Nu's difficulties with Kyaw Nyein from 1956 to 1958, before the two split politically, were partly occasioned by his feeling that he was not getting the recognition he deserved. In his 1956 letter to Kyaw Nyein, he wrote that he, as well as Aung San, had played "an important part in the independence struggle, and I have a desire that the people should know about this."[73] Nu was also annoyed when British Prime Minister Anthony Eden, on a stopover in Rangoon during a trip to the Far East, cabled Nu to meet him and to bring Kyaw Nyein and Ba Swe, his top lieutenants, with him. "Why Ba Swe and Kyaw Nyein also?" Nu is reported to have said. "I am the Prime Minister and the President of the AFPFL."[74]

Nu, however, is willing to admit his mistakes publicly: At a reception at Methodist English Girls High School in Rangoon he stated that at the height of the 1948–51 insurrections he had wrongly attacked the Anglican Bishop, the Rt. Rev. George West. And he can be forgiving: On his 1955 visit to the United States he told Secretary of Agriculture Ezra T. Benson, who had kept him waiting in his office, "I, too, am one of those people who can't keep appointments."[75] "According to our Buddhist scriptures," Nu has said, "there is none on the 31 planes of existence except Pisakha Buddha and the Arahants who does not err. There are no perfect beings even in the celestial abode of the *nats* and *brahmas*."[76] But, once again, Nu has acknowledged his awareness of the political advantages of this point of view: "The Burman is all for the person who has the courage to admit his errors. . . . So long as one understands this fact of Burmese psychology, it is easy to organize politically."[77]

PART THREE

❀

PREMIER NU

NINE

❀

GAINING INDEPENDENCE

THAKIN NU[1] looked forward to the day of Burma's independence not only as the hour of national deliverance but also as the time when he could retire from public life. He had accepted the post of head of the interim government from Governor Sir Hubert Rance with the condition that he would serve only until independence was acquired. Sir Hubert accepted this condition, albeit reluctantly.[2] Nu's colleagues and friends, however, insisted that he serve as Premier for the first six months of independence, and, yielding to their arguments, he promised them and the Governor that he would.

Nu, who assumed his new position uninvolved in earlier schisms among the Communists and others within the AFPFL, now had the opportunity to work for a reconciliation among the estranged elements. On the day of the assassinations Nu met with top Communist leaders, including Thakin Than Tun, who spoke of the desirability of unity among the longtime nationalist colleagues.[3] Two days later, at a meeting at Nu's house, the Communists Than Tun, Ba Tin, and Ba Thein Tin, Ko Ko Gyi of the Socialist Party, Bo Let Ya (second to Nu in the new government), and Nu himself discussed the matter of closing ranks.[4] The assassinations had frightened both the AFPFL and the Communists, who saw a threat from non-leftist diehards.

The discussions with the Communists concerned, among other matters, the possibility of their participation in the government. Nu sought both to woo the Communists back into the AFPFL and to give them representation in the Cabinet.[5] He believed that Than Tun, with whom he had worked so closely through the years, would put Burmese nationalism before his Communism, and tried hard to gain his support.[6] The negotiations failed because of Than Tun's confidence in his bargaining strength and his resulting unwillingness to compromise,[7] and because of the Socialists' efforts to obtain the abolition of the Communist Party as a condition of reunification under the AFPFL banner.[8]

However, on August 2, 1948, a new government was sworn in—but the date was chosen because of astrological considerations rather than because accord had been reached between the AFPFL and the Communists. The hour on which his government had been inaugurated was an inauspicious one, Nu subsequently learned. Governor Sir Hubert Rance was interrupted at golf, his first attempt at relaxation in the two strenuous weeks since the assassinations, by the arrival of the new government at Government House with the request that they be sworn in between six and six-thirty that evening. The Governor did not have a copy of the oath of office, but U Tin Tut, formerly of the Indian Civil Service and a member of the new Cabinet, was able to recall it from memory. The government, which except for Tin Tut was composed exclusively of AFPFL politicians, was duly inaugurated (although, unknown to its members, a couple of minutes behind schedule). The most prominent members of the Cabinet, besides Nu (Premier-designate and holder of the Information portfolio) and Tin Tut (Finance and Revenue), were Bo Let Ya (Thakin Hla Pe of the Dobama Asiayone and the Red Dragon Book Club), Deputy Premier and Defense Minister, and Kyaw Nyein, Home Affairs and Justice.

What effect the inclusion of one or more Communists in Nu's government would have had on its policies will never be known. Differences of outlook between Nu and the Communists on many subjects, including the not yet completed matter of negotiated independence, had certainly existed in the past, however, and unquestionably would have continued. Nu, moreover, sought to identify himself completely with the aims and strategy of the slain Aung San, with whom Than Tun had disagreed vigorously. Nevertheless, in his first major policy address on July 27, Thakin Nu called for unity among his countrymen. "The work outweighs the people," he said, "and it will take all we can give to bring normalcy to our country. Let us all unite in our task."[9] Nu clearly was moved by the spectacle of Chinese fighting Chinese in the wake of Japan's defeat and wished to avoid a Burmese version of such a civil war pitting Communist against non-Communist.[10]

Thakin Nu's efforts to unify the minority peoples and to rally their support of the governing arrangements of the proposed independent semi-federal Union of Burma were a major factor in gaining their acceptance of the new constitution, which was adopted with much fanfare on September 24. The Kachins asked for the large town of Myitkyina, which could justifiably have been retained as part of Burma proper but without which a separate Kachin State within the Union would have been meaningless. Nu not only granted their request but also suggested that Bhamo, another important town, be included in the state and that the head of the Kachin State should always be a Kachin; he also asked the Kachins not to demand the right of secession, and they agreed.[11] There was no Myitkyina or Bhamo to give the Shans, however, and the Shan States demanded and received the right to secede. Nu, however, told them he was certain that they would ask for repeal of this condition in ten years. The Kayahs, who also sought and obtained the right of secession, were nonetheless impressed by Nu's generosity toward the Kachins, and acquiesced in the proposed union more readily because of this. In fact, of the major indigenous minorities who sought separate statehood within the Union, only the Karens, who did not immediately get a state, were seriously displeased. Some Karen leaders, nonetheless, including Mahn Win Maung, who later became President of Burma, identified themselves with the general national cause.

In addition to winning the support of most of the minority leaders and generally shepherding the constitution through the Constituent Assembly, Thakin Nu also played a role in establishing an independent judiciary of the American type. An independent judiciary had been urged upon Aung San by a number of Burmese with experience both as judges and as lawyers, but he and Kyaw Nyein wanted Supreme Court justices to serve eight-year terms and to be reappointed only if their behavior on the bench was consistent with the government's general policies. "We could not get Aung San to budge an inch in this matter," U Myint Thein, later Chief Justice of the Supreme Court, has said.[12] Nu listened to the judges and the lawyers, however, and was convinced of the soundness of their arguments; the result was the constitutional provision for an independent judiciary.

On the whole, however—with the exception of Nu in his dealings with the minority peoples and the constitutional reflections of such deliberations—no single person had a major personal impact on Burma's new basic law. The constitution with which Burma resumed its independence in 1948 was a hastily assembled, largely paste-and-scissors product. Borrowing from the democracies and the Communist countries alike, it sought both to protect and to advance human dignity. In moving its adoption in a speech on September 24, 1947, Nu called upon the members of the Constituent Assembly to "lavish all care and attention" on the "seedling" and to "make it sprout and grow into a great and flourishing tree of magnificent foliage."[13]

Burma's constitution, interestingly in light of the later image of Nu as a veritable holy man, established a state that was clearly secular in character. Aung San had felt strongly on this question, and among the policies of his late friend to which Thakin Nu fell heir was that of a secular basic law and state structure. Nu not only retained Aung San's policy, but also made no reference himself to Buddhism or to religion in his speech moving adoption of the constitution.

One subject on which Nu did speak out at this time, however, was the use of violence to obtain political objectives. "Look at Indochina and Indonesia where blood is being poured out," he declared, "—for what?"[14] Nu announced that all arms and ammunition were to be surrendered to the government by November, and that capital punishment would be the penalty for those possessing them without license after that date. Right up to the hour of independence, and even beyond it, Nu hoped for the non-violent settlement of the differences separating Burma's antagonistic political factions. "The only thing I would ever say against Nu," Sir Hubert Rance has stated, "is that he utterly lacked a capacity for ruthlessness in the months leading up to, and following, independence. If he had been of a more ruthless mold, I think Burma might have escaped a great deal of its postwar insurgent difficulties."[15]

Despite the failure of Thakin Nu's efforts to bring about the return of the Communists to the AFPFL and their participation in the government, Than Tun seemed to be following a policy of cooperation with Nu and the League until the final formalization of the independence arrangements with Britain in mid-October and the subsequent publication of the terms of the various agreements. The Communists' main differences had been with the Socialists anyway, and not with Nu, but Nu was caught in a political vise between the two antagonists. The Socialist Kyaw Nyein, who had succeeded Than Tun as AFPFL Secretary-General, strongly supported a legal approach to the problem of redistributing the land to those who tilled it, while Than Tun favored immediate expropriation without compensation. The fact that Kyaw Nyein's position was reflected in the policies of the Nu government was both a defeat for Than Tun and an opportunity for the Communists to manufacture charges that the AFPFL had sold out the people. In addition, the Socialists had increased their strength organizationally after a slow start. By 1947, under the direction of Thakin Mya (until his death) and Kyaw Nyein, they had eclipsed the Communists in the delta region of lower Burma. The Socialists also were making inroads at the expense of the Communists in the labor field under the leadership of U Ba Swe, who, assuming a larger share of the direction of the Socialist Party with Thakin Mya's death, revealed himself fully capable of meeting the intriguing Communists on their own terms. Their rivalry with the Socialists was probably the chief influence on the Communists' tactics at this time. Nor could Thakin Nu really be neutral in behavior, as contrasted with design; he had to rely, in the last analysis, on the support of the Socialists or that of the Communists. The choice was not easy—but it was clear.

Nu, a member of neither the Socialist nor the Communist faction, nonetheless believed that he had Communist support, and even that the Communists would subsequently "merge with us."[16] Nu and the Communists had "an experimental honeymoon," as one Burmese observer has called it, during which they toured the country for the declared purpose of abolishing violence.[17] Not only Than Tun and other Communists but also the Socialists U Ba Swe and Bo Aung Gyi traveled with Nu. Upon their return they held a joint press conference and made a radio appeal for an end to bloodshed. Their cooperation showed, Nu said, that mutually worthwhile ends might be realized not by "talk, talk, talk, but [by] working together." Subsequently Nu stated that Than Tun "assured me that the Communists would assist the AFPFL in all possible ways in the latter's implementation of the independence program."[18] But the cooperation of the Communists was not sincere, as Thakin Nu was to come to realize. "Although the Communists were loudly condemning terrorism, they were at the same time secretly instructing their followers behind our backs not to surrender their illicit arms," he said later.[19]

The Communists were not the only group that Nu feared might precipitate disunity among the Burmese with the coming of independence. There was also the People's Volunteer Organization, veterans of the resistance movement against the Japanese. Nu had failed to placate them with even a single representative in the Cabinet that Sir Hubert Rance swore in on August 2. The PVO had earlier suffered a decline in political significance with the willingness of Britain to meet Burma's demands connected with independence, while the assassination of Aung San meant even more greatly reduced access to top leadership. In addition, the aggressive Socialists, who had agreed in May 1947 that the PVO should constitute the sole military arm of the AFPFL, were seeking less than six months later to bring the veterans within their mass organizational apparatus.[20] The PVO and the Communists both were concerned over surging Socialist strength.

Nu, aware of the hostility between the Socialists on the one hand and the Communists and the increasingly pro-Communist PVO on the other, tried his "utmost to bring about a union of PVO, Socialist and

Communist Parties."[21] On November 8, upon his return from negotiations in London that had made formal the independence arrangements, he appealed to the contending groups to "unite as one party" making "common cause," since, he explained, the Communists, Socialists, and PVO "resemble one another so closely already that but let them form a committee . . . and in a trice they would find themselves one and the same party."[22] He called for a merger of the Socialists and the PVO to form a "Marxist League" as a first step in this direction.[23] Nu's attempts at reconciliation with the Communists failed again, however, and on November 17 he announced that his efforts to bring the Communists back into the AFPFL would be discontinued. The "Communist protestations of [a] desire for unity," he proclaimed, "are as treacherous as the song of the sirens."[24]

Although the Aung San–Attlee Agreement of January 1947 had committed the British to grant Burma independence, many details had to be worked out before the transfer of authority, and it was for this purpose that Premier-designate Thakin Nu headed a delegation to London in October 1947 for final negotiations with Prime Minister Clement Attlee. No serious differences arose during the talks between Nu and Attlee, who regarded Nu as an "able and pleasant person," and the Nu-Attlee independence treaty, incorporating prior agreements on defense and financial questions, was signed on October 17.[25] Nu's reaction to the results of the negotiations was summed up in his observation that the "admiration for the British people as champions of human rights [has] never been higher in Burma than it is today."[26]

Thakin Nu and his party flew back to Rangoon immediately, and Nu entered the Buddhist monastery at Myathabeik Hill for a brief "religious recess." Upon his return to Rangoon, he found that "the Communists had been pleased to wage [an] unconscionable campaign against the Anglo-Burmese Treaty."[27]

After the conclusion of the Nu-Attlee treaty, the Communists returned to a policy of open opposition to the interim government, possibly as a result of external encouragement by the Indian Communist Party.[28] The Karens, one of Burma's most important ethnic minorities, also were opposed to the agreement—but for reasons different from those of the Communists: they did not want the British to leave for fear of Burman domination. The door for a separate Karen state within the Union of Burma had been left open by the constitution that had been approved by the Constituent Assembly in September, but the leaders of the militant Karen National Union had not been won over.

The Communist attack on the treaty focused primarily on two points: the presence of a British military mission in Burma to help train the Burmese Army, and the provision for compensation for any expropriation of British properties. Burma, moreover, had agreed as a result of the Nu-Attlee talks to "consult with the . . . United Kingdom in advance" in the event of the necessity of action prejudicial to British economic interests, in order to reach a "mutually satisfactory solution."[29] The British recognized that it would probably be necessary for Burma to nationalize the properties of British subjects in Burma, and the Burmese, as seemed only fair to Nu, countered with a promise of equitable compensation.

At his first press conference after returning from London, Thakin Nu described his mission as 90 per cent successful. "The treaty," he later said, was "an Anglo-Burmese compromise, involving give and take on both sides to effect the transfer of power by peaceful means and without bloodshed."[30] Nu also declared that the Burmese had asked for the military mission, "and the British complied." But the Communists rejected Nu's argument that outside aid was necessary to develop Burma's armed forces and that compensation for nationalized British economic interests was the wisest approach in the long run. Burma was not getting real independence, the Communists clamored, but Nu held his ground and the anti-foreign sentiment his adversaries sought to fan did not develop to the degree they anticipated. Of the Communists, Nu publicly stated, "Pray let them not pull passages out of their context and twist them unscrupulously to eke their own praise, and throw dust into the public eye." To Thakin Than Tun in particular, he declared: "It is not proper that a leader, a Communist top man, an exponent of an admirable ideology, should stoop to such chicanery."[31] The last weeks of 1947, however, saw an increase in Communist-instigated unrest among both the peasantry and labor.

The anti-foreign sentiment that the Communists sought with only very limited success to stimulate had one significant result. It completely removed any possibility of Burmese membership in the Commonwealth. Ironically, by mid-1947 Nu had begun to perceive the benefits of Commonwealth association; he even suggested to Sir Hubert Rance the possibility of "associate membership" in the Commonwealth for countries not tied to Britain "by blood, culture or religion."[32] But it was too late; such an association would have been fuel for the fires of Communist propaganda.

There were several reasons for the Communists' severe attack on the Nu-Attlee treaty. The Communist leader Thakin Than Tun, violently anti-British and anti-capitalist, was unquestionably dissatisfied with the results of the negotiations. Cooperation with Nu, moreover, would have meant forsaking a Communist-style revolutionary struggle. In addition, the assassinations of July 1947 had depleted the ranks of the non-Communists while leaving the Communists unscathed. Since many of Burma's ablest surviving nationalist politicians were in the Communist camp, Than Tun felt that his side had the political talent to outmaneuver Nu and the Socialists. Finally, Than Tun, a leader in the wartime underground and one of the leading founders of the AFPFL (as well as a man generally considered superior in ability to Premier-designate Thakin Nu), found himself relegated to a back-seat opposition role in the politics of a soon-to-be-independent Burma; proud, bitter, and jealous, he could not accept this lot.

So it was that independence came to Burma at 4:20 on the morning of January 4, 1948. Originally, the date for the transfer of authority was to have been January 7 or 8, but the astrologers determined that January 4 was a more auspicious day, and the change was made. The hour, too, was the astrologically most propitious. And Premier Thakin Nu was at his magnanimous best as he addressed his free countrymen by radio:

> We need harbor no resentment. We could not forever develop our own culture and maintain our old ways of life without reference to the outside world, a world which was even then growing smaller by the development of the steamship and the railway. The clash with the West was bound to come and if in that clash we lost for a time our independence, we have gained in knowledge of the world and have had time and opportunity to align our civilization and our way of life to what the world demands though we have been careful not to lose in that process our national individuality and the principles which we hold dear.[33]

The Burmese would "part without rancor and in friendship from the great British nation who held us in fee," Nu declared.[34]

※

TEN

FACING THE REBELLIONS

UNLIKE SOME colonial peoples, the Burmese did not have to fight an imperial ruler for independence. Instead, their independence acquired relatively peacefully, they fought among themselves. The Burmese civil war, which began in limited form before the departure of the British, flared fiercely in the first two years of independence, threatening the survival of both U Nu's government and Burma itself. The first revolt was that of Thakin Soe's "Red Flag" Communists in 1946, while the Arakanese Moslem *Mujahids,* an ethno-religious minority, also took to arms in western Burma before independence. But it was the revolution in early 1948 of the "White Flag" Communists, led by Thakin Than Tun, that set in motion the series of events that came perilously close to toppling Nu's government.

It is possible that the insurrections might not have occurred if Aung San had lived, owing to his prestige as the one chiefly responsible for regaining Burma's independence and to the particularly strong backing he enjoyed within the paramilitary People's Volunteer Organization. But Than Tun clearly was opposed to Aung San's leadership and became increasingly jealous of him personally, while the Karens, Burma's most important ethnic minority, were more fearful of the majority Burmans in general than of particular leaders, such as Aung San or Nu. The fact that Nu was new at the helm, inexperienced and unsure, was unquestionably a factor in the deterioration of the Burmese political situation in the wake of liberation from British rule, but serious trouble surely would have arisen anyway.

The legacy of the Japanese years, the lack of consensus among the main political groups in the country, and the personal rivalries that frequently motivated political acts were among the primary causes of Burma's insurrections. Habits of lawlessness and general social demoralization, which preceded the Second World War but were greatly intensified during the Japanese interlude, provided a setting conducive to both rebellion and banditry—the latter frequently masquerading as rebellion. Arms supplied by Britain near the war's end gave rebel and bandit alike the means to oppose authority. The demands of the various competing political groups, moreover, were irreconcilable—the Communists and the non-Communists, the Socialists and the PVO, and the Karens and the Burmans, as well as the lesser rivals. Thakin Soe could not tolerate a role secondary to that of Than Tun, nor could the latter subordinate himself to Aung San, let alone to U Nu. The insecurity of the newly independent Burma and the prevailing absence of discipline, mass and individual alike, provided a tempting opportunity for those who would advance by force their own causes.

Thakin Than Tun's decision to revolt against the AFPFL government was undoubtedly related to international Communism's new hard policy of violence in colonial (and formerly colonial) territories and to his presence, with Ba Tin, at a conference of Southeast Asian "democratic youth" in Calcutta in February 1948 and at a congress of the Indian Communist Party, where the Cominform's shift in strategy was discussed.[1] The Communist leader returned to Burma to intensify his agitation against U Nu and the other members of the ruling party, accusing the AFPFL of being a tool of British imperialism in view of its acceptance of what was called "sham independence." Than Tun had clearly been moving toward a policy of revolt ever since the announcement of the terms of the Nu-Attlee Agreement, but his trip to India appears to have finally decided the issue. Despite Than Tun's provocative behavior in the past, Nu was shocked by the stand of his onetime close nationalist colleague, and moved reluctantly to retaliate against the Communists, even offering to resign the Premiership if Communists, PVO, and Socialists could effect a *rapprochement*.[2]

Subsequently U Nu charged that the Communists revolted because of specific instructions from abroad "for the overthrow of the AFPFL government by violent means."[3] The decision to pursue a policy of violence was made at a meeting of the Central Council of the Burmese Communist Party in February, and a series of major strikes broke out immediately thereafter. The Communist leaders of the strikes said that they "would resist with arms any attempt made by the government to arrest them."[4] Than Tun also predicted that the "bones" of the AFPFL politicians "would fill Bagaya pit to the brim."[5] A turnout of 75,000 peasants at a meeting at Pyinmana in early March had convinced the cocky Than Tun that he enjoyed mass backing for his cause.

Nu and the League tried to come to terms with the Communists, but the latter refused to meet with the AFPFL leaders, who then went themselves to the Communists—but to no avail. The PVO, in addition, offered to mediate the differences between the government and the Communists—and Nu accepted the offer despite the objection of various other AFPFL politicians, who claimed that such negotiations would only give Than Tun more time to prepare his plans to attack the government. The professed goal of the PVO was to get the Communists to suspend their agitation—and the government to postpone any action against them—in order to try to purge the AFPFL, prevent the outbreak of civil war, and unify "White Flag" Communists, Socialists, and PVO. The Communists, however, still avoided meeting those who would negotiate with them, repeatedly postponing the time of talks. Indeed, on March 27 "White Flag" Communists drove about Rangoon in sound trucks declaring that the PVO consisted of "blind patriots having no followers" and that it was attempting to "hang on to the legs of the Communists."[6] Early the next morning, March 28, the police swooped down on the headquarters of the Communists, the government having been informed that they planned a *coup d'état*. But Than Tun and the other main leaders had fled. U Nu had no choice but to take the action he did, although the PVO charged that he moved precipitously. According to Nu, the Communists had "deluded themselves into thinking that the government were quaking in their shoes and that it would hand power over to them."[7]

Nu's hope for a negotiated settlement with the Communists lasted into 1949. There were talks with Communist representatives in late 1948, but the only reply Nu received from these negotiations was the promise that he would be captured alive and tried before a "people's court" for betraying the national cause. Early elections were one of the inducements Nu offered the Communists, promising in April 1949 to hold a vote within a month if Than Tun's rebels would put down their guns—but they would not.

Failing to gain the support of the Communists through persuasion, offers of posts in a caretaker government, and the promise of early elections, Nu tried to prevent any increase in the ranks of the insurrectionists. The Communist revolt probably would not have become critical if the "White Band" faction of the PVO had not subsequently defected. Nu realized this, and his 15-point "Leftist Unity Plan" of May 1948 was a bid more for the retention of PVO support than for the immediate return of the Communists to the fold. In addition to the various policies Nu advanced as acceptable to all leftist elements, he proposed a league for "propagation of Marxist doctrine"—which would "read, discuss and propagate the writings of Marx, Engels, Lenin, Stalin, Mao Tse-tung, Tito, Dimitrov and other apostles of Marxism." Domestic and foreign criticism quickly caused Nu to drop this part of his "Leftist Unity Plan."

Despite his efforts to woo them through unity proposals and a Marxist league, there can be no doubt that U Nu regarded the Communists as agents of a foreign power. "Leftist deviationists," he called them—and accused them of "crying for 'distant aunts while ignoring the mother.'" Why, then, did he try so hard to come to terms with them?

Nu acted as he did in order to save Burma from the devastation of a civil war. And his fears proved well founded: the insurrections resulted in the loss of life and the destruction of property and impeded progress toward stability for the new country. Because of the insurrectionary activity, only 65 per cent of the country's arable land could be cultivated,[8] but Burma needed the earnings of its rice exports for economic development and welfare purposes. An estimated three million refugees were uprooted from their homes by the civil war, and some 22,000 civilians and 5,700 military and other government personnel lost their lives. Damage and destruction to public properties amounted to over $5 million and that to civilian properties to $95 million (through 1955, when the Communist and other rebellions had been at least temporarily reduced to nuisance proportions).[9]

There were also personal reasons why Nu tried so hard to negotiate with the Communists. Thakin Than Tun and many of the others were old friends, comrades in the struggle against the British, "whom he could not bring himself to hate."[10] Moreover, Than Tun, a leading organizer of the AFPFL, was a man Nu had long regarded as genuinely concerned with the welfare of the Burmese people and as a daring advocate of liberation from foreign rule. Surely, Nu thought, such a man could be convinced to fight jointly with the rest for a better Burma. But he was wrong, and as soon as he became convinced of this his posture stiffened and he gave Burma inspired leadership.

Subsequently, following a number of victories for the government, Than Tun's insurrectionists and some of their allies sought to bring about negotiations between Nu and the rebels. "I am at a loss to understand what we have to negotiate for," Nu replied in a speech broadcast in 1956, in which he recalled the Communists' refusal to talk in 1948 and their later rejection of his offers of amnesty and early elections. In 1957, Nu told Thakin Kodaw Hmaing and his "so-called Peace Committee" to plead with the rebels and not with his government, telling them to advise the Communists: "Stop talking nonsense.

You decided at one time that rebellion was right and you rebelled. So, when you now think [rebellion] wrong, why wait for other people's moves? Why not take your own initiative and surrender arms?"

Nevertheless Nu continued to "beckon" the insurgents "to come out of the darkness into the light"—but the Communist leaders steadfastly refused. Amnesty offers were made by the Nu government in 1948, 1949, 1950, and 1955,[11] but they drew only limited response. The first three offers covered only the rebel rank and file, but the last embraced even the leaders who had inaugurated the insurrections. The 1955 amnesty offer contained a multisided appeal to the insurgents and showed the government's extremely forgiving attitude in the circumstances. Its purpose was to permit all persons, irrespective of political affiliation, to participate in the 1956 elections. Attacks upon the insurrectionists were completely suspended during the appeal.

Another aspect of Nu's approach to the problem of the Communist insurrection was his appeal to the people to withdraw their support from the Communists. Without it, he pointed out, the rebellion could not long endure. A character in his play *The People Win Through* explained: "The Government forces didn't want to burn our village. They just couldn't stand by and do nothing when the Communists made it a stronghold. Where do you think the Communists planned all these ambushes against the soldiers round here? All from our village, so the Government couldn't help attacking it. And of course when you fight, you must fight to win."[12]

Nu also employed religion in his battle with the Communists, whom he depicted as opponents of Burma's traditional Buddhist faith. State support of Buddhism developed on a major scale, and religious relics were taken on tours of the country. The day officially beginning the Buddhist lenten season was set aside as a national day of prayer in 1949, and *damasetkya* prayers were chanted in Rangoon and throughout the country, because the Buddha had chanted that prayer and because war had come to an end.[13] Nu's speeches, and his personal conduct as he toured the country—visiting pagodas, offering almsfood to the monks, and propitiating the *nats*—also played an important role in opposing the Communists.

U Nu's survival and assertive performance as Burma's leader in the crucial years from 1948 to 1951 were especially striking when it is considered that his tenure in office was due primarily to the impossibility of finding a successor acceptable to the main groups involved in the stormy Burmese political process: the Socialists, the PVO, and the minority peoples (as well as the Communists). Nu himself hoped that he could leave his official position and devote his energies to guiding the party, thereby setting an example to his colleagues and his foes alike of a politician who would not succumb to personal ambition. In addition, Nu felt that the AFPFL was badly in need of purging, and he wanted personally to oversee the ouster of those whose conduct had set the masses to grumbling about the party. This was a task, he felt, that could be better performed outside the government.

On May 26, 1948, in a radio broadcast, Nu announced his intention to resign from the Premiership on July 20 and to try to unite all of the leftist parties. He subsequently unveiled a 15-point Communist-oriented program proposing increased socialism and closer relations with the Soviet Union and the eastern European countries. Among the policies to be supported by Nu's proposed "United Party of the Left" were land redistribution, nationalization of industry (of which there was very little), state control of foreign trade, rejection of external aid likely to impair Burma's independence, establishment of Soviet-style "popular governments" in the frontier areas, conversion of the Army into a "people's democratic army," "democratic" reform of local administration (including "people's courts"), and inauguration of diplomatic ties with the U.S.S.R. and its satellites.

The reaction to U Nu's "Leftist Unity Plan" was not the unanimous response he had desired. The plan was endorsed by the Socialists and a minority of the People's Volunteer Organization, as well as by those Communists who had not gone underground with Than Tun, including Thein Pe Myint, who had helped Nu draw up the plan.[14] But a majority of the PVO insisted that any such program should be drawn up by all the leftist parties, whether or not they were members of the AFPFL—meaning the Communists. The reason behind the reluctance of most of the PVO to support Nu was apparently not ideological but political, namely, its continued opposition to the Socialists, the increasingly dominant group within the AFPFL.[15] The PVO position was particularly disheartening to Nu because of the numerical strength of the veterans' group within the AFPFL movement and because of its prominent participation in the legislature (the pre-independence Constituent Assembly, which continued to sit until new elections could be held). Nu's leftist unity proposals were not acceptable to the PVO because they did not alter the basic power relationships in Burmese politics—the main concern of the onetime resistance fighters.

Nu's objection to the PVO counterproposal that the Communists participate in the formulation of any leftist unity program did not reflect opposition on his part to negotiations with Thakin Than Tun. Nu, in fact, strongly desired renewed cooperation with Than Tun and his party. But he opposed any talks with the Communists until they had laid down their arms and acknowledged the wrongness of their attempt to seize power by violent means.

On July 2, Nu's leftist unity plan was approved by the Supreme Council of the AFPFL, but the anti-government faction of the PVO refused to accept the League's decision and publicly attacked the AFPFL and its leaders. Bo La Yaung, leader of this majority PVO faction, claimed that he did not oppose Nu's leftist unity plan as such, but that he only wished it to be accompanied by talks with the leaders of the insurrection. However, the attack he directed against the League was clearly an indictment of Nu's leadership. The Supreme Council of the AFPFL subsequently censured the PVO for its public opposition to the decision and threatened expulsion from the League if the PVO did not reinstate those of its members expelled for cooperating with the government. The battlelines were set, and on July 29 the majority faction of the People's Volunteer Organization, known as the "White Band" PVO, went underground. The PVO had been trained for underground fighting; it had opposed demobilization, felt restless in the new setting, and was unwilling to accept a decrease in political importance and influence. U Nu's tactics were applied in vain.

The revolt of the "White Band" PVO was a staggering blow to Nu and the AFPFL, the People's Volunteer Organization being both very well organized and the only paramilitary component of the League. The PVO also maintained close connections with the five Burman regiments of the Army, both groups having been formed from the Patriotic Burmese Forces at the war's end. The government continued to try to woo the "White Band" rebels, and an interim surrender declaration was negotiated between a mission headed by Sir U Thwin and the "White" PVO in October, only to be subsequently repudiated by the latter's Central Working Committee. Other negotiations were conducted between various PVO rebels and certain Socialist ministers and General Ne Win in late 1948 and early 1949 as the threat from a new quarter, the dissatisfied Karen ethnic minority, mounted. The PVO got some arms and ammunition from the hard-pressed government for use against the Karens (although it is not clear that Nu knew all about this)—and later used them against the government.[16]

Having failed to win the backing of either the Communists or the People's Volunteer Organization as a whole for his leftist unity program, U Nu faced a major governmental crisis. Minister of Commerce and Socialist Party Chairman U Ko Ko Gyi, deeply involved in scandal, resigned on July 5 (and fled); U Tin Tut and Deputy Premier Bo Let Ya, who had been Nu's most outspoken supporters in the showdown with the PVO, themselves resigned on July 10, and the rest of the Cabinet turned in their resignations on July 16. Nu and his colleagues, however, agreed at the insistence of the President to serve as a caretaker government until the legislature reconvened on August 15.

Unlike Nu's resignation offers of May and March (and earlier), the various moves of mid-July seem to have been part of a political maneuver that had many faces. Nu himself in his May 26 broadcast acknowledged that "friends in the Frontier States" had sought to restrain him from leaving office in such "critical days" because he was "one of those in whom they place the greatest trust"; Karens, too, had asked him not to leave.[17] Public and press opinion in Rangoon also strongly supported the continuance in office of Nu and his colleagues. Nu ultimately agreed to remain as Prime Minister until the elections scheduled for the next year because he realized that his leaving office would benefit only the Communists. But he surely knew this before mid-July, when he formed the caretaker government, or August 1, when it was announced that he would head the Cabinet until the next elections.

As for the resignations in July of the Socialist members of the Cabinet, these represented a serious bid for power:[18] the Socialists wanted to take over the government, but would have settled for the non-Socialist but more pliable Bo Let Ya as Premier. Bo Let Ya apparently acquiesced in the plot, which is why his political career ended with the Socialist maneuver. The minority groups and independents were hostile to a government of the Socialists (which was already opposed by the Communists and most of the PVO)—and hence the Socialists failed in this transparent bid for political dominance.

Burma's financial position, meanwhile, was rapidly deteriorating, and Premier Nu was moved to reduce the costs of government by cutting pay and reducing the number of ministers. The Cabinet resigned on January 20 in order to make possible the formation of a government of fewer men, but the civil servants balked. A nationwide Ministerial Services Union strike began on February 7, but it was only one of several new challenges to U Nu's government. The executive committee of the "White Band" PVO, which had halfheartedly dispensed with its rebellion to help fight a seemingly imminent Karen insurrection, was again calling for the overthrow of Nu and holding rifle drills in Bandoola Square. Rangoon University students had joined the strikers, as had the Railway Union and practically everybody except the police and the Army. The biggest blow, however, came with the revolt of the Karens, which got under way in earnest in January. Burma's government was now faced with three major insurrectionary foes: the Communists, the PVO (which fought both for and against the government), and the Karens, the country's most important ethnic minority.

The hostility of some Karens to incorporation in an independent Burma, and the distrust by most members of this important minority of the majority Burmans, underlay the Karen armed attacks that broke out in early 1949. Karen-Burman antagonisms existed before the coming of the British, but they were intensified by such British policies as communal representation. The Karens, who number about 1.3 million persons in a population of 20 million, played an important role in wartime resistance against the Japanese—for which they expected British gratitude in the form of continued protection despite the grant of independence to Burma proper. This was a highly unrealistic demand. On the other hand, the Karens had genuine cause to fear the Burmans, as the 1942 Burma Independence Army massacre of Karens tragically showed.

Both Burmans and British were also guilty of according too limited attention to Karen demands before independence. The Rees-Williams Frontier Areas Committee, for example, can hardly be said to have made a genuine effort to settle the Karen problem. Burmese nationalists and the colonial British alike were too concerned with directing the movement toward independence. The Karen National Union, accordingly, boycotted the 1947 Constituent Assembly elections, although the best-known Karen leaders, such as Ba U Gyi, apparently accepted the fact that independence was not possible. Instead, the Karens sought a larger autonomous state within the Union than the Burmans would, or probably could, give them. The trouble was that the Karens formed a majority of the local population in only a comparatively limited area despite the fact that they were the most numerous minority in the country.

The constitution for an independent Burma provided initially for a "special region" of Kawthulay[19] to be followed by the definition by the legislature of a Karen state consisting largely of the backward Salween district and adjacent areas where Karens formed a majority.[20] This was not satisfactory to the Karen National Union, which wanted more territory, including a large part of the delta region (where Burmans and Karens were intermixed). A determined minority of Karens, moreover, organized as the Karen National Defense Organization (KNDO), still wanted outright independence, and these extremists were ultimately able to carry even some of the moderates with them.

As he had done in the case of the Communists and the PVO, U Nu tried desperately to head off a rebellion, and in July 1948 he reportedly received the promise of the chief Karen leaders that they would not seek a separate state except by democratic methods. When incidents among Burmans and Karens increased in mid-1948, Nu met with various Karen leaders and toured the mainly Karen areas with them on behalf of racial harmony; he compared Burma to a big company in which many held shares and from which all derived both benefits and responsibilities. As he himself has put it, "My efforts for Karen-Burman unity earned me the uncomplimentary nickname of 'Karen Nu' from a section of the Burmans."[21] Nu followed up the revolts (and accompanying thefts of public and other property) of Karen soldiers at Maubin, Moulmein, and Loilem in August through September with either a personal visit or the dispatch of top-ranking Karen National Union leaders to these areas. It has been claimed that some Karens planned to kidnap Nu at one of his meetings with their leaders.[22]

A Regional Autonomy Enquiry Commission was appointed in October, and Nu told it, "Please explore the means and ways of satisfying, without hindrance, the legitimate aspirations" of the minority communities.[23] Many of the Karen leaders were impatient, however, as well as suspicious of Burman intentions; others looked at Nu as an appeaser acting as he did out of weakness. A Christmas Eve massacre of Karens by Burmans was the spark that lit the fire of revolt. The KNDO rebellion flared in full in January.

U Nu did not allow the Karens' resort to arms to deflect him from his goal of finding a proper place for them in the Union of Burma. He promised the Karens their state, which the Regional Autonomy Enquiry Commission had recommended in its interim report of February 19, offered an amnesty to all who would lay down their arms, and assured fair treatment of defected KNDO soldiers in the rehabilitation brigades (but would not "consider the reinstatement of mutineers of whatever political color in the national forces"[24]). Negotiations to end the insurrection were held with Ba U Gyi and other Karen leaders in April 1949, but failed almost exclusively because of the intransigence of the rebels. The KNDO rebellion continued, accordingly, and was probably the most important single obstacle to the restoration of peace in Burma.

Nu and the AFPFL leaders in general, on the other hand, cannot escape some responsibility for the Karen tragedy. An amendment to the constitution for a Karen State was not introduced in the legislature until October 1951,[25] and it was not until June 1954 that administrative powers over the several areas of the Karen State were handed over to a Minister for the Karen State. Nu himself, moreover, despite his conciliatory behavior toward the Karens, publicly stated during this period that he was "cent percent in disagreement with the present creation of separate states [for Mons, Karens, and Arakanese]."[26] Such an attitude toward the Mons and Arakanese (some of whom also revolted, as did some Kachins under Naw Seng) was not politically crucial; it was, however, for only too many Karens. Moreover the Karens —who speak a different language from the Burmans and dress differently, and a large number of whom are Christians—were further antagonized by the efforts on behalf of Burmanization by the racial majority.

U Nu called February, March, and April, 1949, the "bleakest" months; "all of us were kept in a terrible state of suspense."[27] He estimated that there were 10,000 rebels in the field in both the Communist and KNDO insurrections, about half of these deserters from the Army, police, and other services.[28] The authority of Nu's government literally ended in the outlying suburbs of Rangoon, and at one point did not even include the whole of the capital city itself. For most of Burma, there was no government.

With the rebel threat at its height, Nu's government was again shaken by more political maneuvering of the sort that occasioned the crisis of July 1948, as the Socialists and "Yellow Band" (or loyal) PVO leaders resigned *en bloc* from the Cabinet. This followed an attempt to turn the government over to the Communists, provided that Nu remained as Premier—an action Nu repudiated (having been in Mandalay when the offer was made to Than Tun). The resigning ministers claimed that they did what they did to convince the rebels of their seriousness in not holding office for its own sake. Nu immediately formed a non-party government that included Army Commander-in-Chief General Ne Win.

Nu's performance under fire was an inspiring one. He admitted the "probability" of the Union's collapse, but sought to provide "decisive leadership" nonetheless; he expressed a "determination to carry on with the struggle, irrespective of success or failure, in the conviction that the course we adopted was the only right course." He asked leaders of the frontier areas to organize emergency units of the "Frontier Armed Forces," which, if necessary, would fight with "sticks and *dahs* [knives]," and, receiving their assurances that they would, "was so overcome with gratitude and . . . so intensely moved that tears welled up in my eyes."[29]

Against the various insurgent elements, Nu's government had only a 12,000-man Army and a three-fighter Air Force, besides its inexperienced and unreliable police and police reserves.[30] Thousands of auxiliary "peace guerrillas" (*sitwundans*) had to be raised by Army Commander-in-Chief General Ne Win (Thakin Shu Maung of the Dobama Asiayone) and able Colonel Aung Gyi, the former Socialist politician, at the height of the emergency. The government barely survived the challenge. In a speech to the legislature on September 28, 1949, Nu admitted that "on one or two dreadful occasions the Union was on the verge of collapse."[31]

On July 19, 1949, the second anniversary of the martyrdom of Aung San and the others, Premier Nu announced the goal of "peace within one year" with the immediate objectives of restoring road and rail traffic between Rangoon and Mandalay and opening up water communications to the rich rice district of Henzada, so that the rice stocks there could be exported. Prospects for the attainment of these objectives seemed limited; the Karens still held Insein, only a dozen miles from Rangoon, as well as Henzada district and Toungoo between Rangoon and Mandalay. The Communists dominated central Burma from their headquarters at Pyinmana, and the PVO controlled the oilfields of the Irrawaddy plain as well as choked the important Irrawaddy River. " 'Peace within one year' is as easy to be talked about as it is difficult to put into operation," admitted Nu,[32] but he and General Ne Win moved to mobilize all available forces in the country to fight the rebels, and by July 19 of the next year the Burmese Army (aided by arms and other war supplies from Britain and India) had broken the backs of the several rebellions.

As U Nu himself later put it, "In the space of one year, the Rangoon Government had once again become the Government of the Union of Burma whose authority extended to most parts of the country."[33] Ever the creator of appealing slogans, Nu on the following Martyrs' Day (July 19, 1950) proposed the goal, "from peace to stability," to make Burma a socialist state by democratic means. The rebellions were by no means over, however, but by the next year, 1951, the insurrectionists could no longer be regarded as possible alternative governments to the AFPFL. By August 1952, accordingly, Nu and his party, overwhelming victors in the staggered elections of 1951–52, unveiled their plans for a Burmese welfare state at a mass conference in Rangoon. Hopes for the early fulfillment of the long-cherished socialist ideals, however, were quickly dashed, as a major security challenge arose from a new quarter—Chinese Nationalist irregulars in Kengtung state who were becoming a menace of pressing proportions just as the government was about to wipe out the other insurrectionists.

U Nu's initial basic tactic in seeking to outwit the Communists, the PVO, and the Karens was probably a valid one : he constantly tried to rob them of their following and their possible allies. The rebellions of the PVO and the Karens on the heels of the Communist insurrection, however, left Nu and his government no choice as to the means to be used against the insurgents. "So long as violent forces are at work," said Nu (who had refused to join the AFO in 1944 because of his opposition to the use of force), "there must be countermeasures to suppress them"; allowing the Communists to triumph by not resisting them, he declared, would be "betraying the masses."[34]

Lack of effective coordination among the rebel armies, which cooperated from time to time in various combinations only to fall out among themselves again, was surely one reason why the government was able to withstand the many-sided assault against it.[35] The fact that they held the capital of Rangoon, however precariously in the worst days of the insurrections, also enabled Nu and his associates to maintain necessary contact with the outside world. Control of the various rice ports permitted the continuation of foreign trade (upon which both the government and some of the rebels depended—which is probably the reason why the Karens in particular did not attempt to block these vital outlets). The success of the government, meanwhile, in enlarging and developing its Army into an effective fighting force enabled it in 1950–51 to turn the tide of victory against the Communists and the Karens, the two most important insurrectionist groups, in the Irrawaddy River plain.

The leadership of U Nu, who had been thrust into the Premiership of independent Burma by Aung San's death, was itself probably the decisive factor in holding the allegiance of the various hill peoples, especially the militarily significant Kachins and Chins.

Nu's chief fear during these years, as subsequently, was for the disintegration of the Union. He was clearly aware of the consequences for China, India, and other countries of internal strife in recent times.

Of the American Civil War, Nu said, "The reason that the United
States is the strongest and most influential nation in the world is due to
the fact that Abraham Lincoln . . . successfully prevented the Southern States from secession, . . . thus consolidating the whole country."[36] Nu regarded his role as paralleling Lincoln's. The Union would
have been partitioned into "three or four parts," he said, but for "the
AFPFL leaders."[37]

ELEVEN

❋

"TOWARDS A WELFARE STATE"

WITH THE COMING of independence on January 4, 1948, Burma's new leaders assumed responsibility for rehabilitating a war-ravaged economy. The output of their land had fallen by about two-thirds as a result of World War II, while half of the country's "man-made" wealth had been destroyed.[1] The production of rice, which accounted for more than two-thirds of all acreage under cultivation, was reviving on the eve of independence, but other important areas of the economy were still critically disabled. The oil wells at Chauk and Yenangyaung had been destroyed by the British at the time of Japan's invasion, as had the largest refinery at Syriam and the pipelines to the other refineries. The Mawchi mines, rich in wolfram and tin, had been demolished, and the Bawdwin mine, a source of lead and silver, also was out of operation. Teak production, which accounted for ten per cent of the prewar gross national product, was just being resumed.

The task of reviving the Burmese economy was a major one and would have tried the abilities of any government. But the leaders of the new Burma wanted to do more than restore; they wanted to remake and modernize the Burmese economy. Development, moreover, was to be for social ends: as U Nu put it in 1952, the objective was "none other than a steady and energetic effort to be exerted by us to exploit the immense natural wealth of the country to benefit the citizens totally and create conditions of contentment and happiness."[2]

Burma's constitution itself was a strongly socialist document,[3] specifically authorizing the government to nationalize "any single branch" of the economy "with compensation and through legal processes." Reflecting its desire to bring about rapid economic changes, U Nu's government set up a Ministry of National Planning even before independence, and a very general Two-Year Economic Development Plan was announced on April 1, 1948 (but was never implemented because of the insurgencies). Burma's dependence on rice exports was evident from the plan, which described the grain as "the currency of the country," setting 1951–52 as the target year for restoration of the prewar level of rice production.[4] The 1948 plan also further revealed the government's socialist intentions—which were fortified by Nu's declaration that he would "nationalize monopolizing capitalist undertakings and . . . administer the resulting national undertakings by partnership between the state and the workers."[5] The plan, however, was more a statement of intent than a set of steps calculated to accomplish particular economic priorities. The revolt of the Communists stiffened Burma's socialist posture, as Nu's 15-point Leftist Unity Plan, announced only weeks after the announcement of the Two-Year Plan, indicated.

Nu's government moved to translate its socialist ideals into reality not only by issuing plans and pronouncements, but also by legislation and other action. On April 20, 1948, the Inland Water Transport Nationalization Act was passed, and the Irrawaddy Flotilla Company (which had largely controlled inland water shipping and transportation under the British) was nationalized on June 1, when the government also took over the extraction of teak from one-third of the areas formerly covered by long-term leases. The state monopoly of rice collection and sales inaugurated by the British after the war (because of the shortage of food throughout Southeast Asia) was continued—and a Land Nationalization Bill was passed on October 11, U Nu declaring that it would "usher in an era whose ultimate objective [was] collective farming."[6] An Economic Council was also created in October to determine which additional economic activities should be nationalized. In September 1949 the government issued a Statement on Industrial Policy which reflected its basic belief that development largely meant industrialization.

During the years from 1948 to 1950 the most extreme socialist legislation of the first decade of independence in Burma was passed, and the period can be considered almost an era in itself in terms of the development of Burmese economic policy. The fulfillment of Burma's ambitious socialist objectives during these years, however, was severely hindered by insurgent activity. Rice output was down 15 per cent in 1949 from the previous year as a result of the insurrections, while the flow of refugees from rebel-threatened areas to the more secure larger towns, including Rangoon, added to the government's economic burdens. The disruption of normal farming activity drastically limited development plans based on the expectation of foreign exchange earnings, and the government could hardly rehabilitate or develop a country that it did not control.

Several bills dealing with agriculture were among the legislation passed in the first months of U Nu's government, including the Tenancy Standard Rent Act of 1947 (enacted before independence), which limited tenancy rent to twice the assessed land revenue. The Communists sharply attacked this bill, promising an end to land rent altogether under Communism. Additional legislation for cultivators enacted during the first year of independence included the Land Nationalization Act, the Agricultural Bank Act, the Agricultural Laborers' Minimum Wage Act, the Tenancy Disposal Act, and the Agriculturalists Debt Relief Act. In addition, in 1950 the government wrote off as uncollectible nearly $15 million worth of agricultural indebtedness and inaugurated new lending machinery and higher per-acre assistance.[7]

The Land Nationalization Act of October 1948, probably the most important of the several pieces of agricultural legislation, was not immediately implemented because of the insurrections. Its significance was considerable, however, because of the legislative development it represented of Section 30 of the Burmese constitution, which declared that the state was the owner of all land; the bill set a 50-acre limit (per family) on land holdings. The act also allowed the government to take possession legally of all land held by persons who did not till the soil themselves. Nearly two-thirds of the land devoted to rice farming was held by non-resident landlords,[8] and most of these were Indian Chettyars,[9] who were more hated individually than the British ever were. Nationalist considerations of the most dynamic sort, accordingly, underlay the demand for change in landholding arrangements.[10] Nonetheless, Nu and his colleagues in the AFPFL government were attacked not only by the Communists—for moving too slowly and not going far enough—but also by Burman landowners for going too far and violating Buddhist precepts in the process.

U Nu replied to his critics among the landowners:

> They assert that according to one of the five precepts of the Buddhist faith, it is a sin to nationalize land or expropriate any other property without the consent of the owner, regardless of whether or not we pay the compensation. Yes, I admit that taking anything without the consent of its owner constitutes a sin under that precept. But who are the landowners in our Union? Is it a Chettyar named Allagappa, or a Chinaman named Akhe-Shoke or a Bur-

mese gentleman wearing a *taungshe pasoe* named U Pyu Gyi? All these persons are ceremonially strutting about, calling themselves owners of the land. But they are in fact not the real owners of the land. . . . The real owners of the land are we, Government freely and gladly elected by the people. . . . During the successive dynasties of Burmese kings, all this land was royal property. After the British occupation of Burma, all land became the property of Queen Victoria and her heirs and successors. When the British transferred power to the constitutionally elected Government of the people, this land became . . . the property of this Government.

The government had "every right to take back . . . its own land," Nu said. "It also has the right to distribute. It can do as it wants with its own property; it can roast it, bake it or do whatever it likes with it."[11]

Nu stated that property was "meant not to be saved, not for gains, nor for comfort. It is to be used by men to meet their needs in respect to clothing, food, habitation, in their journey toward *nirvana*." He told the landlords that it was virtuous to give, and that they would thus make more likely their early arrival at *nirvana*.[12]

By late 1951 the insurrections were fairly well checked, acreage under cultivation had begun to rise, and work could be resumed on the solution of Burma's economic problems. U Nu in his 1952 Martyrs' Day address announced the slogan, "Towards a Welfare State," and promised his countrymen a day when every family in Burma would possess a house, an automobile, and an income of $175 to $200 a month. Burma, he said, was "rich enough to provide these amenities."[13] A highly publicized *Pyidawtha* ("Happy Land") Conference, marked by the unveiling of various economic and social welfare schemes (and plans for the "devolution of powers" and the "democratization of local administration"), was held in Rangoon in August. The speed with which the Burmese government sought to move was explained by Nu to a group of American businessmen in 1955: "We have been in a hurry and we are in a hurry. We have waited for so long and we feel we must accomplish a great deal in a short time."[14]

The Eight-Year Development Plan presented and adopted at the August 1952 *Pyidawtha* conference was based on a comprehensive survey of the natural resources and potential of Burma made by a private firm of United States engineers, Knappen, Tippetts, Abbett, and Mc-Carthy, in association with Pierce Management, Inc., and the economic consulting firm of Robert R. Nathan Associates. The engineering firm had been asked to develop a welfare program for Burma, and the government's $1,575,000,000 Eight-Year Plan was based on its 840-page report.[15] Two-thirds of this investment was to be in productive enterprises and one-third in social services.

The goals of the Eight-Year Plan were highly optimistic.[16] An increase of 78 per cent was envisaged in total national output by 1959–60; per capita national output was to go up 62 per cent, and per capita consumption 52 per cent.[17] Detailed plans were prepared for the achievement of the various *Pyidawtha* goals with respect to industry, power, transport, education, and so on.[18] An Industrial Development Corporation, a Housing Board, and other agencies were created by the legislature to carry out the plans. "Ultimately," Nu said, "all trade and industry must be organized into public corporations and cooperatives controlled and managed by the representatives of workers and consumers."[19]

Prime Minister Nu told the Far East American Council of Commerce and Industry in New York in 1955 that "we are not going overboard for industrialization,"[20] but between 1952 and 1956 his government set up a steel mill, a tile factory, a pharmaceutical plant, a cotton spinning mill, a jute factory, and various lesser industrial projects (for the production and processing of silk, tinned milk, and pottery, and for tea blending). Frank N. Trager, an American aid official in Burma at the time, later wrote, "The drive toward industrialization . . . completely overshadowed Burma's basic economic activity, agriculture."[21] This was in spite of the fact that agriculture was the chief source of vitally needed foreign exchange.

The Five-Year Agricultural Plan which was adopted at the *Pyidawtha* Conference—and which the Agricultural and Rural Development Corporation was created to implement—envisaged, within five years (according to Nu), economic self-sufficiency, the increase of rice exports to prewar levels, and irrigation projects "which will give great benefit to the *ludu*" (people).[22] But the agricultural portion of the *Pyidawtha* Plan went largely unimplemented in the immediately succeeding years—which is not surprising in view of the fact that it was less a plan than a statement of desired production targets.

Primarily as a form of incentive to the farmers, the Nu government passed a second Land Nationalization Act (which really was not necessary) in 1952,[23] but it was not until 1953 that land redistribution programs were actually put into operation in eight pilot districts. The Land Nationalization Act of 1952 promised the redistribution of ten million acres by 1955, but the goal—like others of the *Pyidawtha* era—

was Olympian, and the government came nowhere near reaching it. Nonetheless, in a September 1957 speech to the Parliament, Nu was able to announce the effective nationalization of over two million acres of land in 1,121 villages; 17.2 million acres in 9,000 villages remained to be nationalized.[24] Administration of the land nationalization program, however, was subject to frequent abuse in practice.[25]

The peasantry, on the whole, appears not to have been impressed with the government's farm policy, however, land redistribution notwithstanding. For one thing, the cultivator received only a fraction of the price the government got from the customers to whom it sold the rice he grew. Although Nu claimed that it was possible for a farmer to earn more than $9.50 an acre,[26] farmers were being paid only $28 a ton at a time when the government was selling rice abroad for $140 to $168 a ton. Nu also pointed with pride to the agricultural bank, which was authorized to make loans to local cooperative societies at 6 per cent interest to be reloaned to cultivators at 12 per cent annual interest. But an official survey of almost 275,000 farms in 1954 showed that loans provided by the government amounted to only 36 per cent of the total required working capital, the remaining 64 per cent being provided by private sources at extortionate interest rates.[27] The problem of agricultural credit received far less attention from the Nu government than it warranted.

The KTA report was partly responsible for the optimism of Burma's leaders. Typical of the way it encouraged such optimism was its conclusion that Burma had the "opportunity to telescope within a limited number of years the process of increasing productivity which took generations for other nations to achieve."[28] Burma was "uniquely favored, and will continue to be for some years at least, in the existence of a highly advantageous world market price for her chief export crop, rice," the report stated.[29] The dimensions of the resulting Burmese expectations can be gauged from the fact that more than half of the planned $1,575,000,000 development investment was to come from exports—necessitating a production increase in eight years of approximately two-thirds. That Burma expected a rise in production, rather than in prices, was indicated by U Nu's assertion that the government anticipated a moderate decline in the price of rice.[30] Besides such rice earnings, it was also expected that Burma would be the recipient of considerable foreign technical and material aid and capital investment. Nu declared that Burma "must accept from any country any assistance for the creation of a Welfare State, provided such assistance is given freely and does not violate our sovereignty."[31] But the government terminated American economic assistance, which had begun in 1950 and amounted to $20 million in all[32]—even though it fulfilled the qualifications Nu set—while Nu's remarks concerning ultimate public management of all economic activity were hardly likely to attract foreign investors. (The American aid was ended because of the problem of Nationalist Chinese irregulars operating on Burmese soil.)

Continued high prices for rice were not the only assumption of the government that was not fulfilled. Nu and his associates also antici-pated greater restoration of law and order than in fact occurred, and it expected more success than it achieved in meeting the shortage of technically skilled persons to carry out the Eight-Year Plan.[33] Nu rec-ognized that Burma was "bereft" of "skilled technicians, materials and machineries"; indeed, he said in a radio talk in 1953, "Cost does not come into our consideration in procuring them. The Government has issued directives not to mind the cost."[34] Despite its own greater finan-cial responsibilities that resulted from termination of American aid in 1953, Nu's government dispatched new missions abroad to make fur-ther purchases for *Pyidawtha* projects—in addition to the large orders for capital goods that had already been placed.

By mid-1953 the drain on Burma's foreign exchange reserves had become heavy. These reserves, which stood at more than $365 million in June 1953, dropped to less than $204 million by January 1954 and to less than $112 million by the following January, before reaching their lowest point of $74.5 million in August 1955.[35] The main reason for the drain, even more important than the high level of Burma's foreign purchases, was the drop in the international price of rice. Government-to-government prices had been $140 a ton during the first half of 1952 —i.e., just prior to the August *Pyidawtha* conference—and had even risen to $154 a ton in the last half of 1952 and to $168 in the first half of 1953. Then they dropped—to $100.80 a ton for most government-to-government contracts (and to $89.60 for the important long-term contract with India) by the end of 1953.[36] Burma's leaders were at a loss to explain what was happening; as one senior civil servant put it, "The rice-consuming people were still multiplying faster than increases in rice production, and, as for India's low bid, we thought they were just bargaining—trying to take advantage of us."[37] The Burmese gov-ernment, accordingly, did not lower its prices sufficiently to make up for the drop in price per ton by selling larger quantities. Adequate pro-visions, moreover, had not been made for storing the grain because of the anticipated sellers' market, and Burma suffered additional losses for this reason.

Although the KTA report had anticipated that more than half of the costs of the Eight-Year Plan would be financed out of rice revenues, in fact only two-fifths of the capital outlay in 1955–56 came from taxes or government earnings. One-fifth came from Burma's foreign exchange reserves, a small amount came from reparations, foreign loans, and private savings (in Burma), and nearly two-fifths reflected the government's deficit financing by increasing the domestic money supply.[38]

The goals of the Eight-Year Plan were never achieved. U Nu stated at the January 1958 AFPFL national congress that "it was clear" that the "primary task" economically was to attain the level of production of rice, timber, petroleum, and minerals that had prevailed before the war.[39] This was accomplished by neither the Two- nor the Eight-Year Plan. Indeed, despite the important role assigned to increased rice production in the 1952 plan, it was only in the 1956–57 dry season that the Agricultural and Rural Development Corporation began to seek to expand paddy acreage in the fertile Irrawaddy delta—yet a three-million-acre increase was planned by 1959–60.[40] Yields, moreover, continued to be low—in part as a result of primitive techniques. The level of rice exports in 1956–57 was still 33 per cent less than in 1938–39, timber exports were not even a quarter of the 1937 to 1941 average, and the highest export volume of minerals and ores under the AFPFL government (that of 1954–55) was only four per cent of the level of the period from 1937 to 1941.[41]

The socialist objectives of the Burmese leaders in the first years of independence had failed of fulfillment, U Nu clearly admitted in a 1949 statement in the Parliament on the government's attitude toward foreign capital. An important modification in the economic policies of the Nu government took place at the start of the 1950's, accordingly, in the form of the "joint ventures" accepted by Burma's leaders as a short-term substitute for nationalization and state monopolies. The first of these (the Burma Corporation), which took effect in January 1952, was for the working of the Bawdwin Mines, and this was followed by others, including the Burma Oil Company (1954), Anglo-Burma Tin (1956), and Mawchi Mines (1958).[42] The reparations agreement with Japan also specified the use of certain funds for cooperative enterprises between Japanese firms and the Burmese government.

Explaining the Bawdwin Mines agreement (which gave the government a 50 per cent share), Nu said, "Our intention is to get our people sufficiently trained as administrators, technicians and skilled laborers, without immediately nationalizing these enterprises. Our share of the partnership will be augmented as and when the nature of that training is improved until at last we are in a position to nationalize them."[43] The high priority accorded the joint ventures was indicated in a December 1953 speech by Nu in which he listed the types of enterprises to which "aid and assistance shall be given" in order of priority: state enterprises, joint ventures between the government and private concerns, cooperative societies, limited companies owned by Burmese nationals, limited companies in which Burmese nationals owned 60 per cent of the shares, and private companies.

U Nu and his leading associates ultimately realized many of the shortcomings of their approach to Burma's economic problems. And they had the courage to admit that they had been wrong.

Under the impact of the changing rice market and the related burden of trying to do too much too soon, the Eight-Year Development Plan of 1952 was first modified and then virtually abandoned. In a statement read to the Parliament in September 1957 outlining the government's Four-Year Plan (successor to the Eight-Year Plan) Nu proclaimed a major change in Burma's economic policy. The change had actually been made in 1956 and subsequently had itself been modified in terms of particular priorities. However, according to economist Louis J. Walinsky, chief foreign economic consultant to the government, it was neither necessary nor meaningful to embark on a new Four-Year Plan. "What was necessary," he has written, "was that the Government apply itself to persistent effort to correct the accumulated abuses and weaknesses of the past." Nu had "confused rather than clarified the issues" by his action.[44]

"We wanted to get a thing done in one month which normally should take one year," Nu confessed at a June meeting dealing with the plan. "From practical experience," he said, "I no longer like to see Government's finger in all sorts of economic pies." In the future the government would "concentrate only on key economic projects. . . . In order to step up production in the economic field, the operation of all industrial and mining enterprises, except certain key projects," Nu proposed, "should not be entrusted solely to those who are only interested in getting salaries. They should be entrusted also to those who have profit motives."[45] Accordingly, a cutback in new projects was announced and the invitation for greater cooperation with private capital was renewed.

Nu denied, however, that Burma was abandoning socialism, explaining,

We are . . . modifying somewhat our ideas of what Socialism is, and how it can work effectively in the modern world—and especially in an underdeveloped country like Burma. Socialism has changed, and come of age, in the modern world; and we must change with it. No longer is Socialism necessarily identified with Government ownership and operation of the means of production. . . . Where and when nationalization can achieve these goals better than other techniques can, we shall have nationalization. But where these goals can be achieved better by other means, we shall employ those other means without fear. Socialism and nationalization in every field are not equivalent terms in our thinking any longer.[46]

The new Four-Year Plan reflected another proclaimed change in Burmese economic policy which had been developing for some time. The 1957 Plan, basically a modification of changes in the *Pyidawtha* plan made by U Ba Swe as Premier in 1956 while Nu was voluntarily out of office, placed "a much heavier emphasis than heretofore on the primary sectors of the economy—agriculture, forestry and mining."[47] In his June 1957 speech, Nu pointed out that Burma was not utilizing 54 per cent of its arable land and urged the use of this land for the cultivation of rubber, jute, groundnuts, tobacco, cotton, wheat, coffee, and tea.[48] In his subsequent September address to the Parliament, he declared that "agriculture, tin and minerals must be restored to at least their prewar output before satisfactory gains in other important sectors of the economy can be made and sustained."[49]

Once again, however, there was an air of unreality about the government's policy, in practice. U Kyaw Nyein at one point in drawing up the Four-Year Plan even proposed that various new industrial projects be carried out—without resort either to foreign exchange or to local currency.[50] The completion of various existing economic projects was in fact delayed, while a number of new ones were begun. The words of the invitation to foreign private investors were cordial enough and several investment bills were drafted, but the government never passed any of them. U Nu's government frequently did not do what he said it would.

There were a number of reasons for Burma's failure in the first decade of independence to make a more adequate assault on her economic problems. One of the most important of these was the physical state of the country as inherited from the British; the invasion and counterinvasion of the wartime Japanese period had destroyed at least half of Burma's capital of modern communications and industry. According to U Hla Maung, formerly Secretary of the Economic and Social Board, moreover, "There were too few of them—trying to do too much (because there were too few of them and because there was so much to do) and lacking in time and opportunity to take a long look, backward or forward, at where they had been and where they were going."[51]

The engagement of the overwhelming majority of the Burmese in colonial days in traditional types of work, such as agriculture and crafts, moreover, left them unprepared for the roles they would have to fill with the ending of imperial rule. In 1953 Nu admitted, "We have not sufficient practical experience even for . . . normal administrative purposes, much less for the building of *Pyidawtha*."[52] As a result, expensive equipment for industrial enterprises could not be operated for lack of trained personnel or was ruined because of inadequate care. In a 1955 speech in Bangkok, in which he compared Burma's backwardness with the state of human and technical development in neighboring Thailand, Nu observed that his country "lagged behind so much that for every step forward that Thailand takes Burma needs to take ten."[53]

The result of Burma's lack of administrative and business experience was incompetent direction of the many socialist boards, agencies, and economic enterprises (among other types of activity) set up by the government. Forty per cent of the import licenses granted in the first years of independence went to foreigners, not because the government wanted it that way, but because as Nu himself put it, "our own nationals are finding it exceedingly difficult to even cope with the present allocation of 60 per cent."[54]

U Nu clearly was aware of the hindrance to his government's development aspirations posed by the backwardness of his countrymen; in 1951, for example, he publicly termed "the dearth of capable and sincere workers . . . the greatest obstacle" to the implementation of the AFPFL program.[55] Yet the plans were proclaimed nonetheless.

Nu also blamed the "lack of system in recruiting personnel" for much of the inefficiency of the government's many economic enterprises. But, according to the columnist "Criticus" in *The Nation*, "It was not a lack of system but the existence of a definite, but perverted, system of appointing Party henchmen, or so-called henchmen, in every key post and every post where nepotism and patronage could be exercised."[56] Not only were "party hacks" frequently rewarded with important managerial positions, despite the complete lack of any professional qualifications, but some able men were denied the opportunity of government service because they had not participated in the nationalist struggle. (This was the case for many Burmese who had had genuine administrative experience under the British.) Nu frequently expressed concern for the morale of the civil service, but little was done in practice to improve it.

In a 1957 speech on the Four-Year Plan, Nu—on behalf of his colleagues and himself—admitted to "the launching of our plans without first preparing the ground systematically." Before foundations for industrial buildings were even laid, the machines that were to occupy the buildings arrived and "lay scattered in the sun and rain without any use being made of them." Even after the buildings were completed, "specific plans" had still to be "formulated for the production and supply of raw material."[57] In short, Burma's planners planned badly.

Nu also listed as major reasons "for our failure . . . inadequate care in laying the foundations of our national structure and choosing the materials that went into its building, lack of good and qualified leaders and . . . the fact that many of our leaders and members succumbed to temptation and forgot their noble ideals."[58] Nu recognized in his speeches the need for determination and hard work on the part of leaders and masses alike to achieve Burma's economic goals, but he and his government failed to require sufficient discipline from their countrymen in practice. Students at the University of Rangoon, for example, worked less (and were less disciplined) than under colonial rule. The Bureau of Special Investigation (BSI), formed by Nu to "eradicate termites" from the bureaucracy, rather than ending "managerial constipation," as he called it, probably did more harm in stifling the little initiative the administrative structure possessed than good in locating some (but not necessarily the worst) villains in the government.

However, in Nu's own view the insurrections bore the chief responsibility for Burma's failure to implement her ambitious plans for economic development and social welfare.[59] From 1942 through 1945, Nu explained in 1957, Burma had been a battlefield, "with the result that the machinery for law and order was broken into pieces [and] disruptive forces became rampant all over the country." The launching in 1952 of the *Pyidawtha* economic and social plans, he said, was "a terrible blunder"; the government diverted its attention from the complete restoration of law and order to develop the national economy and social services "instead of adopting the wise dictum 'One thing at a time and that done well.' "[60]

But was the government's policy as unwise as Nu claimed?

The *Pyidawtha* program—indeed, the original Two-Year Plan and even Nu's Leftist Unity Plan—clearly identified the government's orientation and complexion for all to see. This was an advantage in dealing with the Communists in terms both of undercutting their promises and of winning the positive identification of the masses with the national leaders.

Communist, Karen, and other insurrectionary activity of 1948 to 1951 clearly prevented Nu's government from registering accomplishments on the economic and welfare fronts, while continued operations against the insurgents (including the Chinese Nationalist irregulars) after 1952 diverted money and attention from economic and social programs. But the insurrections cannot be blamed for the bad planning (which Nu and the others have admitted), the corruption, and the inefficiency of many of those who directed the growing number of economic enterprises and boards (which caused Nu to establish the BSI), the inexperience of the Burmese people (including U Nu and U Kyaw Nyein, among others) in business and technical matters—or the heady optimism (for example, the automobile for every family that Nu promised in 1952). Nor can the Communists, the Karens, or the Chinese Nationalists be held responsible for the government's failure to provide leadership by deeds, not speeches, in the economic field—or for the "lack of systematic preparation of development projects" and the "weaknesses in the execution of projects" which a former American economic consultant to Nu's government has described in a major study of Burmese economic development during these years.

According to the latter, Louis J. Walinsky, "The 'terrible blunder' had not been in undertaking development without first completely restoring law and order, but rather in not pressing vigorously to suppress civil disorder while economic development was going forward. The twin efforts were complementary and each would have contributed to the other."[61]

Actual implementation of *Pyidawtha* social welfare goals did not get under way until 1954. A Comprehensive Plan of Social Development, drawn up with assistance from United Nations specialists, was completed in 1953, and a Directorate of Social Welfare was established to implement it. A Union Conference of Social Work was convened the next year—and a continuing Union Council of Social Service set up as a link with local participants in the social development program. But the fall in the price of rice in late 1953—even before the government's welfare programs had really gotten off the ground—was a major check on implementation. In 1957, as noted, Nu announced that economic development and the social services would be accorded secondary priority to the restoration of law and order.

However, Nu and his associates consistently gave high priority to education, which was to be free and ultimately compulsory. Nu regarded the education of the Burmese people as essential to the economic modernization of the country and the successful establishment of democratic government. He termed ignorance "a continual invitation to subversion,"[62] and described it as being "in its own way . . . as dangerous to society as hunger or poverty."[63] His government, accordingly, "set out to spread education throughout the country as quickly as possible."[64] New schools were opened at various levels, education was made free (even at Rangoon University), textbooks were distributed without charge to students, a mass education program for the rural areas was inaugurated, and the work of the Burma Translation Society was officially encouraged. The goals, as Nu expounded them in 1952, were to give every citizen a "rudimentary knowledge of writing, reading and arithmetic," to extend "skillful and practical" technical knowledge, and to equip Burmese men and women to fulfill the "manifold responsibilities" of Union citizenship.[65]

The Burma Translation Society (BTS) and the Mass Education Council both sought to make education easily accessible—and digestible—to adults, particularly in the rural regions. The BTS, which was founded in 1947, just before independence was restored, translated and printed a variety of works that were purchased by the government and widely distributed throughout the country.[66] Besides books for adult readers, the BTS also translated many school texts. Nu termed this activity "the root of all real progress for the peoples of this Union," and in 1952 declared that his government had decided "to incur whatever expenditure that may be required for the purpose."[67] Created in 1949, the Mass Education Council trained educational workers to be sent to various parts of the country to "uplift the rural population, improve rural health, develop rural economy, social welfare and education."[68] The primary function of the workers, however, was "fundamental and adult education."

U Nu's personal influence on education was unquestionably beneficial on the whole. World War II left Burma with a most unfortunate legacy in the field of education : three-quarters of the physical plant was destroyed, and it was not until 1953 that there were as many children of primary school age being instructed as there had been before the war.[69] Nu, indeed, had the wisdom, and the courage, to depart from the inherited British pattern for training teachers to meet the emergency needs of a country in which the normal processes of education were all but eliminated during World War II. "Two-month intensive training courses" were established to provide eight thousand primary teachers "in the course of three or four years."[70] As a result of the Educational Plan for the Welfare State, presented at the 1952 *Pyidawtha* Conference, there were 6,891 new primary, 343 middle, and 112 high schools by the end of 1957. School enrollment between 1953 and 1956, moreover, jumped from some 596,000 to 1,155,800 at the primary level, from 54,000 to 144,200 at the secondary, and from 16,000 to 31,700 in high schools.[71] Construction of new schools fell far short of the country's needs, however; the shortage of teachers remained critical, and the level of the education offered and the performance of students compared very unfavorably with the prewar years.[72] Political agitation among students and government pressures on private (including missionary) schools hardly helped the situation.

The number of students attending Rangoon University also increased rapidly—from less than 5,000 in 1951 to more than 10,000 only three years later. New buildings were constructed and changes in curricula made, but academic standards dropped drastically in comparison with the days of British rule. The number of young men and women desiring a higher education also led to the establishment of several new intermediate (two-year) colleges at various locations in the country, while Mandalay College became a university. U Nu was not content to fill his role as Chancellor of Rangoon University only nominally; on several occasions he interfered with the independent operation of the institution.[73] However, although he took note of excesses of student behavior on several occasions, Nu did not provide effective leadership in dealing with the related student problems of indiscipline and political extremism (which were rooted partially in the prewar political agitation at the University of a younger Nu and his nationalist friends).[74] Nu's leadership in this respect did not compare favorably with that of General Ne Win when he was Premier from 1958 to 1960[75] but, on the other hand, it had a human quality that was sorely lacking in Ne Win's administration, as the shooting of student demonstrators during Ne Win's second government in mid-1962 indicates.

Nu felt almost as strongly about progress in the field of health as he did about education. When the Burmese took over the health department, he said, "We found a dearth of many essentials. There were all kinds of deficiencies, in doctors, ambulance personnel, midwives, compounders, vaccinators, health officers, buildings and medicines."[76] The Welfare State Scheme for Health aimed at bringing the national health level up to prewar standards, extending the benefits of modern medical and health facilities to the rural areas (inhabited by 85 per cent of the population), and attaining generally higher standards of physical fitness, nutrition, and sanitation. More than 400 rural health centers were established. Steps were taken to train larger numbers of doctors and public health officers and to increase the supply of medicines, and health education authorities issued posters and literature, showed photographs and films, and arranged lectures as part of campaigns designed to reduce the incidence of malaria, tuberculosis, venereal disease, and other diseases. Twenty-eight new hospitals were built, new departments of Maternity and Infant Welfare and Child Health were established, Women and Child Welfare Centers and dispensaries were opened in various parts of the country, and a National Fitness Council was established. But the goals again were ambitious. A plan "not in consonance" with the resources of a country, U Nu said in 1957, "may be likened to a health scheme which prescribes two eggs and one viss of milk a day and a well-ventilated and quiet house for a poor laborer."[77] But Nu's hopes for 500 to 600 new doctors a year "soon" were of the same order.

One of Nu's pet projects for a while—to illustrate his interest in the health of his countrymen—was the distribution of vitamin tablets to the people. In a ceremony inaugurating the scheme, he declared that "it is up to all of us to persuade the people of the Union to fall back upon 'lone-dee' rice [unpolished rice] which is extremely rich in vitamins. Candidly speaking, I am personally in favor of enacting legislation requiring the milling of 'lone-dee' rice only, so that the people will have no other choice but to eat it. . . . I attempted to get the necessary legislation passed, but I found myself one among many."[78]

An American economist associated with the KTA advisory group subsequently criticized U Nu's government for shortcomings in planning in the fields of education, health, and housing.[79] Of the government's housing plan, for example, he stated that it contained no assessment of "the total size of the job that needed to be done" or of what portion of the job the government planned to undertake.[80] Some housing, primarily for civil servants and refugee squatters, was constructed, however—but usually at costs that bore no relation to the rental rates the intended occupants would be able to pay. About 2,000 housing units were built in the first seven years of independence.[81]

U Nu was unquestionably personally responsible for many of the mistakes of the first decade of independence. He has stated,

> Since I carried the heaviest responsibility amongst us . . . , I made the most mistakes, and repeatedly. But . . . I have never attempted to cover up any of my mistakes; nor have I been afraid of the consequences, or stood in fear of losing the respect of the people because of those mistakes. I admitted my mistakes openly as soon as I became aware of them, and thereafter tried to correct them.[82]

Although many of Nu's speeches after 1957 showed an acute awareness of the nature of his past mistakes, others seemed naïvely oversimplified. For example, in a talk on November 17, 1959, Nu said, "During the past ten years we had not considered the human material very much. We had only considered power. In the future we must pay more attention to human values than to power. If we have good men it does not matter if we have no power. The country cannot be ruined. Whether we get power or not we must only strive to show that the men we have are all good men."[83]

In late 1957, speaking on the new Four-Year Plan, Nu said that it "should be realistically related to available financial resources, should aim at a balance in foreign exchange payments, should make available imports in sufficient quantity to counteract inflationary trends, should be based on clearly defined priorities, and should strive to achieve maximum increases in output."[84] Although these specifications are on the general side, they reflect an analysis that seems clear-headed and to the point. The same might be said of Nu's remarks in the *Pyidawtha* days concerning Burma's monetary, material, and manpower requirements and the need "to export sufficiently to meet all our commitments for expenditure overseas."[85] The cutting of ministerial salaries in 1949 to one-fifth of what they had been under the British was surely an act of realism. And, discussing land redistribution in 1952, Nu asked, "Will this cultivator acquire all the required money simply by getting his land back from the Chettyars?" "Utterly impossible," he replied.[86]

Burma's problem was that U Nu and the other leaders failed only too frequently to behave as wisely as they spoke. This is not to say that Nu, for example, always spoke wisely; much of what he said in the decade from 1948 to 1958 was nonsensical, unduly optimistic, and naïve. But more of it made sense than not, and in his remarks he revealed himself to be a man of considerable wisdom and insight as well as a humanitarian and a patriot. Some of Nu's deeds revealed the same characteristics, but others did not—and in a number of instances no deeds at all resulted from the words. Many of the solid recommendations of Burma's foreign economic advisors in the fields of taxation and organization and operation of the various state-owned boards and corporations, for example, went unheeded.

Burma, nonetheless, made progress in its first decade of independence, and this progress was probably as much the result of U Nu's leadership as of any other single factor. The amount of foreign aid received by Burma from 1948 to 1958 was comparatively small by the standards of the decade, the legacy of trained personnel parsimonious by comparison with other former British colonies. No other ex-British territory faced the virtually complete collapse of law and order that Burma experienced from 1948 to 1950—by no means the fault of Nu, who went to extraordinary but probably necessary lengths to head off the various rebellions.

Economic growth, moreover, was more impressive than many realize,[87] particularly when it is remembered that not until 1951–52 did Burma's economic output return to the level prevailing at the time of independence. Between then and 1956–57, total output increased 29 per cent; per capita output during this time went up 20 per cent, an average increase of four per cent a year (more than twice the rate of Burma's population growth).[88] Exports of rice and rice products rose 70 per cent during these five years (though still not to prewar levels); mining, however, lagged far behind the other sectors of the economy.[89] As for industrial output, it had reached the prewar level by 1954.[90]

❀

TWELVE

LEADER OF THE GOVERNMENT

THE STRUCTURE of Burma's government during the first decade of independence was quasi-federal: five states (composed mainly of ethnic minorities) and Burma proper ruled as a unitary state. All the powers of government were exercised by organs of the Union or central government, except those specifically delegated by the constitution to the Shan, Kachin, Kayah, and Karen States, and the Chin Division. According to the constitution, the primary policy-forming body on the national level was the Cabinet, which was responsible to the Chamber of Deputies (by far the more important house of Burma's bicameral Parliament). U Nu, as Premier, presided over this body. In addition to a Prime Minister, the constitution also provided for a President, whose function was largely ceremonial.

During most of this decade, Nu had four subordinate Deputy Premiers, U Kyaw Nyein, U Ba Swe, Thakin Tin, and Saw Hkun Hkio. The office of Deputy Premier was created to lessen the load on the full Cabinet, the Deputy Premiers meeting with Cabinet colleagues on a sub-Cabinet level to handle problems that did not need to go to the Cabinet. This procedure was only partially successful, however, in limiting the number of questions that came before the Cabinet at its weekly meetings.[1] Kyaw Nyein met with members of the Cabinet and other officials who were concerned primarily with economic matters,[2] and Ba Swe and Thakin Tin consulted with those in the areas of defense and agricultural policy; the procedure was followed least closely by Foreign Minister Sao Hkun Hkio. The arrangements that linked the Deputy Premiers with other ministers and officials were informal, and existed side by side with Cabinet subcommittees, which varied in number from time to time.

Also aiding Nu as Premier was the Office of the Prime Minister, which, though directly responsible to the Premier, was designed to assist other ministers as well. Separate secretaries existed for this office and for the important Economic and Social Board, but the Secretary of the Prime Minister also attended meetings of the Board. The agenda for Cabinet meetings was prepared by the Office of the Prime Minister under the direction of the Secretary in consultation with the Premier. "The Prime Minister had the last word on agenda," Secretary U Win Pe has said. "If he did not want a matter brought up, it could not be brought up."[3]

The manner in which the Cabinet, Deputy Premiers and subcommittees interacted is illustrated by the procedure by which the 1956–60 Four-Year Plan was revised. The preparation of the plan, a further modification of the already modified Eight-Year Plan of 1952, did not really begin until 1956, the year in which it was supposed to be put into effect, and was completed only in early 1957. Nu and the Cabinet, however, decided to streamline it by excluding the less urgent projects, and three committees, charged with submitting revisions within two weeks (neither much time nor, probably, the best institutional means)[4] were set up in mid-1957. The committees dealt with policy in the areas of economic development, social services, and law and order. Five weeks later, *The Nation* reported that only the first committee had submitted its report.[5] The committees were to report to Nu and his four Deputy Premiers, who acted as a sort of sub-Cabinet, and they would pass along the revisions to the full Cabinet. The Finance Ministry stated that the original Four-Year Plan had called for expenditures four times greater than anticipated revenue, but no limiting figure was given the revising planners in the various departments (who were merely asked to drop the less urgent projects). Policy formation in the economic field was generally complicated (and confused) as a result of the proliferation of committees and subcommittees that were designed to supplement, aid, or check the major organs of economic decision-making.[6]

In addition to serving as Prime Minister, U Nu also held various other portfolios from time to time, and was supported not only by the Office of the Prime Minister but also by the Bureau of Special Investigation (BSI). Directly under the Premier, the BSI had the authority to investigate almost all governmental or political activities in the country, although Nu never employed it in a vengeful fashion. Other ministers, too, held more than one position—Kyaw Nyein, for example, headed the Industrial Development Corporation. At a press conference in 1952 Nu had observed that the holding of several portfolios by one man necessarily resulted in inefficiency,[7] and in his September 1957 marathon speech to the Parliament he said,

Over-centralization of authority and responsibility for the Government's far-flung activities means the hopeless overburdening of a relatively small number of people at the very top who cannot give adequate time and attention to the many problems involved, which range all the way from questions of major policy to the smallest detail.[8]

But once again, though he seemed to recognize the problem, Nu did little about it.

An example of this over-centralization was the Economic and Social Board, created in 1952. The Board was originally established under the Minister of National Planning and Religious Affairs, but in 1953 it was placed directly under the Office of the Prime Minister. According to U Hla Maung, formerly its Executive Secretary, the Board was originally not to be concerned with actual planning. It was to supervise and to evaluate the execution of plans that had already been decided upon. Later, however, its duties came to include planning.[9]

Variously termed a "sort of super-Cabinet" and a "subcommittee" of the Cabinet, the Economic and Social Board came to be the highest-level decision-making body for economic and social questions in the Burmese welfare state. According to U Hla Maung,

Since the Cabinet members responsible for economic and social matters sat on it, what it approved was subsequently approved by the Cabinet. Such automatic agreement did not follow, however, in the relationship between the Board and the AFPFL Executive Committee. Decisions were made in the E.C. on political and ideological grounds and by many persons who were not members of the Economic and Social Board. Decisions valid on political and ideological grounds might be opposed by the Economic and Social Board on the basis of lack of technical feasibility.[10]

The Board consisted of from six to eight members, including the governing triumvirate of Burmese politics, Nu, Kyaw Nyein, and Ba Swe, as well as U Raschid, Thakin Tin, and U Win (among others at different times). Any other Cabinet members who wanted to attend meetings of the Board could do so without special invitation, according to U Win Pe.[11] Nu, though seeking to give the Board leadership, did not apparently dominate it. He and Kyaw Nyein were its most important members; they worked well together and Nu frequently deferred to Kyaw Nyein's judgment in matters of economic development.[12] "From the outside it might look as though Nu was running the show, but he was strongly aided in the period from 1952 to 1955 by Kyaw Nyein," Hla Maung has said.[13] Nu, however, clearly had no intention of taking a back seat to Kyaw Nyein or to anyone else in this field. U Win, who served as Minister of National Planning as well as of Culture and Religious Affairs, has said that he accepted the former portfolio "only after I had obtained an understanding with U Nu that he would serve as the main decision-maker in this vital field."[14] As a result, according to former economic adviser Louis J. Walinsky, "the ultimate responsibility for central coordination, both in planning and in implementation, was vested in one person, the Prime Minister."[15]

Nu's personal control over planning was increased in 1957 with the abolition of the Economic and Social Board and the end of the Ministry of National Planning as a separate ministry. Planning became the direct responsibility of the Office of the Prime Minister, which was expanded to encompass also the "departments" of Services (personnel), Projects, and the Council of Ministers (Cabinet). The Economic and Social Board was abolished, it was stated, to prevent overlapping with the Planning Department of the Prime Minister's Office.[16]

The constitution designated the Cabinet as the chief formal decision-making body of the Burmese government. Between 1952 and 1957, however, the Economic and Social Board—in its broad area of activity—was as important as the Cabinet, or perhaps even more important. Throughout the decade from 1948 to 1958, moreover, the AFPFL E.C. was probably more significant as a decision-making unit than either of these two official organs.

Decisions in the Cabinet were made by common agreement; there were no votes.[17] "Nu just asked if there were any objections," U Tun Win has said.[18] On most questions there was no vigorous discussion; only Kyaw Nyein and, to a lesser extent, Ba Swe ever challenged Nu in the Cabinet—and only rarely because the Cabinet was primarily a ratifying organ.[19] After 1952, however, the procedures of Cabinet meetings changed in at least one significant way.

U Sein Win, an informed and honest newsman, has described the change:

> After 1952, the minutes of the Cabinet meetings did not register dissent, as they had before that time. This followed in the wake of Burma's first parliamentary elections in which U Nu was endorsed as Burma's leader in his own right. After 1952 one could not glean from the Cabinet minutes that there had been opposition to any policies, nor had there probably been any expressed opposition. Ministers and secretaries, realizing how U Nu wanted things done,

would go to him beforehand to get his approval or learn of his disapproval for pet projects. They would then be brought up at Cabinet meetings with foreknowledge of how they would be treated—or they would not be brought up. Eventually, even Kyaw Nyein's supporters—and it was Nu and Kyaw Nyein who were the real giants of Burma's ruling elite—would go to Nu beforehand. This obviously antagonized Kyaw Nyein.[20]

Nu's pre-eminent role in the Cabinet was particularly evident in 1955, when the government postponed the presentation of the budget until his return from a trip abroad.[21]

The procedure in the Economic and Social Board was essentially the same as in the Cabinet; i.e., there was no vote, Nu as Premier was the single most important member, and there is no known occasion when a decision was accepted against his will.[22] Nu served as Chairman of the Board and used his position to influence the nature of the decisions taken, although once again there was surprisingly little overt opposition to anything he recommended with any vigor.[23] The confirmation by the Cabinet of the Economic and Social Board's decisions was virtually automatic. But the consideration of the problem by the E.C. always preceded decisions in both official organs.[24] The E.C. usually met on Saturdays and the Cabinet on the subsequent Mondays. The Economic and Social Board, however, met irregularly.[25]

U Nu has acknowledged and defended the influence of the E.C. on the making of official decisions:

The Party, as the entity responsible for the conduct of the government, ought to make the basic decisions—which, unless the government is a coalition one, are then more or less formalized by the Cabinet. This was how it was in the days of the united AFPFL. And this is as it should be. The people did not vote for the government, so to speak, as an abstract entity. The people—in a parliamentary democracy—vote for a particular party and what it stands for. The party, having been so voted into power, must then make the basic decisions as to how to implement its various policies. Government, to my way of thinking, is the device whereby the party fulfills the program supported by the electorate at the polls.[26]

Nu claimed obedience, as well as allegiance, to the E.C. In an exchange of letters with Kyaw Nyein, published in 1958, Nu stated that he had constantly abided by the decisions of the party committee and explained that it was the party—not himself—that had placed various checks (to which Kyaw Nyein had objected) on the ministers.[27] "If the ministers felt these directives were hampering their actions, then the Prime Minister and other ministers who were members of the E.C. could have these directives changed by the E.C."[28] Such was the control of the party over its members in the government. The party, however, was not a representative organ. As Nu himself later admitted, "though elections were held at district levels to the AFPFL hierarchy, these elections ceased in time to represent the real wishes of the people. The same candidates got elected year in and year out, and they were nominated either by the leaders or [by] central organizations."[29]

The significant role of the E.C. in Burmese governmental decision-making is indicated by the fact that "E.C. members who might not be ministers at a given moment might call non-E.C. members who were ministers to report to them," according to Kyaw Nyein.[30] But U Raschid has disagreed that the E.C. was "the real locus of power in the system." According to Raschid,

> The real decision-makers were Nu, Ba Swe, Kyaw Nyein and, to a lesser extent, Thakin Tin. Each had his own sphere: Nu, social welfare and education; Kyaw Nyein, industry; Thakin Tin, agriculture, and Ba Swe, defense and labor. The big decisions were the collective ones of these four. Nu was by no means the single decision-maker.[31]

"One always had the opinion," Raschid said on another occasion, "that these men had talked things over among themselves and had really made up their minds before the rest of us were in the picture. Once [they had] done this, however, the E.C. became the major institutional decision-making agency."[32] And attendance at its meetings was regarded as most important by Nu: according to Raschid, Nu once told him, "I don't care if you miss a Cabinet meeting, but I want you always at the E.C. meetings."

Nu himself, in an address to the Parliament in April 1960, confirmed that decision-making in the first decade of independence was indeed informal. As he put it,

> The practice developed during those years of every major question of policy or executive action being discussed and decided on by two or three leaders who were most concerned with the problem—sometimes by only one person. The decision was then confirmed by the Cabinet without any real discussion and handed down for execution.[33]

Nu was a party to every decision, irrespective of the number of other persons involved. One of Nu's closest staff associates has said of his conduct in chairing the E.C., "He maneuvered the party as he did the Cabinet—not quite in a rubber stamp sense but not too far from it."[34]

Perhaps the most astounding instance of U Nu's influence—and persistence—was the ill-fated yeast tablet scheme of the middle 1950's. During a visit to Scandinavia, Nu somehow got the idea that the people of that part of the world were tall and vigorous because they ate yeast. Deciding that Burma must therefore have a yeast factory, he would not take no for an answer. The United States Government, from whom aid was requested, refused to support the yeast plan. Finally, after being stalled for three years by his colleagues, Nu dispatched a delegation to England with orders to bring back an agreement that included provisions for yeast production. The result was the Burma Pharmaceutical Industry (BPI), which turned out (among other products) one million yeast tablets a day. However, no prior attention had been given to the promotion or distribution of the tablets. Neither the Medical Stores of the Health Ministry, nor the Ministry itself, was able to sell —or even to give away—the tablets in the amounts produced, and the yeast began to deteriorate. The Medical Stores, for one thing, had not been authorized to spend enough money to play its part in what was— from Nu's point of view—a serious effort to combat dietary deficiencies among his countrymen. Although Nu was by no means responsible for all the errors that resulted from the decision to establish the BPI, the yeast tablet affair clearly illustrates how he was usually able to carry the day against the opposition of his colleagues. It also clearly revealed the almost total lack of planning that characterized Burma's government during these years. The scheme that started out to mass-produce yeast tablets ended with great success in making alcoholic beverages— a by-product of the former process—which was quite inconsistent with the Burmese Buddhist prohibition against drinking such beverages.[35]

According to Kyaw Nyein, as the years passed, Nu's attitude toward his colleagues in the E.C. changed. "Nu became increasingly critical of those who opposed him," Kyaw Nyein has said. "There was a time when he would hear out all criticism and be most gracious in this regard. But he changed. He came to think of himself as 'boss' and even questioned the motives of those who objected to his views."[36] A close political associate of many years' standing has added, "Nu took mild disagreement as insufficient reason for changing course—and strong disagreement as insubordination—therefore, it did not occur."[37]

Kyaw Nyein's criticisms of Nu were mild in comparison with those expressed five years earlier by U Tun Pe, who resigned as Minister of

Culture as a result of differences with Nu over the expenditure of $6 million for the Sixth Buddhist Synod. Tun Pe called the expenditure unjustified in view of the rehabilitation needs of the country, but his sharpest criticism was reserved for the way in which major decisions of government were made under Nu. Tun Pe cited the question of establishing a Buddhist university as an example. He had tried to get the matter discussed in the E.C., but, he charged in a fiery pamphlet, "no chance has ever been given . . . the E.C. to discuss the issue."[38] Tun Pe also attacked the method of preparing the government's Budget Estimates. The Budget was "nothing but the compilation of estimates prepared by each department," he charged, and AFPFL members were never "given the chance to review the whole financial picture."[39]

It was unquestionably true that Nu sometimes acted without consulting his colleagues and that occasionally he even refused to accept the majority opinion when it did not agree with his own. However, he even more frequently changed his views to accord with those of his chief colleagues—particularly Kyaw Nyein and Ba Swe—until 1955, when personal suspicions began to exert increasing influence on his actions.

During Burma's first decade of independence it was frequently claimed that there was a division of primary responsibility for governmental activity in various areas—"spheres of influence"—between U Nu and the Socialists. Broadly speaking, the Socialists were alleged to have been given a relatively free hand in economic development, land nationalization, and labor affairs, while Nu concentrated on welfare and cultural matters. Nu, Ba Swe, Kyaw Nyein, and others have consistently denied the existence of such spheres of influence.[40] "How can you say Nu was not interested in economic matters?" Ba Swe has asked. "He was Planning Minister and strongly interested in the job!" Kyaw Nyein has admitted, however, that "particularly at first, Nu had great regard for me and interest in my economic ideas and relied on me to a great extent in development matters."

Though it is clear that Nu and Kyaw Nyein shared responsibilities in the economic field, the partnership between Nu and the leading Socialists was, from the start, an uneasy one. Nu enjoyed no organized mass following like that of the Socialist leaders, but he and other "independents" shared control of the AFPFL headquarters in Rangoon (though the districts were under the domination of the main Socialist leaders). The Socialists themselves ultimately split into "educated" pro-industrialization and "uneducated" agriculture-first factions under Kyaw Nyein (and Ba Swe) and Thakin Tin, respectively. At first Nu tried to remain aloof from the Socialist in-fighting, but he finally came out on the side of Thakin Tin for personal reasons. Though not directly relevant, this matter is mentioned here because it did have an effect on the decision-making partnership that existed among Nu, Ba Swe, Kyaw Nyein, and Thakin Tin. The old cooperation was a thing of the past by 1956. "When I talked to Burma's leading Socialists, Kyaw Nyein and Ba Swe, at this time," a former Socialist International official and student of socialism in the area has said, "there was no doubt that their differences with Nu had reached serious proportions. They complained of the difficulties of working with him. They more or less indicated that they tolerated him because he was necessary to them."[41]

This was not the first of U Nu's splits with Socialists within the AFPFL. In 1950, the so-called "Red Flag" Socialists broke with the League over the question of accepting United States economic aid and the challenge by the then pro-Nu anti-Communist Socialists led by Ba Swe and Kyaw Nyein, to "Red Flag" leadership of the Trade Union Congress (Burma). Major policy differences had long separated Nu and these Socialists, but he had not broken with them previously because he had needed their support during the insurrections.

Much more serious than the defection of the left-wing Socialists (to form the Burma Workers and Peasants Party)—which was really a split more with the main body of the Socialist Party than with Nu—was the resignation from Nu's Cabinet of leading Socialist and "Yellow Band" PVO politicians in April 1949 at the height of the insurrection. Despondency apparently developed among the Socialists (and the PVO) in mid-March—while Nu was in Upper Burma to discuss plans for taking Mandalay from the Communists and the Karen National Defense Organization—as a result of both the government's failure to check the Karens and public criticism of themselves. Four Socialist and PVO ministers resigned, while the remainder in the Cabinet offered to capitulate to Thakin Than Tun if he would permit Nu to remain as Prime Minister and would guarantee them immunity from trial in Communist "people's courts."[42] The cocky Communists rejected the offer, which Nu completely repudiated after a quick flight back to Rangoon. The Socialists and PVO's, who had been seeking Communist and "White Band" PVO assistance against the Karens, informed Nu of their wish to resign for the sake of peace in the country, claiming that this would get the Communists out of the jungle and into the process of nation-building (because of the removal of their arch foes, the Socialists, from the government). "The insurgents at that time claimed that they were only fighting the Socialists and demanded their removal from power," the Socialist U Ba Swe has said.[43]

U Nu told the Socialist (and the PVO) ministers to go ahead and resign; he would run the country alone. Nearly a decade later he told a Union Youth Conference: "When I got back to Rangoon, their decision had already been made, and I had to accept their resignation. But I did not accept their suggestion to write the insurgent leaders to join the Government."[44] He did not, however, discard the latter suggestion without giving it considerable thought. As he himself has said,

> I considered my colleagues' proposal from all aspects. It seemed almost hopeless to disregard it. I felt as if I was wandering in a pitch-dark night with no ray of light in front. . . . I made my decision thus, "This is nothing but the complete surrender of our cherished principles. I will *not* acquiesce."[45]

The remaining six Socialist and "Yellow Band" PVO ministers resigned on April 2, leaving only independents and frontier area leaders in the government; gone were such able figures as U Kyaw Nyein (who had been Deputy Premier and Foreign Minister) and U Win (Minister of Education). Drawing on independents and the Army (represented by Commander-in-Chief General Ne Win) Nu rebuilt his government, and that government held out against the Communists and the other insurgents despite the Socialists' desertion. Key men in the revamped Cabinet were General Ne Win, who held the crucial Defense and Home Affairs portfolios as well as serving as Deputy Premier, and Supreme Court Justice Dr. E Maung, who became Foreign Minister, Minister of Judicial Affairs, and Minister of Health and Rehabilitation.

On the third night after the resignations Nu said in a speech broadcast to the nation:

> I am both sad and happy at the resignation of Socialists and "Yellow Band" PVO's from office. My sadness is due to my sudden separation from those who, since 1936, were my close political colleagues sharing common joys and sorrows. My happiness is due to the fact that in spite of their resignation from office they do not withdraw from the AFPFL.[46]

The fact that the Socialists and the "Yellow Band" PVO's resigned only from the government, and not from the AFPFL, was of major significance, since they remained in the E.C. and continued to support Nu down the line in the Parliament. Since the E.C. was the most important institutional decision-making unit in Burmese politics, in a very real sense there was no parting of the ways. Nevertheless it was also true that the Cabinet—and, equally important, the individual Ministers (particularly General Ne Win)—were more significant as actual decision-makers at this time than at any other point in Burma's first decade of independence.

Less than a year later (in January 1950), the Socialists and the "Yellow Band" PVO's began making their way back into the Cabinet —at Nu's invitation. First to return were U Win, U Kyaw Myint, and Bo Khin Maung Gale, who became Ministers, respectively, of Rehabilitation, Industries and Mines, and Agriculture and Forests.

The field in which U Nu appears to have been most conspicuously the decision-maker was the one in which he ultimately came to be most interested: religion. In 1951 Nu told students at Rangoon University that apathy to religion was the cause of at least 80 per cent of Burma's troubles.[47] This being Nu's feeling, it was not surprising that his government should sponsor a "religious revival [but] not a fanatical campaign on behalf of Buddhism."[48]

In September 1954, at the height of a controversy regarding Buddhist instruction in the schools, Nu stated in a press conference:

> People think that because of the convening of the Synod and the teaching of Buddhism in the schools, etc., the Church and the State have become mixed. This is not so. As I have pointed out, I am not responsible to the Church for any action or policy. I am responsible only to Parliament, and Parliament in turn is responsible to the voters.[49]

But there is no doubt that religious leaders influenced Nu. He himself admitted that instruction in Buddhism was begun in state schools in 1954 in response to a request from the abbots. Nu, however, felt that the government must then introduce instuction in other religions as well. When the Buddhist clergy objected, Nu issued still another directive to stop religious teaching altogether, a decision in which the advice of the Cabinet was sought. This set off new protests, and Nu and the Chief Justice of the Supreme Court flew to Mandalay to confer with religious leaders there. The 8,000 clergymen meeting there, however, were adamant; they passed a resolution urging the government to rescind its suspension of Buddhist instruction under threat of strong action, and appointed a committee to decide what the strong action should be. "If religion is taught at all," Nu defiantly asserted in the midst of this crisis, "all religion must be taught."[50] On his return to Rangoon, he was immediately visited by a delegation of members of the Buddhist Sasana Council (which he had created) and by a group of Islamic leaders; the former joined in the criticism of his actions, but the Moslems suggested that it would be better if the teaching of Islam were dropped. U Nu subsequently ordered the resumption of the teaching of Buddhism in the schools and appointed a commission of inquiry to look into the matter of instruction in other religions. He had committed two mistakes, he admitted in a radio broadcast: He had not explained to the Buddhist leaders that "whereas the teaching of Buddhism was religious, the proposal to introduce the teaching of other religions was political," and he had acted rashly in suspending Buddhist instruction.[51]

Besides the Democratization of Local Government Act of 1949, two of the proposals presented at the 1952 *Pyidawtha* Conference, the Welfare State Scheme for Devolution of Power and the Welfare State Scheme for Democratic Administration, were designed to bring about greater popular participation in the governing of Burma. As for the other *Pyidawtha* schemes, these too would be implemented in such a way that "more people [would] experience the democratic responsibilities of managing their own affairs."[52] The *Pyidawtha* objective was to increase not only the economic and social development of Burma but also the degree of democracy and unity. During his 1955 visit to the United States, U Nu stated that he wanted to "demonstrate to the masses of people in so-called underdeveloped parts of the world that democratic methods can bring increased standards of living under a system of economic and social justice."[53]

Nu later admitted, however, that there were major imperfections in Burmese democracy. These he ascribed to ignorance, especially with respect to the roles in a democracy of the party in power, the opposition, and the civil service; unawareness of the "limitations" on a democratic government's participation in "economic activities"; and the undemocratic organization of the AFPFL itself. As he explained it,

> The parliamentary system . . . is new to Burma. It was unknown in the days of the Burmese Kings, and the diluted form that was introduced during the latter part of the British period taught us little beyond what its outward appearance looked like, and its basic procedures. When therefore we adopted this system in 1948, we were insufficiently aware of the balances and discipline which keep a parliamentary system on an even keel, or the dangers that can

destroy the basically democratic character of the parliamentary system. We were therefore not sufficiently mindful of certain distortions which appeared in our country and posed a threat to democracy and the democratic way of life.[54]

One of the many ways in which Nu tried to encourage democratic government in Burma in the first decade of independence was by holding free and fair elections. As late as February 1949, Nu promised general elections by the end of March, as scheduled at the time of independence. But the insurrections prevented the voting's taking place on time, and it was not until 1951–52 that staggered balloting could be conducted. The ruling AFPFL swept this election, winning 147 seats out of 239 on its own, or 200, if its affiliates are included; the opposition garnered only 30 seats and the rest were scattered among various independents. Well over half the victorious League candidates were members of the Socialist Party (a party within a party), while Nu himself won by a 4,873 to 2,783 margin in a Rangoon constituency over Aung San's brother, Aung Than, leader of the pro-Communist People's Peace Front. The AFPFL and its allies obtained 85 per cent of the seats in Burma's first elected Chamber of Deputies (and 60 per cent of the popular vote). The elections, moreover, were fairly conducted, as far as Nu and his government were immediately concerned; however, efforts were made on the local level by "party, civil servant and military types" to influence the outcome.[55] But this does not mean that the notoriously independent Burmese voter did not cast his ballot the way he desired once inside the secret polling place.

In the second elections in 1956 the AFPFL again won an overwhelming majority of the seats in the important lower house—148 in its own right. The pro-Communist coalition National Unity Front (NUF), however, won in 47 constituencies (and affiliated candidates won in two more), the Arakanese National United Organization won six seats, and independents won nine; the remaining victorious candidates belonged to affiliates of the League. The NUF, in winning its 47 seats, garnered a 1.1 million popular vote as compared with 1.7 million for the AFPFL. Once again, there unquestionably were attempts to influence the outcome of the vote—but they were apparently not sanctioned by the Nu government nor were they of such proportions as to shift in a major way the relationship among the parties in the Parliament.

For a man who boasted of his efforts to establish parliamentary democracy in his country, Nu behaved very surprisingly toward the

Parliament. The newly elected Chamber of Deputies met for the first time on March 12, 1952, but not until almost a year later, on March 2, 1953, did Nu deliver a major address—on the Kuomintang "aggression" against Burma—to the Parliament.[56]

Nu's performance in the 1952–56 Chamber of Deputies was in contrast with the role he played in the Constituent Assembly that served as Burma's national legislature from the first Independence Day (January 4, 1948) until the elections for the Chamber of Deputies in 1951–52. He appeared before the Constituent Assembly on 49 occasions—making speeches or policy statements 18 times, introducing 16 motions, opposing or replying to motions ten times, and answering five questions. His speeches included State of the Union addresses in 1948 and 1949, and his "From Peace to Stability" address of March 8, 1951. Nu also moved the Democratization of Local Administration Bill of 1949 and, on September 5, 1950, introduced the motion approving his government's policy in support of the United Nations' response to aggression in Korea. He spoke in support of the 1948 Land Nationalization Bill, the Buddha Sasana Bill of 1950, and the first economic aid agreement between the United States and Burma in September 1950.[57] After he had succeeded Aung San as Burma's political leader, and prior to independence, Nu appeared before the Constituent Assembly in discussions of 16 issues, and, on September 24, 1947, he introduced the motion to adopt legislation approving the new constitution.[58]

After resigning voluntarily (and temporarily) from the Premiership in June 1956, U Nu failed to attend even a single session of the Chamber of Deputies, though he remained a member of Parliament.[59] Even before his appearances before the legislature became fewer, Nu displayed a certain disdain for the practice of parliamentary give-and-take. When one M.P. charged that the government ignored the remarks of the legislators and gave assurances that it did not keep, he responded: "You put us in power. If you have faith in us, you should be prepared to face difficult times with us instead of blaming us."[60]

Upon resuming the Premiership in March 1957, Nu pledged that he would attend the Parliament regularly in the future and report on all important matters as far as possible. "This has been a dereliction of duty on my part," he confessed, "and I promise to change it."[61]

The fact that Nu did not make major policy statements before the Chamber of Deputies in the period from 1952 to 1956 does not mean that he did not make any at all. Rather he seemed to prefer to explain government policy at fortnightly press conferences, inaugurated at about the same time that he began to neglect the Parliament, and at frequent dinners at which he met with leading editors. It is significant that in 1956, upon his return from border talks with the Communist Chinese leaders in Peiping, Nu immediately met with the press to discuss the Chinese proposals—but that he did not discuss the subject in the Chamber of Deputies (although he did do so at a meeting of the AFPFL E.C. and at a separate session with chief opposition leaders).[62] According to editor U Ohn Khin of the newspaper *Bama Khit*, U Nu used the dinners with leading journalists "to see if the press would be likely to support his ideas and also for the purpose of soliciting from these editors ideas about popular feeling, rumor and the like—the sort of thing that did not make its way into the press or that his advisers might be reluctant to tell him."[63]

Decisions on the subordinate levels of government in Burma during the first decade of independence were made notoriously slowly, but this was not true on the level of Nu, Kyaw Nyein, Ba Swe, and their colleagues; indeed, frequently their decisions were made too rapidly without sufficient consideration of all facets of a problem. The real problem at the top national level in Burma was the implementation of decisions. Neither Nu nor most of his associates were good at implementing decisions.[64] Moreover, there was often political interference with the execution of public policy at various levels, and Nu himself not infrequently interfered with the work of his ministers and their subordinates on quite minor matters, particularly in those fields in which he was most interested. "He interfered from time to time, of course," U Raschid has explained, "but most of the time he left us alone. But when he got hold of an idea, he would really come at you. He didn't ask you what you thought of it or ask you to have your professional experts study it. He instructed you that it should be done."[65] Nu also frequently instructed the ministers directly—bypassing the Cabinet—and sometimes even bypassed a minister to communicate with his subordinates.

One problem that particularly annoyed the senior personnel in the ministries was the fact that "Nu's foreign advisers frequently exceeded their authority—they did not just 'advise' us, they told us what to do."[66] Rather than being advisers to particular ministries or to the National Planning Commission, they became in effect economic advisers to the Cabinet.

U Tun Pe, one of Nu's severest early critics, was particularly annoyed by the fact that a request for American information and public relations experts was made without his knowledge, even though he was Minister of Information; he even denied to the press the existence of such a request. The request, he later discovered, had been sent under direct orders from Nu.[67] In the conduct of foreign affairs, bypassing subordinates to get to Nu directly was a common thing among ambassadors. According to Professor Myo Min, formerly of the Office of the Prime Minister, "Nu did not encourage this, but he did not discourage it either."[68]

Although it has often been charged that Nu did not easily accept advice, the charge is only partly true. In terms of immediate technical advice, Nu relied heavily upon several Secretaries: the Secretary to the Cabinet, the Secretary to the National Planning Commission, the Secretary for the Home Ministry (when Nu headed that Ministry), and the various Secretaries of the departments within the Office of the Prime Minister. U Win Pe, a quiet and cautious man, served Nu well as Secretary of the Office of the Prime Minister, and was generally regarded as a major contributor to stability in the government.[69] According to U Myo Min, former Projects Secretary, however, "there was no single man Nu leaned on for information or policy guidance in the way President Eisenhower leaned on Dulles or Humphrey."[70] Myo Min described U Thant, Nu's old Pantanaw friend and later Secretary-General of the United Nations, however, as "his sort of Harry Hopkins"—before his assignment as Burma's Permanent Representative to the U.N. in 1957. According to U Law Yone, Thant was the only man really close to Nu at that time.[71] Unquestionably the placid Thant was a stabilizing influence on Nu and an intellectually stimulating one whose ideas and good sense helped his friend clarify his own thoughts in such important areas as democracy and foreign policy. It is very easy, however, to overrate Thant's role in view of his subsequent skillful execution of the duties of the Secretary-General of the United Nations. U Thant was not interested in politics, and he did not involve himself in AFPFL in-fighting, let alone electioneering. After Thant's departure in 1957, his place was taken by another old friend of Rangoon University days, the erratic and eccentric U Ohn. Ohn probably provided no positive assistance to Nu, being generally regarded among Burmese politicians as a yes-man. Ohn's succession to Thant's role certainly represented a major change in the character of this type of aid to Nu, but probably did not, as many in Burma claim, begin a decline in Nu's political fortunes.

According to many observers, a definite weakness in Nu as Premier was his indifference to independent sources of information with which to compare the official advice he received. He did not, for example, read the newspapers; "he said he thought they would unduly influence him."[72] According to U Myo Min, "Nu's sources of information were primarily his comparatively impartial and loyal staff and his Cabinet colleagues."[73] Hard as it may be to believe, one official very close to Nu told the author that Nu (then out of office) first learned of Soviet Premier Khrushchev's planned visit to the United States in 1959 from the American Ambassador—well after the news had appeared in the press.

The image of U Nu as government leader has changed considerably with the years. The year after independence one correspondent wrote that Nu was "the only possible Prime Minister in a parliamentary type of government but . . . lacks the personality of a 'national' leader."[74] Another writer called him "a respectable and respected figurehead," and still another described him as "no strong man."[75] All of these characterizations, however, seem to miss the point and to be inaccurate even as contemporary descriptions.

What, then, was Nu in the first decade of independence, and how can his role as a government leader best be characterized? His one-time lieutenant U Ba Swe has written that in the drama of the Burmese revolution "everyone from Thakin Nu downwards are but actors taking their part in the entire play, each discharging the responsibility assigned to him."[76] This Marxist interpretation may be correct in the subordinate role it assigns to men as actors in a drama, but it is highly inaccurate in implying that Nu played the role assigned to him. This, indeed, was just what Nu did not do—unless one postulates a mystical (but illiterate) puppeteer of history who, unaware of the contents of the script, lets his chief marionette do as he wants.

U Nu's weaknesses, on the whole, were those of his countrymen in general, including Kyaw Nyein and Ba Swe, among others. Although Nu might have given his nation better leadership in several respects, it is questionable whether he can reasonably be expected to have done so in view of his and Burma's particular legacies derived from their recent colonial past. It is also doubtful that a different kind of leadership on Nu's part would have appreciably changed the system in which he functioned. U Raschid has described that system as follows:

Government in Burma is like nothing in the West. The degree of non-coordination and the casualness with which officials take their responsibilities is unimaginable to one who has not been outside the United States or Western Europe. There was a time, for example, when we sent five missions in a single month to China. The non-Communist embassies were much alarmed; they feared we were becoming pro-Communist. The truth is that nobody knew we had five missions visiting China at the same time.[77]

The Rangoon newspaper *The Nation,* often a source of friendly criticism of Nu, has said that there has never in fact been planning in Burma—but only project-creation [and] scheme-drafting.[78] Seemingly the only major effort at effecting genuine coordination during the first decade of independence was made through the Secretary to the Minister for National Planning (the Prime Minister). But the Secretary had virtually no staff and, sitting as he did on the boards of directors of all the major governmental industrial corporations and joint ventures, he had not nearly enough time to coordinate effectively the far-flung economic and related activities of the Nu administration.[79] Nor was his task made easier by Nu's habit of making a decision himself in a particular minister's area of responsibility and not even informing the minister of this decision. Nu's behavior in this respect varied from frequent interference with the work of his subordinates in some fields to almost complete disregard of the activities of the responsible ministers and officials in others. The interference was more the norm than the exception in the government of Burma during the first decade of independence.

But perhaps the single most important reason for the limited effectiveness of policy implementation in Burma was the lack of able and trained personnel. The government's economic and welfare ventures called for personnel in numbers far beyond those available, and many untrained (but politically acceptable) people were elevated to positions of responsibility in excess of their technical and administrative competence—and, quite frankly, frequently of their integrity.

Yet Nu was a major supporter of the unanimously passed Democratization of Local Government Act (1949), which allowed local politicians an unparalleled opportunity for interference in the administration of many national programs of the AFPFL government.

Given the limited experience of both the supporting political leaders and the administrative structure, Nu exercised a surprisingly large amount of control over his government.[80] The charge that he sought to dominate the Burmese government—a true one—may be explained in terms of Nu's realization of the need for a control device in the absence of any other effective means of control. The Ne Win military administration of October 1958 to April 1960 was more effective than Nu in this regard, but on the other hand it was not a politically responsive government.

The editor U Law Yone has said of Premier Nu:

> He probably was the best possible Premier, given what he had to work with. He would have been a good Premier or President—possibly a better one—in any other country. It was not that he, as a general, was not adequate. His troops were not up to par—nor, frankly, were his officers. There was a limit as to what he, as Prime Minister, could do about this. Ba Swe or Kyaw Nyein or any other alternative leader would not have done any better. The administrative personnel were inadequate for running the country—in terms of training and morally; this was largely the problem. There were politicians, in addition, in the Parliament who not only lacked the ability to be good M.P.'s but also were unscrupulous to the core. What could Nu have done about this? No, we were lucky to have U Nu. The fault was not his, but Burma's.[81]

THIRTEEN

POLITICAL LEADERSHIP

BEFORE THE SPLIT that divided the AFPFL into two roughly equal factions in 1958, Burma had what was in name a multiparty system. But none of the other parties showed any strength at the polls until the elections of 1956, when the Communist-oriented National Unity Front (NUF) emerged as a second important party—although the League still held a commanding majority in the Parliament. The assault on the legal party system, however, was by no means the only political struggle in the country. Throughout the 1950's the insurgent Communists and Karens constituted a greater threat to the government than any of the minor parties, their dissatisfaction with the AFPFL being expressed directly with bullets rather than ballots.

A major result of the AFPFL domination of the government and the parliamentary politics of Burma until 1956 was the absence of an effective legal opposition. U Nu's government did practically everything it wanted in the way of legislative and executive policy-making during these years—the press being far more of a real check upon the AFPFL than any would-be parliamentary opposition. After the 1956 elections, the NUF (aided by the Arakanese National United Organization, some independents, and the smaller parties) provided sufficient legislative opposition to the AFPFL to make Nu and his party at least explain the major measures they brought before the Chamber of Deputies. This situation was still very much short of being a two-party system, however.

This government party, which faced such limited legislative opposition during the first decade after the British departure, was an independence movement turned political party. It included a variety of mass organizations, ethnic groups, and independent members, as well as the entire Socialist Party. At first the AFPFL represented practically every shade of political opinion in Burma, but gradually the more extreme leftist elements were ousted from the organization—the Communists in 1947 and the pseudo-Communist "Red Socialists" in 1950. Nu called the League a "people's front,"[1] but his vigorous critic, U Tun Pe, charged that the Socialist Party dominated the organization. "Independents to which I belong," Tun Pe said, "do not form an organized body nor have they been allowed to do so by the Socialist Party."[2]

In matters concerning the formation of national policy, the machinery of government and party overlapped to such an extent that it was not always possible to distinguish the two. U Nu was Premier and President of the AFPFL; Ba Swe a Deputy Premier, League Vice President, and chief executive official of the Socialist Party as well as of the Trade Union Congress (Burma); Kyaw Nyein was Deputy Premier and AFPFL General Secretary, and Thakin Tin Deputy Premier and President of the All-Burma Peasants Organization (ABPO). Although the Executive Committee of the League unquestionably made the chief policy decisions for the country, it did not exercise a monopoly of authority over AFPFL political activity in the country at large, partly because various component bodies of the AFPFL—the ABPO, the TUC(B), the Women's Freedom League, and the All-Burma Youth League—had affiliates throughout the land. So also, at the start of independence, did the People's Volunteer Organization, which actually had more local branches than the AFPFL when colonial rule ended. Branches of the AFPFL party, however, controlled from above (one indication being the strong influence of the national E.C. on the selection of local candidates), came ultimately to dominate the Burmese political landscape.

The AFPFL Executive Committee derived its authority from the party's national congress, but there was no congress between 1947 and 1958. Theoretically, the members of the E.C. were to be appointed by the League's Supreme Council, which therefore would be more powerful than the E.C., but this was not the case in practice. The E.C., which had 15 members, was a much more important organ than the Supreme Council, a body of 200 delegates representing the district E.C.'s (themselves drawn from township committees made up of representatives from village committees). The township E.C.'s also selected the delegates to the national congress. Elections to the E.C. were held in 1947, but vacancies were subsequently filled by co-option.[3]

U Nu was clearly the leader of the party, a somewhat remarkable situation in view of his having no personal political organization within the League. However, the actual distribution of power was complicated

and shifting. Nu shared power with Ba Swe, Kyaw Nyein, and Thakin
Tin of the Socialist Party, the best-organized component of the League
(which accounted for 60 per cent of the AFPFL seats in Parliament,
held nine out of twelve top Cabinet posts, and constituted a majority
in the League E.C.). The central apparatus of the party was controlled
jointly by Nu, aided by various independents who were loyal to him,
and the Socialists. But the organization outside Rangoon was dominated by different segments of the Socialist Party, which described itself
in 1952 as a "cadre party [with] cells in the AFPFL branches."[4] Nu
survived as party leader in part because of differences among the
Socialists, and he used the threat of resignation to provoke new stir-
rings of this disunity among his mutually jealous would-be successors.[5]

Of the other major constituent bodies of the League, the ABPO
was probably the most important; in 1957 it accounted for some 550,000
of the AFPFL's reported 1,287,290 members.[6] Thakin Tin, who became a Deputy Premier, was perennial ABPO president, and Thakin
Kyaw Tun came to be one of his most important associates; the ABPO
leaders were considered more or less the "uneducated" wing of the Socialist Party. The Federation of Trade Organizations (FTO), headed
by Thakin Pan Myaing, accounted for 100,243 members of the AFPFL,
and the TUC(B) for another 60,584. The "mass organizations," according to an official report in the early 1950's, were "organized and
led by the members of the Socialist Party."[7] Independent political
leaders and leaders of the various racial minorities also figured promi-
nently among the League's leaders—usually on the side of Nu, providing help in offsetting the Socialist numerical predominance.

During the party's heyday, from 1950 to 1955, political views within
the AFPFL ranged from the far (but not extreme) to the moderate left.
The wide range in ideology and the varying degrees of commitment to
the socialist cause among party leaders do not seem to have been a
major source of instability. The organization of the AFPFL, since it
depended on the relative strength of the leaders of the member groups,
was much more a source of friction. Each of the top AFPFL leaders
except Nu controlled strong followings in the various constituent bodies,
which had organizations parallel to that of the parent AFPFL on levels
from the national down to the village. There was no clearly drawn
dividing line between the sphere of the AFPFL and that of the other
mass organizations, and what faintly discernible line existed suffered
continuous violation. This meant that the AFPFL central apparatus
had no effective control over much local political activity associated
with its banner, and, because U Nu lacked a constituent organization

of his own, his ability to direct the party (and its parts) throughout most of the country was limited in practice. Ba Swe, Thakin Tin, and Kyaw Nyein all controlled stronger organizations than did Nu in the secondary party structure.

The nature of the AFPFL organization, besides being a source of friction among the top leaders, contributed to the dictatorial nature of the party. "Dictatorial methods, misuse of power and funds, political persecution, irresponsibility and malpractices by AFPFL adherents, and the overall political decline of the organization are mainly due to lack of frequent conferences and proper organization," Nu declared in May 1955. He underscored the need for annual conferences at various levels and for the regular election of members of the executive committees of the party at all levels. Nu explained that the insurgencies had interfered with the holding of such elections, but pointed out that "failure to hold elections has enabled district AFPFL adherents to become E.C. members simply by obtaining certification from the Rangoon headquarters."[8] The insurrections, which had led to the recruitment of much "riff-raff" by the AFPFL to counter the numbers of the various rebel groups, had thus resulted in a deterioration in the character of the party's membership.[9] At the same time the best of the party's members assumed governmental responsibilities, "leaving," in Nu's words, "organization work to less able men."[10]

The AFPFL also lost strength in the 1956 parliamentary elections, in which the pro-Communist NUF won an unexpected 47 seats in the 250-member Chamber of Deputies as compared with the 30 seats that had been captured by the combined opposition in 1951–52. Nu blamed corrupt elements within the League for popular dissatisfaction with the party, and his largely unsuccessful efforts to purge the AFPFL, which brought him into conflict with some of the other top leaders, were an important factor in the 1958 split.

U Nu's efforts to consolidate the party in 1958 strained the relationship between him and some of the Socialists still more. Nu had earlier discussed with Aung San "the possibility of having in the AFPFL fold only those who hold one definite idea or principle," but the question was "shelved" because of the "pressure of other urgent matters."[11] The Socialists wished to retain their separate status, working "within the framework of the AFPFL as the united national front for the purposes of carrying through (the) socialist revolution."[12] But in January 1958, at the first national congress of the AFPFL since 1947, Nu publicly declared that the League was no longer a coalition or a front, but a distinct party in its own right, requiring acceptance of its ideology and deference to its superiority from all its affiliates.[13] Thus Nu, in effect, challenged the Socialist Party to cease being a party within a party. The congress seemed to end on a unified note—but the Socialists subsequently dispatched organizers to the districts for the specific purpose of building up their party.[14] This was the answer of Kyaw Nyein and Ba Swe to Nu's challenge, and the end of a united AFPFL.

Although the AFPFL split did not occur until 1958, there had been differences between Nu and the Socialists, the most important component of the League, almost from the start of independence. Socialists participated in the drafting of Nu's controversial 15-point Leftist Unity Plan in 1948,[15] but the departure of a majority of the PVO to join the insurrectionists following the failure of this conciliatory effort left the Socialist Party the major force in government and party—and the Socialists pressed Nu for control of both. This was why Nu resigned in July 1948,[16] only to return to office immediately when the various minority representatives refused to acquiesce in a Socialist government. The resignation of the Socialists from the Nu government in April 1949, however, was the result of both fear and the desire not to be the major stumbling block to internal peace (which both the Communists and the Karens claimed that they were).[17]

Nu did not want the Socialists to resign, and subsequently proved most willing to welcome them back into his Cabinet. Nevertheless, by no means did he trust them fully—nor they him—despite their Rangoon University days together. For one thing, they did not regard him as a real Socialist despite his having played the single most important role in the attempt to establish a socialist state in Burma.[18] Nu seemed always to keep an arm's length from the Socialists politically, never associating himself directly with their party. Moreover, in the eyes of some of the Socialists, he had participated to only a limited extent in the formation of the Anti-Fascist Organization (which became the AFPFL). Some Socialists, in addition, questioned whether Nu was as strongly anti-Communist as they—a strange question in the light of their resignations from the government in 1949 at the height of the Communist threat and their 2,000-word policy statement issued later the same year "rejoicing" in the Communist victory in China.[19]

Despite their differences, Nu accorded considerable deference to the wishes of the Socialists. He invited them to nominate candidates for particular portfolios, and automatically accepted their recommendations. Moreover, on the two occasions when he wished to dismiss Socialists from his Cabinet, Nu asked the Socialist Party to make the dismissals.[20] And in the first half of the 1950's he frequently denied rumors of Socialist plots against him. In 1951 he told a press conference, "I myself suggested to U Kyaw Nyein that he should accept the Premiership, and his response was 'Do you think anyone can be Premier just like that?' " It had been difficult enough getting Ba Swe to run for the Parliament, Nu said; he "agreed finally, but after we had put pressure on him."[21]

Rather than seeming to fear being ousted, Nu stated in 1954 that he would like to have each of his three chief lieutenants in the government and party—Ba Swe (AFPFL Vice President), Kyaw Nyein (General Secretary of the League), and Thakin Tin (head of the ABPO)—serve a turn as Premier before he finally stepped down from office. (One objective was to ensure that his successor would not come to the Premiership as inexperienced as he himself had been.) But Nu would not do away with the AFPFL as the Socialists asked him to, according to Ba Swe, and allow the League to be replaced by the Socialist Party. "Most of the component parts of the League, or front, had long since left it," according to Ba Swe in 1960, "—it was a purposeless political organization. But U Nu seemed to fear throwing in his lot with us. He thought that he would have less political leverage in such an arrangement."[22]

There were also differences among the Socialists themselves, however, even before the middle 1950's. The division into two fairly well-defined camps of Socialists was a political reality by 1953, when the "Thakin Tin Socialists"—including Thakin Kyaw Tun and Thakin Pan Myaing—refused to participate in the Rangoon Asian Socialist Conference. The division was, in a very real sense, between the "college" Socialists and the *"pongyi-kyaung"* (or monastery school) Socialists—the "educated" and the "uneducated" Socialists, as they were also called. The college group was made up largely of those Socialists who had been student agitators together at Rangoon University in the 1930's, who had worked together during the war and the early pre-independence years, and who were concerned chiefly with the industrial development of the country, holding Cabinet posts dealing with this phase of the economy. Kyaw Nyein and Ba Swe were the leading personalities in this faction.

Most of the *pongyi-kyaung* Socialists were not University graduates, nor were they members of the inner clique of wartime and postwar intriguers. They were generally concerned with the agricultural development of the country and held the Cabinet posts related to agriculture and rural affairs. Thakins Tin and Kyaw Tun of the numerically strong ABPO, and Thakin Pan Myaing, who headed the FTO, were leaders of this group.

Various factors underlay the struggle between these two groups.

They clearly represented different interests that were competing for the limited resources of the Burmese state. The extravagant goals of the 1952 *Pyidawtha* program postponed a showdown between the two Socialist groups by promising everything to everybody. A more realistic statement of the goals in 1956–57, on the other hand, heightened the conflict. At the same time personal jealousies among the competing groups had grown stronger, particularly the conflict between Kyaw Nyein and Thakin Tin as well as the differences between Nu and Kyaw Nyein (upon which Tin played). The efforts of the district and township ABPO branches to dominate the equivalent AFPFL affiliates further alienated the opponents of Thakin Tin and his ABPO allies.

The three most important persons in Burma's government between 1948 and 1958, besides U Nu, were unquestionably U Kyaw Nyein, U Ba Swe, and Thakin Tin. Kyaw Nyein, eight years Nu's junior, had known Nu well in their days as leaders of the Rangoon University Students' Union and the students' strike of 1936. Although Kyaw Nyein had not been active in the Dobama Asiayone, he had been a leading founder in 1939 of the Burma Revolutionary Party, which later became the Socialist Party, and he was active in the wartime resistance and a prominent participant in the launching of the AFPFL. In 1946, he succeeded Thakin Than Tun as General Secretary of the AFPFL, a post he held until 1956, and he became General Secretary of the Socialist Party when Ba Swe assumed its Presidency with the assassination of Thakin Mya in 1947.

Of the four leading AFPFL politicians, Kyaw Nyein was the most widely read and the most clear-headed in his economic thinking; he was considered the "brains" of Burma's drive toward socialism. A Marxist who moved steadily in the direction of pragmatic Western socialism as the decade of the 1950's advanced, he was far more sophisticated than his Socialist Party colleague U Ba Swe. Far less of a traditionalist in philosophic outlook than Ba Swe or Nu, he also differed with them in their attempt to reconcile socialism and Buddhism. Widely respected for his intellectual ability and drive, Kyaw Nyein was also feared more than any other member of the ruling group; he was generally considered to be ruthless, devious, and possibly corrupt. Kyaw Nyein was not regarded, however—nor did he seem to regard himself— as an aspirant for the Premiership.[23] He seemed content with influence as distinct from office.

In the first years of independence Kyaw Nyein and Nu genuinely cooperated with one another. Their subsequent drifting apart was gradual, and difficult to date for this reason. Nu seemed visibly annoyed with objections raised by Kyaw Nyein in the E.C., the Cabinet, and the Economic and Social Board by 1953–54, but the objections were probably not the reason for the annoyance, since Kyaw Nyein had always acted in this manner. Some of Nu's friends suggest that he was upset because various Socialists, led by Kyaw Nyein, would get together and criticize him privately.[24]

The first major overt clash between the two men occurred in 1954, although there had been a strongly expressed difference of opinion previously over the boundaries between the domains of pro-Kyaw Nyein Minister of Cooperatives U Tun Win and pro-Thakin Tin Minister of Agriculture and Forests Thakin Kyaw Tun, both of whom claimed jurisdiction over fisheries. In the 1954 quarrel, Nu questioned Kyaw Nyein's integrity in connection with the sale of 150,000 tons of State Agricultural Marketing Board rice stock by a Cabinet subcommittee of which Kyaw Nyein was a member. In the transaction, Kyaw Nyein had proposed reducing the required security waiver, and, when U Ba San of the Board advised that the Premier's consent should be obtained on such an important matter, Kyaw Nyein argued that this was not necessary in view of the presence of several ministers at the meeting (and Nu's absence on a trip to China). According to Nu, however, U Ba San was "brow-beaten" into accepting Kyaw Nyein's point of view.[25] U Raschid, the minister within whose jurisdiction the matter technically fell, also backed the Kyaw Nyein proposal. "U Nu's charge boiled down to an accusation that Kyaw Nyein, acting for reasons of personal advantage, influenced the other ministers and myself," Raschid, long one of Nu's closest associates, has said. "I offered to resign, but Nu would not hear of it. I think he may have been laying for Kyaw Nyein."[26] This was the interpretation that Kyaw Nyein, too, placed on the incident, regarding it as a deliberate move by Nu to discredit him.[27]

U Ba Swe, the man who became Kyaw Nyein's chief ally in his 1958 split with U Nu, was (like Kyaw Nyein) eight years Nu's junior and a man of action rather than an intellectual or a planner. He was neither as respected nor as feared as Kyaw Nyein, but was widely liked; his integrity, moreover, was never questioned. Leader of the Trade Union Congress (Burma), Ba Swe was an outspoken advocate of all-inclusive nationalization. Alleged by some to harbor a desire to oust Nu as Premier,[28] Ba Swe was probably too lazy to engage in the amount of groundwork necessary for the successful execution of such a venture.[29]

The clash of strong-willed, easily irritated, and suspicious personalities was probably the major factor that underlay the developing showdown between U Nu and U Kyaw Nyein, both of whom were beset by fears for their personal security born of the years of intrigue against the British and the Japanese. The factor that brought the feud between the two men fully to a head, however—and without which the course of recent Burmese history might have been very different—was U Nu's easily wounded ego. Few political observers in Burma will deny that Nu was constantly annoyed by articles by foreign newsmen which indicated that Kyaw Nyein and Ba Swe were the real powers in his country. Whenever Nu traveled abroad, he was asked about the relationship among the three men, and he resented what he felt to be the implication that he was a kind of puppet. As a result, Nu decided that he would—in fact—be boss politically in Burma. From about 1953 on, he sought to dominate E.C. and Cabinet meetings. Nu even refused to take either Kyaw Nyein or Ba Swe with him to the 1955 Bandung Afro-Asian Conference "because it would then be claimed that he was not able to make decisions himself without constantly consulting us."[30] This highly personal consideration—U Nu's almost consuming desire to appear to be boss (heightened by his fear of dislodgment)—was the most important factor in the rupture of a political partnership that had been shaped in the struggle for independence from colonial rule.

Thakin Tin, the third member of the triumvirate that served as Nu's chief lieutenants in the early and middle 1950's, was four years older than Nu and lacked a university education. A member of the Dobama Asiayone before any of the other major politicians of independent Burma, Tin was associated with the mass ABPO from its inception and became its perennial President. He joined the Cabinet as Minister of Forests and Agriculture following Aung San's assassination in 1947, but was ousted from the inner ranks of the AFPFL in 1950 at the time of the departure of the so-called "Red Socialists" from the Socialist Party and the League. A Marxist of nearly Communist complexion as recently as the early 1950's, Tin developed less along the pragmatic lines of Kyaw Nyein and others of the "educated" Socialists as the decade progressed—partly because he was not much of a thinking politician. Personable but a political opportunist, Thakin Tin also drank fairly heavily and enjoyed a reputation for having numerous love affairs. Tin's differences with Kyaw Nyein appear to have had their roots in the fear that Kyaw Nyein was out to get him and in the conflict between urban and rural interests that the two men represented.

Although Thakin Kyaw Tun never achieved the power of U Nu's three chief lieutenants of the middle 1950's, he was a close associate of

Thakin Tin in the ABPO and his main ally in the AFPFL. The son of a farmer and the same age as Kyaw Nyein and Ba Swe, Kyaw Tun was not a university graduate nor was he intellectually inclined. In 1956 he became Secretary-General of the AFPFL, worked closely with U Nu in the latter's efforts to reorganize the League, and was subsequently advanced within the ranks of the party by Nu.

Less important as individuals but very important collectively in Burmese politics under Nu were the various independents—either non-members of the AFPFL or members of the party but not of any of its component mass organizations. Perhaps the most important of these was Nu's friend since Rangoon University days, the Indian U (or M. A.) Raschid. Intellectually and technically one of the most qualified persons in Burmese political life, Raschid was distrusted by the Socialists because he remained a businessman and disliked by many Burmese because he was an Indian. Despite the fact that Raschid was an extremely likeable person, to a certain extent only Nu trusted and wanted him in the government. Nu's feelings stemmed from his realization of Raschid's value to the government as well as from long-standing friendship, but also probably partly from the recognition that Raschid had no one else to turn to and would for this reason if no other remain personally loyal. Nu unquestionably used such independents to counterbalance the formidable Socialist component of the AFPFL.

Similarly, Nu used his standing with the minorities to counterbalance the Socialists within both the government and the party. The Shan leader Sao Hkun Hkio, for example, served more or less continuously as Nu's Foreign Minister in the middle 1950's and was accorded a Deputy Premiership, making him technically the equal of Kyaw Nyein, Ba Swe, and Thakin Tin. Most of the Socialists were more conspicuously Burman in their attitude toward the minorities, and Nu used minority fears of "Burmanization" to help maintain his hold on government and party.

U Nu publicly attributed his position as the leader of Burma's government and the head of the Anti-Fascist People's Freedom League to forces beyond his control; Aung San's death had catapulted him into a role of leadership in Burmese politics. "Man proposes, God disposes," he said in 1949, pledging his intention to retire from "the mundane world" to a life of contemplation "as soon as I get the opportunity."[31]

Various factors underlay Nu's survival as Burma's chief political figure during the first decade of independence. Foremost among these was his nationalism. Nu's neutralist foreign policy and his request that

American economic aid be terminated in 1953 were indications of this nationalism, which, although it never really became xenophobic, gave no quarter to foreign powers. Supporting the general public image of Nu as the almost ideal Burmese nationalist was his progressively more passionate devotion to Buddhism, the national religion. Many Burmese also regarded Nu as a sort of father of the nation, but not in the "founding father" sense of George Washington or Aung San. "In every Burmese house," according to a Burmese political scientist, "a certain amount of respect accords to the father, however able he may or may not be. This applies to U Nu in a national sense."[32] "There is no doubt about it in my mind," U Kyaw Nyein said in 1960, "the public image of U Nu is his greatest political asset."[33]

In the first decade of independence Nu as a politician also displayed an almost uncanny sensitivity to the aspirations of the Burmese people. He clearly knew what they wanted—and how to appeal to them, being unquestionably Burma's best political speaker. U Ba Swe, Thakin Tin, and others of Burma's leading politicians were also extremely personable men and had followers who would back them irrespective of their policy positions, but none compared with Nu in mass appeal.

U Raschid, U Win, U Tin, U Thant, U Ohn, and others through the years aided Nu—directly and indirectly—in maintaining his position of political prominence. But many of the tactics and certainly the timing were Nu's personal contributions; he knew how to accept assistance, but was probably more resourceful a political strategist than all his advisers combined.

Nu's great public appeal as well as his support by the non-Burman minorities explain why his rivals (and his colleagues) resisted the efforts he made from time to time to resign the Premiership. There was general agreement up to the 1958 split in the AFPFL that it was necessary to have a truly national figure heading the government and leading the country in order to maintain unity. All agreed that U Nu was the only man for the job.

FOURTEEN

A PARTING OF THE WAYS

AFTER THE STRONG showing of the pro-Communist National Unity Front in the 1956 elections, Nu resigned the Premiership. "It was only after the Sixth Synod had been completed and I was meditating in the Sacred Cave that I felt all the barriers melt away, and I knew I would carry out my resolve," he told a press conference, referring to his resolution of many years earlier to leave public office.[1]

According to Nu himself, his decision had nothing to do with the results of the election, but was motivated by his desire of long standing to devote himself to purging the AFPFL of corrupt elements. He had to threaten to resign both the Premiership and party office, he explained, to get his way. As he put it, "They allowed me one year to give undivided attention to the political organization."[2]

"We begged Nu not to step down," Kyaw Nyein has said, "I more than anyone else. When the meeting at which he announced his decision ended, he put his arms around Ba Swe and myself and said, 'When I become the next Buddha, you two will be my faithful right- and left-hand disciples.' Buddha was supposed to have had two particularly close disciples. I jestingly said, 'Who knows—I may turn out to be your brother-in-law.' Buddha, you know, was alleged to have been betrayed by his brother-in-law."[3]

Nu had tried previously, with little success, to rid the AFPFL of undesirable elements, and his 1956 resignation was, to a certain extent, an act of desperation. He was virtually obsessed with the fear that Burma would go the way of Chiang Kai-shek's China unless various types of selfish behavior were checked.[4]

Nu's approach to reforming the AFPFL by no means met with the full approval of the E.C., but none was more outspoken in his criticism than Kyaw Nyein, who agreed with Nu that the AFPFL needed reform, but objected to the manner in which Nu sought to go about the task.[5] As one of Kyaw Nyein's closest allies, U Tun Win, put it, "Kyaw Nyein thought Nu would wreck rather than revitalize the party."[6]

Nu's departure from office was followed by an acrimonious exchange of letters between the two men (published two years later at the time of the formal split in the AFPFL) in which Kyaw Nyein accused Nu of seeking to divide the Socialists and to substitute his own followers for them in the League leadership.[7] A general purge would leave the AFPFL in ruins, Kyaw Nyein charged, probably reflecting a genuine fear for the fate of the organization as such. But he was also concerned about his own future, claiming that Nu sought to "expose him as a man who employed corrupt people and therefore a corrupt man himself."[8] Nu, who had questioned Kyaw Nyein's integrity again by bringing up the 1954 rice incident, claimed that his longtime nationalist colleague was moved by unnecessary fear.

According to Kyaw Nyein, Nu had complained to him that "the people have been led to believe that nothing can be done without Ba Swe and Kyaw Nyein and that Thakin Nu is only a simple fool." Kyaw Nyein also accused Nu of refusing to take him along on a visit to China "because the Chinese Government may think that I dare not do anything unless you Socialists are there to back me up. . . . If you want to visit China," Nu is alleged to have said, "you can go on your own."

"If I wanted to get at the Socialists," Nu replied to Kyaw Nyein's charges, "don't you think I would be more effective while holding both the jobs of Premier and AFPFL President?" Indeed, Nu claimed, he had offered to step down from both positions to become "Patron" of the party with Kyaw Nyein as Premier and Ba Swe as AFPFL President, "but you did not want to go over Ba Swe." Terming Kyaw Nyein's allegations "serious ones," Nu sent the correspondence to the E.C., urging the members "to personally investigate them and, if they are found to be correct, to take decisive action against me."[9] This, of course, was never done.

U Ba Swe succeeded U Nu as Premier in June 1956. U Kyaw Nyein, Thakin Tin, and Sao Hkun Hkio were Deputy Prime Ministers. Nu insisted, however, that there must be a separation of governmental and party responsibilities, citing his own behavior as an example, and that the Deputy Premiers should devote their full time to their official duties. This, again, seemed to Kyaw Nyein to be a move directed primarily against himself, since he was the only one whose power would be curtailed. Ba Swe as Premier would have greater power than he had previously possessed as Deputy Premier and Defense Minister, even if he stepped down as leader of the TUC(B). And Sao Hkun Hkio, a Shan leader and not a contender for top governmental leadership, would suffer no diminution of influence. Kyaw Nyein charged in his correspondence with Nu that the attempt to separate the tasks of political organization and governmental administration was "an excuse." What made him particularly suspicious was the fact that Thakin Kyaw Tun, a key supporter of Thakin Tin, was not required to resign as Minister of Agriculture and Forests or to sever his organizational ties with the ABPO, although he was at the same time designated Secretary-General of the AFPFL itself.

Probably neither Nu nor Ba Swe foresaw the problems that might attend Nu's return to office. The Ba Swe government had revised what remained of the *Pyidawtha* plan, and still another revision by Nu upon his resumption of the Premiership in 1957 indicated differences over priorities.[10] Socialist strength also seemed to increase in the government during the Ba Swe administration, and various men close to Nu were demoted or left the Cabinet altogether. Nu himself, meanwhile, encountering difficulties in his efforts to reform the party, reacted in a way that only compounded the confusion. In mid-July he termed his job "beyond the task of one man or even one body of men,"[11] an admission which followed by three days his announcement to student journalists that the following January he would resign as President of the party.[12]

The question of U Nu's position in the government as well as in the party came to a precipitous head in late 1956 as a result of a proposal made by Ambassador to China U Hla Maung, at an informal meeting, that Nu not return to the Premiership but assume the role of a non-controversial national figure, as President of the AFPFL, on the model of Chairman Mao Tse-tung of China. No objection was expressed to the proposal at the meeting, and Hla Maung and Army Commander-in-Chief General Ne Win were deputed to explain it to Nu upon his return from a religious pilgrimage to Ceylon. Thakin Kyaw Tun got to Nu first, however, and told him to proceed immediately to see Thakin Tin, then hospitalized, before talking to anyone else.[13] Tin had not been at the meeting at which the Hla Maung proposal had been discussed, but a delegation had subsequently gone to Rangoon General Hospital, where he was a patient, to tell him of it— an act which did not seem to suggest an anti-Tin conspiracy.

According to Thakin Tin, however,

Kyaw Nyein convinced Ba Swe to hold on to the Premiership for the remainder of the parliamentary term. It was the duty of Kyaw Tun and myself to tell Nu of this conspiracy to kick him upstairs. U Nu was our first national leader in many hundreds of years, and it seemed an act of major folly to us to push him aside in favor of second-rate politicians.[14]

Nu seems to have believed Thakin Tin and Kyaw Tun, and he decided to return to office immediately.[15] But Ba Swe has said that Nu did not really accept the Tin–Kyaw Tun charge, but only used it to resume the Premiership and play the two Socialist factions off against one another.[16] Ba Swe, however, offered no resistance to Nu's resuming the office of Prime Minister. He has stated that at the first E.C. meeting at which the question was discussed, in late December, only Thakins Tin and Kyaw Tun spoke in support of Nu's return to office.[17] It was only at the second meeting, when Ba Swe announced that he would step down, that the other members of the party executive acquiesced in Nu's resuming the Premiership.[18] Several Socialist ministers, including Kyaw Nyein and his close ally, U Tun Win, were away from Rangoon and did not participate in the deliberations. However, in the official announcement of Nu's planned resumption of office, Kyaw Nyein was named as one of a committee of four who would determine the composition of the new Cabinet—the others being Nu, Ba Swe, and Thakin Tin—suggesting a temporary healing of the breach. Nu actually did not resume office, although he wanted to do so immediately, until March 1, an astrologically propitious date. The Burmese constitution, however, accorded authority to nominate the Premier to the Chamber of Deputies, not to the E.C., and the legislature was not in session.

The December 1956 succession incident clearly left Nu more suspicious than ever of Kyaw Nyein—and of Ba Swe. As he later put it, "When I wished to resign, they did not want me to go; but when I proposed to return, they did not want me to come back. . . . If I did not come back, all that I had done for the government during the past ten years would have gone to waste."[19] Ba Swe, who by all accounts preferred the easier life of not being Prime Minister, had willingly stepped down, and Kyaw Nyein had not sought to resist Nu's return. Yet Kyaw Nyein came to be regarded as a major threat to Nu, and Ba Swe also became suspect in Nu's eyes as Kyaw Nyein's collaborator, while simultaneously Nu felt a debt of gratitude to Thakin Tin and Kyaw Tun for informing him of the alleged plot against him.

The all-Burma national congress of the AFPFL that began in Rangoon on January 29, 1958, was the first such session since December

The Nu of today is still recognizable in this cartoon satirizing the 1936 Rangoon University students' strike.

U Nu, looking relaxed, only six weeks before the second military *coup* of March 2, 1962 (Wide World Photos).

At the *balinatsa* ceremony in 1959 (while he was out of office) U Nu tells followers of the role of *nats* in helping him fight the insurgents.

U Nu, as Premier, taking part in the Burmese New Year's Water Festival in April 1960

U Nu, his hands folded in prayer, participates in the 1961 ceremonies marking the anniversary of the death of the Buddha.

Pictures on this and the next two pages: Wide World Photos, Inc.

After his induction as an honorary Tenderfoot, Nu, appropriately attired, inspects Boy Scouts at a ceremony in Rangoon in 1961.

Superstitious Nu prays for the avoidance of world-wide war and disaster, which was predicted by an Indian astrologer in February 1962.

Nu, probably the most genuinely neutral of the attending neutralists, as he appeared at the Afro-Asian meeting in Bandung, Indonesia, in April 1955.

Premier U Nu pats a baby rhinoceros, a gift from Nepal, at a christening ceremony in Rangoon in 1962.

1947. Ideologically, the congress seemed to reflect a willingness among the top party leaders to reconcile their differing points of view. U Nu as League President was the main speaker. He vigorously rejected Marxism (saying that it was identical with Communism) on the grounds that it was incompatible with Buddhism, and strongly endorsed democratic socialism.[20] The speech, which lasted some four hours and ran to 180 foolscap pages, had been approved at a day-long session of the E.C. (from which Thakin Tin was absent*) on January 25. Nu's views as contained in this address were closer to those of Kyaw Nyein than to those of any of the other top leaders. Kyaw Nyein's chief foe among the Socialists, Thakin Tin, on the other hand, did not want to endorse Nu's anti-Marxist speech.[21] Nu's assertion that Marxism and Buddhism were not compatible, moreover, ran contrary to Ba Swe's view that the two were the same in concept. Nu, indeed, may have sought common ideological ground with Kyaw Nyein, partly in the spirit of compromise,[22] although there is no question that he had been moving for some time in the direction of the public position he took in January 1958.

Nu's ideological stand at the congress was that Marxism (i.e., Communism) was not "a doctrine that is infallible and true without reservation." Because the AFPFL approved "of only some parts of the Economic Doctrine of Marxism," Nu declared, it rejected Marxism as its "guiding political philosophy." The League did believe, however, that "commodities should not be produced for profit-making, but for the consumption and use of the people." As Nu put it, "The AFPFL ideology or political philosophy [was] neither Communism (Marxism) nor State Capitalism, but Socialism." Marxism, Nu stated, required adaptation to time and circumstances and could not effectively be applied to Burma. He objected to both the doctrine and the methods of Marxism.[23]

The reaction of the delegates to Nu's speech was good but by no means unanimously approving. Some delegates objected to Nu's emphasis on ideology, claiming that he should not have laid down an ideology for the AFPFL, since it was not really a party but a coalition. To the latter view, however, Nu took exception, claiming categorically that the League was a political party and not a "united front." This assertion ran counter to U Ba Swe's plans for an early reorganization of the Socialist Party.[24] But although Nu's image of the party was not unrelated to the main divisive issue, it was not this claim that nearly split the AFPFL at this time.

* Tin was in Arakan to accept the surrender of insurgent forces.

U Nu's leadership of the party was never at issue as his resumption of the Premiership had been in late 1956. He was the only nominee for the League Presidency and was re-elected unanimously. A Secretary-General, however, was not to be chosen so easily. Kyaw Nyein strongly endorsed his supporter, Thakin Tha Khin, while Nu backed Thakin Kyaw Tun, close ally of Thakin Tin (who was Kyaw Nyein's chief adversary). Efforts to resolve this conflict in advance of the congress failed. Twenty-four hours before the congress began, the E.C. had not reached a decision on whether Kyaw Tun should remain as Secretary-General or be succeeded by someone else.[25] Nu frankly justified his support in terms of his debt to Kyaw Tun for informing him of the 1956 "plot" to prevent his return to the Premiership.[26] But Kyaw Nyein threatened to split the Socialist element of the League if Kyaw Tun retained his post.[27]

The compromise solution that seemed to be accepted was the handiwork of the peace-making Ba Swe. Kyaw Tun, Ba Swe announced at a January 29 press conference, would remain as Secretary-General and Tha Khin would be "Joint Secretary." Moreover, Ba Swe thought that he had Kyaw Tun's agreement to step down from his post in 45 days.[28] U Nu himself was not a party to this agreement and later, when Kyaw Tun refused to honor it, Nu failed to see its importance in terms of the threat this represented to Kyaw Nyein in particular but also to Ba Swe and others.

Nu clearly played a role, however, in the January compromise settlement. His agreement to allow Kyaw Nyein to form his own mass organization for youth and to accept this body into the AFPFL was unquestionably a concession to the Socialist leader—the more significant in view of Nu's frequently stated opposition to the use of such organizations by their officers for partisan advantage. And his decision in favor of Kyaw Nyein for the purpose of political balance—the only possible justification under the circumstances—was resented by Thakin Tin, Kyaw Tun, and Pan Myaing as favoritism to their main rival. Kyaw Nyein, for his part, realizing that he possessed a limited base of political support among only the "educated" Socialists, began to raid the territory of Thakin Tin's backers for new members of his youth organizations—conspicuously in Insein and Mandalay, two of the strongholds of Tin's ABPO. Kyaw Nyein's actions, however, seem to have been in retaliation for Thakin Kyaw Tun's failure to step down from the AFPFL Secretary-Generalship after 45 days and for Nu's apparent unwillingness to try to do anything about it.

The issue of corruption, long a staple with Nu, also played a part in the final showdown that led to the split in the AFPFL. On March 14, two days after he had stated that there would be no reshuffle in the AFPFL executive ranks (i.e., that Kyaw Tun would not step down as party Secretary), Nu authorized the first in a series of mass arrests that were to be regarded as a threat both by the Thakin Tin faction and by Kyaw Nyein and his followers. According to Nu, the Army had complained that there were "persons who were murdering, raping, kidnapping, trafficking with the enemy, or abetting persons who were doing these things" but that "no action could be taken against them because they had political protection."[29] The complaints were raised at the high-level National Defense Council, and Nu himself ordered the arrest of all suspected criminals regardless of their political affiliation.[30] However, the members of the Council, including, besides Kyaw Nyein, Home Minister Thakin Tha Khin (who had lost to Kyaw Tun in the struggle for the AFPFL Secretary-Generalship) and Kyaw Nyein's Socialist colleague Defense Minister Ba Swe, were clearly sympathetic to Kyaw Nyein.

Although followers of both Thakin Tin and Kyaw Nyein were arrested, the number of supporters of the Tin faction—especially persons closely associated with Thakin Kyaw Tun—who were detained was far greater. Some top ABPO leaders, including the President and General Secretary of the Insein branch, and even an M.P., were among them. *The Nation* reported: "There is a strong belief that the arrests are not merely a purge of bad elements but an elimination contest between warring factions of the AFPFL in a secret struggle to the death."[31] Nu, who admitted at an April 22 press conference that there was serious factional fighting within the League, claimed that the arrests were an altogether different matter; he said that he did not want the two issues linked. The fact is that they were linked—by Kyaw Nyein and Thakin Tin, both of whom were convinced that their followers were being attacked.

Nu also struck out at corruption in public life with a policy of personnel retrenchment in the government service aimed primarily at uprooting dishonest persons. He was obviously displeased when some of those who had been expelled from the government service were recruited by Kyaw Nyein's new youth organization. This only confirmed Nu's suspicions that Kyaw Nyein was consciously harboring dishonest elements among his supporters, and counterbalanced, for Nu, the number of followers of Kyaw Tun and Thakin Tin who were involved in the arrests of March and April. There is no evidence, however, that Nu's anti-corruption drive, launched in March, was directed against

Kyaw Nyein (or Thakin Tin, Kyaw Tun, or anyone else). It was another instance of Nu's taking action without considering thoroughly the possible political consequences of what he did.

Nu's behavior during March and most of April also suggests that his ultimate decision to side with one of the two main factions was not carefully planned. The E.C. announcement of March 15 that there would be a six-day meeting of the party's Supreme Council at Taunggyi during the last week of May appeared to indicate that any intraparty conflicts would be decided within the party and according to formal procedure. The announcement of March 31 that Dr. E Maung of the Justice Party would shortly visit China and the Soviet Union on a mission for the Premier, and that U Ohn, Nu's chief personal confidant, might travel to the two countries at the same time hardly suggested that Nu was preparing for a major political showdown. Dr. E Maung was becoming one of Nu's most valuable political allies, and presumably Nu would have wanted the faithful Ohn also at his side in the event of trouble.

The Thakin Tin–Kyaw Tun faction objected to Nu that the arrests of their followers in March and April were unjust in view of their support of Nu when he had been threatened by Kyaw Nyein in 1956. Whether they threatened Nu with withdrawal of their support is not certain. Nu, however, already regarded Kyaw Nyein and his followers as foes; the loss of the backing of the Tin–Kyaw Tun faction would have left him in disfavor with the two most vigorous components of the League, both the "college" and the *"pongyi-kyaung"* Socialists. Nu's plan to visit Thailand in late April (en route to Japan), the subject of a public announcement the first week of April, suggests that he did not anticipate a political crisis. But apparently pressures from the Tin–Kyaw Tun group increased as the month advanced.

Following his participation in the opening of the Burmese New Year's celebration in Rangoon in mid-April, Nu flew to Moulmein, where he spent three days and met with Ba Swe. However, he did not discuss his plans with Ba Swe,[32] who had earlier volunteered to take over the post of party Secretary-General himself as a compromise in the Kyaw Nyein–Kyaw Tun quarrel. But Nu had not been able to agree "to Thakin Kyaw Tun being knocked out because Thakin Kyaw Tun stood by me once before when the others tried to push me out," he himself later explained.[33] Nu's possibly unjustified suspicions of Ba Swe, stemming from the Tin–Kyaw Tun 1956 allegations and Ba Swe's organizational efforts on behalf of the Socialist Party, may have fathered his biggest miscalculation in the April jockeying for power. If Nu had agreed to remove Kyaw Tun as party Secretary in favor of some compromise candidate, Ba Swe (and others) might have supported him, even if the differences between Nu and Kyaw Nyein were not resolved to the latter's satisfaction. Ba Swe, who had played the role of peacemaker in January, was not committed to Kyaw Nyein before the split. Nu's recognition of the factionalization forced Ba Swe to take sides.

On his return to Rangoon on April 22, Nu decided to side with the Thakin Tin–Kyaw Tun faction of the AFPFL (and the Socialist Party) —which meant a split in the ruling party. "If the parties were determined to part," Nu said later, "would not enforced propinquity aggravate enmity and lead to bloodshed?"[34] Accordingly, Nu summoned Thakin Tin's group on April 23 and announced his decision. He spoke separately to Ba Swe, who—according to Nu himself—told him that he would be pouring kerosene on the fire. Ba Swe, who still sought to unify the badly divided governing party, asked Nu to reconsider his decision and, at the least, to postpone the split until the 1960 elections.[35] Nu refused.

Nu's next move (on April 25) was to recall Home Minister Thakin Tha Khin, who was en route to New Delhi on a trade mission. After dispatching the cable, Nu "discussed" his action with Ba Swe, still a Deputy Premier; Kyaw Nyein, also a Deputy Premier, was out of Rangoon all this time and was not informed either of Nu's decision to side with Thakin Tin and Kyaw Tun or of the recall of his close ally, Thakin Tha Khin. On April 26 Nu formally removed Tha Khin as Home Minister and assumed the portfolio himself. He explained Tha Khin's dismissal and his own assumption of the Home Minister's portfolio in terms of the rising tension in the country; the Union Military Police came under the Home Ministry, and Nu wanted this force within his immediate control.[36]

On April 27, three days after he had informed Thakin Tin and Ba Swe of his decision to side with the Tin faction, Nu met with Kyaw Nyein for the first time since his return from Moulmein. Kyaw Nyein had been away from Rangoon all this time, and had returned to the capital only that day. Nu summoned him to his residence and informed Kyaw Nyein of his decision to take sides against him and his political supporters. Kyaw Nyein was taken by surprise. He had not expected such a move by Nu—at least not at this time (with the Communists and the other insurgents still in the field)—nor had he apparently been forewarned of Nu's decision, even though Ba Swe had known of it for three days.

Nu probably did not side with Thakin Tin and Kyaw Tun because of a fear of Kyaw Nyein or out of gratitude to the two *"pongyi-kyaung"* Socialist leaders for informing him of the 1956 plot. The success of Kyaw Nyein's organizational efforts in March and April 1958, plus the arrest of some of Kyaw Tun's supporters, caused Tin and Kyaw Tun to put pressure on Nu to side with them.[37] Nu's claim that the split was there and that he had to recognize it was valid. Thakin Tin and Kyaw Tun unquestionably indicated their intention to resist the suppression of their faction. Nu decided to ally himself with Tin because of Tin's control of the ABPO, the largest organized component of the AFPFL.

The AFPFL split over the issue of control of the mass organizations that comprised it. U Nu did not split the party. The rivalries among his chief lieutenants did, however—rivalries to which he had contributed through the years. The paradox is that Burma's governing party should fall apart because of organizational considerations, when party organization was (in Hugh Tinker's words) "inchoate" and provided only the "cloak" rather than "the skeleton and the nervous system of the body national" as it did in many other countries.[38]

Policy-making and most other aspects of government came to a standstill with the split in the AFPFL. The Cabinet, divided between the supporters of Nu and Thakin Tin and those of Kyaw Nyein (to whose support Ba Swe rallied), ceased to meet. The national bureaucracy, centered in Rangoon, was immobilized, fearing to offend whichever group might ultimately be victorious.

The Swe-Nyein faction, as Kyaw Nyein's and Ba Swe's group came to be called, insisted on a showdown with Nu and his allies in the Chamber of Deputies. Nu, not wanting to confront the country with elections, agreed. The Swe-Nyein suggestion had originally been advanced because of a fear that the large ABPO representation in the AFPFL Supreme Council would make a victory over Nu within the party itself impossible. Kyaw Nyein and Ba Swe, however, became concerned over their chances of winning in the Parliament when the pro-Communist NUF (with a solid bloc of 45 votes) declared in favor of the Nu-Tin group. The Swe-Nyein faction demanded that Nu let the AFPFL M.P.'s decide who should be Prime Minister, but Nu refused. So it was that an essentially intra-party quarrel came to be decided in the national legislature—with the balance between the two factions held by what had been until late April the opposition (the NUF).

The last meeting of the Cabinet attended by both the Nu-Tin group and the Swe-Nyein group was held on May 5. The lines of battle were clearly drawn two days later when Ba Swe, addressing the Supreme Council of the TUC(B) as its President, labeled Nu a power-mad dictator who had destroyed the AFPFL. The charge that Nu had split the party for his own advantage was really the only one the Swe-Nyein group could level against him—for they had been members of his government and shared the responsibility for policy and its execution. Nu merely countered that the split already existed; he had only recognized it.

The next five weeks were marked by a mud-slinging campaign the like of which Burma had never before known. Although both sides promised the monks that they would not resort to violence, there was still widespread fear that force might be employed. General Ne Win, Army Commander-in-Chief, promised that the military would not become involved in the struggle for power. Nu and Kyaw Nyein, once such close friends, published letters they had exchanged in 1956 at the time of Nu's decision to resign the Premiership temporarily. The letters showed clearly that the formal cooperation of the previous two years had not reflected genuine trust and confidence among Burma's top leaders. Ba Swe's and Kyaw Nyein's expressed fears of "disorder and bloodshed" were interpreted by Nu as threats to the foundations of constitutional government in Burma.

The struggle for power inevitably involved the M.P.'s from the several states, dividing the minority representatives among themselves— one of the comparatively few occasions on which the lesser ethnic groups appeared to be seriously concerned about a genuinely national question. In order to win the backing of the rightist Arakanese National United Organization (ANUO), headed by the capable U Kyaw Min, in the parliamentary vote, U Nu, who only a few weeks earlier had proclaimed his opposition to the creation of more ethnic states, came out in support of an autonomous Arakanese state. The Swe-Nyein politicians tried to match the Nu-Tin group in appealing to the minorities, but they had to contend with the very favorable image of Nu long held by the non-Burman ethnic groups. Late on the evening of May 25, sixteen Shan deputies and two from the Kayah State declared for Nu, who had been trailing the Swe-Nyein faction up to this time, bringing him abreast of his opponents.

The statistics of support for the two AFPFL factions were issued daily and carried in serial-like fashion by the press. A majority of the AFPFL legislators backed Ba Swe and Kyaw Nyein, but the combined endorsement of the NUF, a majority of the Shan deputies, and the Arakanese M.P.'s provided a counterweight to Nu's lack of support within the party over which he had presided for more than a decade. The pro-Communist NUF backed Nu largely because of its opposition to Kyaw Nyein, who was generally regarded as a more uncompromising anti-Communist than any of Burma's other top leaders.

A major issue was the much-discussed possibility that U Nu might dissolve the legislature if he were defeated, an act which the Swe-Nyein group claimed would be illegal. The debate involved the interpretation of Sections 57 and 119 of Burma's constitution, the latter of which stated: "The Prime Minister shall resign from office upon his ceasing to retain the support of a majority in the Chamber of Deputies unless on his advice the President dissolves the Parliament under Section 57 and on the re-assembly of the Parliament after the dissolution the Prime Minister secures the support of a majority in the Chamber of Deputies." Nu declared in a June 1 rally in Aung San Stadium in Rangoon, "Up to the present we have not decided to dissolve Parliament and hold fresh elections, but let me publicly declare that, if the need should arise for the dissolution to be made, I shall not hesitate to use the power conferred by the Constitution and order the dissolution."[39] Nu's position was probably technically correct, and was presented with great skill. There is no reason to believe that Nu did not intend to recommend dissolution in the event of a vote against him.

The day of the vote, June 9, was a suspenseful one. The city of Rangoon itself was largely under guard, and Army, Navy, and Air Force personnel surrounded the compound in which the Parliament building was located. The outcome of the vote still seemed in doubt; there had been eight defections from the Swe-Nyein camp to the Nu-Tin bloc on June 3, but one AFPFL M.P. and another from the NUF subsequently switched over to the side of Ba Swe and Kyaw Nyein. Each legislator had his own bodyguard, provided by the government, a reflection of the fears of the hour. Nu had demanded that the Swe-Nyein ministers resign from the Cabinet by June 4, and on the morning of June 5 the new members of a Nu-Tin government were sworn in. The Swe-Nyein ministers, meanwhile—led by Ba Swe and Kyaw Nyein—drove to a statue of the late Aung San, where they proclaimed a six-point complaint against U Nu and promised to save the nation from the dangers to which Nu had exposed it. Kyaw Nyein and Ba Swe, "both Monday-born and therefore propitiously oriented," also led a caravan of supporters to the Shwedagon Pagoda for prayer in advance of the important vote on June 9—a Monday.[40]

The debate in the Parliament on June 9 began at eleven in the morning and lasted until seven in the evening. The proceedings were broadcast nationally, and those who did not have radios clustered about the doors and windows of homes and shops that did have them. The debate was surprisingly calm. There was even a touch of humor in places, and the occasional interruptions of the speeches were polite and friendly. The final vote was 127–119 in favor of Nu—a margin of only eight ballots.*

Only slightly more than a third of the members of the party over which Nu had presided for so long voted for him. The decisive factor in the balloting was the support of the NUF, the dominant group of which was the far left Burma Workers and Peasants Party (often called the country's "aboveground Communists"). Two of the NUF deputies, who had been jailed and not allowed to participate in the previous session of Parliament, were released in order to take part in the balloting—so much was the outcome in doubt, even down to the parliamentary vote itself.

The irreversible character of the split became evident in the wake of the vote in the Chamber of Deputies, as Ba Swe and Kyaw Nyein, enjoying the support of a majority of the AFPFL M.P.'s, read Nu and his colleagues out of the party that had regained Burma its independence. U Nu and Thakins Tin and Kyaw Tun, for their part—chief officers in the AFPFL and its main component, the ABPO—subsequently expelled the Swe-Nyein faction from their portion of the party. In fact there were now two AFPFL's—the self-styled "Clean" AFPFL led by U Nu, and the Ba Swe–Kyaw Nyein "Stable" AFPFL. Each in turn had its own satellite organizations after the model of the pre-split AFPFL: the "Clean" AFPFL its Union Labor Organization and Union Women's League, for example, and the "Stable" AFPFL its Trade Union Congress (Burma) and Women's Freedom League.

* Of the attending 248 members, 246 voted. The vote was as follows:

	Nu-Tin	Swe-Nyein
AFPFL M.P.'s (Burma proper)	51	97
National Unity Front	44	1
Arakanese National United Organization	6	0
Shans	16	9
Kachins	3	4
Chins	3	3
Kayahs	2	0
Karens	2	5
	127	119

U Nu remained Burma's chief political leader—indeed Burma's hero—despite the fact that nearly two-thirds of his own party deserted him in the June 1958 no-confidence vote. Besides being a leader of Burma, however, Nu had also emerged during the first decade of independence as a world figure. It is to a description and analysis of Nu's role as Burma's chief spokesman abroad that this study now turns.

❀

FIFTEEN

WORLD FIGURE

AT THE START of independence Nu stated that the three most influential factors in shaping Burma's foreign policy were geography, the pro-British orientation of some of the minorities, and the great regard of a majority of those in effective political life for the Soviet Union, especially its economic achievements and orientation. Cataloguing Burma's weaknesses, Nu noted that "she has only a population of 17 millions, national unity is far from being on a firm basis, and she has been reduced to ashes as a result of the war passing over her twice." Because the Burmese "suffered the most by the war," according to Nu, the nation "seeks peace for the whole world. . . . We shall support any measure for securing unity between Britain, the United States, Russia and other Powers."[1]

Nu's bid for unity with the Communists failed, and the subsequent insurrection of PVO, Karen, and other factions moved the government to seek both economic and military aid, first from the Commonwealth of Nations and then from the United States. Nu's first request for financial and arms assistance was considered in late February 1949 at a meeting of Commonwealth representatives in New Delhi. It resulted in the proposal that the Burmese seek to conciliate their differences with the Karens with the aid of Commonwealth mediation.[2] Nu saw this as unwarranted interference in Burma's internal affairs, and sharply rebuffed the offer. However, in April Nu flew to Delhi and Karachi to explain the Burmese situation to Jawaharlal Nehru and Liaquat Ali Khan before their departure for a meeting of Commonwealth Prime Ministers in London. They agreed to ask the other Commonwealth Premiers to grant Burma's request for economic help. A loan of nearly $17 million was ultimately agreed upon, but this credit was never actually utilized, although direct arms assistance given earlier by both India and the United Kingdom was used.

Burma's increasingly favorable orientation toward the West during these years was probably caused in part by events in China. U Nu, in a December 1948 radio speech, expressed concern over the influx of refugees from China, describing them as a threat to peace in his country. Nu dispatched his Foreign Minister, Dr. E Maung, to Britain and the United States to discuss the Chinese Communists' rise to power and the problems it posed for Burma's government. Upon his return in August 1949, E Maung reported that the Burmese, British, and American governments had agreed to confer on Communist advances in Southeast Asia.

The inauguration of the Commonwealth loan negotiations and the return of Dr. E Maung from his mission were followed by Burma's recognition in December 1949 of the new Communist government of China. Thus Burma was the first Asian country to take this step. The Socialists were the strongest component in the government in favor of recognition.[3] However, Dr. E Maung stated in a radio broadcast that recognition did not mean approval. Recognition, moreover, was followed by Nu's announcement in March 1950 that Burma had approached the American government for military and economic aid. Said Nu: "The Union Government considered that greater advantage lies in closer relations with the Western democracies and it will be our endeavor to obtain aid of various kinds from the West, i.e., the United States and Britain."[4] Nearly a year earlier, U Nu had declared, "It is now time that we should enter into mutually beneficial treaties or arrangements, defense and economic, with countries of common interest. The Union Government is at present considering this question in all its aspects."[5]

The Socialist U Kyaw Nyein, formerly Foreign Minister, had criticized Nu's view, quoted Indian Premier Nehru in support of his plea for a neutral foreign policy, and warned his colleagues of the dangers of becoming associated with power blocs. Nu, in reply, had admitted that the ideal course would be to remain strictly neutral, but, he had pointed out, foreign capital and technical help were needed to develop the nation economically and to pull the country together from the chaos created by the insurrections. Considerations of profit and security might not attract capital to Burma, he had observed, but there were both nations and individuals who might aid the country in order to maintain it as a democracy.[6]

United States economic aid was not accepted without opposition, and U Nu had to deny that its acceptance represented a policy of alignment in the cold war. He offered to accept Soviet as well as American and British assistance, but the U.S.S.R. under Stalin made no effort to extend aid to Burma. An economic assistance agreement between the Burmese and the American governments was signed in Rangoon on September 13, 1950; it provided for eight to ten million dollars in Economic Cooperation Administration grant aid for the year ending June 30, 1951. This was less than one-fifth the amount Nu was reported to have requested of U.S. roving Ambassador Philip C. Jessup during the latter's visit to Burma in May 1950.[7] The parliamentary debate over the aid pact was a heated one, and the opposition of the "Red Socialists" was a factor in their ouster from the AFPFL.

The cessation of American aid in 1953, at Nu's request, was the result not of Burma's fear that she had become too closely identified with the United States, but mainly of the presence of Chinese Kuomintang irregulars, originally refugees from the Communists, on Burmese soil—Chinese supplied by Chiang Kai-shek who had allied themselves with some of Burma's indigenous insurrectionists. The self-supporting policy that Burma's leaders chose to pursue with the termination of American aid was short-lived, however. As the international demand for rice started to drop before the end of the year and foreign exchange reserves began to decline, Nu announced, "Burma is willing to accept United States economic aid, but we do not want it free. We prefer to pay for it as this forms a more solid basis of friendship than acceptance of grants." He urged the United States to buy Burmese rice for allocation to nations in Southeast Asia with food deficits; Burma would use the money to hire American technicians and to buy machinery from the United States to assist in fulfilling her development program. The United States, however, would not negotiate an aid agreement based on rice purchases, and hence Burma entered into the much-publicized trade agreements with the Communist countries, including China, for the disposition of her rice surpluses and the acquisition of the equipment and technicians she needed. The United States resumed economic assistance to Burma in 1956 with the successful negotiation of a $21 million surplus agricultural commodities agreement, and this was followed by other types of help. Nu hailed the beginning of a new relationship between the two countries.

Although Burma's official foreign outlook since the early 1950's has been described as one of positive neutrality, there is reason to believe that this policy was not a first choice. At meetings in Rangoon, Moulmein, and Mandalay in late 1950 U Nu stated, "We must find out which country or countries have common interests with us and if we find any it is up to us to work together with them."[8] There was never any question, however, of Burma's becoming a political camp follower of any nation or group of nations. As Nu put it at the time of his clash with the "Red Socialists," "We cannot allow ourselves to be absorbed into any power bloc."[9] And in 1951, he declared, "The sole criterion for all our decisions is our sense of what is right and proper."[10]

By 1952, Burma's foreign policy had taken the neutralist form that was to characterize it for the rest of the decade. In his opening address to the *Pyidawtha* Conference, Nu identified four main elements of Burmese policy: friendly relations with all nations, acceptance of any aid from abroad that did not infringe on the country's sovereignty, the determination of all issues on their own merits, and assistance to any country needing help.[11] In an address to the National Press Club in Washington in 1955, Nu described Burmese non-alignment as a policy "of actively seeking to discover through negotiation and compromise and accommodation some acceptable basis on which the peace of the world can be secured."[12]

U Nu's quest for friendly relations with all nations was closely related to his belief in peaceful coexistence. In 1955 Nu stated, "It may sometimes happen that our methods differ although our goal is the same, and we fully recognize the right of all countries to adopt their own methods which they consider best."[13] At the 1955 Bandung Afro-Asian Conference, he declared:

> More than ever, [man] needs to exercise courage, patience, tolerance and imagination. Fear, which for so long has been the counsellor of man, is today man's mortal enemy. Suspicion and mistrust are likewise greater enemies of the human race than ever before. In this new situation, how are the nations of the world to be guided in their relations with each other?
>
> I believe that the answer is to be found in the five principles comprising respect for sovereignty and territorial integrity, non-aggression, non-interference in the internal affairs of another state, equality, and mutual benefit. The sum of these principles adds up to our concept of coexistence.[14]

On his visit to Communist China in 1954 U Nu counseled Chinese leaders to learn to coexist with the Americans. In the United States in 1955 he rejected the suggestion that peaceful coexistence only provided an opportunity for would-be aggressors to prepare themselves. In Moscow the same year he told his Soviet hosts,

> So long as . . . fear and suspicion exist, peaceful coexistence will be meaningless. Sincere efforts should therefore be made by all par-

ties concerned to liquidate such fear and suspicion. Coexistence with that kind of fear and suspicion will be like the association of two men who are shaking hands, while their other hands are still hidden at their backs, grabbing a dagger and a revolver respectively.[15]

Discussing Sino-Burmese relations in August 1956 in the wake of the public revelation of Chinese incursions across the Burmese border, Nu asserted that the Burmese could not blind themselves "to the fact that, regardless of the system of government which might obtain in either country at any time, we are destined to exist side by side as next-door neighbors."[16]

There was one type of governmental arrangement, however, that Nu could not accept: colonialism. Although an admirer of Britain as a nation, and of its people in general, he could not countenance British policy toward Kenya and other African territories or Britain's retention of control over Malaya. In a speech in September 1955, he termed colonialism the "root cause" of the world's problems; without its eradication there could be no peace—even if the differences among the great powers of the world diminished. During his visit to the United States earlier the same year, Nu indicated that his major disagreement with American foreign policy concerned the stand of the United States on colonialism. He also stated that if the British had not wisely and generously given Burma its independence, "I might have been a camp follower of Communism myself." And at a reception in his honor in New York, he said, "We have often been told that colonialism is not as dangerous as Communism, but I regard colonialism as an instrument that paves the way for Communism."[17]

"Although 'a sesamum seed will not produce oil,' as the saying goes, a quantity of sesamum seeds will certainly produce oil." So spoke U Nu on November 2, 1949, of the benefits of international cooperation through the United Nations.[18] The fact that Burma's "first major act in the international field was to apply for membership in the world organization" indicated the strength of Nu's belief in the U.N.[19] At the time of the parliamentary debate on the Korean War in September 1950, he declared:

When we joined the United Nations Organization, we were not prompted by considerations of financial aid, medical aid, educational missions to plan our educational program and such other benefits likely to accrue from membership. . . . What was foremost in our minds was the expectation of U.N. assistance when our country should be subjected to aggression by a stronger power.[20]

The Charter of the United Nations, Nu declared before the National Press Club in Washington in 1955, "is in effect one great mutual security pact." He added: "We say that the system has not broken down, but merely that it has not been made to work; that the remedy is not to push the United Nations aside but to strengthen it and put more life into it."[21] Nu spoke equally vigorously on other occasions of the benefits of economic and social cooperation through the United Nations. "To us," he said in a 1952 broadcast talk on the U.N.'s Economic Commission for Asia and the Far East, "the United Nations is not a faraway organization."[22]

However, Nu was aware also of the shortcomings of the United Nations. In 1956 he recognized that, "unless the leading powers consent to a particular course of action, nothing substantial can be achieved." Moreover, Burma itself—according to Nu—had been less than fully faithful to its U.N. obligations. "Even we ourselves . . . failed to observe the United Nations embargo about shipments of rubber (to Communist China). The tonnage that we shipped was insignificant but nonetheless . . . it was failure on our part to abide by the United Nations decision."[23] Nu also was visibly embarrassed when Burma failed to vote in 1956 for the resolution condemning Soviet intervention in Hungary; he later explained that instructions on how to vote did not reach the Burmese delegation on time. On a subsequent vote Burma did join in condemning the Soviet action despite the abstention of such other neutrals as India, Indonesia, and Cambodia.

In 1955, during his visit to the United States, Nu summed up his government's feelings about the role of the United Nations:

Despite its failure to come up to our expectations, our faith in the United Nations remains undiminished. It remains the main hope for mankind in this atomic age. If it were considered essential ten years ago, it is even more essential today. A divided world stands in greater need of a common forum to discuss differences than a world united. I believe that if the United Nations did not exist today, the world would be working feverishly to establish it or something like it. Our task therefore is to strengthen it, and to make it the effective organization which had been planned by its founders.[24]

Nu's affirmative reply to U.N. Secretary-General Dag Hammarskjöld's request for Burmese troops for police duties in Lebanon in 1958 showed that the Burmese Premier was willing to back his words with deeds. Nu had also done this in 1950 at the time of the Communist aggression in Korea at the expense of a serious domestic political split during a time when his country was already badly divided. "It was very clear . . . that the North . . . was the aggressor," Nu explained, "and we deemed it right to oppose the aggressor."[25]

The reasons for Burma's action were clear. As Nu himself stated in 1952, "our position is not so different from that of Korea. We are within an arm's reach from . . . Soviet Russia and Red China as well as from the British and the United States sphere of influence."[26] According to the Executive Committee of the AFPFL, three factors underlay the government's decision to support the U.N. intervention: the need to protect Burma from aggression, the government's policy of non-partisanship, and the requirements of fair play. If Burma expected U.N. help in its hour of need, according to Nu, "we felt a reciprocal obligation to contribute our mite to the United Nations when that great organization tackles any aggressor in any place at any time."[27] Subsequently Burma sanctioned the crossing of the 38th parallel into North Korea by the United Nations forces and supported the "Uniting for Peace" resolution sponsored by the United States (which established procedure for future consideration by the General Assembly of aggression in the event of Security Council inaction).

The Burmese were apprehensive about the intentions of their large neighbor, China, from the very re-inauguration of independence.[28] This fear was not lessened by the presence in Burma of a Chinese minority estimated at more than 350,000, who were receiving various forms of aid from the Chinese Communists—including financial support for Chinese schools.[29] "Han, Manchu, Nationalist, Communist—it makes no difference to the Burmese," a former Burmese Ambassador to Peiping told the author in 1960. "A Chinese is a Chinese—and to be feared. U Nu fully accepts this view."[30] Nu himself admitted in 1949, after the Communists' accession to power, "Our relations with China could not be said to be cordial." According to U Nu, "the new Chinese Government seemed inclined to give our Communists their moral support, apparently regarding us as stooges of the West." China also provided sanctuary and training for some of Burma's insurgents (as Nu told Premier Chou En-lai in Rangoon in 1954).[31] But "as the years passed, and the Chinese saw from our actions that we were stooges of nobody, that we were embarked on an independent policy in international affairs, they changed their attitude."[32]

Fear of possible friction with China was a factor in Burma's decision in 1949 to become the first country to recognize the Communist government. According to the Indian diplomat-author K. M. Panikkar,

U Nu's government requested India to delay its recognition of China so that Burma might be first.[33] Burma also was one of the first of the non-Communist countries to urge the "return" of Formosa to the new Chinese government. But Burma also was willing to criticize China when it seemed appropriate to do so (as it did when Information Secretary U Thant, in a radio broadcast, expressed regret over Chinese military action in Tibet).

The policy of Communist China toward Burma before 1954 was neither friendly nor overtly hostile. The Chinese received at least four delegations from Burma's Communist rebels, but did not acquiesce in their requests for major aid against U Nu's government.[34] An air of anxiety existed nonetheless, encouraged also by the large number of Chinese immigrants and Communist agents that crossed the Sino-Burmese border illegally.[35] The first sign of a change in this atmosphere seemed to come with the visit of Chinese Premier Chou En-lai to Rangoon in June 1954 (en route home from the Geneva Conference on Indochina and following a meeting with India's Nehru in New Delhi). It was at this time that Nu and Chou endorsed the five principles of peaceful coexistence, which had been enunciated by Nehru and Chou in India, and issued a joint statement that asserted, "The people of each nation should have the right to choose their own State system and way of life without interference from other nations. Revolution cannot be exported."[36]

To critics of his endorsement of these principles, Nu had this to say:

There are some who say that only knaves or fools would place all their faith in these five principles, and that some kind of guarantee or deterrent is necessary to ensure their observation by all parties. In other words, they work on the assumption that the other party is not to be trusted. As we all know, mistrust begets mistrust, and suspicion begets suspicion. It may have been permissible in the days of conventional weapons for nations to live in a perpetual atmosphere of suspicion and mistrust. But in the nuclear age, such a concept is obsolete. We cannot afford to live in mistrust of our neighbors. We have to learn to live with them in mutual trust and confidence, and when this happy state has not existed in the past, someone has to break the ice. For trust also begets trust, and confidence begets confidence.[37]

Following Chou En-lai's stopover in Rangoon, U Nu accepted an invitation to visit China later the same year. Arriving in Peiping on November 30 for a two-week tour of the country, Nu met with Mao Tse-tung and Chou En-lai (among others), made an extensive tour of Manchuria, and spoke out boldly in the spirit of the truly uncommitted.

At a farewell banquet, he openly and courageously identified himself as a friend of both China and the United States; as such, he said, "We want these two countries to be on the friendliest terms. . . . I will exert my utmost to bring about an understanding between the People's Republic of China and the United States of America."[38] He also declared that, "although Burma by itself may be ineffective in meddling with China's internal affairs, it may be able to create trouble in China if it allows itself to be used as a stooge by the enemy."[39] This thinly veiled threat was accompanied by Nu's assurances that the Burmese would "under no circumstances be stooges of any power . . . We will never turn false. . . . We want peace more than any other thing."[40]

China, for its part, promised to continue a policy of non-interference in Burma's domestic affairs—a promise that was violated in 1956, for example, when the Chinese Embassy in Rangoon financially aided pro-Communist candidates in the elections. Upon his return from China in 1954, however, Nu reported: "The leaders of Communist China have a code of honor. They will not break a pledge once given. In regard to Burma they have given a pledge of friendly relations, and I believe that they will sincerely honor that pledge."[41]

During his visit to the United States six months later, Nu praised the good will and peaceful intentions of China's leaders, observing, "Believe me, I cannot afford to be naïve or indulge in wishful thinking about this. You are far away from China; we are next door. Therefore we have much more to lose in the event that I am wrong in my estimate of Chinese sentiment."[42]

There was widespread public shock in Burma in the wake of the announcement in mid-1956 that Chinese troops had crossed the frontier between the two states and were moving in the general direction of Myitkyina in the Kachin State.[43] Both Premier U Ba Swe and U Nu—temporarily out of office but still President of the AFPFL—responded calmly to the news. Nu urged his countrymen not to be alarmed, cited Chinese good will toward Burma (noting as evidence Peiping's purchase of 200,000 tons of damaged Burmese rice), and wrote a personal letter to Chou En-lai—which he dispatched with the widow of Sun Yat-sen. However, in September more troops were reported in another part of the country, the northernmost part of the Kachin State. In November, following his return from a trip to China, Nu claimed that the Chinese crossings had been a mistake—the result of the fact that the Sino-Burmese frontier was undemarcated. The Burmese government, however, had long viewed with concern Chinese maps showing various parts of Burma as belonging to China.

"There is nothing reliable to show that the boundary between China and Burma was ever completely defined at any time in history," Nu claimed, "not even during the British period." The Chinese government had never ratified the 1914 border agreement negotiated with Britain, he said, while the Chinese were in no position to resist British pressure for rectification of the frontier in 1941.[44] Diplomatic correspondence took place through normal channels, and on October 2 Premier U Ba Swe was able to announce that China had agreed to accept the "1941 line" as a basis for negotiations. Nu, meanwhile, in a letter to Nehru, asked the Indian Premier to use his influence to obtain the withdrawal of Chinese troops from Burmese soil.[45] The troops, however, were not withdrawn prior to Nu's departure on October 23 on an "informal and personal" visit to Chinese Premier Chou En-lai.

Nu minced no words with the Chinese. "The Chinese people would defend to the last the preservation of their honor and dignity," he told a large audience. "The Burmese would do likewise and any infringement would be resisted."[46] Nu and Chou engaged in lengthy private talks for nearly a week, and the resulting proposals were dispatched to the Burmese Cabinet in Rangoon. A Burmese mission — with full powers to negotiate the border controversy—left Burma for China on October 30, and Nu told newsmen upon leaving China that a final settlement was in sight.

A joint communiqué issued by the two governments and statements by U Nu and other Burmese leaders at a press conference in Rangoon on November 10 indicated that at least provisional agreement had been reached by Burma and China on three major points. The three northern Kachin villages of Hpimaw, Gawlum, and Kanfang (forcibly occupied by the British in 1913 but over which Britain itself had never claimed sovereignty) were to be recognized as Chinese territory, and Burma's perpetual lease of the strategic Namwan Assigned Tract in the southern Kachin State (obtained by the British in 1897) was to be abrogated. China, in return, would accept the rest of Burma's version of the frontier. Burmese troops would withdraw from Hpimaw, Kanfang, and Gawlum, which command important mountain passes leading to China, before the end of the year, and the Chinese would evacuate to territory west of the 1941 line.

Implementing the provisional border agreement proved to be more difficult than U Nu had anticipated. When he resumed the Premiership on March 1, Nu announced his determination to bring the controversy to a close, and shortly thereafter visited Chou En-lai in Kunming, China for further talks.[47] It soon became clear, however, that the

Chinese were stalling, and Nu had to tell a press conference in April that there were details that still needed to be ironed out. No border agreement was reached in fact before Nu's ouster as Premier in September-October 1958, but the general view in Burma at the time was that a settlement would be effected and that Nu would make additional concessions if these were necessary.

Burma's recognition of the People's Republic of China in 1949 did not end the problem of dealing with the Chinese Nationalists. Indeed, this was Burma's most important foreign policy problem in the early 1950's. A number of Chinese Nationalist troops had crossed the border in fleeing from the Communists in 1950, and subsequently engaged in marauding Burma's countryside. Some of them even aligned themselves with the insurrectionists opposed to Nu's government.

In April 1951 the Kuomintang forces, numbering some 4,000 men, led by General Li Mi and supplied from outside Burma by air, had grouped themselves along the Burmese-Thai border. By the end of the year the number of KMT soldiers had increased to 6,000, and the Nationalists had expanded the area of their operations into the Wa State and along Burma's border with the Chinese province of Yunnan. These Kuomintang elements became even more active (and numerous) in 1952, moving further southward and westward as they crossed the important Salween River; they also joined forces with the rebellious Karen National Defense Organization, the largest of Burma's several indigenous insurgent groups.[48]

According to U Nu, there were three courses of action open to Burma in dealing with the KMT forces: the government could bring the matter before the United Nations, it could negotiate a withdrawal of the Nationalist troops through a friendly nation that had diplomatic relations with Formosa, or it could defeat the Kuomintang aggressors on the battlefield with its own Army. Nu clearly feared that an appeal to the U.N. might result in the dispatching of foreign troops to Burma, which might "antagonize the People's Republic of China and make the present simple case of aggression a much more complicated issue." The Burmese government at first waived taking the matter to the United Nations and only changed its mind in March 1953 as a result of an increase in the number of "nefarious deeds" of the "aggressors." "In order to dispel possible misunderstanding," however, Nu told the Chamber of Deputies on March 2, he had "made arrangements by which our representatives can meet the representatives of the People's Republic of China to have full and frank discussions whenever the occasion arises."[49] In his major policy address to the Parliament in September 1957, Nu said, "Considering that the Kuomintang forces were openly proclaiming that it was their intention to 'liberate' Yunnan, the Chinese Government could, were it so minded, have made difficulties for us."[50]

In addition to complicating relations with Communist China, the Kuomintang problem strained Burmese-American ties. As Nu later put it, "We found ourselves in the anomalous position of receiving aid from the United States Government on the one hand, and on the other fighting against an enemy which was controlled and supplied by the Formosan authorities whose continued existence was dependent on large-scale American aid."[51] At no time, however, did Nu suggest that the United States Government itself supported the Kuomintang aggression. Indeed, Nu sought American help in persuading the Kuomintang government on Formosa to evacuate the KMT forces in Burma, but his efforts were unsuccessful. Equipped with modern American arms, the KMT soldiers were able literally to outgun their Burmese Army adversaries, and by March 1953 the Burmese government was forced to concentrate five-sixths of its defense forces against the Nationalists. It was in this context that Nu informed the United States on March 17, 1953, that his government did not wish American foreign aid after June of that year.

On April 14, 1953, Burma officially charged Nationalist China in the U.N. with aggression, on the grounds that the Formosan regime exercised control over the refugee KMT soldiers, whose numbers had by this time increased to 12,000.

U Myint Thein, arguing Burma's case, declared that the condemnation of the KMT aggression by the U.N. "will stop the dispatch of further supplies and reinforcements and will also, we hope, force neighboring countries to keep a more watchful eye on the border traffic in their countries."[52] However, Burma did not want physical intervention in the quarrel on Burmese soil.[53] On a visit to Premier Nehru of India in late March, U Nu stated his hope that the U.N. would order the Nationalist soldiers in Burma to give up their arms and submit to internment.

An amendment to the Burmese resolution, proposed by Mexico and backed by the United States, branded Formosa an "aggressor" (but not by name), called for the evacuation or internment of the "foreign forces," and requested all states to respect Burma's territorial integrity and abstain from supplying aid of any kind to these foreign forces. Backed by most of the Asian, African, and Latin American countries, this resolution was adopted by the General Assembly in a vote of 59 to 0 with China abstaining. A four-nation military commission—comprising Burma, the United States, Thailand, and Formosa—was set up to effect the evacuation.

However, the Assembly resolution did not end Burma's KMT problem, which was to endure in mitigated form throughout the decade. The Burmese government withdrew from (and later returned to) the Bangkok meetings of the military commission, raised the matter again in the U.N., and even appealed directly to American President Dwight D. Eisenhower before the formal ending of the internationally supervised evacuation operation in May 1954. More than 6,000 troops and dependents had been removed by this date, but another 6,000 remained. In October 1954 Nu stated that Burma realized that the "evacuation represented the limit of what could be accomplished by international action," and recognized that the final disposition of the KMT elements still in the country was her own responsibility.

Under U Nu's leadership, Burma's relations with the United States were generally cordial. According to Nu, the Burmese thought at first that the American government "harbored some doubts about us because she felt that we were too 'progressive.' "[54] Shortly after independence, Nu has said, certain advisers proposed to him that "the Government of the Union of Burma—a Government possessed of a navy consisting of a frigate, an air force comprising some fighters and an army of a few partially equipped infantry battalions—should declare war on Britain and the United States. In reply, I unrolled a world map before them and told them to study it closely. They then asked me whether a token declaration of war could not be made even if an effectual declaration was not possible. It was only when I told them that there was no such thing as a token declaration of war—that once a war is declared you *are* at war—that they went back with their decision."[55]

This sort of sentiment notwithstanding, Burma drew steadily closer to the United States. The far left of Burmese politics accused Nu of partiality toward the United States (and Britain), but this did not seem to be borne out by such actions as Burma's recognition of Communist China, support of the seating of the Communist Chinese in the United Nations, opposition to the American U.N. resolution to brand China an aggressor because of its intervention in Korea, and refusal to attend the San Francisco Conference for the purpose of signing a Japanese peace treaty. The refusal of further American aid in 1953 was hardly the act of a client state!

Despite his friendship for the United States, Nu never hesitated to disagree with the American government when he opposed its foreign policies. The Southeast Asian defense alliance (SEATO), sponsored by the United States, he said, "increases the chances of a third world war because it heightens the tensions in Asia, intensifies China's fear of American encirclement and diminishes the chances of peaceful cooperation."[56] Nu clearly was opposed to SEATO from the start, but he apparently was willing to meet with the leaders of the other Colombo Powers in Rangoon to discuss alternatives to the type of regional grouping proposed by the United States. Indian Prime Minister Nehru, however, influenced him to turn his back on even a discussion of alternatives (as proposed by Ceylon's Premier, Sir John Kotalawala).[57] Privately, however, Burma's leaders were not unhappy about the implicit SEATO guarantee of their country's security.[58]

Following his visit to Communist China later the same year (1954), Nu stated publicly that if the United States withdrew its forces from the Formosa Straits, "then the possibility of peacefully liberating Taiwan would arise."[59] The American government valued Nu's friendship, however—despite disagreement over such questions as SEATO and the Formosan problem—as its invitation to him shortly thereafter to visit the United States indicates. During this 1955 visit, Nu met with President Eisenhower and Secretary of State John Foster Dulles, addressed a joint session of Congress, appeared before the United Nations in New York and the National Press Club in Washington, visited the Grand Canyon and the Tennessee Valley Authority, and was shown such assorted segments of Americana as a baseball game, a five-and-ten-cent store, and the Empire State Building.

Nu minced no words during the visit. He told the Overseas Press Club in New York, for example, that Asians could not understand the American "preoccupation with Communism."[60] And he created more than a little stir by the frankness with which he reported his impressions of the views of various American leaders. "I think Mr. Dulles is considering my proposal to have direct talks with China," Nu stated.[61] He also felt that most responsible persons in Washington were not opposed to seating Communist China in the United Nations.[62]

The attitude of the U.S.S.R. toward Burma at the inception of independence was not hostile, but it was not nearly so friendly as that of the British and the Americans. The Soviets did not oppose Burma's admission to the United Nations, but they did seem to regard the newly sovereign former British colony as "on probation." Subsequently, Nu himself put it, "as the Communist rebellion gathered momentum," the attitude of the Soviet Union "underwent a change, and indications were that she came to look upon us as reactionaries standing in the way of the people's liberation."[63] Nu's play *The People Win Through* leaves no doubt about his belief that Burma's Communists' resorting to insurrection was externally ordered.

The death of Stalin in 1953 was followed by a change in Soviet policy toward Burma. The willingness of the U.S.S.R. and its satellites as well as China to buy surplus Burmese rice in 1954–55, when the international price for the grain dropped and Burma's ambitious development plans seemed doomed, marked the beginning of a new era in Burmese-Soviet relations. During a 14-day tour of the Soviet Union in late 1955, his third major trip abroad in a year, Nu strongly praised the Soviet Union for having saved Burma, as he put it, by purchasing its surplus rice in an hour of great need—and he urged the Soviet leaders to accept Burmese rice in exchange for factories, machinery, and other equipment, as well as technical help. Nu also announced that his government had asked the U.S.S.R. to build in Rangoon a sports stadium, capable of accommodating 100,000 persons, and a large hall for international conferences.

The joint communiqué that Nu and Soviet Premier Nikolai A. Bulganin issued at the conclusion of the visit seemed to reflect Nu's endorsement of many of the stated main aims of Soviet foreign policy: an unconditional ban on nuclear weapons, the restoration of Formosa to the government of mainland China, the seating of the People's Republic of China in the United Nations, and a general reduction and control of all armaments. The two leaders also praised the policy of nonalignment.

On his return to Rangoon, Nu said at a press conference, "Soviet Russia understands and appreciates Burma's foreign policy." Asked the question, "What is the attitude of the Soviet leaders towards the Burma Communists?," he replied, "We did not discuss the matter."[64]

Nu's trip to the U.S.S.R. was followed—the very next month—by the visit to Burma of Soviet Party Secretary Nikita S. Khrushchev and Premier Bulganin. The Soviet leaders used the occasion to denounce the colonial countries of the West and to play the role of friends of the Burmese people. The visit ended with a joint statement, reminiscent of the earlier Moscow communiqué, in which the Burmese and Soviet Premiers reaffirmed their confidence in the five principles of peaceful coexistence, their concern over the armaments race, and their opposition to the policy of creating blocs. A Burmese-Soviet trade pact was also signed, providing for Russian agricultural and industrial aid in exchange for Burmese rice. An extension of this agreement was negotiated and initialed during the visit to Rangoon four months later of Soviet Deputy Premier Anastas Mikoyan; this pact extended the 1955 agreement from its original one year to five years and provided for the shipment of 400,000 long tons of Burmese rice to the U.S.S.R. each year. Less than a year later—in January 1957—still another aid agreement was signed between Burma and the Soviet Union, this one providing for a Soviet "gift to the people of Burma" of a technical institute, a hospital, a theater, a hotel, a stadium, an exhibition hall, a conference hall, and a swimming pool. The Burmese agreed to reciprocate with a "gift" of rice to the U.S.S.R.

The view that these and other actions represented a pro-Communist tinge in Burmese neutralism was not supported by Nu's prior or later behavior. The trade agreements, which did not satisfy the Burmese,[65] resulted from economic necessity; indeed, Burma from the start preferred cash sales to barter transactions with the Communists.[66] The joint statements represented a sincere effort to find common ground with an adversary (whether so described or not).

Burma's relations with India, unlike those with China and Russia, were cordial from the start of independence. In a policy address in September 1955, U Nu acknowledged that he had asked for "substantial help from India on three different occasions": in 1949 he had traveled to New Delhi to ask for more arms and ammunition, in 1954 India was asked to buy surplus rice "on our suggested terms and . . . came to our rescue," and "now again we are in need of money and asked India for help."[67]

"The reason we can approach India for help in our time of need," Nu explained, "is because there is firm Indo-Burmese friendship."[68] This was in part the result of the close friendship and usually similar outlook of Nu and Indian Premier Nehru. The two had occasion to visit one another quite frequently during Burma's first decade of independence and also met often with other Asian leaders at such meetings as the Bandung Conference and the gatherings of the Colombo Powers Premiers. Nu solicited Nehru's advice on a number of occasions (in 1951, for example, he visited Delhi to talk to the Indian Premier about Burma's refusal to participate in the multilateral conference, sponsored by the United States, to draw up a Japanese peace treaty). Nehru, for his part, frequently spoke on questions more directly Burma's concern than India's—for example, his remarks in 1953, after an exchange of views with Nu, that he would be surprised if there were direct American governmental aid to the Chinese Nationalist irregulars fighting the Burmese government.[69] Nu also asked Nehru for aid in soothing Sino-Burmese relations in 1956 at the time of the Chinese border incursions into Burma. Nehru himself has said that he asked Chinese Premier Chou En-lai to invite Nu to visit him in 1956 for a discussion of the frontier troubles between the two countries—and Chou did.[70]

One of the settings in which Nu and Nehru met was at meetings of the group of South and Southeast Asian countries known as the "Colombo Powers"—which, according to Nu, "at moments of crisis has been able to exercise a moderating influence and help avert catastrophe for mankind." The first meeting of the Colombo Powers— Indonesia, Pakistan, Ceylon, India, and Burma—took place in late April and early May 1954 and resulted in a communiqué that vigorously supported efforts to obtain peace in Indochina at the Geneva Conference then in session. At subsequent meetings, views on the Anglo-French-Israeli invasion of Suez were shared, Soviet intervention in Hungary was discussed, and groundwork was laid for the 1955 Afro-Asian Bandung Conference. According to Nu, the latter meeting "made history by proclaiming to a startled world that Asia and Africa had come of age and were now ready and able and determined to play their part in deciding the future of the world."[71] The five Colombo countries disagreed over Communist China's participation at Bandung, but Nu insisted that China be invited. He even went so far as to say that Burmese participation was doubtful if the Chinese were not invited.[72] Nu also fought for the inclusion of Israel, first with Nehru's support and then alone, but unsuccessfully.[73]

U Nu did not deliver the speech he had prepared for the opening of the Bandung Conference—because of impatience to get on with the business of the meeting—but it was printed and circulated. In it, he said:

> Man . . . is now at the cross-roads. The stupendous advances of science face him with the alternatives of total annihilation or unprecedented prosperity. But in this form, it seems strange that there should be any doubt as to which he will choose. But the sad fact is that the doubt does exist. The choice has still to be made. The countries which are represented at this Conference, with more than half of the world's population between them, could play an influential and even decisive role in the making of this choice. It is my earnest prayer that we shall be able to rise to our individual and collective responsibility not only to ourselves, but to future unborn generations who run the risk of remaining forever unborn unless the present generation chooses right.[74]

The twenty-nine-nation Bandung Conference produced a 5,000-word communiqué which—not surprisingly—roundly condemned colonialism and also emphasized economic cooperation among the participating states. U Nu's role at the meeting was a fairly active one and included secret talks with China and other nations about the still unsettled problem of Indochina. He was also a strong supporter of a declaration calling for the lifting of the United Nations trade embargo against Communist China. This problem (among others) produced divisions among the participating countries along cold war lines, which Nu found disturbing. Behind the scenes, Nu endeavored to fashion some kind of accord out of this disunity and to draw the several Asian nations, in particular, closer together[75]—with limited success. Nu also opposed efforts by the Arab countries to obtain the support of the Bandung Conference for their position in the quarrel with Israel. But he was unable to keep the Israeli issue out of the final communiqué, although he did bring about a considerable modification of the Middle East passage in that declaration.

At the Bandung Conference Nu played a more important role in private than at the public sessions, where he said little.[76] Even privately, however, Nu "seemed bored frequently when talk focused on details. He was at his best in talks with important political leaders—like Premiers Nehru and Chou En-lai—or when conciliation was called for."[77] His voice was probably one of the more influential ones raised at Bandung (despite his defeat on such questions as the Israeli issue), and he "seemed to gain in stature" as Indian Prime Minister Nehru appeared to falter (as a result of his annoyance over the same cold war differences that disturbed Nu).[78]

Indonesia, site of the 1955 Bandung Conference, was the first of the nations of Southeast Asia with which U Nu's government developed close relations. Nu himself proposed the 1949 New Delhi Conference on Indonesia, and his government banned Dutch planes from flying over Burma during the military action against the Indonesians—an action repeated with respect to the French during the late stages of the French-Indochinese war. Indonesia subsequently became an important customer for Burmese rice, an active participant in the Colombo Powers group (the only other Southeast Asian nation among these countries), and the main moving force behind the Bandung meeting.

The genuineness of U Nu's quest for peace was illustrated by his efforts in the middle 1950's to develop friendly relations with neighboring Thailand, traditionally an enemy as well as a country that followed a foreign policy of alignment with the West in contrast to Burma's neutralism. Relations between the two countries seriously deteriorated in 1953, after the accidental bombing of Thai territory by Burmese military aircraft pursuing Chinese Nationalist forces. Thai Prime Minister Phibun Songkhram spoke publicly of Burma's "general unfriendliness," and dispatched anti-aircraft units to the border. Stopping in Bangkok in late 1954, en route to a Colombo Powers meeting in Bogor, Indonesia, Nu disarmingly apologized for past Burmese "misdeeds" against Thailand, such as the sacking of its onetime capital of Ayuthia in pre-colonial times. Subsequently, in 1955, Nu and Thai Premier Phibun exchanged visits, and in October of that year Burma waived all claims on Thailand for damages suffered during World War II, in view of the new "friendly relations between the two countries."

The conclusion of the 1954 Geneva Conference on Indochina, which ended French colonial rule there, was followed by Burma's recognition of the states of Cambodia and Laos (Theravada Buddhist lands like both Burma and Thailand). King Norodom Sihanouk of Cambodia visited Rangoon shortly thereafter, and Nu stopped off in the Cambodian capital of Phnom Penh on his way back from China later the same year. Laotian Premier Prince Souvanna Phouma was subsequently a guest in Rangoon.

Although Nu's government extended *de jure* recognition to both Cambodia and Laos, it accorded only *de facto* recognition to Communist North and non-Communist South Vietnam. The 1954 Geneva meeting —at which the non-Communist Vietnamese were not represented— agreed on elections by 1956 to re-unify the country, but South Vietnam's Ngo Dinh Diem claimed that free elections were not possible. Nu publicly called on Diem to allow elections, even if this meant a Communist victory.[79] Despite disagreement on this question, in 1956 Nu accepted an invitation to visit President Diem in Saigon and "found him an outstanding person."[80] Diem, in turn, visited Nu in Rangoon in 1957. But Nu also met with North Vietnamese leaders in both Hanoi and Rangoon and expressed the highest regard for the Communist leader Ho Chi Minh.

The inauguration of diplomatic relations with Japan, Burma's wartime ruler, was delayed by the Nu government's refusal in 1951 to sign the multination Japanese peace treaty encouraged by the United States because, as Nu put it, "We felt that it did not sufficiently take into account our reparations claims against Japan." The state of war between the two countries was officially ended on April 2, 1952, however, and a reparations agreement and peace treaty were signed on November 5, 1954. Under the former agreement Japan agreed to provide reparations in the form of products and services worth $250,000,000 over a period of ten years. "I would not be frank were I to say that we were completely satisfied with this agreement," Nu told the Chamber of Deputies in September 1957. "Compared with the damage done by the war in our country, the amount was small. But we had to be realistic. We were not the only country which had claims against Japan."[81] Later, however, Burma felt that it had struck a bad bargain in view of Japanese settlements with other countries, and sought additional reparations.

After the threat of insurrection had been reduced, Burma's government assumed a more active role in international affairs, and U Nu sought to mediate the differences between the leading nations of the two great power blocs. In a speech on New Year's Day 1955, Nu stated that he would seek, as a mediator, to save what he could of the world's shipwreck. Nu had already begun his own personal attempt to bridge the gulf separating Communist China and the United States with his warm remarks about Americans during his visit to Peiping in 1954. On his way back from China in December, Nu said publicly that he would visit Washington on a "peacemaker mission" if the United States invited him; "I have strong reasons to believe the Formosan question can be solved peacefully," he stated.[82] Chinese Premier Chou En-lai had assured him, Nu declared, that if the United States made the friendly gesture of sending a good-will mission to Peiping, it would be well received. At a subsequent press conference in Rangoon, Nu said that he had a "definite plan" for promoting a Sino-American *rapprochement*, "but it would be premature to disclose it."[83]

During his talks with American leaders in Washington, Nu has stated, he "suggested the advisability of direct negotiations between the representatives of Peiping and of Formosa towards peaceful settlement of the Formosan problem."[84] Nu also recommended "diplomatic talks between the United States and China."[85] The Burmese Premier told the National Press Club in Washington that his government was willing to mediate the Formosan dispute if requested to do so by Peiping and Washington. Indeed Nu has stated, "I even went a step further," offering to "arrange a meeting of representatives of Peiping and Washington."[86] The result, according to Nu, was the ambassadorial conversations (between the United States and Communist China) in Geneva.

Another of Nu's efforts to mediate international differences was his suggestion to the United States during the period of the correspondence between President Eisenhower and Soviet Defense Minister Marshal Georgy Zhukov that the American government invite Zhukov to Washington for "discussions at the highest level, particularly disarmament. This particular project failed."[87] In 1955, Nu was successful in arranging talks between the government of adjacent Laos and the leader of the rebel (Communist) Pathet Lao movement, Prince Souvannavong, although the talks did not result in an immediate reconciliation between estranged Laotian political factions. En route to the United States in 1955, Nu stated in the Middle East that he was willing to seek to mediate Arab-Israeli differences, "if both sides want it."[88] Nu also sought on more than one occasion to ease the ruffled relations between India and Pakistan.[89]

"U Nu was his own Foreign Minister—it was he who made Burma's foreign policy. His colleagues influenced him—occasionally even got him to change his mind. But he made foreign policy—not the Foreign Office, not the Cabinet, not the party." So stated a former member of Nu's immediate official staff, and a personal friend, in 1959.[90] "He is regularly briefed, primarily on 'hot spots,' by the Foreign Office, which is his chief source of information about Burma's external relations," James Barrington, formerly Permanent Secretary of the Foreign Office, has said.[91] "U Thant is probably the only man who can be said to have been a personal adviser in the foreign field," according to a top official under Nu. "Barrington was the permanent official with the closest contact with him, but he was never a personal adviser," another has said.

Burma's Cabinet had a Subcommittee for Foreign Affairs (and others for several other policy areas). Nu, who played a leading role in forming foreign policy, chaired this committee. Foreign policy questions also were discussed regularly in the E.C., but not always with Nu's blessing.

According to U Kyaw Nyein,

When U Nu went to Peiping in late 1956 in his capacity as President of the AFPFL, he did not seek—indeed, he refused—a briefing on the border question from Foreign Minister Sao Hkun Hkio, who had asked to fill him in on various details. The Foreign Office was definitely worried about what Nu might do in China, and so were various members of the E.C. I was more or less the person on the E.C. who concerned himself with foreign affairs, and I took it upon myself to deliver a 45-minute briefing on the border question as part of the E.C. meeting preceding Nu's departure on his trip. Otherwise, he would have gone to China singularly uninformed.

According to Kyaw Nyein, Nu took matters into his own hands in Peiping, even though he was no longer Premier. "Nu was clearly instructed not to negotiate. He could discuss anything he wanted, but the E.C. told him not to bargain. Yet he did. He came back and announced that he and Chou En-lai had agreed that three Kachin villages would go to China."[92]

U Myint Thein, formerly Ambassador to China and later Chief Justice of the Supreme Court, has also stated that "U Nu made his own foreign policy—perhaps too much of it." According to Justice Myint Thein, "This explains some of the difficulties he got into with his colleagues. He agreed, for example, to the so-called Soviet 'gift projects' on his own and committed us to many, many more *lakhs* than we should be spending on such activity."

Myint Thein has also said that U Nu "had all but consummated a border agreement with the Chinese before his ouster from office in 1958, but Kyaw Nyein kept blocking it." He has explained, "Kyaw Nyein did not want to give the Chinese anything in return for the Namwan Assigned Tract. I do not think it was a matter of principle. I think he just wanted to keep Nu from getting the credit. Ne Win was able to get Kyaw Nyein's—as well as Nu's and Ba Swe's—acquiescence during the 1958–60 military caretaker government, and that is why we got a border pact with China under the military administration and not previously."[93]

Kyaw Nyein's remarks about the "new imperialism," at the 1954 Kalaw conference of the Anti-Colonial Bureau of the Asian Socialist Organization, suggested to some a foreign policy orientation different from Nu's, but this was not true. Although more outspoken than Nu on the subject of Communist imperialism, Kyaw Nyein was nonetheless a vigorous advocate of a policy of nonalignment with either of the two major power blocs.

Nu himself has admitted that Burma's foreign policy was influenced by India's, stating that Burma wanted to recognize Communist China before it actually did so but postponed doing so at the request of Indian Premier Nehru.[94] According to Nehru, however, Nu "was not a follower in international meetings in which I participated with him. He had definite ideas of his own and pursued them."[95]

Nu also developed close personal ties with Communist Chinese

Premier Chou En-lai, and some have suggested (Kyaw Nyein, for example) that Nu frequently fell victim to the charm and persuasive powers of Chou. However, U Myint Thein, former Ambassador to Peiping, has said:

> U Nu unquestionably regards Chou as a close personal friend. Without doubt he believes Chou likes him. Yet this does not prevent him from identifying what he regards as the Burmese national interest, pursuing it, and questioning Chinese intentions toward Burma. He spoke out in a way in Communist China in 1954, for example, that practically no one else would have dared to do. Can a man as good-hearted and sincere as Nu, a man so lacking in sinister intention, really understand, and effectively deal with, a man like the Communist Chou En-lai? That is a big question. It is one I have often thought about. I suppose that one might argue that a negative reply is almost inevitably in order, but personally I would not give such a reply. I think Nu can hold his own with Chou.[96]

"There are good and bad points in every nation," Nu said in 1952. "Why, then, must we join any group when these are all devoid of the right outlook and are consciously or unconsciously trying to destroy the world?"[97] The big powers "are not working for the interests and benefit of anyone else," Nu observed. "They are working purely for their own interests."[98]

Burma, as Nu saw it, was "hemmed in like a tender gourd among the cactuses."[99] Emphasizing the good qualities of Burma's neighbors, including China, Nu sought cordial relations both with countries of like orientation, such as India, and with countries that had different approaches to the cold war and other important questions, such as Thailand. In his attempt to lift relations among nations to a higher plane, Nu endeavored to convince such neighbors and other states, particularly the big powers, that war in the mid-twentieth century was impractical in addition to being morally indefensible. The basic principle in U Nu's foreign policy, *The Nation* stated in 1955, is that external interference in Burma's affairs "can be avoided if this country shows its sincerity and determination to live in peace with the rest of the world, regardless of differing ideologies in various countries."[100] Neutrality, Nu told a National Day mass rally in 1954, had saved Burma from becoming a second Korea, Indochina, or Guatemala when Chinese Nationalist troops were present on her soil.[101] Another war, he said at Bandung, might make "redemption impossible," even if a given country "should be spared total annihilation"[102]—a reference to the drying up of sources of foreign aid, among other consequences of such a war.

The policy of good relations with all nations was clearly a reflection of Nu's Buddhist ideological orientation.[103] International understanding and cordiality among nations were more than a matter of self-interest. Tolerance and forbearance were qualities taught by Buddhism, and Nu sought to apply these to Burma's relations with other countries. Burma's close ties with Ceylon stemmed largely from their common religion. Nu also stated once that he found in the Israeli *kibbutz* the same kind of denial of the "ego" that characterized Buddhism.[104] Burma's relations with Israel were extremely cordial—as were those with Yugoslavia (chiefly for ideological reasons in both cases).

Although a strong believer in the value of "close personal contacts among peoples" and an outspoken supporter of disarmament, Nu admitted that such means alone could not bring about world peace.[105] Nu assessed the value of summit meetings conservatively when he observed in 1955 of the meeting of the Chiefs of State of the United States, the U.S.S.R., Britain, and France:

> As I see it, the world today is like a clock whose spring has been wound so tight that it is in danger of snapping if an attempt were made to wind it any tighter. Equally, any attempt to release the spring suddenly is likely to cause it to snap. In this situation what is required is to let the spring unwind itself slowly and gradually so that the clock keeps on ticking all the time. The Geneva Conference could represent the moment at which the spring of the clock *begins* to unwind itself.[106]

PART FOUR

❁

END OF AN ERA

❁

SIXTEEN

THE FIRST COUP

THE 1958 SPLIT in the AFPFL changed the character of the Burmese party system significantly. During the three-and-a-half months of the government of Premier U Nu and Deputy Premier Thakin Tin, Burma had a multiparty system in fact for the first time since independence. It also had bad government—the worst of any in the first decade following release from colonial rule.

During this period, U Nu's chief political ally was Thakin Tin. A traditionalist in most ways, despite his Marxist economic outlook,[1] Tin enjoyed a somewhat unsavory reputation—which was in part undeserved. Tin was a good organizer, and he carried out the AFPFL government's land nationalization policies with a minimum of corruption for Burma. Moreover, of Burma's top leaders at the time of the split, only Nu himself lived more modestly than Thakin Tin.[2]

Nu's other political associates during this period were a varied lot, and included many opportunists who had no difficulty changing their economic and political philosophies whenever they saw the possibility of personal gain. However, Bo Hmu Aung, a leader of the PVO faction that had remained with the AFPFL, shared U Nu's increasingly traditionalist orientation, and was loyal, though outspoken, in his relations with Nu. U Ohn's influence on Nu was generally minimized by both Nu's political friends and his foes, but, Dr. E Maung stated in 1960, "Ohn was probably the person closest to Nu personally, seeing him more frequently than any of the rest of us."[3] E Maung himself, plain-spoken like Bo Hmu Aung, was another of the most influential persons in Nu's entourage; he was competent, and conservative in his economic philosophy. Thakin Kyaw Tun, protégé of Thakin Tin (and later detained for alleged involvement in a political kidnapping and murder), was another traditionalist ally of Nu, to whom he promised more moral behavior in the future. U Raschid remained a confidant, too, although he was also concerned with his personal business ventures throughout this period. Bo Min Gaung (ex-PVO), Chan Tha (a recruit to politics from the bureaucracy), the respected Daw Khin Kyi (widow of Aung San), and U Win also helped Nu during the Nu-Tin period.

The opposition to the Nu-Tin, or "Clean" AFPFL, government was led by U Ba Swe and U Kyaw Nyein. Ba Swe became President of the "Stable" AFPFL, which included a majority of the AFPFL M.P.'s as well as of the party's Supreme Council, in addition to 20 of the 22 Parliamentary Secretaries in the pre-split government. But the "Stable" was denied many of the means of expression available to the opposition in developed democracies, much as the pre-split AFPFL had denied the use of the state-operated radio and other facilities to its political opponents in the past.

The denial of such facilities to the opposition "Stable" AFPFL was indicative of the tactics of the Nu-Tin government. Much of what the "Clean" AFPFL did, however, was what any government in power would have done, and surely what the "Stable" itself would have done. Opposition parliamentary and private secretaries and members of government boards, councils, and committees were removed, and the newly formed pro-"Clean" Union Labor Organization was distinctly favored over the "Stable" Trade Union Congress (Burma.)[4] Although the Swe-Nyein party held majorities in the Kachin and Karen State Councils, Nu selected pro-"Clean" ministers as Heads of State. Because the Kachin, Karen, and other ministers were members of the central government as well as heads of their own state administrations, Nu's move was probably politically necessary. Less defensible were the directive ordering all public libraries to stop subscriptions to the pro-"Stable" *Mandaing Daily,* onetime official organ of the united AFPFL, and the fact that many of the policies of the Nu-Tin government, particularly its intentionally obvious favoritism toward the pro-"Clean" labor organization, were almost certain to result in violence.[5]

During the time his government was moving to undercut the strength of the "Stable" party as much as possible, Nu was talking of ways of lessening internal conflict in the country.[6] Partly to distract the Communists from their policy of revolt, he proposed a national convention, which would include as participants members of both factions of the AFPFL as well as of other opposition groups, and the insurrectionists (if they surrendered), to draft a "national charter" that would define the rights and duties of the government, the opposition, and all organizations and individuals in a Burmese democracy. Such a document, he stated, would become an ethical yardstick for all Burmese and the "foundation of democracy" in the country. Attacking his own past administration for basing policy on consultation with too few people, Nu promised to broaden the basis of policy formation and execution. More than 2,000 representatives of 16 different fields, including business, industry, religion, labor, art, journalism, education, and government, attended an eight-day consultative conference on national planning held in July. The conference was labeled a psychological device to allow people to "let off steam"[7] and a "clever stunt, just before the elections, to win votes for his party,"[8] but Nu probably genuinely believed, as he put it, that this was a way to right past wrongs and set an effective course for Burma in the future.

Nu's political position, however, was precarious. A change of only four votes in the Chamber of Deputies would have cost him his parliamentary majority.* The consultative conference was also unquestionably designed to increase support for Nu by presenting him as a leader who was aware of his past mistakes and sought to make amends.[9] The Nu-Tin government's desire to make itself attractive to the left by acting to end the insurrections and establish internal peace was part of the same general design. Hundreds of *détenus,* mainly students and political suspects, were released by the government; the re-instatement of students expelled from schools for political reasons was officially encouraged; and Nu-Tin ministers revealed themselves more tolerant of far leftist views and were more accessible to all sections of Burmese political opinion. U Nu clearly was endeavoring to broaden the base of his political support—by including in his government such conservatives as the able Dr. E Maung of the Justice Party and representatives of minority interests (e.g., the also conservative U Kyaw Min of the Arakanese National United Organization) at the same time that he was making such an obvious bid for backing from the left. Many of those who came to occupy government posts during the Nu-Tin period were persons Nu would have called "bad hats" in the past.[10] Hence it is not surprising that many of the policies of the Nu-Tin government were ambiguous.[11]

Planning an election in which the country would choose between

* According to U Ba Swe, Nu had lost his majority by mid-July.

the "Stable" AFPFL and his faction of the party, Nu took to the political stump—accompanied by Daw Khin Kyi, widow of the revered Aung San, among others. Nu talked largely of the "five precepts," the others of politics. The last of these tours started on September 4 and ended September 22, absenting Nu from Rangoon during one of the most critical periods in the politics of independent Burma.

Nu's stumping was accompanied by attempts to expand the membership and activities of the satellite Union Labor Organization, Union Youth League, and other such bodies. Nu's longtime friend U Raschid and the aggressive Bo Min Gaung directed the "Clean" AFPFL's organizational efforts in the labor field, and it was widely reported that Nu also intended to develop a mass organization after the model of Thakin Tin's ABPO or U Ba Swe's TUC(B).[12] But Nu did not do so—presumably for the reasons that underlay his prior denunciation of personal political organizations. Moreover, the task of seeking to organize practically all types of associations throughout the country on a pro-"Clean" basis—in opposition to the "Stable" AFPFL—occupied the time and energies of Raschid, Bo Min Gaung, and the others. The result of these efforts was to split every past AFPFL affiliate into competing factions—right down to the grass roots level. In an amazingly short time, every town and village in the land came to have its "Clean" and its "Stable" organization.

The insecurity of U Nu's support in the Chamber of Deputies, where he had won the no-confidence vote of June 9 by only eight votes, led directly to a major constitutional wrangle in August. The approaching end of Burma's official fiscal year meant that U Nu needed a new budget, but defeat in the legislature on one or more sections of his budget would not serve Nu or his party well in the anticipated elections. The National Unity Front, which in order to retain Nu's dependence on its support was trying to avoid dissolution of the Parliament, proposed an all-party compromise budget—to which Nu turned a deaf ear. On July 28 Nu made a surprise announcement that the Chamber of Deputies would meet in budget session on August 28, and the Chamber of Nationalities, the upper and less important house, on September 15. Even more unexpectedly, he declared on August 19 that the budget session had been canceled and that the budget would be passed by presidential ordinance; clearly Nu felt that he had lost his parliamentary majority.[13] On September 22, the day he returned from an apparently beneficial 18-day political tour of the Kachin State, Nu announced that the Parliament would be dissolved September 29, the budget proclaimed by ordinance September 30, and elections held in November. Despite Swe-Nyein charges to the contrary, Nu's actions were probably constitutional, though possibly not in keeping with the democratic spirit of Burma's basic law. Nu's goal was clear: political survival for himself and the values he cherished, even if it meant endangering those very values by the tactics he chose.

The "aboveground Communists" played a balancing role in the Chamber of Deputies, much to Nu's political distaste, and now the Communists in revolt seemed capable also of shifting the balance of power in the country at large. The split in the AFPFL had been followed almost immediately by a more belligerent attitude on the part of the Communist rebels, who took heart from the division in the ranks of the anti-Communists. The hard-pressed insurgents had written Nu clandestinely just before the split in a more conciliatory spirit than on any previous occasion since the outbreak of their insurrection in 1948.[14] Nu's AFPFL government had turned down Thakin Than Tun's offer to "come in" on March 28, the tenth anniversary of the Communist resort to arms, because Than Tun had not yet renounced the policy of armed struggle. Than Tun wrote to Nu again the day the break-up of the AFPFL was announced in April,[15] and on May 20, he sent a particularly arrogant note demanding face-to-face negotiations (instead of obeying the demand of Nu and the AFPFL that he surrender). Than Tun even insisted that his rebel army be made legal.[16]

After the defeat of the no-confidence vote against him on June 9, U Nu, it has been charged, paid his debt to the NUF by opening new negotiations with the Communist rebels and promising them complete amnesty, party legalization, and new elections.[17] Nu made such promises, but not as repayment to the NUF and not without demanding that the Communists disavow their policy of armed revolt, cut all connections with any of their comrades remaining underground, and participate in a national convention to draw up a charter reaffirming the principles that "the sovereign power of the Union of Burma lies with the people" and that the "Government derives its legislative, administrative and judicial powers from the people." Nu was fully aware of the risks involved in his policy. "Although the insurgents may give up their arms, they may do it only in token form," he admitted. His government, as a result, would be "the target of a two-pronged attack from both the underground forces and the section that has come into the light."[18] The unsatisfactory Communist reply took the form of an offer to meet with Nu on equal terms to reach a political settlement.

On July 31, despite the uncompromising response of the Communists, the government promulgated a decree granting full amnesty to all surrendering insurgents for crimes committed during the insurrections and promising to restore all political and other rights upon their renouncing the policy of rebellion.

Accused of appeasing the Communists, Nu subsequently stated:

> To get peace, I did my best in granting amnesties and concessions to the insurgents. I do not deny this. But, whatever amnesty we gave, and whatever concession we made, I always consulted the Army and secured their concurrence first. . . . I went even to the length of showing all my announcements and all my speeches concerning the insurgents to the Army leaders, and issued the announcements only after their concurrence had been obtained and delivered the speeches only after the Army leaders had made the changes they wanted to make in the speeches. . . . I was convinced that, if we could manage to get peace as quickly as possible, the danger of the country turning Communist would be averted.[19]

Most of the remaining rebel PVO's (numbering several hundred) quickly surrendered, renounced rebellion, took the name of the People's Comrade Party (PCP), were legalized, and shortly thereafter announced their intention to work for the establishment of a Communist state. Nu hoped to win the support of some of the PCP. But the PCP and its friends inside and outside the "Clean" AFPFL seemed more concerned with discrediting the anti-Communist Army, thereby driving an important wedge between U Nu and the military.[20] Nu did not name any of the Communist members of the NUF or the PCP to positions in his government, however. The only other insurgent group surrendering in large numbers at this time was the Mon People's Front, which (like the Karen rebels of earlier years) sought a separate state in the Union. More than a thousand Mon rebels turned themselves in— less because of the amnesty apparently than in response to U Nu's promise to facilitate the creation of a Mon state if a majority of the Mons wanted one. Nu had earlier made a similar promise to the Arakanese as part of his effort to enlarge the ranks of his supporters. The Mons, however, had never posed a security threat as large as that of the insurgent Karens, Communists, or PVO's.

Nu remained anti-Communist, and the anti-Communist Army leaders realized this, but many of the top military figures still questioned the wisdom of Nu's policies toward the Communists. Many soldiers (and others) believed that Nu's concessions only encouraged the Communists to demand more concessions.[21] According to Nu himself, "Some people spread the rumor that these concessions were intended to pave the way for an alliance between us and the Communists, and the anxieties within the Army grew all the greater."[22] The 1958 amnesty, however, resulted in an immediate, if short-lived, improvement in the security situation of the country,[23] but some of the above-ground leftist elements continued to demand face-to-face negotiations with the insurgent Than Tun Communists.

Burma's Army made no move in support of either the "Clean" or "Stable" faction at the time of the AFPFL split in April 1958, although General Ne Win warned both groups against the use of violence. Military neutrality in the political struggle, however, did not extend to the Communists. The Army's mounting distrust of U Nu's attitude toward the NUF, the PCP, and the Communist insurgents following the split was matched by a growing fear on the part of the "Clean" AFPFL that the military leaders were sympathetic to its "Stable" rival. General Ne Win cautioned U Nu against relying on NUF backing in the legislature, and he vigorously rejected suggestions that surrendered rebels be inducted into the Armed Forces.[24] Ne Win also warned Army personnel against becoming involved in political quarrels. However, the attempt by the Armed Forces to abolish the *pyusawhtis,* a popular militia formed earlier to help fight the insurgents, could not help but involve the military in the political rivalries, since some *pyusawhtis* were armed supporters of the contestants in the struggle for power.

The second echelon of leaders of the "Clean" AFPFL, clearly infiltrated by some individuals with Communist leanings, would not allow the Army to remain aloof from politics, and sought actively to discredit the military both in order to reduce the importance of an alleged "Stable" ally and to increase the likelihood that some of their political sympathizers still in revolt would regain legal status.[25] The Army, indeed, was labeled Public Enemy Number One at a "Clean" convention in U Nu's official compound in early September—a label that Nu subsequently denied in a radio broadcast. A widening break in the ranks of the NUF indicated that support for Nu from this quarter was weakening. The Army, meanwhile, charged pro-Communist elements with plotting a *coup* against the Nu-Tin government, encouraged by the leniency of that government.[26]

Nu's intentions seemed clear enough. As late as September 26, the day of the Army *coup, The Nation* predicted editorially that elections would be held before November 28. Nu's intentions notwithstanding, the political situation deteriorated almost daily throughout September, reaching seemingly explosive proportions. The event that brought the tension to a head was the attempt to transport to Rangoon pro-"Clean" units of the para-military Union Military Police (UMP) from Mandalay—significantly, perhaps, while Nu himself was on tour of Upper Burma.[27] The UMP elements fell within the jurisdiction of the ambitious Bo Min Gaung, and it was he, apparently, who was primarily responsible for the troop movements. By mid-September the Army was visibly more partial to the "Stable" party, and Bo Min Gaung and some other second-line leaders wanted pro-"Clean" armed personnel in the Rangoon area. A person very close to Nu quoted Nu on the eve of the change of governments as saying of UMP units outside his residence, "I don't know whether they're here to guard me, or what."[28] Nu had earlier disclaimed any knowledge of anti-Army statements in many of the speeches at the all-Burma convention of his "Clean" AFPFL the first week of September. "It is clearly possible that he did not know what was going on while he was in Upper Burma on tour," a leading journalist has said. "But surely he knew at least some of what was happening after his return."[29]

U Nu returned to Rangoon on September 22 with the avowed intention of keeping a promise made to his friend and counsellor U Ohn: he would retire to a monastery to meditate and rest.[30] He arrived at two in the afternoon and convened a Cabinet meeting two hours later "to dispose of all important matters" before proceeding to "keep continuous sabbath for a number of days."[31] This session of the Cabinet decided to dissolve the Parliament on September 29. The budget would then be passed by presidential ordinance the next day, and general elections would be held in November.

According to Nu, about half an hour after the meeting had started he received a message from Bo Min Gaung's residence asking him and Bo Hmu Aung to go there immediately. Bo Ming Gaung wanted the Cabinet session adjourned immediately, but Nu would not adjourn it because, he said, he did not want any flurry.

> When only I myself, and such AFPFL leaders as Thakin Tin, Bo Hmu Aung, and Thakin Kyaw Tun were left and others had gone, Bo Min Gaung told us that he had it from a reliable source that there would be a *coup d'état* by the Army, and that arrangements had already been made in Rangoon and the districts for such a *coup*.

He said that the *coup* would take place that night. Nu tried to contact General Ne Win, but Ne Win was at a party. So Nu retired for the night with only the instruction to the security officer at his official residence not to take any action "without awakening me and getting orders."[32]

The next day Nu met with Colonel Maung Maung, one of Ne Win's top aides, who told him that all Army units had been alerted, since it was rumored that General Ne Win, Maung Maung himself, and other leading soldiers would be assassinated, that the government would then disband the Army, and the surrendered People's Comrade Party would rearm, raid, and occupy key positions.[33] Colonel Maung Maung said later that "the Army knew of the widespread existence of arms and ammunition in Burma before the change of governments, but the politicians, especially on the local level, kept us from doing anything about it."[34] The weapons were hidden by surrendered insurgent elements, the Army claimed, for later use against the government. The movement of UMP elements into Rangoon (frequently in disguise and their presence inexplicable even by the Inspector-General of Police) and the shifting of Karen rebel headquarters to within nine miles of the capital city,[35] the flight of families from the town of Khayan to Rangoon (recalling the refugees of 1948–49) and messages to the main newspapers of troop movements in various parts of the country,[36] Communist rebel boldness in moving nearer Rangoon and the fact that weapons were known to be hidden (particularly in the area between Prome and Rangoon) seemed to set the stage for a return to the chaotic conditions of a decade earlier. Civil war among the anti-Communists was a real possibility; indeed, fighting had already taken place between followers of Thakin Tin and those of U Kyaw Nyein.[37] "Surely," one of Rangoon's most respected foreign diplomats has said, "U Nu and the rest knew that Ne Win and the Army could not put up with this sort of thing."[38]

On September 26, 1958, when the city of Rangoon was almost completely encircled by Army units—and these, in turn, were surrounded by Union Military Police—U Nu announced that he had asked General Ne Win, Commander-in-Chief of Burma's Armed Forces, to form a caretaker government. Bo Min Gaung, as Home Minister, ordered the UMP action, but the fact that he was not prosecuted under the subsequent military government would seem to suggest that this was a defensive action rather than an attempt at a *coup* of his own (as many in Burma have suggested). According to "Clean" Minister Dr. E Maung:

> The Army moved first, but not on orders from Ne Win, Maung Maung or Aung Gyi, but at the initiative of younger officers, many of whom were related to the Swe-Nyein faction. These officers

forced the issue with Maung Maung and Aung Gyi [and hence with Ne Win], who had to move to get Nu out or suffer serious consequences within the Army.[39]

Nu himself publicly ascribed the Army's action to concern over the weapons the surrendered PCP's had concealed before turning themselves in. "I was told of these events within three to four hours of my return on September 22," he has stated. "I therefore called the Army authorities in and asked them questions. They said the Army harbored very deep suspicions, but that they were doing everything to control the situation." Nu has said that he asked himself, "after their departure, whether in such a situation free and fair elections would be possible."[40] Aung Gyi's version of the change of governments was that he and Maung Maung visited Nu to complain of the deteriorating security situation. Nu replied by asking them if they knew anyone to whom he might turn over power for a caretaker period during which law and order could be restored and free elections held. "They gulped and said, 'Why yes, as a matter of fact there is—General Ne Win.' "[41]

Colonels Maung Maung and Aung Gyi visited Nu on September 24, and the decision was made to establish a caretaker government headed by Ne Win. A formal exchange of letters between Nu and Ne Win took place on September 26, and that evening Nu made a public announcement of the transfer of authority. According to U Nu's letter to Ne Win, the main purpose of the caretaker administration was "to provide all the necessary conditions and requirements that would ensure the holding of a free and fair general election before the end of April 1959."[42] All this can be fully documented.

In a press conference on September 30, U Nu himself vigorously insisted that his exchange of letters with General Ne Win described things as they actually happened; he had asked Ne Win to form an interim government to prepare for free and fair elections, and he had advised the President to summon the Chamber of Deputies to meet on October 28 to receive his resignation. But Dr. Ba Maw, Burma's wartime Premier, termed the change of governments a "*coup* by consent."[43] According to Deputy Premier Thakin Tin, "Maung Maung and Aung Gyi discussed with U Nu the problems of the day, and Nu came up with the answer to the situation. He was not told to get out."[44]

One of the persons closest to Nu at the time said subsequently: "Yes, Nu almost had to go along. It was he, however, who supplied the formula for the switch—because of his strong desire to maintain the forms of democratic government. He probably could have held out a little longer. But there might have been bloodshed. Also, if he had been toppled in an outright *coup,* there would be the question of the legitimacy of the successor government. This would not have augured well for the stability of Burma politically, and so Nu went along."[45]

General Ne Win apparently did not initiate the change of governments. In their conversations with Nu, Maung Maung and Aung Gyi were Ne Win's advocates at first, not his emissaries. On the other hand, as one of the more able foreign ambassadors in Rangoon put it, "Ne Win did not become Prime Minister just because two of his chief lieutenants wanted him to."[46] His decision was apparently a reluctant one, however. He consented to the *coup* only when he became convinced that there was no other way to avoid splitting both the Army and the country. Ne Win was not a politically ambitious person; indeed, he was more than a little on the lazy side. The 1958 *coup* was not a grab for power for its own sake—at least not by Ne Win.

Nu's decision to turn over the reins of government to Ne Win was his own.[47] At his September 30 press conference, he stated that his tour of Upper Burma had raised doubts about the wisdom of holding early elections in view of the shootings, killings, and general sense of insecurity throughout the country. As he put it, "Democracy works in such a way that leaders must act frequently on their own. When I go abroad I often sign agreements on my own. When I return I put the matter up before the Cabinet. If the Cabinet disagrees I have to resign. But we do have to shoulder responsibility and do things unilaterally."[48]

According to Dr. E Maung of the Nu-Tin government, "Nu asked us what to do at a meeting of the Cabinet—that is, he told us of the approach of Aung Gyi and Maung Maung and his desire to ask Ne Win to form a government. I said impetuously, 'Hell, no! Let's fight this thing out!' Nu strongly implied that this was not a very wise course of action."[49]

The Arakanese politician U Kyaw Min, also a Minister in the Nu-Tin government but not a member of the "Clean" AFPFL, has stated of this important Cabinet meeting:

> Nu announced that he had something to say and told us of his offer to General Ne Win and Ne Win's acceptance. We were astounded —that is, the non-"Clean" members of the Cabinet [the "Clean" people obviously already knew]. E Maung asked: "Why wasn't the Cabinet consulted?" Nu said that there was no chance. It was put to him point blank: he had to decide.[50]

"The amazing thing," the ANUO's Kyaw Min has said, "was that U Nu—with a *coup* staring him in the face—had said in effect, 'All right, you can have your *coup* but not until next month.' "

Publicly, Nu declared, as he prepared to leave office, "There is no failure of democracy and no question of its abandonment. There is no Western type. Democracy took hold in the West after many painful years. It will take time here. As for guided democracy, I don't believe in it."[51]

On October 28 General Ne Win took office as Prime Minister of Burma, and immediately formed a non-parliamentary Cabinet of 14 persons—only five of whom, representing the state governments, were politicians. The others were judges, civil servants, or educators. Ne Win himself was the only soldier in the Cabinet.

❀

SEVENTEEN

THE COMEBACK

THE SITUATION inherited by General Ne Win from the civilian politicians was chaotic. Security conditions in the country were the worst they had been since the dark days of 1949–51. By September 1958, government in Burma had all but come to a standstill, political considerations were seemingly the only ones that influenced official decision-making, and the public was obviously and increasingly losing confidence in the ability of the Nu-Tin administration to direct the nation's affairs. In addition there remained the chronic problems of indecisiveness in policy formation and ineffectiveness in implementing government decisions. Burma needed a new—and steadier—hand.

The governance of Burma under the Ne Win caretaker administration was efficient, honest, frequently inspiring, and equally often frightening in its authoritarian character. The insurrections were reduced in importance, but by no means eliminated, as a result of the more efficient direction of, and the elimination of political interference with, the anti-rebel military effort. Divisional and district security councils were established throughout the country, giving local military commanders new authority to coordinate anti-insurgent activity within their jurisdictions. The number of insurgents was reduced by about 5,000 persons, or nearly one-half. The reduction would have been greater except for the rebellion of some Shans (largely in response to the high-handed behavior of Burma's new soldier-rulers).[1] Of some 56,500 arms "seized or recovered," almost 52,000 were said to be from sources other than actual insurgents or surrendered personnel[2]—a situation that illustrates the threat hanging over Burma before the Army took control. The ordinary crime rate was also significantly reduced.

On the economic front, such state-operated enterprises as the Thamaing cotton textile plant, the sugar mills, and the Insein steel mill were placed on a profit-making basis. Regulations on trade in rice (as well as in rubber, timber, and cotton) were liberalized, private participation was encouraged, and exports of rice soared to a postwar high. A particular target of the caretaker regime was the so-called "economic insurgents"—persons engaged in subverting the state through various kinds of commercial manipulations. Two-thirds of the registered importers lost their registration. The government also moved to lower the cost of living by attempting to control prices, increase the supply of goods, and improve the system of distribution. The cost of living was reduced—but apparently not permanently: An 11 per cent advance in the cost-of-living index between March 1959 and March 1960 followed a drop of 18 per cent in the period from September 1958 to February 1959.[3] The Ne Win government made no major changes in development policies, although the caretaker administration did reverse U Nu's policy of not accepting foreign grant aid.[4] The Army's Defense Services Institute emerged as the country's most important economic organization during this period, however, becoming a major importer of a vast variety of goods ranging from coal to automobiles, and operating banking, shipping, construction, fish, and transportation businesses as well as the country's largest department store.[5]

Largely as a result of the appointment of senior military officers to the major departments and boards, governmental administration improved. The capital city of Rangoon, a place of considerable natural beauty but disgustingly dirty during the AFPFL era, was cleaned up and made more attractive. In an effort to reduce the ever-present danger of fire in Rangoon, thousands of squatter huts were torn down and some 200,000 persons were moved (far from willingly) to the "satellite towns" of Okkalapa and Thaketa. The Ne Win government also effectively restored discipline to troubled Rangoon University—at the expense, however, of free discussion, even in the classroom. Some student political agitators were detained, while others went into hiding for fear of detention.[6]

The foreign policy of the Ne Win caretaker administration differed from that of the previous AFPFL and Nu-Tin governments only in emphasis, for the most part, although the military regime was able to register one major accomplishment, in particular, that had eluded the civilian politicians. This was a border agreement with the neighboring Communist Chinese. As Premier, General Ne Win, like U Nu before him, followed a policy of nonalignment; indeed, the government responded to China's suppression of the Tibetan uprising in 1959 (which produced in Burma a vigorous popular reaction against Peiping) with a conspicuous silence. Ne Win, however, was willing to cancel five of the eight "gift projects" from the U.S.S.R., which had been arranged under U Nu's government, because they would cost the Burmese too much, while coming to an agreement with the United States on grant assistance for a new Rangoon University campus. Burma and the United States also agreed to a preliminary survey in preparation for the construction, with American aid, of a Rangoon-Mandalay road.[7]

The Sino-Burmese border agreement, which settled the question in principle, recognized Burma's version of the frontier except for changes made by the pact itself: the "return" to China of the three Kachin villages of Hpimaw, Gawlum, and Kanfang, and the exchange by Burma of an area in the Wa territory of the Shan States for the previously leased Namwan Assigned Tract.[8] The Ne Win–Chou En-lai frontier settlement, which provided for subsequent demarcation by a joint commission, was accompanied by a treaty of friendship in which Burma agreed not to enter into a military alliance directed against China.[9] China apparently hoped to use its border settlement with Burma as leverage in the more important frontier controversy with India. The pact was also possibly the first step in a new offensive to draw Burma within a Chinese sphere of influence.[10] Burma, however, got what it wanted: Chinese recognition, for the most part, of the border as Burma claimed it should be—and this in writing!

In the political realm, the Ne Win regime established a network of National Solidarity Associations throughout the country. These were ostensibly designed to inculcate civic virtue, but were really intended to keep future civilian governments in check, and hence to eliminate in the future the need for the Army to assume control of the whole government.[11] Businessmen, who at first responded negatively to the caretaker administration, were nonetheless pleased with some of its specific actions, such as the elimination of the official monopolies of trade in various commodities.[12] Popular reaction to the Army government, however, was almost universally unfavorable, largely as a result of its authoritarian methods: the soldiers, for example, failed to obtain court orders when they raided warehouses of suspected hoarders or forced owners of safe-deposit boxes to reveal their contents.[13] The lowering of prices (for chicken, for example) resulted in increased demand, and hence in the necessity for lining up to buy goods—a type of discipline resented by the Burmese masses. The arbitrary requisitioning of personnel, vehicles, and equipment outside Rangoon (Rangoon was least subject to excessively provocative behavior on the part of the military) antagonized many Burmese and was an important factor in the Shan revolt.[14]

As had been true during the AFPFL and the Nu-Tin regimes, the main decisions of government during the 1958–60 Ne Win caretaker administration were not made by the Cabinet (despite the fact that it was constitutionally the chief executive organ of the state). During the AFPFL administration, the locus of real decision-making power had been the Executive Council of the party in power, or, more correctly, the Council's leading members. The chief decision-making section of the first Ne Win government was the Military Staff Council, of which Brigadier Aung Gyi (onetime Socialist politician) and Colonel Maung Maung were the most important members.[15] General Ne Win, although Premier and Commander-in-Chief of the Armed Forces, was not a member of this body. Ne Win's views and those of his chief military subordinates, which sometimes differed, were formally reconciled in the Cabinet. Only rarely were other opinions, such as those of the civilian ministers, recognized. Aung Gyi, Maung Maung, and Brigadier Tin Pe were also members of the important Economic Advisory Committee of the Cabinet—which did much more than advise. The chief decision-maker, however, was General Ne Win himself, probably to an even greater degree than U Nu had been before him.

Nu, largely for political rather than for policy reasons, was disturbed about the wide range of activities of the caretaker administration, which he had thought would concern itself almost wholly with restoring law and order preparatory to holding elections. Military infiltration of the civilian administration and the fear of his partisans in the districts to participate in politics particularly concerned Nu. Before the six months for which Ne Win had been officially "asked" to serve as Premier had expired, Nu informed him that conditions in the country had improved sufficiently for elections to be held, but the General disagreed. If his party won, Nu promised, key portfolios in his government would go to top soldiers, but still Ne Win refused to hold elections.[16]

Nu did not want to oppose amending Burma's constitution to allow General Ne Win, not a member of Parliament, to continue in office— for fear of being labeled pro-Communist or of creating a situation that might elevate "Stable" leader U Ba Swe to the Premiership. Equally important, he feared defections from his "Clean" party. His party, as a result, voted for amending the constitution to permit a non-M.P. to be Premier for more than six months, but Nu himself was absent from the Parliament on February 27, the day of the vote.

The Ne Win caretaker government was clearly anti–U Nu. Efforts were made to smear Nu, and a number of his followers were arrested for alleged criminal offenses or on charges of being in contact with the insurgents. But "bad hats" in the "Stable" camp were not similarly treated. As J. S. Furnivall, longtime observer of Burmese politics, stated, "All the bad fellows were not in the 'Clean' AFPFL, but the officially encouraged press coverage was designed to suggest this."[17] According to Thakin Tin, even he and U Nu feared that they might be arrested—"not to mention Bo Min Gaung for his alleged September 1958 plot against the Army."[18] The government released copies of Communist documents urging opposition to the Swe-Nyein "Stable" AFPFL in any future elections. Documents that purported to reveal Communist infiltration into the "Clean" AFPFL were also publicly released.

Nu responded to the personal attacks on himself[19] and the arrest of his followers with a campaign against "fascism." He had no alternative but to attack the Army government in terms of its authoritarian character; he could hardly have been in favor of "economic insurgents," and against "clean streets" and "honest government." Nu's active efforts to return to power began during the North Burma "Clean" AFPFL District and Township Representatives' Conference held in Mandalay in December 1958. He distinguished the three rival paths— fascism, Communism, and democracy. Appealing for "Stable" support against "fascism," he proposed a three-man committee acceptable to both factions of the once-united AFPFL to lead in restoring democratic government to Burma. Nu got no backing from the "Stable," however, and had to stand alone.[20]

In February 1959, at the same time that he acquiesced in giving the support of his "Clean" AFPFL party to the amendment that would permit General Ne Win to remain as Premier, Nu began to prepare for a passive resistance campaign against the same Ne Win. "Don't give us privileges," he declared, "but stop victimizing and harassing us."[21] Nu set no date for the start of his passive resistance campaign, but he left no doubt that he intended to begin it if the injustices about which he had complained were not remedied. The major speech of Nu's preparatory effort was delivered on May 1—symbolically at Martyrs' Hill, resting place of Aung San and the other assassinated comrades of July 19, 1947. One hundred thousand persons turned out, and Nu was repeatedly cheered. Many leading "Clean" politicians had scattered about the country in the event of repercussions to Nu's address, and possibly for the purpose of launching the civil disobedience campaign itself, if necessary. In his speech, Nu complained of "the un-

fair and exclusive distribution in the Burmese Army of those newspapers which are the stooges of our opponents and which are devoting
themselves to daily attacks on us, . . . the one-sided propaganda that
is being conducted against us by some of the instructors in the training
classes and refresher courses for government servants [and] the way
witnesses are forced by beatings and tortures to make confessions . . .
to involve some 'Clean' leaders in criminal cases."

Typical of the content and tone of the address was Nu's charge:

> In some localities, the authorities call up the local leaders of the
> "Clean" AFPFL and ask them first to change over to the "Stable"
> AFPFL. If that is complied with through fear, that is the end of
> the matter. But if that request is refused, then the leaders are asked
> to leave the "Clean" AFPFL and to remain neutral and inactive.
> But if that request is not complied with, the persons concerned are
> after a time arrested and detained on some pretext or other. Some-
> times there is so much haste and eagerness in arresting these politi-
> cal leaders, that the arrests are made under the wrong sections of
> the acts, and the sections cited have to be changed several times.
> In some localities, the arrested person is tortured by having a mild
> electric current passed through the body; finger nails are loosened
> with small pliers or tweezers; the arrested person is made to lie on
> the floor and water is continuously poured on his face till he is nearly
> suffocated; sand is put into a nylon stocking and the stocking is
> used as a black-jack to beat the sides of the body, so that no ex-
> ternal injury would appear. Interrogation of the arrested person
> is by third degree; the person under interrogation is not allowed to
> sleep a single wink throughout the 24 hours, while the officials con-
> ducting the interrogation take it in turn; the person so interrogated
> for an extended time at last says what he is wanted to say by his
> inquisitors, and then this is taken down as a confession by the
> arrested person.[22]

Moreover, according to Nu, "in some places the 'Clean' AFPFL
leaders are taken out of their homes, and then ruthlessly shot down."
He also complained of the requisitioning of cars by forcible order and
of recruiting forced labor on days of "Clean" political rallies. Sometimes "Clean" members of local governmental units were placed under
arrest, he charged, in order to give the "Stable" party a majority in
electing officers or in reaching a particular decision.[23]

In a scarcely veiled reference to the Ne Win government's vigorously pursued reformism, Nu said, "In the totalitarian system, the only
thing that is taken into account is the accomplishment or completion of
what the dictator or dictator-group wants." He declared:

As our Union of Burma is a democratic country, the power of the government is derived from the people. This is explicitly stated in the Constitution. Therefore, in this country the Government must exist for the people only; the people should not exist for the government. The government cannot or should not by force impose on the people all that it wants to do. The public should be first informed and educated. The leaders of the people should be asked to discussions and consultations. If there are differences of opinion, compromises and concessions should be made on a give-and-take basis.[24]

The alternatives as Nu saw them were: "Firstly, the road of compliance, taking the attitude that nothing can be done in the present circumstances. Secondly, the road of violent retaliation, taking the attitude that force must be met by force. Thirdly, the road of Non-Violent Struggle for Democracy."[25] The last approach involved meeting "anger and hostility [with] love and amicableness on our side," the "course of conduct approved by the Buddha." Some persons would participate in mass meetings, processions, and collective prayer-meetings. Others would just pray according to their own religions for the "preservation of democracy from threats and dangers," while still others would go about doing meritorious deeds, such as "offering alms to monks," and "buying up live fish from the market and letting the fish go unharmed back to rivers and lakes." The mass meetings would have the effect of drawing public attention to oppressive actions—such as unjust arrests, torture, or killing.[26] "I myself am quite resolved and am firmly determined in the cause of democracy to face and endure without flinching any danger, any risk, whether it is arrest, torture, or death," Nu said.[27]

The object of a campaign of passive resistance, Nu said, was to bring about a change of attitude on the other side. "For instance," he explained, "look at the hornbills. They always stay in couples of males and females. If a bird hunter shoots down either of the two, the remaining hornbill dives to the ground close to the dead hornbill and gives up its life. The bird hunter who witnesses the scene changes his mind and gives up his bird-hunting."[28]

The civil disobedience campaign did not begin, however, with Nu's May Day speech, although many expected that it would. The government's reaction was negative, but not oppressive (despite the arrest of some persons for shouting extracts from Nu's address). At a press conference on May 15, Colonel Maung Maung, Chairman of the National Security Council, said of Nu's speech: "He is not placed above the law; at the same time, he is an ex-Prime Minister who has recently lost his job, who is naturally prone to be reckless and bombastic for the sake of recovering his lost ego and bolstering up his supporters."[29]

Nu would not enjoy immunity permanently, Colonel Maung Maung asserted; the government would wait to see how far he would go. The government's attitude toward newspapers and political leaders was described as tolerant; action had not been taken against anyone for casual errors or sudden and impulsive outbursts. Maung Maung also reported that only 228 arrests had taken place so far in 1959 under section 5 of the Public Order Preservation Act, as compared with an annual average of 2,449 during the first ten years of independence. Yet Nu's particular allegations, charges of specific acts of political persecution, were not directly rebutted.

As for Nu's intentions, he probably did not plan to lead a national passive resistance campaign unless the situation failed to improve or elections were not held. This is not to say that U Nu was not a man of his word. He was the only Burmese to speak out frequently and vigorously against the abuses of Army rule during the caretaker period. He came to believe that free elections would be held, however, possibly in advance of the official announcement. He probably would have led a civil disobedience campaign if he had deemed one necessary.

During the caretaker period U Nu sought to rebuild both his political organization as such and the public image of his party. During the Nu-Tin period, the fact that Nu had won the no-confidence vote and was in power had attracted recruits to the "Clean" AFPFL from the defeated "Stable" party, but desertions from the party followed the transfer of power to General Ne Win. The "Stable" party, led by Ba Swe and Kyaw Nyein, had been weakened in the wake of the June 1958 parliamentary showdown, but the first months of the Army government seemed to provide it with an opportunity to increase its strength at the expense of the "Clean." Nu also faced the problem of restoring public confidence in the integrity of his party. Politics was a worthy job, he declared again and again in the campaign for the 1960 elections, and men of high moral character were needed to "carry it out." (Kyaw Tun and Pan Myaing, arrested for major crimes by the Ne Win government, would be expelled from the party—if found guilty—he promised.)

Nu also pledged "not to develop our party into a colossus which will dominate every aspect of life, and to prevent the growth of one-party rule in Burma."[30] The opposition should be treated with tolerance, he declared: "Whatever the members of the opposition, either themselves or their colleagues, might have done to us in the past, we must not look upon them as our enemies."[31] Nu promised that the opposition and other interested groups would be consulted on many questions before policy decisions were made.[32]

"A party in a democratic society," Nu said, "must be organized on strictly democratic lines and imbued fully with the democratic spirit."[33] The "Clean" AFPFL, he declared during the election campaign, would "protect workers and peasants from those who exploit them for their own purposes"—that is, from such satellite organizations as comprised the pre-split AFPFL.[34] However, the All-Burma Peasants Organization, it was announced after the elections, would not be dissolved (although it would not be affiliated directly with the Union Party, as the "Clean" AFPFL was renamed).

U Nu not only remained a democrat during his year and a half out of office, but also seemed to become more aware of the subtleties of the democratic approach to the problem of governing—particularly in an underdeveloped country like Burma. The "Clean" AFPFL, he said in a speech at Insein on the eve of the 1960 voting, "could not establish democracy in Burma by itself." If his party won the elections, he declared, "it would need the cooperation of the 'Stable,' and vice versa, since it was only through working together that the future could be saved for democracy."[35] Nu also remained a socialist, despite "Stable" charges to the contrary—although socialism had now become for Nu "the final goal, attainment of which we must strive for relentlessly." He declared the "impossibility of turning Burma into a socialist state within a short period of time"; even in the U.S.S.R., he stated, "where dictatorial methods were used, developments were far from satisfactory, and it would be far slower and more difficult in Burma where democratic methods will be used for development."[36]

On the eve of the 1960 Burmese parliamentary vote, the veteran Arakanese politician U Kyaw Min stated:

The Army is holding elections for the very same reason General Ne Win withdrew the Army team from the football league a couple of years ago; he doesn't want the Army booed. Some of his top associates opposed elections, but Ne Win—wisely, I think—decided the Army should quit while it was still ahead. No matter how anti-Communist it should remain, the Army would be serving Communist purposes if it remained in power and grew in unpopularity, providing the Communists with a convenient whipping boy. This is why the Army decided to hold elections.[37]

There were other reasons, too. The Army had taken over the government because of the imminent collapse of law and order with the resulting threat to the country's very existence and to the Army itself, stemming in part from the Communists. The Army had restored law and order to a major degree by September 1959, when plans for elections were officially announced. A number of top Army leaders did not wish to see U Nu returned to office, and hence Nu continued to suggest to General Ne Win that senior soldiers fill prominent posts in the government in the event of a "Clean" AFPFL victory in the elections.[38] Brigadier Aung Gyi and Colonel Maung Maung in particular hoped that independents would hold the balance between the "Clean" and the "Stable" party in the new Parliament and that such independents would be susceptible to control by the military. The National Solidarity Associations were part of the same plan for influence without responsibility.[39]

Other reasons for the withdrawal from office by the Army were Ne Win's belief that the military would be weakened by protracted neglect of its main mission, Ne Win's lack of personal political ambition, general support of constitutional and civilian government by most of the top Army leaders,[40] and probably fear that U Nu would launch a civil disobedience campaign (which would not serve any of the Army's objectives). Burma's soldier-rulers also may have realized that they were becoming more like the civilian politicians they had displaced, slowly compromising their standards and differing among themselves[41] —the result in part of the environment of political problems and traditions that they inherited.[42] The fact that the elections were held, however, was a tribute both to the selflessness of the Army and to the effectiveness of U Nu's opposition.

Nu opened the campaign for the "Clean" AFPFL with a marathon speech inaugurating a four-day all-Burma meeting of the party's Supreme Council on September 26, 1959, at Kaba-Aye near the Peace Pagoda and man-made cave he had constructed for the 1954–56 Buddhist synod. The huge tent in which the meeting was held was packed despite the worst weather of the year's rainy season and the fact that Nu and the "Clean" were still being harassed by some officials of the caretaker government. Nu outlined the party's program, which included a promise to make Buddhism the state religion, a pledge not to negotiate with the insurgents, and a vow to resume the task of building the welfare state.[43]

In one of the best-received political speeches of his career, Nu declared:

We are at the crossroads of history, and we must today look back and take stock of both our successes and failures, and seek the reasons therefor. During the first decade of our independence, we have had many achievements of which we may be proud, but we are still far short of our ultimate goal of a strong and firmly based democratic state, a level of prosperity commensurate with our natural wealth, and a standard of morality and discipline befitting an independent nation.

The promises Nu made during the election campaign were far from universally approved. His pledge to consider statehood for the Arakanese and the Mons was criticized by the "Stable" (and by non-partisans, too) as resembling what was alleged to have been the "divide-and-rule" policy of the colonial era. Nu's vow not to negotiate with the rebels was contrasted with his installing the pro-Communist President of the Rangoon University's Students' Union on the very day of the opening of the "Clean" All-Burma Conference. Neither of these issues, however—nor even the question of a state religion—compared in importance with dissatisfaction with Army rule or with U Nu's personal popularity as real factors in determining the outcome of the election.

U Nu's personality dominated the campaign; it was literally a contest between Nu on the one hand and the alleged Army-"Stable" coalition on the other. According to Nu's close friend (and a well-known editor), U Ohn Khin, however, "Nu did not even want to be a candidate. He wanted to be 'the power behind the scenes,' playing a role analogous to his position as AFPFL Vice President before the assassination of Aung San."

Ohn Khin has said:

> We convinced Nu that we could not win without him. In the public's eye, we told him, he would be less a part of the campaign if he were not a candidate himself. He asked me, for example, three times if I did not think it better if he did not run for office. The idea of making the campaign one of personalities from our side—which it definitely was—was the idea of our "brain trust." Nu did not care much for it.[44]

Convinced that he should run for the Parliament, Nu decided to contest U Ba Swe's seat personally, Thakin Tin having already offered to oppose U Kyaw Nyein. "We thought this a little too risky," Dr. E Maung has said. "There was at least the limited possibility that he might get beaten. So I offered to stand against Ba Swe, and finally [Nu] acquiesced."[45] E Maung denied the opposition's claim that Nu set Tin and himself up for certain defeat; he also stated that some of the other "Clean" political leaders—Bo Min Gaung, U Win, U Ohn, Thakin Kyaw Tun, Thakin Pan Myaing, Bo Tin Maung Gyi, and Daw Khin Kyi—offered not to stand for election in order to work to strengthen the party.[46]

Describing the character of the campaign then in progress, U Nu declared in a speech at Insein on January 18, 1960:

> The whole country is aware of the mistakes committed by the "Stable." Their first mistake was to believe they can frighten the masses into support by threats, that they can disperse the "Clean" leaders by the same method. They have intimidated those who are not scared by threats in the belief that they will not be able to stand up to intimidation, and this is their second big mistake. They also believed that they can win with mass support through all forms of bribery, and this is their third big mistake.
>
> Whenever the "Stable" committed these errors—whether in town or in the country—the people veered round to support the "Clean." The result of these errors was to create support for the "Clean"—it was almost as if they were acting as our organizers! This has been so evident that one can hear all over the country given in jest to us: "Why bother yourselves? The "Stable" are doing it for you.[47]

The "Stable" charge of corruption in the ranks of the "Clean"—of which Nu was fully aware, his opponents alleged—failed to impress the voters. As a veteran foreign diplomat observed, "The jailing of the likes of Kyaw Tun and Pan Myaing actually helped Nu: It conveniently got them out of the way for him."[48]

Nu's appeal to his countrymen as a long-time nationalist and an outspoken critic of the Ne Win government was matched by the overwhelming attraction of the public image of Nu as a holy man—one on the way to becoming a Buddha, some believed. This was probably even more important than Nu's promise to introduce legislation in the first parliamentary session after the election, if possible, to make Buddhism the official faith of the land. Since partisan exploitation of religion was specifically prohibited by the Burmese constitution, the "Clean" AFPFL did not include the state religion question as part of its formal platform. But Nu assured his countrymen that the party would implement the promise despite this fact.[49]

The "Stable" AFPFL charge that U Nu raised the religious issue only to garner votes was probably untrue. Although Nu undoubtedly realized that his stand would increase his popular support, he had been pressing for making Buddhism the state religion, apparently sincerely, since 1956, when he stated at the conclusion of the Sixth Great Buddhist Synod that he had a "burning desire" to do so. He would "carefully, conscientiously and above all justly make Buddhism the state religion," he said, as soon as there was no longer a danger of disunity stemming from non-Buddhist opposition to such a move.[50] Two years later, at the national consultative conference of July 1958 (during the Nu-Tin period), Nu again stated that as soon as all "possible grounds for breeding fear and misunderstanding" were removed, "the way should be open for the declaration of Buddhism as a state religion."[51]

Nu also urged his fellow "Clean" politicians to be good Buddhists—indeed, to become *thawtarpans,* who never degenerate into lower beings and who could even, after seven more lives at most, attain *nirvana.*[52] And he entered a monastery for six weeks in October 1959—three months before the election. The image—and the man—were unbeatable.

As the Ne Win caretaker period progressed, it became clear that Burma's military rulers lacked genuine political affection for either group of civilian politicians—who had so misgoverned the country for a decade in their eyes. The military was not pro-"Stable," as some have claimed. The Ne Win government, indeed, inquired into some of the undertakings of the Industrial Development Corporation, of which U Kyaw Nyein of the "Stable" formerly had served as Chairman. But there was a limit to how many civilian politicians the caretaker administration could discredit if it intended to give up office at an early date. Accordingly, the Army favored the "Stable"—not because it regarded that faction with real respect, but because it was the lesser of two evils. The "Clean" AFPFL was ridden with pro-Communist elements, the military leaders seemed to believe, and it was under a government headed by U Nu that the security situation had so rapidly deteriorated in September 1958. U Ba Swe, by contrast with U Kyaw Nyein, enjoyed personal popularity with the soldiers, stemming from his past cooperation with the military leaders as Minister of Defense.

The "Stable" AFPFL, unaware of the degree of popular dissatisfaction with the military government until it was too late, unwisely decided to cooperate with Premier General Ne Win and the colonels.[53] U Nu's offer of key portfolios to soldiers in any future government that he might head is evidence that he considered the same opportunistic course, but Ne Win would not aid the man he had dislodged from power, whom he blamed for many of Burma's problems. Army backing seemed to help the "Stable" at first, but it ultimately proved to be a veritable "kiss of death" politically. The "Stable," moreover, led by some of Burma's most competent politicians and alleged to be much better organized than the harassed "Clean" party, seemed to fail altogether to communicate with, and to mobilize, the masses. The "Stable" leaders took U Nu far less seriously than the Army, and their initial approach to the campaign for the 1960 elections suggested overconfidence. It was Nu's party that chose the issues, which ranged from charges of "fascism" (directed against both the Army and, by implication, the cooperative Swe-Nyein group) to state religion and statehood for the Arakanese and the Mons. The "Stable" AFPFL offered a more consistent and sophisticated platform, but it was never made understandable to the voters. Moreover, the Swe-Nyein faction employed more effort in countering Nu's promises than in propagandizing its own.

The municipal elections of November and December 1959, in which popular support for U Nu and his party was clearly demonstrated, resulted in changes of both policy and pace on the part of the "Stable" AFPFL. But the changes were too late and too swift. The promise of "Stable" leader U Ba Swe that he would send the colonels back to the barracks, if elected, was popularly interpreted as a bribe spoken by a man who feared defeat. The attempt by Ba Swe and particularly by Kyaw Nyein to imitate Nu's religious behavior—observing the sabbath, offering almsfood to the monks, and such—did not accord with the past behavior of the two leaders. Nor were the last-minute efforts of the "Stable" politicians to put their much-vaunted organization to work sufficient to stem the tide of victory for Nu.

The elections of February 6, 1960, were both free and fair. And, when the votes were finally tallied, the "Clean" AFPFL and its allies in the states—the Shan States United Hill People's Organization, the People's Economic and Cultural Development Organization (Kachin), the Chin National Organization, and the Kayah National United League—had swept to a majority of more than two-thirds in the Chamber of Deputies. The two leaders of the "Stable" party, U Ba Swe and U Kyaw Nyein, had been defeated. Dr. E Maung had beaten the one, and Thakin Tin the other (his archfoe, Kyaw Nyein). Most of the other top leaders of the "Stable" also were defeated, leaving the party virtually leaderless as well as short-numbered in the Parliament; the Swe-Nyein party and its allies among the minorities won only 45 seats.

The pro-Communist National Unity Front won only three seats as compared with 47 in 1956. The dimensions of the victory were overwhelming: nearly three out of four of Rangoon's voters, for example, had voted for Nu's party. However, these very results were somewhat embarrassing in the light of Nu's prior declaration that one-party supremacy had led to misgovernment in the past. Moreover, the consultations with the opposition that Nu had promised in the campaign would be difficult without significant parliamentary representation for his opponents.

The victory was a personal triumph for Nu—personal in the sense that the voters had endorsed the "Clean" party because it was his party, and also because it had been a hard, uphill fight. "Each day U Nu is out of power," I was told again and again in Rangoon in June 1959, "the further removed he is from office." Yet those who said this failed to take into consideration two important factors: the public image of Nu as semi-divine, and the traditional enmity of the Burmese toward government. The five chief evils of mankind, according to historic Burmese belief, are water, fire, the thief, the ill-wisher, and government. The Ne Win government—which, paradoxically, gave Burma the best government it had known since (and possibly before) independence— was regarded by the masses as such an evil. Its reforms had been too much for most Burmese to accept—particularly when carried out, as they frequently were, in an unnecessarily bullying way.

The triumph of his party gave Nu—as undisputed "Clean" leader— a far more solid political base than he had known in the ten years of the united AFPFL or the precarious three and a half months of the ill-fated Nu-Tin government.[54] Nu, who had wanted to renounce politics at the war's end (and had voiced this sentiment repeatedly in subsequent years), found himself with the most obvious—and most vigorous —public mandate a Burmese leader had ever possessed. The Army, moreover, which had not wanted his return, was apparently willing to acquiesce in his resuming the Premiership. It was, indeed, a triumph for Nu and his party—and for the principle of freely chosen government in Burma.

❀

EIGHTEEN

A SECOND CHANCE

WHEN U NU became Premier again on April 4, 1960, Burma was faced with "16,000 problems," he subsequently stated,[1] but her machinery for meeting them he compared to a broken-down jeep without tires or even the essential parts of the engine. "I can't drive this affair at 160 miles an hour," he declared.[2] Yet Nu continued to speak of the future in terms of a greatly—and quickly—improved standard of living. In mid-1961, the government announced a 16-year plan that would quadruple Burma's national income and advance the economy to the "take-off" level by 1978.[3] The promises continued to be at variance with reality, however, as reflected, for example, in the steady rise in prices, which amounted to more than 10 per cent in the first year and a half of Nu's new government.[4] Nu told a press conference in mid-1961 that the high cost of fish would encourage the people to stop eating it[5]—a highly meritorious thing from a Buddhist point of view.

Burma's pressing economic problems were not accorded priority treatment by the Nu government, which was occupied primarily with the state religion question during its first year and a half in office, and with minorities difficulties subsequently.[6] The passage of the Constitution (Third Amendment) Act, 1961, by both houses of the Parliament in a joint sitting on August 26 fulfilled U Nu's promise to make Buddhism the state religion.[7] It also proved to be the prelude to the bloodiest demonstration of religious intolerance post-colonial Burma had experienced. Paradoxically, there might have been even more violence if Nu had not honored his pledge. Once the promise had been made, it had to be kept.

The threat of bloodshed had been raised in connection with the religious issue during the 1960 parliamentary budget session, and Nu had replied: "I am not a man of violence, and therefore I cannot match the threat to kill anyone or let anyone's blood, but I am determined to bring in State Religion, even if I have to die in the attempt."[8] Nu told the Chamber of Deputies in August 1961 that there were three reasons why he had taken such a strong stand on this issue: his own "overpowering desire" to perform this "great deed of merit," his belief that most of his countrymen shared his feelings, and a fear that failure to make Buddhism the official faith would feed religious fanaticism.[9] Nu's strict enforcement of party discipline in his Union Party, as the "Clean" AFPFL had been renamed, in the vote on the amendment was an indication of the intensity of his feelings on the subject.[10]

The National Religious Minorities Alliance, formed to represent the interests of Burma's three million non-Buddhists, acted with restraint—but this was not true of all opponents of the amendment. Kachins, for example, stoned an official investigating commission. Police aircraft dropped leaflets over Rangoon before the vote on the amendment, warning of harsh action if non-Buddhists provoked violence over a state religion. On the day of the vote, armored vehicles surrounded the governmental compound of which the parliamentary buildings were a part. There was no violence.

Burma's Army, which had so recently relinquished control of the governmental machinery, also opposed making Buddhism the official religion of the whole country, urging Nu to limit the state religion to Burma proper. There was even talk in some military quarters of a new Army takeover if the divisiveness occasioned by the issue affected the unity and discipline of the Armed Forces.[11]

"If the Government encourages religion," U Nu told the Chamber of Deputies on August 17, "the people in the country too will encourage and support religion."[12] To the Chamber of Deputies on August 23, he said: "If the Government provides for the welfare of the people in such matters as education, health and economic prosperity in the short span of life in this existence, it should provide for their welfare in the inestimably long future existences." But he also warned that "laws alone cannot prevent the fears of non-Buddhists from materializing. It is necessary for the hundreds of thousands of Buddhists to attain the right view and to restrain themselves in speech, act and thought in all matters which concern non-Buddhists."[13]

In September, Nu moved to establish new legal safeguards for non-Buddhists in the form of the Constitution (Fourth Amendment) Act, 1961, despite the fact that the Burmese constitution already protected the rights of believers in any religion to practice their faith.[14] Extremists among the clergy objected to the amendment, and on September 17, approximately 100 yellow-robed monks besieged the Premier's residence in protest. In a radio broadcast, Nu explained that the second constitutional amendment was not a religious action, but one aimed at preventing bloodshed, civil war, disintegration, and loss of independence. He declared that he would resign if the amendment were defeated, and threatened to expel from the party any Union Party M.P. who voted against it.[15] Although the amendment passed both houses of the Parliament by a unanimous vote on September 25, some 500 Buddhist monks picketed the parliamentary building, which was protected by 2,000 policemen armed with bayonets and automatic weapons.

Although it has been claimed that the amendment establishing Buddhism as the state religion made little or no difference in view of the already recognized special position of the faith in the constitution, it did have the effect of stimulating at least some *pongyis* into political action and leading to bloody intercommunal as well as religious rioting. There have probably been about 100,000 monks in Burma at any one time in recent years, some of whom have merely taken their vows temporarily.[16] Although most monks have generally not been politically inclined, the more militant younger *pongyis* have been—and it was these who led the November 14, 1961, riots in the Rangoon suburb of Okkalapa, which resulted in four deaths and the arrest of 279 persons, including 92 monks. The *pongyis* were demonstrating against the government's decision to allow the construction of additional mosques at Okkalapa, and the lynching of two Moslems by a mob led by monks was the shameful highlight of the disturbances. Nu himself was rudely denounced over loudspeakers controlled by the rioters. Subsquently 1,500 monks demonstrated against the detention of the arrested persons, and Nu was accused of being a bogus Buddhist and urged to resign.

Ethnic unity in Burma following U Nu's return to office was still an unattained goal. The dissatisfaction of the minorities with domination by the largely Burman-controlled central government produced talk of state legislatures and even of militia.[17] The Shan insurrection was the most obvious sign of the growing discontent of the ethnic minorities. A conference of minority peoples held at Taunggyi in June 1961 passed resolutions endorsing a proposal by Shan leaders of a more genuinely federal form of government.[18] The Shan insistence on changes in Burma's governing arrangements, particularly endorsed by some Kayah leaders, was probably stimulated partly by the general anticipation of a rearrangement of the curious semi-federal constitutional structure of Burmese government. U Nu had promised both the Arakanese and the Mons their own states within the Union, if a majority of these ethnic minorities wanted them, in order to broaden his political backing in the critical middle months of 1958, and had reiterated the pledge for the same purpose in the campaign for the 1960 elections. Arakanese and Mon leaders demanded the fulfillment of these promises after Nu's return to power, and, like the state religion issue, the questions of how many states to create and what powers they should be given produced more discontent than satisfaction. Both the state religion question and the minorities question had been settled constitutionally in 1947, before independence, although they were raised again from time to time. Further airing of the different aspects of both problems in 1960–62 seriously disturbed what political tranquility the troubled Union of Burma had, and for this U Nu must bear a major part of the blame.

Nu sought to be as democratic as he could in dealing with the demands of the minorities, but he would not be forced into concessions. Some of the minorities, however, or factions of them, employed force. The small-scale insurrection of the Kachins, who were largely non-Buddhists, was inspired in part by the state religion issue. The Karens continued their rebellion, driven apparently in desperation to join forces with the Communist rebels.[19] The threat of Shan insurgence continued to grow, the number of Shan rebels increasing from 800 in 1959 to 3,000 in 1961.[20] These rebels allied themselves with the Karens[21]— despite Nu's willingness to meet with the Shan State Council on the subject of federalism and to appoint a committee to study the question. Security conditions were clearly deteriorating, and a year after the transition from military to civilian rule the government was forced to establish local law and order councils, reviving, in effect, the security councils that had operated so well in coordinating civilian and military action against the insurgents during the previous Ne Win regime. At the end of 1961, Nu admitted that rebels controlled one-tenth of the country.[22]

The numbers of the once-formidable Communist insurrectionists were small,* however, and the rebels, led by Than Tun, were located in generally remote areas. Nu continued to refuse to negotiate with

---

* According to Colonel Than Sein of the War Office, the various insurgent groups in March 1961 included 1,610 "White Flag" and 690 "Red Flag" Communists, 4,100 Karens, 2,850 Shans, 400 Mujahids, 50 Mons, and 50 Kayahs. (*The Nation,* Apr. 1, 1961).

the Communists and the other insurgents because negotiating would make a kind of sport of rebellion, with insurgents gaining power if they succeeded and suffering no ill consequences if they did not. Than Tun, nonetheless, wrote Nu in January 1961, his first such letter in more than two years, declaring that he would not surrender under the amnesty offer the government had made the previous August.

Concern with both the political and the constitutional aspects of the state religion issue and the minorities issue accounted in part for the limited attention U Nu's government accorded economic problems during its first year and a half in office. On April 5, 1960, in his first speech to the Parliament as Premier again, Nu promised that state participation in the economy would be limited, and pledged that no existing private enterprise would be nationalized during his four-year term of office. He also endorsed Burmanization of trade and industry as far as possible, and the operation of import agencies was in fact legally restricted to Burmese nationals. The new Four-Year Plan, slow in making its appearance, confirmed the Nu government's announced decision not to stress new state economic enterprises; the emphasis of the plan was on consolidating and rationalizing public projects already in being.[23] An average annual gross capital investment of more than $230 million was anticipated. Over half of this amount, which was more than double the past actual investment and hence was probably too high, was to come from the private sector. Public-sector investment was to increase 154 per cent over the previous Four-Year Plan for social services, 49 per cent for agriculture and industry, and 56 per cent for transportation and communications. In addition, an Industrial Development Bank was established in late 1961, and foreign investment legislation was liberalized, but the effects of these developments were not to be felt during U Nu's second premiership.

The economic problem that attracted greatest attention, and for which the government was most criticized, was the rising cost of living. Nu established *prahita* (selfless service) shops to sell consumer goods at low prices, and he set up a price-lowering committee—but prices continued to spiral upward. Some of the government's policies seemed to have effects opposite from those generally desired; increases in customs duties and the sales tax in 1961, for example, doubled the cost of many foodstuffs.

The economic record of the previous Army caretaker regime and a fear of military domination of the economy were factors in the government's establishment of the Burma Economic Development Corporation in 1961. The purpose of this organization was to take over most of the businesses operated by the Defense Services Institute. The D.S.I. was Burma's most important economic operation, a holding company run by the Army. Nu's problem was to obtain the benefits of its experience and demonstrated competence without Army control of the economy. Chaired by Brigadier Aung Gyi, the board of directors of the Burma Economic Development Corporation included three other officers and three civilians, including the Secretary of the Defense Ministry. In December 1961, Nu proposed creating a second Economic Development Corporation staffed by members of the Burmese civil service, which suggested that he might be moving gradually to reduce the Army's influence over the economy.

The "16,000 problems" of which U Nu spoke would take over 20 years to solve, he claimed.[24] Political unity and a strong national civil service were necessary in order to begin to solve them effectively. If such unity could not be created and if "successive governments set aside the program of the previous government to devise new ones, the finances of the Union will not long be able to withstand the successive changes," Nu told the Parliament. A National Planning Committee under the chairmanship of Finance and Planning Minister Thakin Tin of Nu's Union Party was subsequently formed, with three representatives each from the Union Party, the Ba Swe–Kyaw Nyein AFPFL, and the pro-Communist National Unity Front (and one from the Arakanese National United Organization), as well as a number of others drawn from the states, the civil service, the armed forces, and the professions.

To the civil servants Nu appealed for loyalty to the government, not the ruling party, promising that his administration would not treat them in a partisan way and that they would be rewarded according to the merit principle. He also appointed an inquiry committee, headed by Supreme Court Justice U Chan Htoon Aung and Chief Secretary U Shwe Mra, which was to examine public-service conditions in European countries and to make recommendations for improvements in Burma. The commission made its report in 1961,[25] and on the basis of the report, Nu strongly endorsed a constitutional amendment specifically protecting the rights of civil servants (despite the opposition of the other parties in the Parliament, the Army, the junior ranks of the civil service, and even some members of his own Union Party). The Premier explained that the matter had become "an obsession with me."[26]

Nu also realized that Burma's development as a viable state depended on the establishment of better conditions of law and order than had existed under his previous governments.[27] He sought to stabilize the security situation, in part by absorbing special police reserves into the regular Union Military Police, and he initially abolished the local security councils, which had served to coordinate civilian and military anti-insurgent efforts in the past but which had been misused in some instances for political reasons. The need for greater coordination of security efforts, however, became increasingly and painfully clear with the Karen derailment of the Rangoon-Mandalay express train on March 26, 1961, in which 17 persons were killed, about 100 wounded, and another 80 taken hostage. The train incident was followed by a marked increase in the number of Karen raids in lower Burma, which created such fear in Insein, only ten miles from Rangoon, that there was a sizable exodus of inhabitants to the capital. On April 10 it was announced that law and order councils, similar to the former security councils, would be formed in certain divisions and districts. Nu, as Home Minister, served as chairman of a coordinating central council.

In February 1961, anti-American riots organized by the Rangoon University Students' Union broke out in Rangoon following the disclosure that Nationalist China was continuing to supply the Kuomintang irregulars in Burma with arms and ammunition made in the United States. On this occasion Nu spoke out more strongly than ever before about what he termed "mobocracy." "A cult has grown up in our country whereby a few persons with grievances, real or imaginary, . . . collect a crowd, demonstrate, throw stones or set motor cars on fire," he stated. "If it is allowed to flourish, Burma will disintegrate."[28] Such mob violence, he promised, would be suppressed as far as the law allowed. Nu clearly was aware of the problems posed both by the insurgents and by mob action; the question was whether he could, or would, do anything about them.

One important factor in what has been called Burma's "government by inaction" was the reliance of the country's political leaders on an unnecessarily large number of committees. During Nu's second Premiership the situation grew even worse. Among the numerous committees created were the Union Party Steering Committee and the Advisory Committee of elder statesmen. The former comprised four Cabinet members, including Nu, and seven members of the Union Party E.C., and was designed to advise the government on both policy and administration; the latter, composed of three former judges and two former ministers, was supposed to advise on legal and constitutional questions. The elder statesmen were given the thorny political chore of examining the demand of Arakanese and Mon leaders for statehood. There were also committees dealing with state religion, constitutional revision, promotion of parliamentary democracy, lowering of prices, and practically every other political, economic, social, and administrative question with which the government was concerned. In addition, there were committees within the Cabinet dealing with the "administration and stabilization of democracy," foreign affairs, economic planning, and social welfare. The government also proposed having two Cabinets, one for national questions and the other for questions involving the states. The Swe-Nyein AFPFL parliamentary opposition attacked the Advisory Committee of elder statesmen in particular, but encouraged the creation of parliamentary committees, which were conspicuously absent from the otherwise committee-ridden Burmese government.

Yet all roads still seemed ultimately to lead to U Nu. The Burma Economic Development Corporation, for example, was directly responsible to him. Nevertheless he found it possible to withdraw completely from his public responsibilities from time to time, just as he had in the past: In May 1961 he went into meditation at Mount Popa for no less than 45 days!

Nu's chief political objective after his return to office was probably to prevent the kind of split that had earlier plunged Burma into military rule—and China, Laos, and other lands into even worse fates. Nu promised his defeated AFPFL opponents that they would be accorded full democratic rights and that he would consult them on important issues, and he kept both promises. A six-point agreement on the use of governmental facilities and authority by the party in power was signed on March 11, 1961. It included a number of reforms that Nu had already put into practice. Nu's policy was one of "forgive and forget," but supporters of both parties in the districts and villages were slow to follow their leaders.

The restraint Nu showed in his relations with the AFPFL was evident also in his attitude toward those Army officers and civil servants who had misused their positions to work against him in the campaign for the February 1960 elections.[29] However, after his return to power Nu held the Defense portfolio—presumably as a precaution. Some senior officers in the Army were far less compromising than Nu in their suggestion that it might be necessary to restore military rule.[30] The political divisiveness of this suggestion, plus other differences of opinion among General Ne Win's immediate subordinates,[31] led Ne Win to insist on the resignation of the officers involved.[32] Brigadier Maung Maung, one of the chief figures in the September 1958 *coup d'état,* and Brigadier Aung Shwe, who headed the important Southern Command, were assigned to ambassadorial posts abroad, while five senior colonels were made military attachés and another five announced that they were going into business or politics.[33] The 1961 resignations by no means ended the military threat to Nu's continuing in office, particularly since the National Solidarity Associations, set up by the soldiers as a check on the returning civilian politicians, were inconsequential politically less than six months after Nu's return to office— although they probably could not have prevented the situations that appeared to alarm the Army in late 1961 and early 1962 anyway.

Nu remained as President when the "Clean" AFPFL was renamed the Union Party in 1960, but announced that he intended to become an ordinary member although he would remain as Premier. This step was in keeping with his frequently expressed view that one person should not hold both a top governmental and a top party post and with his hope to develop a party that was not dependent on his leadership and popular appeal. The difficulties of Nu's task were heightened by the heterogeneous character of his party; it was no longer a federation of mass organizations, but it was still clearly a coalition of diverse and unreconciled personalities and interests. Its commanding majority in the Parliament, moreover, limited the need for unity, and led to Nu's public admission that the numerical strength of the Union Party was "somewhat of a headache to me."[34]

Three groups, two of them formally allied, comprised the Union Party: the Thakins, the Bo's, and the U's. The Thakins, who took their name from the Dobama Asiayone of the 1930's, were the professional politicians and the least educated faction of the party. The Bo's were some of the political survivors of the "Thirty Comrades" and those who had subsequently associated themselves with the onetime resistance fighters and their heirs. The U's included most of the professional persons among the top party leaders, and were, on the whole, the most administratively experienced element. Each group claimed to be superior to the others in political competence, patriotism, education, and other factors.

The U's and the Bo's joined forces, so that there were really only two factions: the Thakins and the U-Bo's. Among the Thakins were Tin, Kyaw Tun, Pan Myaing, Tin Maung, San Way, and Chan Tun (and Bo Tin Maung Gyi), largely the "uneducated Socialists" who had played a major role in the AFPFL split of 1958. The U-Bo group included Win, Min Gaung, Hmu Aung, Hmu Bala, Chan Tha, Zin Yaw, Ye Gaung Nyunt, Myint Swe, Tin Kyi, Ba Tin, Chit Pe, and Tin U. U Raschid and U Thwin backed the U-Bo's, but the opportunistic Dr. E Maung and U Ba Saw tried to straddle the fence between the two factions. Both groups wanted U Nu to be "Party Leader," a position that Nu had conceived as one from which he might maintain control of (while not really leading) the party. The Thakins and the U-Bo's each had their own candidates for party President and Secretary, however. The Thakins proposed Tin and Kyaw Tun, and the U-Bo's, U Win or Bo Hmu Aung, and Bo Min Gaung.[35] Rivalry between the two factions became intense, particularly in the districts— even less than a year after the smashing "Clean" AFPFL election victory—and Nu had to visit Mandalay, Moulmein, Prome, and other places to seek to contain the competition.

U Nu's call in late 1960 for an all-party conference to select a "Leader," the growing realization within the top party ranks that he would not stand for the post himself, and his specific declaration on December 20 that he would not, heightened competition between the rival Union Party factions. Thakin Tin and Bo Hmu Aung each suggested that the other should assume the post of "Party Leader" (neither presumably wanted to appear to be seeking to succeed Nu, even in a job that he was now voluntarily leaving, probably in part to avoid provoking his jealousy). Like Nu, Tin even declared his intention to remain an ordinary member of the party. This declaration followed his resignation as President of the All-Burma Peasants Organization in November 1960, which indicated that he had been asked by U Nu to take charge of the Union Party.[36] The U-Bo's opposed Tin's directing the party, further increasing tensions within the ruling group.

Nu declared publicly that he would not side with either faction, but whether he fulfilled this promise is open to question. In a manner that recalled the spirit, if not the specific events, of the first four months of 1958, each faction revealed fears that Nu really wanted its rival to win the struggle for power. Be this as it may, on March 14, 1961, U Nu shook his political associates by submitting his resignation as President of the Union Party. Because of Nu's great national popularity, the 29-man Executive Committee of the party had no choice but to resign en bloc and let Nu choose his own executive to serve for a year until an all-Burma conference of the party could be held. During this period Nu was to attempt to reorganize the party, a task he had not been able to perform in 1956 for the pre-split AFPFL. To Thakin Tin, who had remained at his side in the troubled times of 1956–60, Nu offered the position of party Secretary, but Tin said that he could not accept it in clear conscience, meaning that he could not take the post away from his ally Thakin Kyaw Tun (even if Kyaw Tun were going to lose it anyway). Nu downgraded the job, called it "Organizing Secretary," and assigned it to his reliable confidant U Ohn. He also formed a three-man temporary E.C. comprising himself (as party President), U Ohn (as Organizing Secretary), and Chin Affairs Minister U Zahre Lian (as Treasurer), and a four-man Consultative Committee composed of Thakin Tin (of the Thakin faction), Bo Hmu Aung (of the U-Bo's), and the neutrals Dr. E Maung and Kachin Minister Sama Duwa Sinwa Nawng. The members of both groups together comprised a third committee, which was to supervise all future party elections—village, township, and district. In addition, a six-man committee representing equally the Caretaker E.C. and the Thakin and U-Bo factions of the old E.C. was set up to devise a plan for party reorganization.

Nu apparently reluctantly undertook to form a three-man "caretaker" E.C. He wanted to couple this action with the announcement that he would retire from politics altogether at the end of the period for which his government was elected (i.e., in 1964), but the Cabinet and the three-man Advisory Committee of elder statesmen at first dissuaded him from doing so.[37] Bo Hmu Aung, one of the two Vice Presidents of the Union Party, publicly stated that Nu intended to retire from political life in 1964, however,[38] and Nu himself confirmed his decision (long rumored and much discussed in top Union Party circles) at a press conference March 20.[39] His plan was to step down as head of his party at the All-Burma Union Party Conference scheduled for early 1962. In public remarks in late 1961 Nu reconfirmed his intention to "quit politics" altogether in 1964 "to go to India to propagate the Buddhist faith."[40]

Upon his return to office, Nu accorded highest priority to the consummation of the border settlement that the Ne Win government had reached with Communist China. A treaty implementing the Ne Win–Chou En-lai Agreement in detail was signed by Premiers Nu and Chou in Peiping on October 1, 1960 (at the astrologically propitious hour of 5:50 P.M.), and Chou visited Rangoon in January 1961 for the exchange of ratifications. The January meeting between the two leaders was also the occasion for the announcement that China had awarded an $84 million interest-free loan to Burma (to be paid off in ten equal installments starting ten years later) and that Nu had bestowed upon Chou a newly created title, personally chosen by Nu himself and the highest in the land: Supreme Upholder of the Glory of Great Love. In October 1961, Nu and Chou signed yet another document, a protocol to the original boundary agreement, indicating that a joint boundary committee had "successfully completed the task of surveying boundary lines between the two countries" and had erected markers to demarcate the border.[41] In addition to the border agreement and the 20-year loan, China also agreed to purchase some 350,000 tons of Burmese rice in 1961 at a price well above that of the prevailing market, but U Nu vigorously denied that Burma was forsaking its neutralist ways.[42] Imports from China rose by more than 60 per cent in 1960.

Premiers Nu and Chou En-lai met again in Yunnan during Nu's "holiday" in that Chinese province in April 1961, and the two leaders agreed in a joint communiqué to cooperate against the threat posed to both their states by the presence of Chinese Nationalist irregulars on Burmese soil.[43] Nu explained in a subsequent press conference that what was envisaged was the sharing of intelligence on the problem, and discussions when necessary—the same kind of cooperation, he said, that had been taking place regularly between Burma and Thailand.[44] Chinese Communist troops, however, began crossing again into Burma in the northern Kengtung area in late 1960 (despite government denials at first).[45] A military spokesman termed their numbers "insignificant," but reports placed the figure as high as 5,000, and it was by no means clear that they were on Burmese soil by prearrangement with the Rangoon government.[46] The Chinese subsequently departed,[47] but their entry surely left its imprint on Nu's mind.

The border agreement, the aid pact, and Nu's suggestions to Chou En-lai in Yunnan in April 1961 that Burma could be an overland outlet for the products of that part of China[48] reflected Burma's fear of future aggressive moves by the Chinese. The Sino-Burmese agreement to consult on the problem of Kuomintang irregulars in Burma was made at a time when the government had said that there were only 600 of the Nationalist Chinese marauders left in the country, the lowest number in a decade of struggle against them.[49]

Concluding the border pact with the Chinese had repercussions for Burma's usually cordial relations with India. In view of the strong feeling in India that China had illegally occupied Indian territory, there was obvious irritation with U Nu's holding up the Sino-Burmese frontier treaty as a model for settling the dispute between the Indians and the Chinese.[50] Of more immediate concern to the Indian government was the map attached to the Sino-Burmese treaty, which showed the frontier separating Burma and China ending where China (but not India) claimed the Sino-Indian border started. There were also reports in the Indian press that Burma and China would jointly build a highway that would join a road the Chinese had been building in what India considered its territory. Nu, anticipating a negative reaction from Indian Premier Nehru, went to New Delhi to explain the situation—but was unsuccessful in placating Nehru.[51] It was reported that he also sought to mediate the India-China border dispute, but Nu emphatically denied this.[52] Nehru told his Parliament in early 1961 that his government could not recognize "erroneous depictions of tri-junctions" in the map attached to the Sino-Burmese treaty because these had adverse implications for the territorial integrity of India.[53] Nu subsequently told Nehru, who protested officially to both Burma and China,[54] that the Burmese did not accept the map as binding.[55]

Burma's concern over China's intentions, combined with its continued indignation over foreign support of alien military activity on its soil, underlay the renewed strain on Burmese-American relations over the problem of the Kuomintang irregulars. The Burmese Army's capture of Mong Pa-liao airfield in February 1961, which resulted in the discovery of arms and supplies bearing American foreign-aid markings, and the subsequent death of a Burmese Air Force lieutenant in an aerial duel with an unidentified transport aircraft were followed by anti–United States rioting in Rangoon, where two persons were killed and 50 wounded, and in Mandalay. Burma's response to the growing evidence of renewed Nationalist Chinese "aggression" was to cable the United Nations Secretary-General urging the cessation of all assistance being given the aggressors. U Nu also stated that representatives had discussed the subject with the government of the United States "at the highest level." Nu's views on American involvement in the KMT problem were declared anew in a speech before the Chamber of Deputies in which he charged:

> The Kuomintang regime would not . . . exist on . . . Formosa but for the large-scale assistance, military and economic, furnished to it by the United States. We believe that this fact imposes on the United States certain responsibilities. One is to ensure that the Formosan regime does not misuse the military equipment which the United States provides to it.[56]

The United States responded to Burma's representations by effecting yet another airlift of Nationalist Chinese to Formosa, but not without the expression of deep-seated bitterness from Burma and from Nu.

The re-emergence of the Kuomintang controversy did not push the Burmese government into any dependence upon the Communist countries for arms. Indeed, U Nu indicated in late March 1961 that Burma wanted to purchase more arms from the British—or from the Americans, if British equipment were not available—for use against the Karens and the Kuomintang marauders. Agreement also was reached on American aid for modernization of the road to Mandalay, the United States made an outright grant of $6 million to Burma for the construction of a new "intermediate college" in Rangoon, an additional $9.25 million was loaned to the Burmese, and the General Exploration Company (an American firm) was licensed to conduct geological surveys for oil in 10,000 square miles of central Burma.

Nu's willingness to accept American aid despite his ire over the Kuomintang affair indicated that he was aware that Burma still needed external economic and technical help for development purposes. The future of Burma "is basically our own responsibility," Nu told the Chamber of Deputies in September 1960, but this responsibility could not be discharged "by us with our own resources. To make headway, we need to use every available resource, including foreign assistance."[57] Still smarting from the knowledge that other formerly occupied Southeast Asian lands had made more profitable reparations arrangements with Japan, Burma asked the Japanese in 1961 for $200 million more in reparations payments (a request that Japan refused).

Another problem about which Burma could do little, despite a number of determined efforts by Nu, was that of adjacent Laos. "We believe that a durable solution to their problem can be worked out only by the Laotian people themselves under the umbrella of the Geneva Agreement on Laos of 1954," Nu said in the Parliament in September 1960, "and we appeal to all the Powers concerned to help promote such a settlement."[58] According to Nu, "Strict neutrality in foreign affairs [was] the only realistic policy for Laos, given her geographical situation and other circumstances."[59] Yet he himself did not follow a strictly neutral policy toward the Laotian internal struggle for power, selling the blockaded government of Prince Souvanna Phouma petroleum in September 1960 and allowing it to be airlifted from Burmese fields.[60] When the military tide temporarily turned against the Souvanna Phouma government in December 1960, however, Burma turned a deaf ear to the requests of refugee officials for help—because all factions in the Laotian civil war were supported by major participants in the cold war.[61] Nu also declined an invitation from Laotian King Savang Vathana for Burma to become a member, together with Malaya and Cambodia, of a commission to visit Laos and confirm its neutrality. To do so, Nu said, would amount to recognizing the government headed by Prince Boun Oum.[62]

Burma, its Foreign Ministry said in an official statement on December 20, 1960, "considers that the fall of Vientiane [to the pro-Western Boun Oum–Phoumi Nosavan faction] does not mean the end of the Laotian civil war but the beginning of a much more serious conflict which may involve the two power blocs. . . . In these circumstances the Government of the Union of Burma considers that it might be helpful if the United Nations can appoint a commission composed of neutral countries which are acceptable to the parties involved in the Laotian civil war and charge it to find ways and means of solving the present conflict in Laos."[63] Subsequently, Nu called for "free and fair elections" in Laos "to be supervised by a commission of uncommitted states acceptable to all the Laotian parties." Burma, he said, "would be happy, if requested, to serve on such a commission."[64] The importance of Nu's views on the Laotian problem was underscored in late April 1961 when the American, British, and French Ambassadors called jointly on the Burmese Premier to urge him to encourage the other nonaligned nations to support an immediate cessation of hostilities in Laos.[65] There was even a possibility that he might "go abroad to a few places in connection with the cease-fire in Laos," Nu told members of his Union Party on May 7, but he said no more. Burma, having originally refused to participate in a 14-nation conference on Laos (suggested by Cambodia's Prince Norodom Sihanouk), subsequently agreed to take part in the Geneva parley on the Laotian problem, which began in mid-May 1961. Burma's Foreign Minister Sao Hkun Hkio declared that his government would welcome a continuous stretch of nonaligned states from India in the west to Laos and Cambodia in the east (a plan suggested also by Prince Sihanouk). The Geneva Conference made what was generally regarded as progress in its efforts to bring about international agreement concerning the future of Laos, but fared less well in its attempts to reconcile the opposed factions within the country.[66] The key to the Laotian problem, as Nu had predicted, lay with the Laotians themselves. Nu also realized, however, that even with internal reconciliation, peace in Laos (and Southeast Asia) depended on the support of the big powers. This was why he sought Chou En-lai's endorsement of "genuine neutrality" for Laos in the joint communiqué that followed the April 1961 meeting at Yunnan[67]—and why, also, he provided facilities for a meeting between

United States roving Ambassador W. Averell Harriman and Laotian Prince Souvanna Phouma in Rangoon in September.

Nu's behavior on the international scene in 1960–62 was also governed by a growing doubt that a nuclear war between the two blocs in the cold war was as unlikely as he had once believed.[68] His feelings were particularly evident at the Belgrade conference of nonaligned states held in September 1961. However much the great powers "may want peace," Nu said in the Parliament following the Belgrade meeting, "there are too many other considerations which enter the picture, one of the most important being that of national prestige. Therefore, despite their own yearnings for a peaceful world, the leaders of the Great Powers need support and backing."[69] This was why Nu urged the Belgrade nations to encourage the leading Communist and anti-Communist countries to set a "cooling-off period," and why he called on them to use "a large heart and a level head" in the way they went about opposing the evils of colonialism and racial discrimination and to "obey the golden rule of forgive and forget."[70]

Not all of the leaders attending the Belgrade meeting agreed that their countries should make an effort to bridge the gap dividing the world's great powers. Among those whose agreement was not obvious was the host, President Tito of Yugoslavia. The African countries in particular wanted to use the conference as a device for berating the West. Indian Premier Nehru, however—ably seconded by Nu and assisted by Mrs. S. W. R. D. Bandaranaike (Ceylon's Premier) and Archbishop Makarios (President of Cyprus)—succeeded in reducing the anti-Western feeling of the Belgrade meeting.[71] Nu himself, in addition, threatened to "publicly dissociate himself from the conference" in order to prevent the passage of a strong anti-Israeli resolution instigated by the Arab states.[72]

In January 1962, at the national congress of his Union Party, U Nu stepped down as Party President, although he remained as Premier. At the same convention the Thakin wing of the party decisively defeated the more moderate U-Bo's in the contest for domination of the new E.C. The Thakins, led by Thakin Tin, won all the seats on the E.C., seemingly settling for the time being the question of control of the party machinery. The split in the Union Party was similar to the rivalry for control of the united AFPFL before April 1958. The goal of both factions was to gain control of the party apparatus, and their struggle involved personality differences and rival political machines as well as a clash of interests. On the whole, the Thakins, less educated and more traditionalist in most ways, were paradoxically the more extreme socialists, while the U-Bo's, more educated and Westernized, were far more cautious concerning the state's role in the economy (though they were by no means anti-socialist).

Party differences had been one of the factors preventing the implementation of the new Four-Year Plan, virtually nothing having been done to put it into operation[73] despite the urgency Nu expressed in an address to the Parliament[74] in August 1961. Another cause of the government's immobility, however, was its preoccupation with the growing discontent of the minorities with the country's governing arrangements and with the policies of the Burman-dominated central government. In a conference on minority problems in Rangoon, Shan leaders had even threatened to secede from the Union,[75] and, according to Brigadier Aung Gyi, the Kayahs, numbering only 87,000 persons, had also talked of independence.[76] There was a feeling in the country that the Nu government was unwilling or unable to deal strictly enough with such talk of secession.[77] These considerations, coupled with lagging economic development and the decline in governmental efficiency that followed the return of the civilian politicians to office, seemed to move Burma once again toward the brink of chaos. In addition, the announcement that the Nu government intended to nationalize foreign trade as of March 1, 1962, aroused the ire of the Rangoon business community and contributed to the growing ranks of the dissatisfied. Monks had attacked U Nu following the adoption of new constitutional guarantees on behalf of non-Buddhists, ethnic minorities were more aroused than at any time since independence, and now businessmen, too, were voicing discontent with the Nu government.

So it was that on March 2, 1962, General Ne Win and the Army returned to power in a lightning-like *coup* that contrasted sharply with the constitutionally camouflaged seizure of power in 1958. Forming a 17-man Revolutionary Council of senior officers to govern the country, Ne Win declared in a radio broadcast that the Armed Forces "had taken over the responsibility and the task of keeping the country's safety owing to greatly deteriorating conditions in the country."[78] In a press conference on March 7, Brigadier Aung Gyi, next in importance to Ne Win in the new government, explained:

> In Burma we had economic, religious and political crises with the issue of federalism the most important reason for the *coup*. . . . A small country like Burma cannot afford division. The states enjoy autonomy and the right of secession guaranteed by the Consti-

tution, but if secession were to be exercised, small and newly independent Burma would sink like Laos or Vietnam.[79]

General Ne Win declared that the constitution had grave defects,
and he unilaterally and illegally abrogated it. He also dissolved the
Parliament and the existing state governments.

As for U Nu, he was placed under detention—together with most
of the other top members of the government, Union Party leaders, and
various Shan political figures. This was not Nu's first detention; he
had been jailed by the British on the eve of World War II. Then he
was only a young nationalist agitator; in 1962 he was Burma's Premier and a world figure. In 1962, moreover, he was detained by some
of his own countrymen following his second ouster from the Premiership at the hands of the Army. The second detention was unquestionably the more painful, followed as it was by his successor Ne Win's
abrogating the constitution, discarding (at least temporarily) even the
forms of democratic government in Burma, and disestablishing Buddhism as the state religion (in effect, since its status derived exclusively
from a 1961 amendment to the country's basic law). Nu's lot was failure and disappointment on many fronts.

NINETEEN

EXIT?

As Burma's Premier, U Nu sought reconciliation with his foes both within and outside Burma. He tried to show his countrymen—and the world—the relevance of love and truth to the solution of human problems. Typical of his approach was the speech he made to the 1960 graduating class of Rangoon University, in which he said:

> Man is a creature who lives in a community. . . . Only when a man wins the love and respect of his community can he be called eminent. . . . That which wins the love and respect of fellow humans is not worldly goods; it is truth, probity and practical benevolence towards others which wins the love and respect of fellow humans. If a man acts on every occasion with an honest mind, just and unshaken principles, and with the welfare of the ward, the village, the town, the country and the world at heart, this person will win the love and respect of the human world.[1]

The words revealed the character of the man, but they did not solve the "16,000 problems."

According to Dr. Ba Maw, the trouble with Nu was that neither by temperament nor by training was he a revolutionist. The Burmese revolution continued to smolder, but Nu and his associates were unable to channel its demands effectively, and hence contributed to "a general feeling of frustration and betrayal."[2] This feeling was particularly strong among members of Burma's armed forces, who were becoming increasingly important politically.[3] They were a different kind of man from Nu and the old-line revolutionaries—and in their own eyes were better equipped for the difficult tasks of leading the multi-sided Burmese revolution.

Several months after Nu's return to office in 1960, *The Nation,* the

influential Rangoon daily newspaper, assessed him and his government
in an editorial titled "Best Prime Minister, Worst Administration."
"Where he fails," the newspaper said of Nu, "is in finding lieutenants
with the capability to fill in the appropriate pictures, to color and shade
them into a composite whole. . . . It is a tragedy of U Nu's career
that he finds himself surrounded, either through personal selection or
force of circumstances, by mediocrities and wrong-headed types."[4] Nu's
leadership was largely leadership by example; as he himself put it, "I
have intended and hoped that my resolutions and conduct would be as
a beacon transmitting timely reminders."[5]

Shortly after his return to office in 1960, Nu attributed his country's woes to "a perverse sense of values. . . . Men everywhere are
attaching prime importance to material success," he said, "and resorting to means and methods, in order to achieve that success, which our
forefathers would hold to be dishonorable or questionable."[6] In order
to encourage right values, he wrote another play, *The Wages of Sin,*
which was serialized in *The Nation* in February 1961.[7] In this play Po
Thoung, a young Communist, says of his father:

> My father, though a minister, does not behave like one. He drinks,
> gambles, womanizes and takes bribes. One day my mother caught
> him with a prostitute. She slapped him. My father being drunk
> and without self-respect put up a loud howl. The neighbors sick
> to death of his drunken uproars threw stones at him. The incident
> made newspaper headlines the next day. After that I didn't dare
> show my face anywhere. At school the walls were covered with
> posters which said: "Boozing Minister," "Whoring Minister,"
> "Gambling Minister," "Money-eating Minister." Eventually my
> desk too was plastered with these posters. My schoolmates began
> to shout these words after me. I had to stop attending school. I did
> not dare go out. It seemed to me that everyone was looking at me
> and saying, "Here comes the son of the whoring minister." I didn't
> know what to do till Mya Than told me about the school [Commu-
> nist] here and I came over. I am very ashamed of my father. One
> of these days I will either kill myself or kill him. This is why I have
> bought this dagger.[8]

Another character in the play, Tin Tin, tells the minister, U Po
Lone, that he is "paving the way for a Communist takeover" by his
conduct.[9] Again and again Nu drove home the message that evil would
befall evildoers and that good would ultimately triumph.[10]

Nu's desire to establish Buddhism as the state religion was part of
his attempt to strengthen the moral fiber of his countrymen. But Nu's

religious outlook also affected his performance as Premier in other ways. In May 1961 he began a 45-day period of prayer and meditation at Mount Popa at a time when the Laotian crisis was still far from resolved—although he did postpone the start of his retreat in order to consult with the American, British, and French Ambassadors on the possibility of an extension of the war in neighboring Laos. When he did go into retreat, he left strict orders not to be disturbed. Later the same year the Cabinet voted to erect a large *nat* shrine at Mount Popa, superseding a previous decision to build two such shrines, one in Rangoon and one in Mandalay. The $2,000 allocated for the two shrines would be used to build a larger one at Mount Popa. In late 1961 the Ministry of Religious Affairs appropriated more than $12,000 for the building of pagodas of sand, symbolizing purity.

In his second Premiership U Nu was clearly more traditionalist than revolutionary, but this had not always been so. Through the years Nu has shown many facets. Nationalist, modernizer, traditionalist, humanist, religionist, and, sometimes, superb politician—Nu was all of these. He became Burma's political leader largely by chance. Dr. Ba Maw liked him—at least better than any of the other young Thakins—and he became a member of the wartime government, partly to escape prosecution by the Japanese. He was elected to the Constituent Assembly in 1947 to fill a seat vacated by the accidental death of its occupant. He became independent Burma's first Premier because the assassinations of Aung San and the other top leaders left nobody else.

However, Nu's emergence as Burma's chief governmental decision-maker within half a decade of his rise to the leadership of his country, and his position as its most popular citizen, were not the result of chance. They stemmed from his keen understanding of his political colleagues in particular and his countrymen in general. The colleagues —U Ba Swe, U Kyaw Nyein, and the rest—were younger than Nu and hence accorded him great deference; they also were less sure of themselves—including the Army leaders, even after the 1958 and 1962 *coups*. Nu's countrymen, on the other hand, came to love and respect him as Burma's ranking nationalist, a devout Buddhist, and a man who increasingly displayed a personal cultural orientation at one with the way the average Burmese viewed the world about him. Nu consciously played upon the attitudes of both groups.

As political leader of his country, U Nu was genuinely successful until the spring of 1958; he unified his countrymen, inspired them, and had the courage to fight when necessary for what he believed in. As chief governmental administrator, he was never a success; Burma in the decade from 1948 to 1958 was badly governed, and the two years following Nu's return to office in April 1960 were no improvement. Although this situation was in part the result of the limited legacy of administrative experience left by the British, it was also the result of political interference with administration, the caliber of Nu's chief lieutenants, and the tendency on Nu's own part to interfere on all levels of the government.

U Nu's role in the development of the political personality of renascent Burma took five forms. Nu made his first contribution to the evolution of an emancipated Burma in the middle and late 1930's as President of the Rangoon University Students' Union, member of the Dobama Asiayone, and leading figure in the Red Dragon Book Club. This role was an important one, but it probably could have been filled as well by someone else; the forces stirring Burma at this time were powerful ones, and Nu was only one reflection of them. But as a unifying force in Burma in the wake of independence, Nu played a much more important role; he, and he alone, kept the government together after Aung San's assassination and the early Communist and other rebel successes in 1948–50. Equally important, Nu served in the years after independence as a link between the Burmese past and the dream of his political associates and countrymen alike of a better future. Some of his colleagues—U Kyaw Nyein possibly or some of the Army leaders —were more competent technically to chart the course for the modernization of backward Burma. But none of them could have translated socialist aims into the Burmese folk idiom as successfully as Nu. Nu, moreover, was a symbol of Burma and its Buddhism, its hopes, and its groping. Finally, Nu was not only Burma's spokesman on the international scene but also the voice of the underdeveloped countries and nonaligned lands in general (a role he assumed consciously), or so he seemed to many. There was a difference between Nu and most of the others, however; Nu had lost—or controlled—the hatred derived from past mistreatment.

When he resumed the Premiership in April 1960, U Nu was the most popular Burmese political leader of all time and possessed greater potential influence than any other person or group, including the Army, in his land. During both of Nu's administrations his personal influence on Burma's government and the Burmese political process was strong. Yet, far from being a dictator in either word or act, of all the leaders of the countries whose independence had been gained after the Second World War, U Nu was one of the most convinced and understanding democrats. But he failed to retain the Premiership for even two years, and he was not effective in solving Burma's problems.

U Nu's first months under detention were by far the most difficult for him. Although the military government claimed that he was being well treated, he was able to see his wife for only the second time in late August. Nu posed a problem for the ruling Revolutionary Council just as he had for the caretaker administration in 1958–60: he would not quit politics. "Don't you know that it is illegal to arrest the Prime Minister?" Nu is alleged to have said during the second Army *coup*[11] on March 2. Nu was asked to proclaim publicly his resignation from the Premiership and his retirement from public life. He vigorously refused—despite his announcement in late 1961 that he intended to leave politics in 1964. Nu wanted sorely to retire to a life of fulltime meditation and propagation of the Buddhist faith and to set an example as a leader who had renounced power at the height of his glory. But Nu was not at the height of his glory on March 2, 1962, when for a second time in less than four years he was ushered none too gently out of his nation's highest political office. Repeatedly, in subsequent months, the military government asked Nu to disavow political life; "I am still Premier," he is said to have stated with continued firmness. His political office had been taken from him, but Nu's spirit had not been bent.

The Revolutionary Council could not afford to release Nu, a man of great energy and remarkable political resilience as well as of frequently demonstrated courage and shrewdness. Nu is probably still the most popular Burmese of all time with the masses of his countrymen, and the passive resistance campaign that he had planned in 1958–59, if he had decided to revive it in 1962 or later, would have threatened the survival of the Ne Win government. Nor could the Army try the popular and honest Nu both because he had broken no laws and because his trial, let alone conviction, would have made him a political martyr. This led some of his friends to fear for his life. "He could meet with an 'accident' in captivity," a longtime close friend said in Rangoon in August 1962. But this, too, would have aroused the country, and it is grossly unfair to accuse Burma's dedicated military leaders of a capacity for political homicide.

The circumstances left the government only two courses of action: to continue to confine Nu and to erase his image from the public mind —the former the easier to accomplish. "U Nu will not be released until after 1964," a former Cabinet member stated in 1962. "Then he will no longer be able to claim that he is Prime Minister, his term having expired." The exhibition in newly built Envoy Hall in 1962 depicting

Burma's path to independence included only one picture of the deposed Nu, standing to one side as the Union Jack was lowered and the new Burmese flag raised in its place on January 4, 1948. The picture of General Ne Win, Chairman of the Revolutionary Council, was everywhere. Nevertheless, the task of erasing his image would take time, and presumably it would stand a better chance of success if a substitute for Nu could be found.

General Ne Win, a minor nationalist figure before the war who gained fame as one of the "Thirty Comrades," was no substitute himself. He ruled with an iron hand, revealing the very opposite philosophy from U Nu's approach to the governing of man. The tragic slaughter of 16 students in a bloody demonstration at Rangoon University on July 7, 1962, in which another 42 young men and women were wounded, lost for the soldier government the respect of many educated and responsible Burmese who had previously not regretted U Nu's departure from the Premiership. Indeed, the second Ne Win government seemed to have developed the art of political alienation to a fine degree. Chairman Ne Win berated civil servants (many of whom appreciated the order and stability of his previous administration), offended many judges and lawyers by his abrogation of the constitution and replacement of Western-style judicial institutions with "special crimes courts," deprived the Rangoon and Mandalay University faculties of tenure and the right to govern themselves, and similarly displeased other sections of the Burmese elite. The parliamentary politicians could hardly be pleased at being displaced, nor could students (and their familes and friends) be enamored of a government that shot at them. Burma had no shortage of discontent as 1962 ended—a major reason for U Nu's continued confinement. Once before in 1958–60, Nu had used popular dissatisfaction with a military government as a springboard to return to power in Burma.

Despite its shortcomings, the Ne Win government did initially try to win political backing. To the strife-weary Burmese people it promised the establishment at last of law and order in the country, and it vowed to improve the distribution of various goods and to lower prices; the Adjutant-General even issued a directive informing military personnel how to behave toward civilians. Surrendering Shan insurgents were told in September that the "people's administration" would not exploit them as their *sawbwas* (hereditary chieftains) had done,[12] while businessmen were assured that Nu's plan to nationalize import trade would be delayed for at least two years. The pro-Communist National Unity Front, against which the soldiers had moved so vigorously in 1958–60, was now wooed by a military government that seemingly sought to end the nearly 15-year-old Communist insurrection by indicating to the extreme leftists that there was still a place for them in "revolutionary" Burma.[13] When U Nu had done essentially the same thing in mid-1958, however, he had been accused by many of the same soldiers of appeasing the Communists.

The Ne Win regime at first moved cautiously in its approach to various problems. Initially, it seemed that the soldiers did not want to compromise their chances of success by hasty action, but when they later moved to nationalize the economy, they did so with a vengeance. The Revolutionary Council, however, stated its support of socialist goals, declaring that it did not believe that man would "be set free from social evils as long as pernicious economic systems exist in which man exploits man and lives on the fat of such appropriation." Liberation would come only when "a socialist economy based on justice is established," the Council stated in a major, if vague, policy declaration, *The Burmese Way to Socialism*.[14] The lack of any definite statement of what the "Burmese way to socialism" was left an "emptiness in our midst," as Dr. Ba Maw, under the pseudonym of Po Thu Daw, wrote in *The Nation*.[15] One thing was clear about the new government's economic policy, however: it would place a greater emphasis than ever before on agriculture,[16] which U Nu had also proclaimed his intention to do as early as 1957.

Politically, the soldiers who ousted Nu in March 1962 tried, as he, too, had done, to limit political factionalism, and its consequent weakening of the government, by encouraging a single national party. To this end, they proclaimed a Burma Socialist Programme Party, which had the support of the anti-democratic NUF but of neither the recently deposed Union Party nor the Ba Swe–Kyaw Nyein AFPFL. The new party was described as a "transitional" and "cadre" one, which would be "constituted on the principle of centralism."[17] Parliamentary democracy had failed, the Revolutionary Council charged in April 1962, declaring: "The nation's socialist aims cannot be achieved with any assurance by means of the form of parliamentary democracy that we have so far experienced."[18]

In November 1960, in a speech before the Indian Council of World Affairs in New Delhi, U Nu sought to answer the question, "Are Asians fit for democracy?" He said:

If we take a good look at the nations of the West, we find that barely half of them are practicing democracies today, and that in only a handful of them has democracy been firmly established. In view of this state of affairs, it would be just as permissible for us to ask, "Are Westerners fit for democracy?" But of course we do not ask it because we realize that it would not be a fair question. It would not be fair because we know that the democratic system of Government, though the most desirable, is at the same time the most difficult form of Government to operate. No amount of academic study of democracy will by itself produce a democratic society. Democracy simply cannot be forced on a people, however enlightened the rulers may be. The basic principles of democracy have to be applied in each country in such a way as to suit local conditions, local beliefs and local customs. This means a slow process of gradual growth, and of education of the people. That is why, if we look into the record of those countries in which democracy has been firmly established, we will find that it has taken them hundreds of years to get where they are today. Most of the countries of Asia have been independent for just over a decade. This fact makes doubly unfair the question, "Are Asians fit for democracy?" I suppose the correct answer to this question, even if it sounds a little facetious, is: "Ask me in a few hundred years' time, and I will tell you not only whether the Asians but all the other peoples of the world are fit for democracy.

. . .

In the final analysis, the success or failure of a democratic experiment depends on the human element. Good men are essential to the successful working of a democracy. As I see it, human frailties, and particularly addiction to one or more of the main human vices—wine, women, gambling and corruption—are the greatest threat to democracy in Asia today. Having come to power by democratic means, many of our leaders have fallen prey to these evils and have thereby forfeited the confidence of their peoples. In a long-established democracy, such a Government would be thrown out by the electorate at the next election if not before. But in countries where a long tradition of democracy does not exist, these same corrupted leaders are only too often tempted to evade the democratic consequences of their conduct by adopting unfair means to perpetuate themselves in power. . . . In Burma we have a saying, "Only a gold cup is good enough to hold a lion's fat." Similarly, only good men can successfully operate a democratic system of Government.[19]

U Nu was a good man, but he did not make democracy work in Burma. With so many problems and the resources at hand so limited, what could one man—even a good man—do? More, perhaps, than Nu did: Nu "talked a good game," as the saying goes, but he did far less.

Indeed his goodness may have stood in his way; he lacked the ruthlessness that seems necessary even for the purposes of democracy. He seemed, moreover, to regard democratic government as an end in itself rather than as a means to other ends. And his revolutionary spirit unquestionably diminished between 1936 and 1962.

General Ne Win and his subordinates who took over from Nu in March 1962 were not by any means more able to direct the Burmese revolution. Nor would theirs be any easier task; if they lacked most of Nu's weaknesses, they also lacked many of his assets—and they would have to function, at least initially, in the same Burmese environment.[20] The tragedy was that U Nu and the Army were never able to form a political alliance, despite Nu's efforts in 1960–62 to remain on good terms with the military. But Nu could not control the various civilian political forces, and so he failed.

Early in Nu's first Premiership, when he was leading the fight against the Communists and the other insurgents, the Burmese writer Dagon Taya wrote a "little verse," as he called it, about Nu. In a biographical sketch of Nu,[21] published in the middle 1950's, Dagon Taya used this unfinished verse to characterize Nu's career:

> In the blast of the whirlwind,
> A leaf caught up, spinning;
> Whirling and eddying,
> And floating in the wind.

The times had brought Nu to the center of the stage, and the times had taken him away. But during his appearance he dominated the stage and played his part better, under the circumstances, than most others would have. The part, however, was too big for him. A different role might have suited him better—and may do so still.

TWENTY

A THIRD CHANCE?

FROM MARCH 2, 1962, to October 27, 1966, U Nu was a prisoner of the Burmese state he had helped to bring into being. During those years, Burma, which had tried to be a democracy under Nu's leadership, was one of the most rigorously autocratic regimes in Asia. General Ne Win, who served as caretaker ruler of the country in 1958–60 and later ousted Nu from office for the second time in four years, declared repeatedly that democracy was not an appropriate political instrument for solving Burma's problems. The narrowly nationalistic "Burmese Way to Socialism" which he proclaimed, however—to eradicate "the last vestiges of capitalist exploitation"—resulted in greater mass economic hardship than the Burmese people had experienced since the wartime Japanese occupation. The release of U Nu from detention in late 1966 seemed to be, at least in part, a reaction by Ne Win to the dislocation and decline of Burma's economy and the functional bankruptcy of its political system.

U Nu probably should have expected the army *coup* that catapulted him from power in March 1962, but the action caught him completely by surprise. Almost incredibly naïvely, Nu persisted in claiming that he was Burma's Premier—and ordering his captors to release him—as he was carried away to confinement. There was no doubt in his mind, however, that this time the military takeover was not an improvised one (as had been the case in 1958) and that democracy was at least temporarily dead in Burma. For the first two days after his arrest Nu was absolutely miserable, he later said, but then he remembered that Buddhism teaches "that you shouldn't be too happy when you're up or too unhappy when you're down." Early in his detention, accordingly, Nu established a rigorous daily routine of reading, writing, and meditation, a schedule not particularly different apparently from those of the other arrested former political leaders. Nu's onetime political lieutenant and later rival, U Kyaw Nyein, very much the agnostic in the past, studied Buddhist philosophy as well as history and politics, while Bo Let Ya did more than 100 oil paintings and Bohmu Aung practiced meditation and read religious literature.[1]

For four and a half years U Nu lived alone in a small house, his visitors were few and infrequent, and his letters were only slightly more numerous. The letters, including several written through the years to General Ne Win, were inevitably signed "Maung* Nu, Prime Minister of Burma." There were rumors from time to time that Nu had been freed for this or that holiday or, once, that he had been let out for a personal reason, but there is no evidence that he was ever released—temporarily or under guard—during the 55 months of his arrest. Reports also varied greatly as to how well he was treated during his captivity, but he made no public charges of mistreatment when he was released in October 1966. When freed, moreover, Nu showed few signs of any ill effects from his long detention. He was a little less rotund than formerly, and his hair had noticeably grayed. He also complained of occasional dizzy spells. But he was 59 years old and had otherwise lived a hard and trying life. Nu seemed older but not particularly more so than might otherwise have been expected.

Burma as a country showed greater signs of deterioration than did Nu as a result of the years that followed the soldiers' March 1962 takeover. Economic decline, which began early in the Ne Win administration, accelerated as the years passed. By 1968, two years after Nu's release from detention, rice exports had reached a record peacetime low of only 330,000 metric tons. In 1962, the year in which Ne Win toppled Nu from power, Burma had exported 1.8 million tons of rice, six times more than it did in 1968. Foreign trade had dropped by 1968 to half of its level six years earlier. Land under cultivation also declined, and there were chronic shortages of cooking oil, cloth, and other necessities. The cost of living nearly doubled in the decade 1958–68 (during only two years of which U Nu was Prime Minister), but incomes remained nearly static.[2] As one Rangoon newspaper put it in 1968, "We can hardly say we are enjoying prosperity."[3]

There was also an increase in corruption—the direct, if not the intended, result of the rigorously applied nationalization policies of the Ne Win regime. The distribution system in the country was all but wholly nationalized by the mid-1960's, although there was subsequent-

---

* Nu continued to sign his name "Maung" (not "U") Nu—a less honorific form of the prefix "Mr."—through the years.

ly some relaxation. People's Stores, created to replace the formerly private enterprises, persistently lacked goods, even everyday necessities, which led, in turn, to the establishment of a thriving and profitable black market. Prime participants in the black market enterprises were the managers and other employees of the various People's Stores.

General Ne Win's highly eulogized "Burmese Way to Socialism" made some progress, not least of all in the field of education (including the reorganization of the very outdated and ineffective University of Rangoon). The nationalization measures enacted by the soldier regime, moreover, ended—at long last—alien Asian domination of key areas of the national economy (particularly retail trade). Indians and Chinese in the thousands were deprived of their businesses as the government nationalized most of the economy as a means of reclaiming it from foreign hands. Nearly 200,000 Indians left the country for India in the years that followed Ne Win's assumption of power and subsequent nationalization moves, leaving behind only about 350,000 Indians in a land in which there had once been more than 900,000 members of this commercially astute minority. More than a quarter of Burma's 400,000 or so Chinese also left the country, many of them going to the People's Republic of China (planes to China being booked a full year ahead in mid-1967). Both minorities (but especially the Indians) had long been feared and hated by many Burmese, and the way they conducted their businesses was rarely designed to benefit Burma or the Burmese people. On the other hand, the Indians and the Chinese possessed skills and talents not yet developed among the Burmese, and the economy and the Burmese people were the worse off in the short run for their exodus. The paucity of Burma's capital and human resources was starkly shown in the wake of the departure of such large numbers of Indians and Chinese.

Economic conditions under U Nu's leadership admittedly often left much to be desired, particularly during his second Premiership in 1960–62, but they were never as bad as during the post-1962 years of Ne Win's rule. In addition, the economic decline accelerated in the second half of the 1960's; exports in 1967, for example, being only one-third of what they had been in 1965, only two years earlier. Economic decisions were taken by the Ne Win government, moreover, with almost no comprehension of their most likely consequences. It was not anticipated, for example, that the nationalization of Rangoon's retail trade in 1965, which had been planned (if not well), would merely drive goods out of the capital city, which is what happened. The government then precipitously nationalized retail trading throughout the land—with no provision whatsoever for any immediate substitute institutions for the nationalized former private traders. The quickly emergent black market was literally a functional necessity.

Burma's economic development, halting though it was in the 1950's, looked impressive in retrospective comparison with the economic decline and dislocation of the 1960's. General Ne Win must bear a very large share of the responsibility for the economic decay of the years 1962–69—but not all of it. Similarly, U Nu cannot be credited for all of the sometimes substantial accomplishments of the united AFPFL years (or blamed for all of their various shortcomings). The records of the two decades, the 1950's and the 1960's, stand in stark contrast to one another, however, and this fact cannot be dissociated from the leadership that the country experienced during these years.

The foreign policies of the U Nu and Ne Win governments also contrasted sharply in important respects. Both leaders pursued avowedly and actually neutralist foreign policies, but there the policies' similarities mainly ended. Nu's foreign policy—one of participation in the 1955 Bandung Conference and of efforts to reconcile Sino-American, Indo-Pakistani, and Arab-Israeli differences—was very much an activist foreign policy. Ne Win's was not. Burma's foreign policy under Ne Win in the years after 1962 was one of withdrawal. In May 1967, Ne Win actually said publicly that he wished he had "an atomic scissors so that I could cut this country off from Asia and have it towed out to sea away from those . . . up north"[4]—meaning Communist China.

Ne Win made a strong effort to establish cordial relations with Peking in both the caretaker years 1958–60 and after 1962, as evidenced by the border agreement he negotiated with the Chinese in 1960 and his willingness to use Chinese foreign aid at a time when he was turning his back on more assistance from the United States. China's behavior in June 1967, however—and subsequently—made a façade of its professions of friendship toward the Rangoon government. In June 1967, officials of the Chinese embassy openly encouraged students in Chinese schools in Rangoon to wear Maoist armbands and other insignia in defiance of government prohibitions. The worst rioting that post-colonial Burma has ever known followed; some 50 persons, almost all of them Chinese, lost their lives. The Chinese aid program was subsequently discontinued (by China) and Sino-Burmese diplomatic relations were almost broken. Leaders of Burma's Communist insurgency shortly thereafter appeared on Peking television, and China's support for the "White Flag" Communist rebels was at last out in the open.

Burma's difficulties with China encouraged General Ne Win to move closer to two of his country's other neighbors, India and Thailand. The Chinese Communists not only supported Burma's "White Flag" rebels (whose longtime leader and onetime political and personal friend of U Nu, Thakin Than Tun, was murdered by a subordinate in September 1968), but Peking also gave increasing aid to various ethnic minority insurgencies against the Burmese government. General Ne Win met with Indian Premier Mrs. Indira Gandhi in both New Delhi and Rangoon to discuss the problem of Chinese support of tribal insurrections in both of their countries. Burma subsequently pursued a policy of active cooperation with India in an attempt to thwart Chinese efforts to assist Naga tribesmen (to be found on both sides of the Indo-Burmese border) in their revolt against the New Delhi government. Ne Win's regime also held talks and reached a border agreement with neighboring Thailand, a SEATO member and a Vietnam war ally of the United States, in 1968.

General Ne Win's assessment of the strategic situation in South and Southeast Asia was best summed up in remarks made in April 1968. He said: "In Southeast Asia today there are powerful forces at work—forces which have their origin outside the region. The interplay of these forces will influence the future of Southeast Asia. Though the conflict between the forces from outside the region casts its shadow across the political scene, we in Burma believe that ultimately only forces of the region will prevail and play a vital role in determining the kind of Southeast Asia we shall have to live in."[5]

These words might have been spoken by U Nu. The difference between Nu and Ne Win as foreign policy leaders was not in their fears, perceptions, or aspirations. It was in their means and, to an even greater extent, their styles. U Nu feared China no less than Ne Win. Nu was cautious, however, where General Ne Win was timid—in his foreign policy behavior. In 1956 Nu did not intend to reveal the illegal presence of Chinese troops on Burmese soil, but *The Nation* broke the story. Nu, however, pursued his country's rebel insurgents relentlessly in all parts of the country. Ne Win also aggressively hunted down the different rebels, but he publicly stated in 1968 his reluctance to push such efforts too vigorously in the northern reaches of the country (where a combination of Communist and minority insurgents was led by the Peking-trained Kachin Naw Seng) for fear that "our bullets may end up in somebody else's country."

When the Union Jack came down for the last time in January 1948, U Nu thanked the British for drawing—indeed, forcing—Burma into more active contact with the rest of the world. Burma under Nu met regularly with India, Pakistan, Indonesia, and Ceylon as the Colombo Powers and took stands on Korea and other issues. There was always a seeming hesitation underlying Burmese foreign policy, however, even in Nu's day, among those who felt that Burma should interact less actively with other nations of the world. These forces came to a head under General Ne Win's leadership—perhaps because of it—after 1962. They were not able, however, to protect Burma from the pressures of the world beyond it, as the bloody Chinese-provoked demonstrations of June 1967 (and their aftermath) indicated. The difference was not major, but it was nonetheless real: Burma seemed to have less security (and fewer friends) in the Ne Win years than in the two periods in which U Nu served as premier.

The biggest difference between "U Nu's time" (as Burmese nostalgically referred to the period before 1962) and the second Ne Win Premiership was in the pattern and style of its domestic politics. Burma's was a most authoritarian soldier regime following the March 2, 1962, ouster of U Nu. The army, led by the forceful and quick-tempered General Ne Win, literally ran the full apparatus of government. Only one member of the 13-man ruling Revolutionary Council was a civilian (Foreign Minister U Thi Han). Soldiers headed every government agency or board or maintained a watchful eye over those who nominally provided such leadership. The old political parties were forbidden (but few of the old politicians joined the new single government party, the Burma Socialist Program Party). The soldiers, moreover, clearly profited from their privileged political status, as evidenced by their automobiles and comfortable housing.

General Ne Win disavowed altogether the democratic approach to politics so passionately pursued by U Nu. Parliamentary democracy had proved itself unsuitable to Burma's needs, he declared. The Communist-style, cadre-type Burma Socialist Programme Party that he proclaimed was to be the main political instrument for the achievement of a new and more just socialist order (a goal that Nu also pursued, albeit democratically and far more humanely). The basic document outlining the government's aspirations for the new Burma was "The System of Correlation of Man and His Environment," a narrowly ideological and jingoistic treatise that showed no evidence that Ne Win or any of his advisers had ever read Karl Marx. The main reason for the failure of the "Burmese Way to Socialism" was probably not the fact that the new military leadership got lost as a result of its confused (and confusing) ideology, but that ideology certainly provided Burma no subsequent guidance at all out of the ever-worsening economic and political plight in which the Ne Win government found itself.

Rigid in its approach to both economic decision-making and the development of political support (through slowly formed peasants' and workers' councils), the Ne Win regime was no less heavy-handed in its treatment of the country's chief indigenous minorities, the Kachins, Shans, and Karens. The Burmese military and police forces which pursued the insurgents numbered more than 165,000 men, but they were not able after more than seven years of army rule (1962–69) to extend the government's effective writ beyond the approximately two-thirds of the country controlled by U Nu's regime at the time of its overthrow. However, the "White Flag" Communists, less than 3,000 men strong in mid-1969, suffered some of the worst defeats of their 20-year-old insurgency in 1968. But their place as Burma's most dangerous insurrectionary group seemed to be taken in 1969 by another Communist force, which was led by the Kachin Naw Seng and included members of other minorities as well as Kachins and Communists, along the country's northern frontier with China. The various other Karen, Kachin, and Shan insurgencies worsened during the 1960's, as they had done in the years (1958–60) of Ne Win's earlier caretaker regime.

Xenophobic in his nationalist outlook, Ne Win was much more of a Burman than Burmese nationalist. The problem he chose to face head-on was a real one: the making of a nation in fact where one had previously probably existed only in form. But Ne Win's concept of the Burmese nation was a veritably imperial one. It meant the Burmanization of Burma as contrasted with the slower multicultural encouragement of a widespread feeling of being Burmese and of belonging to the Burmese nation. The minorities realized this, and Ne Win, who seized power from U Nu allegedly to prevent the fragmentation of the union, did little in the seven years after 1962 to forge a more perfect union. In fact, he probably weakened the union, imperfect as it was, of Burma's diverse peoples.

Ne Win ruled by the force of his vigorous personality and his singlemindedness of purpose. He was not a dictator, however, after the fashion of a Mao Tse-tung or even a Sukarno; few leaders in modern history have seemed to try to shun the public eye as much as he has done (or to revel less in their paramount position). If he had a model or even a parallel, both of which are unlikely, it would be one or another (or perhaps a composite) of the other military leaders who governed such soldier-run states as South Korea, the United Arab Republic, or Pakistan (under Ayub Khan). Revolutionary by self-decla-

ration, Ne Win also was attracted by the simple and austere life traditionally lived by the Burmese peasant. Living himself unostenta-
tiously, he ruled partly by example—many Burmese appreciating his
integrity if not his policies—but partly also by fear and secret police.
Perhaps the most efficient—certainly the most feared—of Burma's
public agencies was the Military Intelligence Service, whose informers
were quick to tell Ne Win's chief subordinates of suspicious behavior.
Persons were even known to have been jailed for not reporting the
arrival of a relative from the countryside or even for falling asleep and
failing to stand for the national anthem. Of legitimate political opposition, not surprisingly, there was none in Ne Win's Burma.

Such a system could not endure indefinitely, and, increasingly (if
spasmodically), General Ne Win seemed to realize this. In October
1966, a month after his return from a visit to the United States, Ne Win
released U Nu from confinement, 55 months after he had ousted him
from the Premiership. U Ba Swe, Nu's onetime lieutenant and briefly
Premier in 1956 (when Nu had stepped down to "clean up" the
AFPFL political organization), was freed at the same time, and by
February 1968 most of the remaining detained ex-political leaders
were also released: Aung Gyi (once Ne Win's political right arm),
former Deputy Premier U Kyaw Nyein, the dying wartime *Adipati*
Dr. Ba Maw, *The Nation's* longtime editor U Law Yone, ex-Foreign
Minister Sao Hkun Hkio, and such other politicians as Dr. E Maung,
Bohmu Aung, U Raschid, U Win, and Bo Let Ya (among others).

How many of these former political prisoners sought to influence
General Ne Win to change the static, draconian Burmese political system is not known, but two of them at least offered their views in writing to the Revolutionary Council's soldier chairman: U Nu and ex-
Brigadier (and onetime Socialist Party leader) Aung Gyi. Their
letters probably influenced Ne Win's September 1968 address, one of
his comparatively few public appearances, in which he described his
regime as "different from the armies of despots in history." "Politics
belongs to the people," Ne Win declared, adding, "We cannot monop-
olize politics." The "only viable course," as he proclaimed it, was to
enlist the support and influence of those "old politicians who had come
to appreciate the cause for which we stand." Strongly implying prob-
able early political alteration of the decaying Burmese state, Ne Win
asserted, "We are now in a transition period and a lot of things remain
to be done ... including drawing up a constitution."

U Nu, whose pleading probably influenced Ne Win's September
1968 speech, was in less of a mood for compromise than the General

appeared to be. In November 1968 he told a newsman, "Nothing short of a return to parliamentary democracy will satisfy me if they want my support." That Nu could speak so freely was one measure of the change that had already taken place in Burma, but the road back to open politics and personal freedoms remained a long one.

The release of U Nu from detention took place on October 27, 1966. There had been earlier indications, however modest, of Nu's possible liberation (and of related political changes), but of political liberalization there was literally none in the first four years of Ne Win's rule. There were several reasons for this: Ne Win himself (not to mention other less selfless officers) had grown accustomed to power, not all the army officers were by any means anxious to get back to the field and the weary task of fighting the insurgents, there was always the hope that the measures introduced under the "Burmese Way to Socialism" might yet prove successful (though this was a vain hope), and, by no means least important, there was an almost unbelievable degree of inertia that seemed to hold back any kind of political change.

In addition, there was the attitude of U Nu and most of the rest of the detainees. For the most part, they were unwilling to do or say the kinds of things that General Ne Win at first wanted them to do or say in order to gain their release. Whether Nu ultimately made any kind of deal to gain his freedom is unknown, but it appears improbable. Upon his release, however, he did state that he would abstain from political life,[6] but just what he meant is unclear. Subsequently, in early 1969, when Nu suggested the immediate termination of the "unconstitutional" Ne Win regime, he proposed that he himself serve as Premier —because, as he saw it, he was still legally Prime Minister—but he also said that he would hold no public office afterwards. At the time of his release from confinement in 1966, Nu also stated that he would consider the Ne Win regime "illegal" until "Constitutional government" had been restored.[7]

Nu's liberation followed General Ne Win's visit to the United States in September 1966 and talks, while in that country, with his distinguished countryman (and onetime Nu adviser), United Nations Secretary General U Thant. Presumably the American government did not seek to intervene on Nu's behalf, although this possibility cannot be discounted, but surely Thant did speak for the release of his longtime friend and former teaching as well as political colleague. In any event, in the first of a series of events which the Burmese quickly tabbed the "three 27th's," Ne Win—on September 27, 1966—an-

nounced on the eve of his return from the United States the "de-
control" of some 34 commodities whose sale by private traders had previously been illegal. On the second "27th," October 27, U Nu and U Ba
Swe were released from detention. And on November 27 cooking oil
was "decontrolled."

These moves were designed to relieve some of the pressure, economic as well as political, that the Ne Win government was beginning
to feel. The 10 percent increase in the price paid the peasant for his rice,
announced on November 31, was part of the same pattern, which was
to accelerate, at least politically, in 1968 with the release of most of the
rest of the political prisoners. Burma clearly had been approaching a
breaking point. There had been rice rationing in parts of the country in
1965, in a land that had once been the world's leading exporter of the
grain. There was genuine hardship in many parts of the nation and
mounting resentment against the government, though this took no
overt (or known) political form because of the ever present soldiers
and police (and the effective absence of alternative political leadership).

U Nu was released primarily because of these building pressures.
U Thant had earlier sought his release, with no success. Nu made no
concessions in 1966, any more than he had been willing to make them
earlier. The change in 1966 (as compared with 1964 and 1965) was in
the perceptions and conclusions of General Ne Win. If parliamentary
democracy had failed Burma (as Ne Win sincerely believed to be the
case), so, too, had army rule (though this was not to be admitted publicly). Changes were necessary, Ne Win realized, but he had not decided what kind of changes (or how many of them). Ne Win's release
even of Nu was opposed—as much as anyone would directly oppose
such a dictator—by the extreme left-wing (Brigadier) Tin Pe faction
within the ruling Revolutionary Council.

When U Nu was released from detention in 1966, he stated that he
would devote his full energies and time to Buddhism. Nu at first did
so, spending long hours in religious meditation and also beginning a
projected ten-volume history of the world in colloquial Burmese. It
was not long, however, before the seemingly irrepressible Nu was out
again among the Burmese masses (for whom he had demonstrated
such compassion in his years in power). He traveled about the country
and gave sermons on Buddhism. There was nothing political in his
speeches—at least not overtly—but the Burmese are past masters of
the art of double meanings, and many read much into Nu's remarks
(in some instances probably too much). What Nu said was very ortho-
dox Buddhism: there was nothing permanent in this world and exis-

tence—and everything would change in time. This simple message both supported, and contrasted with, the slow, if sporadic, changing political orientation of General Ne Win. Despite his public speeches over the previous two years implying impending changes, very little had happened that really altered the operation of the Burmese political system under Ne Win. But Ne Win implied ultimate change, and so did Nu. On the other hand, while U Nu was allowed to travel freely about the country to deliver his religious lectures, his onetime close associate (and later rival) U Kyaw Nyein was still not permitted to meet openly with his former followers.

Nu vigorously maintained that his words had no political meaning. But "I can't sit idle," he said. "I feel that I must do something for the good of my people, if not in politics, at least in religion."[8]

Nu's behavior seemed more political as time passed. In May 1968, when an unusually destructive hurricane hit the Akyab region of western Burma, leaving anywhere from 1,000 to 3,000 persons dead, Nu organized the "Central Committee for Arakan Cyclone Relief." Nu gathered together many of his former political associates and asked them to aid him in raising funds for the survivors (and the relatives of the deceased) of the Arakan storms. When several of his friends offered generous donations, however, Nu refused to accept them. The Arakan flood relief campaign must be a response of the whole Burmese people, Nu told them; nobody would be allowed to contribute more than one *kyat* (about 22 cents). Nu carried the day, as he was accustomed to doing in such circumstances in the old days, and he and the other politicians embarked on an extensive tour of the country to raise funds for the cyclone victims. When the campaign ended in July, they had raised 400,000 *kyats*—at no more than one *kyat* a contributor—a generous response of the Burmese people. The experience, however, had also given U Nu his greatest mass exposure since his release from confinement in late 1966.

General Ne Win was out of the country when U Nu began his cyclone relief activity. His wife required medical attention, and Ne Win had accompanied her to London. Although Nu's efforts were at first criticized in the government-controlled press and he and the other politicians were watched all of the time by the Military Intelligence Service, there was no interference with either their travels or their speeches. Replying to the charge that he was politically exploiting the misery of his countrymen for personal advantage, Nu characteristically commented, "How can anyone think that? The people were suffering. What else could we do?"[9]

In the first years of U Nu's detention, the government did all it could do to make the people forget their onetime political hero. Exhibitions on national holidays and other such activities rarely included pictures that showed U Nu.[10] By mid-1968, however, Nu was very much back in view again. The people, in fact, had never forgotten U Nu.[11] His effective return to public visibility in 1968, however, revived him as a man of immediate public importance and reminded his countrymen of his continuing great concern for them.

One of the charges leveled against Nu was that his cyclone relief committee represented the beginning of a new "rightist front."[12] Nothing could have been further from the truth. As usual, Nu was not unaware of the political consequences of his actions, but there is no evidence to suggest that he planned to bring into being a new political organization, which would have been illegal anyway. Quite the opposite may in fact have been the case. U Nu may have had his political inclinations stirred by his cyclone relief activity rather than having engaged in this activity for a political purpose. He was visibly moved by the quite depressed economic conditions he saw, openly terming them "almost unbearable." "There must be a relaxation of economic controls," he told a newsman, one of his rare indulgences in public criticism of the policies of the Ne Win government.[13]

General Ne Win, in his September 1968 speech, suggested the likelihood of early political changes, possibly even the participation of some of the old civilian politicians in the government, but for the two years previously there had been suggestions of changes, not least of all after the release of U Nu and U Ba Swe in late 1966. It came as a considerable surprise, consequently, when Ne Win on November 29, 1968, called on the man he had twice displaced as Prime Minister, U Nu, and 32 other former political leaders to serve on a National Unity Board to make recommendations to the government to further the unification of the country and its political development. The membership of the National Unity Advisory Board read like a who's who of onetime Burmese political leaders: U Kyaw Nyein, U Ba Swe, Thakin Tin, Bo Min Guang, Thakin Tha Khin, Bohmu Aung, and former Union President Mahn Win Maung, among others. The board was to complete its work by the end of May 1969. General Ne Win asked the public to send suggestions to the committee concerning the possible form of a new constitution. And Ne Win, who had thrown out the constitution with which Burma began its independence when he ousted U Nu on March 2, 1962, even indicated that a revised version of the old charter might be acceptable to the country's military leadership.

"We"—meaning the ruling Revolutionary Council—"have no intention to make power exclusive to ourselves," Ne Win told the National Unity Advisory Board. The board was instructed to submit to the Revolutionary Council "advice on the means of building a national unity that would benefit the politics, economics, social, and nationality affairs of the working people of the Union of Burma. " Such advice, he said, "should . . . be of use for a constitution that would be drafted for the Union of Burma in the future."[14] Ne Win certainly seemed sincere in the call he made to the old politicians to help him and their country, but, as in 1958–60, there were other soldiers who did not favor the restoration of civilian government in any form whatsoever.[15] Moreover, the creation of the National Unity Advisory Board was followed in late 1968 and early 1969 by new nationalization measures, including the nationalization even of movie houses as well as of privately owned sawmills and 160 "industrial firms."[16] Brigadier Tin Pe and others of the more extreme socialists on the Revolutionary Council clearly had not relaxed their pressure for still more state ownership of the economy. The moves contrasted with Ne Win's professed political open-mindedness and raised the question of whether his still paramount power may not have been diminished a little.

Nu and the other former political leaders, however, set to work on their new task almost immediately. Meeting almost daily in the old stucco colonial dwelling that served as the Prime Minister's house in U Nu's two periods as Premier, the politicians reviewed the constitutions of various nations, Yugoslavia, the United States, France, South Korea, and the Soviet Union among others. In all, the National Unity Advisory Board met 93 times. At its seventh session, on December 30, 1968, U Nu submitted a memorandum to the board urging the immediate formation of "a national government" headed by himself. An amended version of this proposal was discussed in the four meetings held January 30–February 3, 1969, but was never voted on. Nu's memorandum and a report of the discussion on it were submitted to General Ne Win on February 5.[17]

In his memorandum, U Nu called for the resignation of General Ne Win and the Revolutionary Council as the government of Burma and the appointment of himself as interim Prime Minister pending a constitutional change permitting Ne Win to be elected new President of the Union of Burma. (Nu was obviously disregarding the fact that Ne Win had thrown out the constitution when he seized power in 1962.) No solution of the nation's many pressing problems, Nu said, can be effective without the cooperation of political personalities, General Ne Win, or a form of parliamentary democracy. "Immediately" after his designation as interim Premier, Nu stated, "I shall summon Parliament into session" to amend the constitution to permit itself to elect General Ne Win "President of the union" with "full executive powers as distinct from legislative and judicial powers." Ne Win's earlier order banning all political parties except the Burma Socialist Program Party would be lifted. Besides Ne Win's immediate election as President (for a term of unspecified length), the General would be eligible to serve two further terms. "In advising that the (new) constitution . . . be based on a form of parliamentary democracy," Nu stated in his memorandum, "I do so as I cannot accept any other form of government."

Nu's own future political role would be a very modest one, his memorandum suggested, but he did apparently envisage a role for himself. "As soon as Parliament elects the President," he said, "my government will resign and cease to hold office." Suggesting that many of the former political leaders would want to seek office again, Nu stated that there would also be "those who, like myself, will remain outside the government but who will cooperate" with it.[18]

The demand by U Nu for a legitimate transition from the self-established military dictatorship of General Ne Win to an elected republican government—headed by the same General Ne Win as President—was consistent with his past insistence on form and his demonstrated dedication to democracy. Independence had to take effect at precisely the astrologically most propitious hour in 1948 (as did his temporary departure from the Premiership in 1956). When Ne Win demanded that he quit the Premiership in 1958, Nu made the General postpone his coup a month so it would not appear that he was being forced out of office. In 1969 Nu said, "Unless the Revolutionary Government hands over power (to himself), it will retain the character of a government that has assumed power through force." "Whatever new shape or form that government may take," he declared, "it will remain in the sight of the people a government originating in the exercise of force."[19]

There can be little doubt of the continuing dedication of U Nu to democratic political ideals, but there is doubt respecting what he sought to accomplish in offering a proposal that seemed such a direct repudiation of General Ne Win and his regime. After his proposal had been considered by the National Unity Advisory Board, the last such discussion taking place on February 3, 1969, Nu ceased to attend meetings of the board altogether.[20] Having had his say, so to speak, was he unwilling to participate in further deliberations, or was this a tactic designed to protect the other politicians from possible retribution if Ne

Win or others of the military leaders reacted strongly against his proposal? Nu's resumption of his public lectures on Buddhism (attended by ever-larger crowds in Rangoon, Mandalay, Moulmein, and others of Burma's bigger cities), which took place after he stopped attending sessions of the National Unity Advisory Board, suggested that he was in fact making a serious comeback bid. But the charge that Nu used religion for his personal and political advantage was an old one, and those who offered it in the past often failed to appreciate the almost compulsive quality of his dedication to his beloved Buddhism. In February–March 1969, the fact that private buses were offering reduced fares to take the faithful to hear Nu's sermons suggested that the popular ex-Premier had some financial (and other) backing for his religious—or political—activity.[21]

Nu's proposal to the National Unity Advisory Board—and, no less so, his public lecturing on Buddhism (while the constitutional comittee was still in session)—came under vigorous attack from one of the leading figures in the Ne Win regime (and widely reputed heir apparent to the General's military and political power). Brigadier San Yu, vice chief of staff of the army, strongly criticized those who sought political power under a "cloak of religious activity," his attack taking place while General Ne Win was in London for a medical checkup. The government's *Working People's Daily* linked the "old politicians" with Communists and black marketeers as the chief scourges of the nation,[22] and the once liberal *Guardian*, named after the famous English paper, sought to smear the former political leaders by accusing them of having been handmaidens in the past of foreign capitalists "including the Indians and the Chinese."[23] The attacks against both U Nu and democracy seemed designed to protest any possible recommendation by the National Unity Advisory Board for the termination of the existing military regime. At the time of the press attacks on Nu, which took place in April, his memorandum had been in the hands of the government for more than two months, but the National Unity Advisory Board was still sitting—and what its recommendations would be were not known (though perhaps suspected).

The personal attack on Nu by Brigadier San Yu—and the general press assault on democracy as a political answer to Burma's problems—unquestionably played a part in U Nu's April 11 departure on a pilgrimage to Buddhist shrines in India. Nu's health also seemed to be failing somewhat, however, and there can be no doubt of the genuine attraction for him of visiting Buddhist temples and holy places in India. Whatever the relative importance of these influences, the fact remains that

U Nu took the strongest possible practical stand against the continuation of Ne Win's army dictatorship, an action that offended many of the country's top soldiers (if not Ne Win himself). There can be no doubt that Nu would be safer in India than in his own Burma. Ne Win probably would not have jailed him right away again, but there were other ranking Burmese soldiers who would have argued for such action. From a political standpoint, moreover, Nu may have wanted a neutral sanctuary from which to plot his next assault against continued dictatorial rule in his native Burma.

The full 68-page report of the National Unity Advisory Board, completed without U Nu's participation, was submitted to General Ne Win on June 2, 1969, the first working day after the committee's designated term of office ended. Its majority report or two minority reports were signed by all the members of the board except Nu, who was in India.

The strongly ideologically oriented language of both the majority report and the main minority report was consistent with the past political outlooks of those who signed them. The majority report proclaimed a "democratic socialist state as the goal," with "democratic socialism as the axis"; the main minority report proposed a "socialist state as the goal," with "socialist democracy as the axis." The 18-member majority report represented the views of such ex-Union and AFPFL party leaders as U Ba Swe, Mahn Win Maung, Bohmu Aung, U Kyaw Min, Thakin Tin, Bo Min Guang, Bo Khin Maung Gale, and Bo Khin Maung, as well as various minority leaders. These democratically oriented socialists wanted a return to parliamentary democracy, with "a republican form of administration with a strong center." The main minority report (signed by 11 less well-known former political figures, such as Thakin Lwin, Thakin Sun Myint, and other ex-National Unity Front and left-wing Socialist and Communist politicians) "did not favor parliamentary democracy as practiced in the past." The "red Socialists," as they used to be called, favored a one-party state based on "democratic centralism."

There was greater similarity between the majority report and U Nu's memorandum than between the latter document and the minority report of the "red Socialists." The majority recommendations also called for the transformation of Ne Win's Revolutionary Council government into a "national government" including "persons from politics and the nationalities as well as the armed forces." "Pending the convocation of a constituent assembly or the holding of a referendum," the report stated, "party politics are to be allowed at a suitable time through fair and suitable elections." In the "long term," the National Unity Advisory Board's majority, like Nu, favored an elected "President" and a "multiparty system that permits opposition and human rights." In the "short run," however, a "National Front" should be formed—headed by General Ne Win. There was no suggestion of any interim government, however, based on that led by U Nu at the time of Ne Win's March 1962 takeover, to be headed by Nu. Philosophically and even tactically, the majority agreed with Nu's democratic goals for Burma. But the majority apparently saw no immediate role for Nu himself in Burma's politics. His ex-colleagues (some of them later also his rivals) did not seem to support a return by Nu to political power. But then things have not always been as they seemed in sometimes politically indirect Burma.

The majority and main minority reports also differed in terms of their economic philosophy. The majority, which gave top priority to Burma's industrialization, raised the question of some possible future "denationalization," despite the new nationalization moves of late 1968 and early 1969, and supported a private sector as well as the acceptance of foreign aid (in which the Ne Win regime had shown only the most modest interest). The minority was obviously not enthusiastic either over the economic state of the country, proposing to "re-examine measures taken under the 'Burmese Way of Socialism,'" but it called for the complete abolition of capitalism and landlordism in the country. The differences in economic position involved basically a choice between a modified democratic socialist approach (the majority) and a Communist-style socialist economy (the minority). The latter much more closely resembled Ne Win's demonstrated orientation.

The second minority report, signed by former Deputy Premier (and ex-"Stable" AFPFL leader) U Kyaw Nyein, Thakin Tha Khin, and Thakin Chit Maung, differed from the majority report only with respect to the indigenous minority peoples of the country. The majority had recommended the re-creation of the old Shan, Karen, Kachin, and Kayah states and the former Chin Special Division and the establishment in the "short term" of Mon and Arakanese Affairs Councils. The majority would re-establish the pre-March 1962 political ethnic subdivisions, ultimately creating, in addition, new Mon and Arakanese states. The Kyaw Nyein minority report opposed separate states of the old sort and vigorously endorsed the idea of a "strong unitary state."[24]

Referring to the proposal to form a "national government" (with

participation of civilian politicians and representatives of the minorities
as well as of the armed services), as both the majority and minority reports (and U Nu's memorandum) recommended with variations, General Ne Win stated on June 3, 1969: "We shall not hesitate to form
such a government if we can be sure of its benefits."[25] Standing with
Ne Win as he received the several reports of the National Unity Advisory Board were the other chief military figures of the regime—Brigadier San Yu, Brigadier Tin Pe, Colonel Hla Han, and Colonel Than
Sein—to each of whom had been attributed opposition to the civilianiza-
tion and liberalization of Burma's politics and economics. Ne Win
promised, however, to hold "nationwide discussions" on the proposals.

Missing altogther from the scene—personally—was the man who
had once been Burma's Prime Minister and who had taken the strongest stand on behalf of the early democratization of Burma's politics on
the National Unity Advisory Board, U Nu. Nu was missing only in
person, however. His memorandum and the majority and minority reports of the board were carried in their entirety within days in the Rangoon press, a reminder of the years when Burma's was an open political
system and its press one of the freest in Asia (and an indication perhaps
that the country was again moving, however slowly, in that direction).
Ironically, the June 6, 1969, *Working People's Daily* carried, besides its
continuing serialization of the National Unity Advisory Board's reports, a dispatch from New Delhi that U Nu would shortly don the
robes of a Buddhist monk in India. "I have always felt that we owe
deep gratitude to India which gave Buddha to the world," Nu said.
"The time has come to repay this. I have decided to retire from politics
and embark on the religious mission. Now religion is the most important thing for me."[26]

The prospect that U Nu would soon again return to a direct and
open role in Burmese politics seemed to dim in the immediate wake of
General Ne Win's receipt of the several reports of the 33-man National
Unity Advisory Board, but the evidence continued to contain contra-
dictions. The press reaction was markedly unfavorable to the 21-man
majority (including the Kyaw Nyein–led minority which accepted most
of the majority report), not to mention U Nu's memorandum, in the
weeks that followed the termination of the board's responsibilities.
Praise, on the other hand, was accorded the 11-man "red Socialist" report which accepted, according to the press, both the purposes and the
institutional structures of the "Burmese Way to Socialism."[27] The appointment of Brigadier San Yu (Ne Win's most likely soldier successor
and Nu's outspoken critic in the concerted April press attack on the for-

mer Premier) as Minister of National Planning on June 18 also did not
suggest an early liberalization of Burmese politics. On the other hand,
the resignation the same day of civilian Foreign Minister U Thi Han,
accepted regretfully by Ne Win, implied a more active political role for
Thi Han in the future. Thi Han gave as the reason for his resignation
the fact that "some ex-politicians and ex-army officers" had sought his
help on "personal and other matters" and his expectation that they
"will continue to seek such help in the future,too."[28]

The June 2, 1969, presentation of the various recommendations of
the different factions of the National Unity Advisory Board may have
marked the beginning of a new era in the post-colonial political, economic, and social development of Burma. General Ne Win, who asked
33 of his country's leading former political figures for their advice on
shaping Burma's future, presumably would not have done so if he had
not been willing to listen to their ideas. There is no reason to believe
that U Nu, U Kyaw Nyein, U Ba Swe, or any of the rest of the onetime
leaders gave Ne Win any indication that they had basically altered
their political thinking while in confinement. Ne Win asked 33 men to
advise him on how to direct Burma along more suitable lines than the
country had followed in the years after the March 2, 1962, coup d'etat.

Ne Win received three and a half answers to his request : the majority report, the main minority report, the Kyaw Nyein minority report
(which agreed with the majority report except for its approach to the
minorities), and U Nu's memorandum of December 30, 1968, which,
modified, was transmitted to Ne Win on February 5, 1969.

When U Nu left Rangoon on April 11 for India, the question was
when, how—and if—he would return. The sincerity of his Buddhist
proselytizing efforts notwithstanding, Nu clearly hoped that he would
someday return in political triumph—ideally to play at least the short-
term role he designed for himself in his memorandum to the National
Unity Advisory Board. There was also the possibility, however, that he
might return later to participate in elections for a new Burmese parliament. And, finally, there was the possibility that he might never return.

Nu, however, remained only a short while in India—or in the saf-
fron-colored robes of a Buddhist monk. Encouraged by support from
anti–Ne Win Burmese exile elements outside the country, he flew in
mid-1969 to Thailand's capital city of Bangkok, where the largest community of Burmese expatriates is to be found, and from there, on August 23, to London—where he had completed the constitutional negotiations for Burma's independence nearly a quarter of a century earlier.

The purpose of his flight to London, he said, was to define more fully his opposition to the continuation of the Ne Win military government in Burma. There was no little irony in the fact that Nu, who had once so vigorously attacked the British presence in Burma and had even burned the Union Jack as a young nationalist, should return to London to dramatize his continuing commitment to freedom for his countrymen. There was even speculation that Nu would establish a government-in-exile in London as a further means of forcing concessions from the Ne Win regime on behalf of more liberal political institutions. One thing was sure: confronted once again with the choice of the contemplative life of a Buddhist monk or the challenge to serve his countrymen as democracy's champion, U Nu had once again—as he had so frequently done in the past—made his decision in favor of political service. With Nu's August 23 flight to London, the Burmese political battle seemed once again to be joined. The outcome, however, was still very much in doubt.

On August 29, 1969—nine months to the day following General Ne Win's request to U Nu and the 32 other formerly jailed civilian politicians to serve on the National Unity Advisory Board—Nu met the press in distant London and launched his self-proclaimed campaign to restore democracy to Burma. He was still legally Burma's Prime Minister, Nu declared (as he had stated consistently since his overthrow and detention on March 2, 1962), calling on Ne Win "to relinquish the power which he had illegally usurped." The situation in Burma, he told the newsmen, was "such as to break my heart." "I am compelled," Nu said, "to resort to other means to save my country." The Burmese masses would remain patient and watchful for the time being, U Nu predicted, but he would not rule out the ultimate application of force to drive Ne Win from office. As for his own future political intentions, the still most popular of all Burmese leaders said that he would not rest until democracy had been restored in his country.

U Nu told newsmen in London that his August 29 statement was being distributed clandestinely in Burma—which turned out to be unnecessary, as it was printed only a few days later in the government-controlled press in Rangoon. Nu did not intend to establish a government in exile, he said in London, but he did announce the reestablishment of the political party which he headed at the time of his overthrow in 1962 (and which had been banned along with all other parties except the officially sanctioned Burma Socialist Programme Party). Nu admitted that General Ne Win had not yet rejected the majority report of the National Unity Advisory Board, although he had spurned Nu's own proposal that power be returned to himself as caretaker leader preparatory to establishing an elected republican regime with Ne Win at its head. Nu tried to equate the latter action with a rejection of democracy or liberalization altogether[29]—which, while possibly true, was difficult to determine in light of the lack of public knowledge of the real feeling of the majority of National Unity Advisory Board members respecting U Nu's proposal (submitted to Ne Win on February 5). This rejection, however, according to Nu, left "the elected leaders of Burma with no option but to call on the people to oppose his (Ne Win's) regime of hate and oppression with all means at their disposal."[30] U Nu hoped that his campaign of opposition from abroad would move Ne Win to relinquish power peacefully, but he left no doubt of his willingness to resort to force if necessary.[31] There was more than an element of sadness in the fact not only that the peace-professing Buddhist Nu might himself join the ranks of Burma's insurrectionists, whose resort to the gun he had so vigorously attacked in the past, but that he would also be willing to accept at least limited foreign help, presumably in the form of arms and supplies, which he clearly indicated to the press in London that he would do. Nu, however, also felt that prolonged application of force would not be necessary in light of the allegedly overwhelming opposition to the Ne Win government inside Burma. From London Nu flew on to the United States, determined to press his unique campaign there before returning to Thailand by way of Japan and Hong Kong. Whether the Thai would permit him to remain in Bangkok, however—in active opposition to a friendly and neighboring government—was highly problematical.

The years 1962–69—most difficult ones for Nu (despite his great peace of mind, the result of his Buddhist philosophy)—demonstrated at least two things. U Nu and his chief lieutenants of the united AFPFL era, U Kyaw Nyein and U Ba Swe, governed Burma much better in the decade 1948–58 than Ne Win ruled the country after his second ouster of Nu in 1962. Nu, indeed, was a better leader in the brief period 1960–62 than was Ne Win subsequently. The detention years 1962–66 and those that immediately followed also provided additional insight into the essential Nu: a man who held out against great odds those long four and a half years in detention and who tried again to come back—and to revive democracy for Burma—in the tense political climate that still existed even after General Ne Win had created the National Unity Advisory Board.

Nu's behavior after his October 1966 release from detention was not dramatically different from that on previous occasions. Nu had not sought a role of leadership at first during the years of Dr. Ba Maw's ascendency, when the Japanese occupied the country in World War II.[32] He also tried to retire from politics after the war. Even after his ouster from office by General Ne Win in September–October 1958, Nu did not play an overtly oppositionist role until his fiery May Day 1959 speech. After that, of course, particularly after the September 1959 announcement that elections would take place the following February, he showed outstanding skill and courage as he sought almost singlehandedly to restore Burmese democracy. Few in Burma, however, predicted his successful February 1960 victory and comeback,[33] but he won the 1960 election and became Prime Minister again.

U Nu's effort was an even more singlehanded one in 1969, when he sought to convince his National Unity Advisory Board colleagues to support his plan for an interim government headed by himself. He found no allies on the board—or at least he seemed not to find any. Few in Burma (or elsewhere) in mid-1969 would predict his return to political leadership in Burma again—or even to an active political role in the country.

The political obituary of U Nu, however, has twice already been prematurely written. When he was first ousted by General Ne Win in 1958, there were those who declared the end of his political career more than a little too soon. His overthrow by the same Ne Win for a second time in 1962 was again proclaimed as the end of the career of a man who tried to govern Burma but lacked the requisites of leadership in a country that badly needed—and needs—leadership. Burma in mid-1969 had probably not seen the last of U Nu—unless grave and unexpected tragedy were to overtake him. Nu may not again be Burma's Premier. But he will probably be a figure of influence for some time to come. The debate concerning democracy's relevance for Burma—which took place in the marketplaces and bazaars as well as in the National Unity Advisory Board (and among the members of the Revolutionary Council) during the first half of 1969 (and which is probably not yet resolved)—was stimulated, more than anything else, by U Nu's memorandum forwarded to General Ne Win in February of that year. U Nu may not have a third chance to govern his country, but he was experiencing in 1969 a third chance to influence his nation's political development— even if he was temporarily to wage his battle for freedom from distant Britain.

NOTES

For publications cited only once, publication data are given in full in the Notes. For full publication data on publications cited in short form, see the Bibliography, pp. 279–91. Places and dates of the interviews are listed on pp. 290–91.

CHAPTER 1

1. Soe Maung, p. 10.

2. *Ibid.,* p. 13.

3. *Ibid.,* p. 11.

4. Letter of Sept. 14, 1960, to the author from Myanaung U Tin, authorized by Nu to reply to certain questions asked of him.

5. Nu, "Author's Preface," pp. 9–10.

6. U Tin Letter (1960).

7. Quoted from written answers by Nu to questions submitted by the author. These answers, undated, were received in Rangoon on Dec. 15, 1959. Hereafter referred to as "Nu's written reply (1959)."

8. Nu, "Author's Preface," p. 10.

9. *Ibid.*

10. Nu, *If You Want to Be a Front-Line Leader,* pp. 175–76.

11. Nu's written reply (1959).

12. Soe Maung, pp. 12–13.

13. One of several who remember U San Htun from these days, and with whom the author talked, is U Kyaw Min, Member of Parliament in the post-independence period and formerly of the Indian Civil Service.

14. See Hunter, biographical introduction, in Nu, *The People Win Through,* pp. 7–8.

15. U Tin letter (1960).

16. See Maung Maung, *Burma's Constitution,* p. 15.

17. Nu's written reply (1959).   18. *Ibid.*

19. Soe Maung, p. 15.   20. *Ibid.*

21. *Ibid.,* pp. 17–18.   22. Nu's written reply (1959).

23. Cady, *History,* p. 220.   24. Nu's written reply (1959).

25. This incident was related to the author by Nu in Rangoon on Sept. 29, 1959.

26. Particularly prominent among Nu's Myoma contemporaries have been U Thein Han, later librarian at the University of Rangoon, who was interviewed in Rangoon on Feb. 5, 1960, and Myoma Saya Hein, longtime friend and an official of the Burma Translation Society, interviewed on Jan. 6, 1960.

27. Nu's written reply (1959).

28. Nu, "Author's Preface," p. 8.

29. U Myint Thein, later Chief Justice of Burma's Supreme Court, was interviewed in Rangoon on Feb. 24, 1960.

CHAPTER 2

1. The author discussed this group with Thakin Ba Thaung on Mar. 30, 1960, in Rangoon. He also talked to more than two dozen of Nu's undergraduate contemporaries on this and related subjects.

2. Interviewed, respectively, on Jan. 22, Apr. 1, and Feb. 23, 1960.

3. Nu's written reply (1959).

4. U Tin, a friend of Nu's since their undergraduate days, is a main source of information included in this section. Tin was asked by Nu to assist the author. He was interviewed in Rangoon on Dec. 15, 1959.

5. Tinker, "Nu, the Serene Statesman," p. 122.

6. Ba Nyunt interview (1960).   7. U Tin interview (1959).

8. Interview (1960).   9. U Tin interview (1959).

10. *Ibid.*   11. Nu, "Author's Preface," p. 10.

12. Trager, "Our Visitor," p. 8.

13. Interview (1960). Tinker also notes that Nu was "not recognized as an outstanding scholar." ("Nu, the Serene Statesman," p. 121.)

14. Nu, "Author's Preface," p. 8.   15. Interview (1960).

16. Nu, "Author's Preface," p. 8.   17. *Ibid.*

18. Nu, *Burma under the Japanese,* p. 28.

19. *Ibid.,* p. 29.

20. Nu interview (1959).

21. Nu, "Author's Preface," p. 11.

22. *The Nation,* July 15, 1955. From a speech by Nu to an audience about to view one of his plays at the Pasadena Playhouse in California in 1955.

23. Nu, "Author's Preface," p. 11.

24. Ba Thaung interview (1960).

25. Tun Pe, *Sun,* p. 32.

26. U Thant interview (1960).

27. Maung Maung, "U Thant," p. 28.

28. Nu, *If You Want to Be a Front-Line Leader,* pp. 177–78.

29. This account represents a synthesis of the several versions of the elopement told the author in Burma. It has been confirmed by Nu's very good friend, U Thant, who did not, however, assist Nu in his elopement (as is commonly believed).

30. Soe Maung, p. 31.   31. U Thant interview (1960).

32. Nu, "Open Letter," p. 11.   33. Hall interview (1960).

34. Dr. Tha Hla, who was Rector of the University of Rangoon in 1961–62, was interviewed in Rangoon on Sept. 3, 1959.

35. Raschid, longtime friend of Nu and an important Cabinet member in the post-independence period, was first interviewed in Rangoon on Sept. 16, 1959.

36. "Extracts Vice-President's Preliminary Report," p. 19.

37. Sloss interview (1960).

38. Maung Maung, "M. A. Raschid," p. 29.

39. See "Extracts Vice-President's Preliminary Report," p. 19.

40. Sloss and Hall interviews (1960).

41. Interview (1959).

42. Tha Hla, "1936 Strike," Part I, p. 8.

43. Nu's inaugural address as President of the Students' Union is related in Thein Pe Myint's fictional account of the 1936 students' strike, *Student Boycotter,* I. This quotation appears on p. 143. Thein Pe has remained a friend of Nu through the years, even though he is a Communist. The book in question, moreover, was edited by Maung Nu. A second edition of the two-volume work was issued in 1961. Nu's editing of the book would seem to testify to the general authenticity of the material quoted.

CHAPTER 3

1. *New Burma,* XVI (Feb. 2, 1936), 12.

2. Raschid interview (1959). In an interview of Sept. 15, 1959, U Nyo Mya confirmed his role.

3. Nu, "Open Letter."

4. U Thant interview (1960). Principal Sloss has denied this interpretation and has written that he recollects no such plan to woo Nu away from his nationalist politics. Promising students who were interested in public affairs and who might make good administrative officers, however, were recommended by Sloss to the Governor for overseas training, sometimes at Oxford, Cambridge, or London University. Sloss, in retirement, had no records of those he recommended, "but U Nu might well have been one of them, as I thought highly of his abilities and knew of his keen interest in affairs." Letter of D. J. Sloss to the author, Sept. 28, 1960.

5. *New Burma,* XVI (Feb. 5, 1936), 14.

6. Tha Hla, "1936 Strike," Part V, p. 13.

7. *Ibid.,* Part I, p. 8.

8. *Ibid.,* Part II, p. 12. See also "Manifesto issued by Publicity Bureau," p. 14.

9. Maung Maung, *Burma's Constitution,* p. 36.

10. *Ibid.*

11. Tha Hla, "1936 Strike," Part II, p. 13.

12. Maung Maung, *Burma's Constitution,* p. 37.

13. "Rangoon University Boycotters Demands," p. 18.

14. Tha Hla, "1936 Strike," Part IV, p. 11.

15. Nu, "Speech to Boycotters, Shwedagon Pagoda," p. 14. Minor alterations have been made for smoothness.

16. Nu, "Speech at Prome," p. 17. (Nu did not then call himself "U Nu," but *New Burma* did.)

17. Maung Maung, "M. A. Raschid," pp. 31–32.

18. Kyaw Nyein interview (1960).

19. See Thein Pe, *Student Boycotter,* I, 19.

20. *Ibid.,* II, 249–60.

21. Interview (1960).

22. Nu, *Modern Plays.*

23. See Hunter, biographical introduction, in Nu, *The People Win Through,* p. 16.

24. Interview (1960).

25. Tha Hla, "1936 Strike," Part IV, p. 12.

CHAPTER 4

1. Soe Maung, p. 38.

2. Tun Pe, *Sun,* pp. 35–38.

3. Thein Pe Myint (as he later called himself) was interviewed in Rangoon on Nov. 13, 1959.

4. Law Yone, *The Nation,* Mar. 2, 1957.

5. Maung Nu, "I am a Marxist," in U Thein Pe, ed., *Communism and Dobama* (in Burmese) (Rangoon: Pyidaw Soe Press, 1954). This book is a collection of essays written in the late 1930's and republished by Thein Pe Myint in 1954. "I am a Marxist" appears on pp. 43–63, and another article by Nu, "What Kind of Independence?," on pp. 69–77.

6. *The Nation,* Jan. 30, 1958.

7. *Ibid.*

8. Furnivall, "Twilight in Burma: Reconquest and Crisis," p. 10.

9. Speech by Nu to Members of Parliament, *The Nation,* June 6, 1956.

10. Nu interview (1959).

11. Tinker, *Union,* p. 7.

12. *Final Report of Riot Inquiry Committee,* p. 291.

13. See Tinker, *Union,* p. 8, and Maung Maung, "Thakin Than Tun," p. 34.

14. Kyaw Nyein interview (1960).

15. The author's main source of information here was Bo Let Ya (Thakin Hla Pe), who was interviewed in Rangoon on Jan. 5, 1960.

16. The records of the book club are held by the Burma Translation Society, whose head, U San Htwa, was interviewed in Rangoon on Jan. 5, 1960.

17. Most of the information here was obtained from Myoma Saya Hein, now with the Burma Translation Society, interviewed in Rangoon on Jan. 6, 1960.

18. *An Asian Speaks* (a collection of speeches made by U Nu during his visit to the United States, June 29–July 16, 1955), p. 45.

19. Nu's literary activities during this period are among the subjects treated in Dagon Taya's sketch of Nu in *Portraits*.

20. Nu, *Modern Plays*.

21. See John Gunther, *Inside Asia* (New York: Harper, 1939), pp. 216–17.

22. Nu, *Ganda-layit*, p. 301.

23. Maung Maung Myint, ed., *Burmese Affairs* (Rangoon: Red Dragon Book Club, n.d.). Nu's essay appears on pp. 97–115.

24. Kodaw Hmaing interview (1959).

25. Foucar, p. 84.

26. See Cady, *History,* pp. 403–4.

27. Ba Maw, "The Making of a Revolution."

28. *New Burma,* XX (Feb. 16, 1940), 16.

29. *Ibid.,* XXI (May 26, 1940), 17.

30. *The Nation,* Oct. 20, 1958.

31. See Aung San, "Burma's Challenge," p. 2.

32. Trager, "Our Visitor," p. 9.

33. Nu, "Author's Preface," p. 12.

CHAPTER 5

1. Nu, *Burma under the Japanese,* p. 10. This book, used extensively as a source in preparation of this chapter, was written between August and November 1945 in the first months of the British reoccupation.

2. For details of an earlier plot to help Nu escape from jail, see Thein Pe, pp. 5–8. This author is not to be confused with the Communist writer *Tetpongyi* Thein Pe (Myint).

3. Nu, *Burma under the Japanese,* pp. 28–30.

4. Ohn Khin interview (1960).

5. Thakin Tin interview (1960).

6. Furnivall, Introduction to Nu, *Burma under the Japanese,* p. xiii.

7. Ba Maw interview (1959).   8. Rose, *Socialism,* p. 101.

9. Maung Pye, p. 57.   10. Thakin Tin interview (1960).

11. Ba Maw interview (1960).

12. Nu, *Burma under the Japanese,* pp. 38–39.

13. See Jones, p. 354.

14. Nu, *Burma under the Japanese,* pp. 60–61.

15. *Ibid.,* pp. 66–67.

16. Rose, *Socialism,* p. 102.

17. Nu, *Burma under the Japanese,* p. 43.

18. Elsbree, pp. 59–60.

19. *The Nation,* June 6, 1956.

20. *Ibid.,* Jan. 30, 1958.

21. Nu, *Burma under the Japanese,* pp. 79–80.

22. *Ibid.,* p. 85. See also *Burma during the Japanese Occupation,* p. 17.

23. Nu, *Burma under the Japanese,* p. 103.
24. Tun Pe, *Sun,* p. 105.
25. Nu, *Burma under the Japanese,* pp. 91–92.
26. *The Greater Asia,* I (Aug. 29, 1943).
27. Nu, *Towards Peace,* p. 226.
28. Nu, *Burma under the Japanese,* p. 35.
29. *Burma's Fight for Freedom,* p. 6.
30. *The Nation,* June 24, 1956.
31. See Tinker, *Union,* pp. 13–14.
32. See Nu, *Burma under the Japanese,* p. 105.
33. *Ibid.,* p. 103.
34. AFPFL, *The New Burma in the New World* (Rangoon: Nay Win Kyi Press, 1945?), p. 2. See also Maung Pye, pp. 82–83. This source includes the text of the "Manifesto of the AFPFL," pp. 177–83.
35. Nu, *Burma under the Japanese,* p. 105.
36. Maung Maung, "U Ba Swe," p. 30.
37. Nu, *Burma under the Japanese,* p. 107.
38. Bo Let Ya interview (1960).
39. Nu, *Burma under the Japanese,* p. 110.
40. See Maung Maung, "U Hla Maung," p. 15.

CHAPTER 6

1. See Mountbatten, *Report.*
2. See *Burma: Statement of Policy.*
3. See Nu, *Premier Reports to the People,* Appendix 1 (a), pp. 47–48.
4. U Win interview (1960).   5. U Ohn Khin interview (1960).
6. See Pu Galay, I, 7–8.   7. *The Nation,* June 6, 1956.
8. *Ibid.,* Oct. 20, 1958.
9. Tinker, "Nu, the Serene Statesman," p. 124.
10. Ba Swe interview (1960).
11. Speech reported in *The Statesman,* Apr. 28, 1948.
12. Sir Hubert Rance interview (1960).
13. Quoted by Thomson, "Marxism in Burma," p. 33.
14. Maung Maung, "U Kyaw Nyein," p. 17.
15. This was stated to the author by U Kyaw Nyein, U Ba Swe, U Win, and others.
16. *The Nation,* June 6, 1956.
17. Nu stated this in a speech to a Union Youth Conference, reported in *The Nation,* Oct. 20, 1958.
18. Ohn Khin interview (1960).
19. Union Youth Conference speech, *The Nation,* Oct. 20, 1958.
20. See Frontier Areas Committee of Enquiry, Part I, 1947.
21. Speech reported in *The Statesman* (Calcutta), Apr. 28, 1948.
22. Attlee, p. 188.
23. Speech of Governor Sir Hubert Rance, reported in *The Statesman* (Calcutta), Apr. 28, 1948.

24. Union Youth Conference speech reported in *The Nation,* Oct. 20, 1958.

25. See Hunter, biographical introduction, in Nu, *The People Win Through,* p. 33.

26. Speech to Parliament reported in *The Nation,* June 6, 1956.

27. See "The Political Evolution of Burma," p. 11.

28. *Burma's Fight for Freedom,* p. 59.

29. Sir Hubert Rance interview (1960).

30. See Tinker, *Union,* p. 27.

31. See press conference remarks reported in *The Statesman* (Calcutta), July 24, 1947.

32. Sir Hubert Rance interview (1960).

33. *The Guardian* (magazine), V (Nov. 1958), 6.

34. Ohn Khin interview (1960).

35. Speech of Jan. 11, 1954, to the Secretaries and Heads of Departments, in Nu, *Forward with the People,* 1955, p. 110.

CHAPTER 7

1. Tinker, "Nu, the Serene Statesman," p. 132.

2. Letter from U Thant to the author, dated Aug. 17, 1961.

3. Nu, "The Dhamma," p. 11.

4. See *New Times of Burma,* May 6, 1951.

5. Remarks made at a press conference reported in *The Nation,* Oct. 26, 1958.

6. See *Time* cover story, Aug. 30, 1954.

7. A sketch of Nu's personal habits appeared in the Rangoon *Weekly Record* (II), Feb. 13, 1960, 3–4.

8. This was stated to the author during his 1959–60 stay in Burma by one of Nu's close friends, who, for obvious reasons, preferred not to be identified. The friend lent some money to Nu.

9. Nehru interview (1960).

10. U Ohn Khin interview (1960).

11. Nu's performance at this party was described to the writer by Maurice Collis, author of many books on Burma, in Maidenhead, England, on May 15, 1960.

12. *The Nation,* Nov. 21, 1959.   13. Law Yone, " 'Mr. Tender.' "

14. Kodaw Hmaing interview (1959). 15. Law Yone, " 'Mr. Tender.' "

16. Law Yone interview (1959).   17. Ba Maw interview (1959).

18. See Nu, "What are the Four Sampadas?" One of six lectures in *Pyidaungsu Niti,* pp. 1–2.

19. See, for example, Nu, *The Law, The Five Precepts,* and *The Monks* (all Rangoon: Burma Translation Society, 1958; all in Burmese).

20. Sarkisyanz interview (1959). 21. Nu interview (1960).

22. See Tinker, *Union,* p. 166.   23. Nu's written reply (1959).

24. *The Nation,* Apr. 18, 1954.

25. See Trager, "Our Visitor," p. 10.

26. See Nu, "Premier's Address of Veneration," p. 28.
27. Ba Maw, letter to *The Nation,* Mar. 29, 1955.
28. Tun Pe, *Why I Resign,* p. 20.
29. Jawaharlal Nehru interview (1960).
30. Daphne E. Whittam, in *The Nation,* July 9, 1955.
31. Nu, *Forward with the People,* pp. 42–53.
32. *The Nation,* Apr. 18, 1954.
33. *Ibid.,* Feb. 3, 1956.
34. See Kingsley Martin, *New Statesman,* LIX (Mar. 17, 1960), 355.
35. Ba Swe interview (1960).
36. Raschid interview (1960). Alaungpaya, founder of the first unified Burmese "state," made Buddhism the official religion.
37. See "U Nu's Lecture on Buddhism," pp. 256–57.
38. Nu, *An Asian Speaks,* p. 34.
39. "Address by the Hon'ble U Nu at Bhubaneswar on the 22nd of November 1956," *Burma Weekly Bulletin,* V (Dec. 20, 1956), 297.
40. Nu, *An Asian Speaks,* p. 43. In this speech, delivered at New York University in 1955, Nu offered to have ten persons as "my guests" in Burma to test the validity of the Buddhist principles of which he spoke (p. 37).
41. There are different categories of precepts: the Five, Eight, Nine Precepts, etc. Most basic are the Five Precepts: refraining from killing, stealing, adultery, lying, and drinking intoxicants.
42. Nu, "The Dhamma," p. 11.
43. Speech at the Asoka Vihara (meditation) Center in India, *Burma Weekly Bulletin,* V (Dec. 6, 1956), 282.
44. Nu, "Lecture on the 5 Precepts," p. 348. (Quoted from the Buddhist *Jataka Tales.*)
45. Nu, "What are the Four Sampadas?," p. 7.
46. *The Nation,* Feb. 1, 1958.
47. Nu, *Summary of speech in support of "Buddha Susana Organization Act,"* p. 3.
48. Nu, *Pyidaungsu Policy,* p. 101.
49. Nu, *Burma Looks Ahead,* p. 67.
50. Nu, *Premier U Nu on the 4-Year Plan,* p. 12.
51. See Nu, "Premier's Address on Resistance Day," p. 5.
52. Nu, *Burma Looks Ahead,* p. 93.
53. Nu, *Premier U Nu on the 4-Year Plan,* p. 11.
54. *The Nation,* July 6, 1956.
55. "Speech by the Hon'ble U Nu to Students of Utkal University at Cuttack on the 21st of November 1956," *Burma Weekly Bulletin,* V (Dec. 13, 1956), 288.
56. Ba Maw, "U Nu Psychoanalzed."
57. U Nu, *If You Want to Be a Front-Line Leader,* p. 135.
58. Nu, *From Peace to Stability,* p. 9.
59. Nu, *Towards Peace and Democracy,* p. 18.
60. Nu, *An Asian Speaks,* pp. 51–52.
61. *The Nation,* Apr. 12, 1958.
62. *Ibid.,* Aug. 8, 1956.
63. *The Guardian* (newspaper), July 19, 1959.

64. U Kyaw Nyein interview (1960).

65. Tinker, "Nu, the Serene Statesman," p. 133.

CHAPTER 8

1. Quoted in Maung Maung, *Burma's Constitution*, p. 254.

2. Interview by C. L. Sulzberger, in the *New York Times*, Nov. 13, 1957.

3. Nu, "What is Socialism?," in *Pyidaungsu Niti*, p. 10.

4. Nu, "Speech at the Regional Autonomy Inquiry Commission," p. 12.

5. Nu, "What is Socialism?," p. 29.

6. *The Nation*, Nov. 17, 1959.

7. Nu, *From Peace to Stability*, p. 75.

8. Nu, *Man, the Wolf of Man* (Chaps. XXII–XXIV), *The Guardian*, II (Jan. 1955), 14.

9. *Ibid.* (Chap. I), *The Guardian*, I (June 1954), 12.

10. *Ibid.* (Chaps. XXII–XXIV), *The Guardian*, II (Jan. 1955), 14.

11. *Ibid.* (Chap. I), *The Guardian*, I (June 1954), 12.

12. See accounts of speeches in *The Nation*, Jan. 30, 1958, and Nov. 17, 1959.

13. Nu, "What is Socialism?," p. 8.   14. *Ibid.*, p. 21.

15. *Ibid.*, p. 29.   16. Sarkisyanz, pp. 59–60.

17. See Maung Maung, *Burma's Constitution*, p. 257.

18. *The Nation*, Jan. 30, 1958.

19. Nu, *We Must Defend Democracy*, p. 21.

20. For Nu's own explanation why non-Communist Asian leaders have tended to refrain from criticizing Communist China, see Singer, p. 17. See also Nu's "A Program for Asia," in *The Socialist Call*, XXII (Oct. 1954), 14–15. Compare this with U Kyaw Nyein's "A Burmese View of New Colonialism," in the same issue, pp. 13–14.

21. *The Nation*, Jan. 30, 1958.

22. Nu, *Towards a Socialist State*, pp. 32–33.

23. Nu, *The Pyidaungsu Policy*, pp. 8–10.

24. Nu, *We Must Defend Democracy*, pp. 42–44.

25. Nu, *Forward with the People*, pp. 52–55.

26. *The Nation*, Mar. 25, 1960.

27. Speech before World Conference on Religion and Freedom (Dallas, Texas), reported in *The Nation*, Apr. 21, 1959.

28. Nu, *The Pyidaungsu Policy*, pp. 7–8.

29. Nu, *We Must Defend Democracy*, p. 26.

30. Nu, *The Pyidaungsu Policy*, pp. 37–40.

31. Nu, *We Must Defend Democracy*, p. 43.

32. See *The New Times of Burma*, July 29, 1959.

33. Nu, *An Asian Speaks*, p. 28.

34. See Nu, *The Pyidaungsu Policy*, pp. 36 and 43–44.

35. See Nu's National Day speech, Nov. 8, 1947, in *Towards Peace and Democracy*, p. 14.

36. Nu, *We Must Defend Democracy*, p. 28.

37. Nu, *The Pyidaungsu Policy,* pp. 11–16.

38. Nu, *We Must Defend Democracy,* pp. 34–38.

39. Nu, *From Peace to Stability,* p. 88.

40. Nu, "The Scourge," *The Guardian,* III (Jan. 1956), 9–11.

41. *New Times of Burma,* Nov. 30, 1955.

42. Nu, *An Asian Speaks,* p. 25.

43. See *The Nation,* May 15, 1955.

44. This source asked not to be identified.

45. See Nu, *Burma Looks Ahead,* p. 63. Nu has also endeavored to encourage an awareness of heroism in general, as indicated by his little book *Heroes* (in Burmese) (Rangoon: World's Literature House, 1946), which includes descriptions of the feats of Alexander the Great and Horatio Nelson, among others.

46. Htin Fatt, "Consultative Conference," p. 3.

47. Nu, *From Peace to Stability,* p. 38. From the conclusion of his address at the opening ceremony of "Mass Education Training Classes."

48. *The Nation,* Sept. 28, 1957.

49. Nu, "Translation of the Speech by the Hon'ble Thakin Nu, Prime Minister of Burma, delivered in Parliament on 14th June 1949" (typescript), p. 3.

50. Nu, *If You Want to Be a Front-Line Leader,* p. 4.

51. *Ibid.,* p. 10.

52. U Thein Han interview (1960).

53. This source asked not to be identified.

54. Jawaharlal Nehru interview (1960).

55. Nu interview (1960).

56. Dr. Hla Pe (of the School of Oriental and African Studies, University of London) interview (1960).

57. See Cady, *History,* p. 576.

58. Speech on the occasion of the award of the Sarpaybeikman literary prize on June 19, 1949, in Nu, *Towards Peace and Democracy,* p. 218.

59. *Burma Weekly Bulletin,* V (Aug. 23, 1956), 145.

60. Maung Maung, "M. A. Raschid," p. 34.

61. *An Asian Speaks,* p. 13.

62. Nu, *Forward with the People,* p. 116.

63. *An Asian Speaks,* pp. 13–14.

64. Nu, *Forward with the People,* p. 38.

65. *The Nation,* May 10, 1958.

66. Nu, *From Peace to Stability,* p. 155.

67. Quoted in Tinker, "Nu, the Serene Statesman," p. 130.

68. See U Law Yone, "A Hard Look at 'Mr. Tender.'"

69. Tinker and the author talked about Nu in London on May 18, 1960 (and again in late December 1961 at St. Antony's College, Oxford).

70. *The Nation,* Jan. 18, 1960.   71. *Ibid.,* May 10, 1958.

72. *Ibid.,* Oct. 21, 1958.   73. *Ibid.,* May 10, 1958.

74. Sein Win, *Split Story,* pp. 17–18.

75. *New York Times,* July 2, 1955.

76. Nu, *Burma Looks Ahead,* p. 75.

77. *The Nation,* Jan. 18, 1960.

CHAPTER 9

1. The name "Thakin" Nu is used again in this chapter, since it is the name by which Nu was still known at this time. He commenced using "U" Nu in 1951, and this name will be used throughout the book after this chapter.

2. This was told to the author by Sir Hubert in Rugby, England, on May 23, 1960. See also Nu's own account in *The Nation,* June 6, 1956.

3. Thakin Nu, "Rebuttal of Communist Allegations Against the Anglo-Burmese Treaty" (typescript), p. 1.

4. Thein Pe Myint, *Political Experiences,* p. 259.

5. Rose, *Socialism,* p. 109.

6. The author discussed this subject at length with Sir Hubert Rance.

7. See Nu's evaluation in the *New Times of Burma,* Nov. 27, 1947.

8. Thein Pe Myint, *Political Experiences,* p. 259.

9. Soe Maung, pp. 108–9.

10. Nu, "Rebuttal of Communist Allegations Against the Anglo-Burmese Treaty," p. 2.

11. This was told to the author by Supreme Court Chief Justice U Myint Thein, who served as constitutional adviser to the Kachins.

12. *Ibid.*

13. Quoted in Maung Maung, *Burma's Constitution,* p. 84.

14. Nu, *Towards Peace and Democracy,* p. 15.

15. Sir Hubert Rance interview (1960).

16. Pu Galay, p. 21.

17. Maung Maung, *Burma in the Family of Nations,* p. 132.

18. *The Nation,* Apr. 24, 1956.

19. Nu, "Rebuttal of Communist Allegations Against the Anglo-Burmese Treaty," p. 1.

20. Cady, *History,* p. 574.

21. Nu, "Rebuttal of Communist Allegations Against the Anglo-Burmese Treaty," p. 1.

22. Quoted in Tinker, *Union,* p. 32.

23. Brimmel, p. 193.

24. Nu, "Rebuttal of Communist Allegations Against the Anglo-Burmese Treaty," p. 3.

25. Lord Attlee discussed Nu with the writer in Oxford, England, on May 20, 1960.

26. *The Times* (London), Oct. 18, 1947.

27. Nu, "Rebuttal of Communist Allegations Against the Anglo-Burmese Treaty," p. 1.

28. See Pu Galay, p. 26.

29. "Treaty between the Government of the United Kingdom and the Provisional Government of Burma regarding the Recognition of Burmese Independence and Related Matters, October 17, 1947," *Treaty Series,* No. 16 (1948), Cmd. 7360.

30. Prime Minister Thakin Nu, "Which Side Will You Follow?" (typescript of speech broadcast on Apr. 3, 1948), p. 1.

31. Nu, "Rebuttal of Communist Allegations Against the Anglo-Burmese Treaty," pp. 2–4.

32. See speech by Sir Hubert Rance, *The Statesman* (Calcutta), Apr. 24, 1948. See also Mansergh, p. 11.

33. Quoted in Maung Maung, *Burma's Constitution*, p. 87.

34. For an account and an analysis of British policy toward Burma from the end of World War II to independence, see Rose, *Britain*, pp. 109–20.

CHAPTER 10

1. Cady, *History*, p. 582.

2. Tinker, *Union*, p. 35.

3. "Premier's Review of Political Situation," *Burma Weekly Bulletin* (mimeo.), No. 30 (covering the week ending 4 Sept. 1949), p. 7.

4. Nu, *Towards Peace and Democracy*, p. 51.

5. Nu's speech to the All-Burma Peasants Organization, in *The Nation*, Sept. 24, 1956.

6. "Speech delivered by Thakin Nu, President of the AFPFL, at a mass meeting BAA ground on 13/6/48," p. 10.

7. Nu, *Towards Peace and Democracy*, p. 52.

8. Nu, *Burma Looks Ahead*, p. 81.

9. Nu, Appendix 1(a) in *Premier Reports to the People*, p. 51.

10. U Win, interview (1960). Others have told the writer essentially the same thing.

11. *Premier U Nu on the 4-Year Plan*, pp. 14–16.

12. U Nu, *The People Win Through* (Rangoon ed.), pp. 36–37.

13. Pu Galay, p. 230.

14. Cady, *History*, p. 585. The writer confirmed this point in discussions with U Nu and U Thein Pe Myint in 1959.

15. See *The Times* (London), May 29, 1948.

16. See press conference remarks of Information Minister Thakin Chit Maung, *The Nation*, July 3, 1957, and Nu's speech to the ABPO, *The Nation*, Sept. 24, 1956.

17. Nu, *Towards Peace and Democracy*, p. 98.

18. See Tinker, *Union*, p. 36.

19. Articles 180 and 181.

20. Cady, *History*, p. 590.

21. Quoted in Maung Maung, *Burma's Constitution*, p. 184.

22. Pu Galay, p. 129.

23. *The Karen Uprising in Burma*, pp. 2–3.

24. Interview, in *The Observer* (London), May 21, 1950.

25. See Nu's speech in Parliament in support of the amendment, in *Burma Looks Ahead*, p. 13.

26. Tinker, *Union*, p. 37.

27. Thakin Nu, "Translation of the Speech by the Hon'ble Thakin Nu, Prime Minister of Burma, delivered in Parliament on 14th June 1949" (typescript), p. 1.

28. Tinker, *Union,* p. 47.

29. Nu, *From Peace to Stability,* pp. 47–48.

30. See *Time* (U Nu cover story), Aug. 30, 1954.

31. Nu, *From Peace to Stability,* p. 13.

32. *Ibid.,* p. 6.

33. Speech to commanding officers, in *The Nation,* Oct. 21, 1958.

34. Nu, *Towards Peace and Democracy,* p. 146.

35. For a discussion of reasons for the insurgents' failure to topple the Nu government, see Cady, *History,* p. 595.

36. See *Burma Weekly Bulletin,* VI (May 16, 1957), pp. 35, 40.

37. Nu, *Premier Reports to the People,* p. 6.

Chapter 11

1. Walinsky, p. 57.

2. Quoted in Trager, *Building,* p. 15.

3. For a discussion of the constitution, see Winslow Christian, "Burma's New Constitution and Supreme Court," *Tulane Law Review,* XXVI (1951), pp. 47–59.

4. Walinsky, p. 64.

5. Nu, *Towards Peace and Democracy,* pp. 130–31.

6. Tinker, *Union,* p. 95.   7. Cady, *History,* p. 603.

8. Trager, *Building,* p. 2.   9. *Ibid.,* p. 90.

10. For a discussion of the objectives of Burmanization of the economy in general, see Walinsky, p. 72.

11. Nu, *Burma Looks Ahead,* pp. 112–13.

12. Maung Maung, *Burma's Constitution,* p. 107.

13. Tinker, *Union,* p. 104.

14. *Ibid.,* p. 382.

15. See Nu, *Forward with the People,* p. 108.

16. See Trager, *Building,* pp. 59–60.

17. Nu, *Premier Reports to the People,* p. 16.

18. See *Pyidawtha, the New Burma,* p. 27–28.

19. Nu, *Forward with the People,* p. 82.

20. Nu, *An Asian Speaks,* p. 26.

21. Trager, *Building,* p. 101.

22. Nu, *Forward with the People,* p. 80. See also Walinsky, pp. 98–99.

23. Lockwood, p. 403.

24. Nu, *Premier Reports to the People,* p. 83.

25. See Walinsky, p. 294.

26. Nu, *Forward with the People,* pp. 21 and 79.

27. Sein Win, "Peasant Problem," p. 599.

28. Knappen-Tippetts-Abbett, *Comprehensive Report,* p. 35.

29. *Ibid.,* p. 20.

30. Nu, *Premier Reports to the People,* p. 16.

31. Quoted in Lockwood, p. 397.

32. Trager, *Building,* p. 18.

33. Nu, *Premier Reports to the People*, p. 16.

34. Nu, *Forward with the People*, p. 16.

35. Tinker, *Union*, p. 120.

36. Lockwood, pp. 399–400.

37. This official, associated with the State Agricultural Marketing Board, asked not to be identified.

38. Nu, *Premier Reports to the People*, p. 18.

39. *The Nation*, Jan. 30, 1958.

40. Lockwood, p. 401.

41. Daw Tin Tin Shwe, "Barter and All That: Foreign Trade Trends 1947–1960," *Far Eastern Economic Review*, XXVIII (Mar. 17, 1960), p. 573.

42. Win Pe, p. 585.

43. Nu, *From Peace to Stability*, p. 140.

44. Walinsky, p. 229.

45. Nu, *Premier U Nu on the 4-Year Plan*, pp. 3–6.

46. Nu, *Premier Reports to the People*, p. 25.

47. *Ibid.*, p. 22.

48. Nu, *Premier U Nu on the 4-Year Plan*, p. 7.

49. Nu, *Premier Reports to the People*, p. 18.

50. Walinsky, pp. 230–31.

51. U Hla Maung interview (1960).

52. Quoted in Lockwood, p. 422.

53. *New Times of Burma*, Mar. 10, 1955.

54. Nu, *Burma Looks Ahead*, p. 84.

55. *New Times of Burma*, Mar. 9, 1951.

56. *The Nation*, May 29, 1955.

57. Nu, *Premier U Nu on the 4-Year Plan*, p. 3.

58. *The Nation*, Sept. 27, 1959.

59. *Ibid.*

60. Nu, *Premier U Nu on the 4-Year Plan*, pp. 1–2.

61. See Walinsky, pp. 228–29.

62. Nu, *An Asian Speaks*, p. 16.

63. Nu, *Resurgence (Premier U Nu at Bandung)*, p. 10.

64. Nu, *Burma Looks Ahead*, p. 50.

65. *Ibid.*, p. 108–9.

66. Nu, *From Peace to Stability*, p. 191.

67. Nu, *Burma Looks Ahead*, p. 46.

68. Nu, *Premier Reports to the People*, p. 81.

69. Tinker, *Union*, pp. 195–96.

70. Nu, *Forward with the People*, p. 59.

71. Nu, *Premier Reports to the People*, p. 76.

72. For a good examination of pre-university education in Burma, see Tinker, *Union*, pp. 196–203.

73. *Ibid.*, p. 204.

74. For a discussion of student political activities, see *ibid.*, pp. 207–10.

75. The author taught at the University during this period.

76. Nu, *Burma Looks Ahead*, p. 77.

77. Nu, *Premier U Nu on the 4-Year Plan*, p. 9.

78. Nu, *Forward with the People,* p. 135.
79. Walinsky, p. 109.   80. *Ibid.,* pp. 102–3.
81. See Tinker, *Union,* pp. 220–21.   82. *The Nation,* Jan. 18, 1960.
83. *Ibid.,* Nov. 17, 1959.   84. *Ibid.,* Oct. 1, 1957.
85. Nu, *Burma Looks Ahead,* p. 116.   86. *Ibid.,* p. 59.
87. For an evaluation of the "outcomes and impact of the development program" in general by one of the foreign consultants advising the Burmese government, see Walinsky, pp. 352–68.
88. Trager, "Political Divorce," pp. 326–27.
89. Nu, *Premier Reports to the People,* pp. 10–11.
90. Trager, *Building,* p. 61.

CHAPTER 12

1. This was the almost unanimous opinion of various officials with whom I talked.
2. Kyaw Nyein interview (1960).
3. Win Pe interview (1960).
4. See Walinsky, p. 229.
5. *The Nation,* July 15, 1957, is the source of most of the information contained in this paragraph.
6. See, for example, Walinsky, p. 205.
7. *New Times of Burma,* Jan. 3, 1952.
8. Nu, *Premier Reports to the People,* p. 18.
9. U Hla Maung interview (1960). For a description of the origins of the Economic and Social Board, see Walinsky, p. 154.
10. U Hla Maung interview (1960). U Win Pe said essentially the same thing in my interview with him (1960).
11. Win Pe interview (1960).
12. This judgment was expressed by all those to whom I talked who had served on the Board or worked closely with it.
13. U Hla Maung interview (1960).   14. U Win interview (1960).
15. Walinsky, p. 126.   16. *The Nation,* Nov. 22, 1957.
17. Silverstein, p. 126. This was confirmed in conversations with various Cabinet members.
18. The AFPFL politician and former Cabinet member U Tun Win was interviewed on Nov. 2, 1959.
19. This was affirmed by almost all the politicians to whom I talked.
20. U Sein Win interview (1959).
21. Silverstein, p. 126.
22. *Ibid.*
23. This was the expressed view of former members of the Board to whom I talked.
24. See Badgley, "Burma's Political Crisis," p. 340.
25. Walinsky, p. 178.   26. U Nu interview (1960).
27. See Silverstein, p. 127.   28. *The Nation,* May 10, 1958.
29. Nu, *The Pyidaungsu Policy,* p. 31.

30. U Kyaw Nyein interview (1960). 31. U Raschid interview (1959).

32. U Raschid interview (1960).   33. *The Nation,* Apr. 6, 1960.

34. This source asked not to be identified.

35. For a description of the yeast tablet scheme, see *The Nation,* Nov. 3, 1957. I have confirmed the details with various officials.

36. U Kyaw Nyein interview (1960).

37. This source asked not to be identified.

38. Tun Pe, *Why I Resign,* p. 6.

39. *Ibid.,* p. 18.

40. This denial and the quotations that follow were obtained in interviews with Nu, Ba Swe, and Kyaw Nyein, all in 1960.

41. Rose interview (1960).

42. See Tinker, "Nu, the Serene Statesman," p. 127.

43. *The Nation,* Nov. 26, 1959.

44. *Ibid.,* Oct. 20, 1958.

45. Nu, *From Peace to Stability,* pp. 202–3. Italics Nu's.

46. Thakin Nu, "Translation of the Broadcast Speech by the Hon'ble Prime Minister on the Night of 5th April 1949" (typescript, n.d.), p. 1.

47. Nu, *From Peace to Stability,* p. 181.

48. Nu, *An Asian Speaks,* p. 15.

49. *The Nation,* Sept. 23, 1954.

50. Tinker, "Nu, the Serene Statesman," p. 131.

51. *The Nation,* Sept. 26, 1954.

52. Nu, *An Asian Speaks,* p. 27.

53. *Ibid.,* p. 28.

54. *The Nation,* Nov. 27, 1959.

55. This assessment was made in an interview in 1960 by Dr. Ba U, former President of the Union of Burma. Dr. Ba U served as Chairman of the Elections Supervisory Commission.

56. *Parliamentary Proceedings, Chamber of Deputies,* III, pp. 296–304.

57. These speeches may be found in *Parliament (Constituent Assembly) Proceedings,* VI, pp. 94–100; VIII, pp. 151–64; XII, pp. 219–31; VII, pp. 252–57; XI, pp. 209–21; VI, pp. 1165–84; XI, pp. 1459–65; and XI, pp. 1602–8.

58. *Parliament (Constituent Assembly) Proceedings,* III, pp. 339–45.

59. See *The Nation,* Feb. 28, 1957.

60. *The Statesman* (Calcutta), Sept. 27, 1949.

61. *The Nation,* Mar. 1, 1957.

62. *Ibid.,* Nov. 11, 1956.

63. U Ohn Khin interview (1960).

64. This was the view of practically all officials with whom I talked.

65. U Raschid interview (1959).

66. This was a general criticism voiced by secretaries and other senior administrative personnel. The Secretary who stated this asked not to be identified.

67. Tun Pe, *Why I Resign,* p. 13.

68. U Myo Min interview (1959).

69. I was told this by various persons about U Win Pe (with whom I also met in Rangoon on January 22, 1960).

70. U Myo Min interview (1959).
71. Law Yone, "A Hard Look at 'Mr. Tender.' "
72. U Nyo Mya interview (1959).
73. U Myo Min interview (1959).
74. Michael Davidson in *The Scotsman* (Edinburgh), June 13, 1950.
75. Respectively, *The Economist* (London), May 13, 1950, and A. T. Steele, in the *New York Herald-Tribune,* Aug. 25, 1948.
76. Ba Swe, *Burmese Revolution,* p. 11.
77. U Raschid interview (1960).
78. *The Nation,* Aug. 14, 1957.
79. See Lockwood, p. 449.
80. For a profound discussion of relevant characteristics of Burmese administrators and politicians, see Pye, especially pp. 211–30 and 244–66. Profiles "in acculturation" of administrators and politicians appear on pp. 231–43 and 267–82.
81. Law Yone interview (1960).

CHAPTER 13

1. *New Times of Burma,* June 3, 1951.
2. Tun Pe, *Why I Resign,* p. 2.
3. Rose, *Socialism,* p. 138. Much of the material in this paragraph is drawn from Rose, who offers one of the best accounts of the workings of the Burmese political process.
4. Quoted by Rose, *Socialism,* p. 121. For a discussion of the party organization outside Rangoon, see Sein Win, p. 13.
5. Sein Win, p. 13. 6. Furnivall, pp. 114–15.
7. See Rose, *Socialism,* p. 121. 8. *The Nation,* May 26, 1955.
9. See Htin Fatt, "Psychology of Fear," p. 2.
10. *The Nation,* May 27, 1955.
11. Nu, *From Peace to Stability,* p. 199.
12. Quoted by Rose, *Socialism,* p. 123, from a Socialist Party document.
13. See Silverstein, p. 117.
14. Maung Maung, *Burma's Constitution,* p. 132.
15. See *The Times* (London), Aug. 16, 1948.
16. Tinker, "Nu, the Serene Statesman," p. 126.
17. Michael Davidson wrote in *The Scotsman* (Edinburgh) of June 13, 1949, for example, that the Socialists left the government "because they were told they would be murdered if they did not." The latter reason, their desire for unity, was mentioned by U Kyaw Nyein in an interview (1960).
18. This was strongly stated to the writer by Saul Rose, author of *Socialism in Southern Asia* and former Socialist International official, in 1960.
19. See Davidson in *The Scotsman* (Edinburgh), June 9, 1949.
20. Tinker, *Union,* p. 81.
21. *New Times of Burma,* Dec. 16, 1951.
22. U Ba Swe interview (1960).
23. See Maung Maung, "U Kyaw Nyein," p. 19.

24. These sources asked not to be identified.

25. *Burma Weekly Bulletin,* VII (Oct. 16, 1958), 210.

26. U Raschid interview (1960).

27. Sein Win, p. 17.

28. See, for example, *The Economist* (London), Feb. 9, 1952.

29. This is the description of U Ba Swe given by most of the persons to whom I talked in Burma. Of Ba Swe, U Raschid said: "He was too lazy to involve himself—on his own initiative—in the struggle for power. His laziness was, in general, unfortunate, for he was a man of considerable ability."

30. U Ba Swe interview (1960).

31. Thakin Nu, "Translation of the Broadcast Speech by the Hon'ble Prime Minister on the Night of 5th April, 1949" (typescript: n.d.), p. 2.

32. Dr. Ong Gine (of the Department of History and Political Science, Rangoon University) interview (1960).

33. U Kyaw Nyein interview (1960).

CHAPTER 14

1. *The Nation,* June 6, 1956.   2. *Ibid.*

3. Kyaw Nyein interview (1960).   4. See Htin Fatt, "Psychology," p. 2.

5. Trager, "Political Split," p. 148. 6. Tun Win interview (1959).

7. *The Guardian* (daily), May 6–10, 1958.

8. Quoted in Furnivall, *Governance,* pp. 117–18.

9. *The Nation,* May 10, 1958.

10. Trager, "Political Split," p. 149.

11. See Rawle Knox in *The Statesman* (Edinburgh), Aug. 21, 1956.

12. *The Nation,* Aug. 18, 1956.

13. Sein Win, *Split Story,* pp. 20–21.

14. Thakin Tin interview (1960).

15. Sein Win, *Split Story,* p. 21. This was also the opinion of U Ohn Khin, the editor and longtime close friend of Nu.

16. U Ba Swe interview (1960).

17. This was hinted at in *The Nation,* Dec. 30, 1956.

18. U Ba Swe interview (1960).

19. Quoted in Furnivall, *Governance,* p. 118.

20. See Trager, "New Temper," p. 179.

21. Trager, "Political Split," p. 150.

22. See *The Nation,* May 7, 1958. For a discussion of the views of Burma's top leaders in connection with this ideological question, see Trager, "Political Divorce," pp. 319–21.

23. For the text of this important address, see U Nu, *Towards a Socialist State.*

24. *The Nation,* Jan. 20, 1958.   25. *Ibid.,* Jan. 28, 1958.

26. Sein Win, *Split Story,* p. 22.   27. See Cady, "Swing," p. 9.

28. Sein Win, *Split Story,* p. 22.

29. Remarks at a press conference, in *The Nation,* Apr. 23, 1958.

30. Sein Win, *Split Story,* p. 23.   31. *The Nation,* Apr. 11, 1958.

32. Trager, "Political Split," p. 150.   33. See *The Nation,* May 4, 1958.

34. *Ibid.,* May 7, 1958.   35. Sein Win, *Split Story,* p. 26.

36. Walinsky (p. 245) states that Nu's assumption of the Home Ministry portfolio "finally precipitated the AFPFL split." Walinsky's interpretation suggests that Kyaw Nyein and his supporters had to "fight back" at this "declaration of political war"—possibly meaning that they would have split with Nu if he had not moved first. I doubt this.

37. According to Hugh Tinker, "The Swe-Nyein group attempted to undermine the Premier from within the government, but finally withdrew." ("The Politics of Burma," in Rose, *Politics,* p. 113.) This is certainly a possible interpretation of Kyaw Nyein's behavior (and consistent with Ba Swe's efforts to build up the Socialist Party). But I do not believe that it is supported by such other evidence as Ba Swe's peacemaking efforts.

38. See Tinker, "Politics," p. 115.

39. *The Nation,* June 2, 1958.

40. Cady, "Swing," pp. 11–12.

Chapter 15

1. Nu, "Speech at a Mass Meeting on the BAA Ground on June 13, 1948," p. 6.

2. *The Times* (London), Mar. 1 and May 14, 1949.

3. See Cady, *History,* p. 599.

4. *New Times of Burma,* Mar. 7, 1950.

5. Thakin Nu, "Translation of the Speech by the Hon'ble Thakin Nu, Prime Minister of Burma, delivered in Parliament on 14th June 1949" (typescript, n.d.), p. 5.

6. See *The Times,* June 15 and 21, 1949.

7. *The Nation,* May 5, 1950.

8. Johnstone, *Chronology,* p. 21.

9. Nu, *From Peace to Stability,* p. 101.

10. *Ibid.,* p. 196.

11. Nu, *Burma Looks Ahead,* p. 98.

12. Nu, *An Asian Speaks,* p. 18.

13. Quoted in Fifield, p. 228.

14. Nu, *An Asian Speaks,* p. 51.

15. *The Nation,* Nov. 5, 1955.

16. *Ibid.,* Aug. 29, 1956.

17. *Ibid.,* July 7, 1955.

18. Nu, *From Peace to Stability,* p. 40.

19. Nu, *An Asian Speaks,* p. 19.

20. Quoted in Maung Maung, *Burma's Constitution,* p. 199.

21. Nu, *An Asian Speaks,* p. 14.

22. Nu, *Burma Looks Ahead,* p. 43.

23. "Hon'ble U Nu's Address at Martyrs' Day Mass Rally," *Burma Weekly Bulletin,* V (July 26, 1956), 114.

24. Nu, *An Asian Speaks,* p. 19.

25. Nu, *From Peace to Stability*, p. 104.
26. Nu, *Burma Looks Ahead*, p. 102.
27. Nu, *From Peace to Stability*, pp. 98–99.
28. This was stated by several officials of the Burmese Foreign Office.
29. Fifield, p. 200.
30. The ambassador was U Myint Thein, later Chief Justice of the Supreme Court.
31. Fifield, p. 199.
32. Nu, *Premier Reports to the People*, p. 36.
33. Panikkar, p. 68.
34. Tinker, *Union*, p. 373.
35. Fifield, p. 200.
36. Quoted in Tinker, "Nu, the Serene Statesman," p. 136.
37. Nu, *Resurgence*, pp. 7–8.
38. Quoted in Tinker, *Union*, p. 374.
39. Rau, p. 21.
40. Quoted in Tinker, *Union*, p. 374.
41. *The Nation*, Dec. 21, 1954.
42. Nu, *An Asian Speaks*, p. 23.
43. Hinton, p. 53.
44. See Nu's broadcast on the Sino-Burmese boundary question, in *Burma Weekly Bulletin*, V (Nov. 15, 1956), 255.
45. *The Nation*, Aug. 17, 1956.
46. Quoted in Tinker, "Burma's Northeast Borderland Problems," p. 246.
47. Fifield, p. 202.
48. For a detailed narrative of the KMT aggression, see *Translation of a Government Statement on Kuomintang Aggression into Burma* (distributed to members of Parliament Mar. 2, 1953), pp. 1–2.
49. *Translation of the Hon'ble Prime Minister's Speech in the Chamber of Deputies on 2nd March 1953* (n.d.), pp. 1–2.
50. Nu, *Premier Reports to the People*, p. 30. See also Maung Maung, *Grim War Against KMT* (Rangoon: Nu Yin Press, 1953), pp. 15–18.
51. Nu, *Premier Reports to the People*, p. 43.
52. Quoted in Maung Maung, *Grim War Against KMT*, p. 80.
53. U Nu interview (1960).
54. Quoted in Maung Maung, *Burma's Constitution*, p. 202.
55. Nu, *From Peace to Stability*, p. 45.
56. *The Nation*, June 15, 1956.
57. See *ibid.*, Aug. 5, 6, 7, and 9, 1954.
58. Rose, *Britain and South-East Asia*, p. 189. Several Burmese said as much to me in 1959 and 1960.
59. Quoted in Tinker, *Union*, p. 368.
60. Nu, *An Asian Speaks*, p. 22.
61. *The Hindu* (Madras), July 7, 1955.
62. *New York Herald Tribune*, July 7, 1955.
63. Nu, *Premier Reports to the People*, p. 41.
64. *The Nation*, Nov. 8, 1955.
65. See Clubb, p. 25. For background, see Allen, pp. 147–63.

66. Hagen, p. 80.

67. *New Times of Burma,* Sept. 25, 1955.

68. Quoted in Tinker, *Union,* p. 355.

69. *Manchester Guardian,* Apr. 2, 1953.

70. See *The Nation,* Sept. 16, 1959.

71. Quoted in Maung Maung, *Burma's Constitution,* p. 200.

72. See *The Nation,* July 21, 1956.

73. Mizra Khan, "Israel-Burma Ties," *The Guardian,* IV (Dec. 1957), 19. This was confirmed to me by Burmese Foreign Office officials.

74. Nu, *Resurgence,* p. 4.

75. James Barrington, formerly Burmese Ambassador to the United States and later Permanent Secretary of the Burmese Foreign Office, interview (1960).

76. See reports of a talk on Bandung by U Raschid (who accompanied Nu to the conference), in the *New Times of Burma,* May 27 and 28, 1955.

77. U Raschid interview (1960).

78. See the evaluation by Robert Alden in the *New York Times,* Apr. 24, 1955.

79. *The Nation,* Nov. 10, 1955.

80. This description of Nu's impression of Diem was provided by James Barrington of the Burmese Foreign Office.

81. Nu, *Premier Reports to the People,* p. 37.

82. *New York Times,* Dec. 18, 1954.

83. *The Nation,* Dec. 21, 1954.

84. *Ibid.,* July 21, 1956.

85. See interview of C. L. Sulzberger with Nu, in the *New York Times,* Nov. 13, 1957.

86. *The Nation,* July 21, 1956.

87. C. L. Sulzberger, in the *New York Times,* Nov. 13, 1957.

88. *The Times of Cyprus,* May 30, 1955.

89. See *The Statesman* (Calcutta), Sept. 8, 1953. For a discussion of Nu's efforts to help India and Pakistan solve the Kashmir question, see Fifield, p. 216.

90. U Myo Min interview (1959).

91. Barrington interview (1960).

92. U Kyaw Nyein interview (1960).

93. Justice Myint Thein was interviewed in Rangoon on February 24, 1960. Kyaw Nyein told me in 1960: "It is true that the main opposition to a border settlement as it was shaping up under Nu came from me. I thought that Nu was giving too much to the Communists. I opposed not only the cession of the Kachin villages but also the territory in the Wa state area."

94. Dr. Krishnalal Shridharani, in the Indian newspaper *Amrita Bazar Patrika,* July 7, 1950.

95. Jawaharlal Nehru interview (1960).

96. U Myint Thein interview (1960).

97. Nu, *Burma Looks Ahead,* pp. 100–101.

98. Nu, *Forward with the People,* p. 88.

99. Quoted in Tinker, *Union,* p. 337.

100. *The Nation,* Apr. 28, 1955.

101. *Ibid.,* Nov. 21, 1954.

102. *An Asian Speaks,* p. 50.

103. See Tinker, "Nu, the Serene Statesman," p. 135. This was also stated by several persons associated at various times with the Burmese Foreign Office.

104. U Thant, "A Burmese View of Israel," *The Guardian* (magazine), V (Aug. 1958), 18.

105. *The Nation,* Nov. 5, 1955.

106. Nu, *An Asian Speaks,* p. 31. For a very good recent analysis of Burmese external relations under U Nu (and Ne Win), see Johnstone, *Burma's Foreign Policy.*

CHAPTER 16

1. According to Kyaw Nyein (and others), Tin "does not understand socialism."

2. Furnivall interview (1959).

3. E Maung interview (1960).

4. See Sein Win, *Split Story,* pp. 64–65.

5. *Ibid.,* p. 66.

6. See Htin Fatt, "The Conference and After," *New Burma Weekly,* I (Aug. 2, 1958), 4.

7. "Rangoon Diary" (Hittalone), *New Burma Weekly,* I (Aug. 2, 1958), 15.

8. *The Guardian* (magazine), V (Aug. 1958), 6.

9. See Htin Fatt, "Amnesty and Election Prospects," *New Burma Weekly,* I (Aug. 9, 1958), 3.

10. Trager, "Political Split," p. 151.   11. See Cady, "Swing," p. 12.

12. Tin Aung, p. 25.   13. See Cady, "Swing," p. 16.

14. *The Times* (London), Mar. 12, 1958. 15. *The Nation,* June 22, 1958.

16. See Htin Fatt, "Peace Plans," *New Burma Weekly,* I (June 28, 1958), 3.

17. Badgley, "Burma's Political Crisis," p. 345.

18. See Htin Fatt, "Peace Plans," p. 4.

19. U Nu, *The Government for the People,* p. 24.

20. Trager, "Political Split," p. 152.

21. See *The Nation,* Sept. 1, 1958.

22. *Ibid.,* Oct. 29, 1958.

23. See Cady, "Swing," p. 13.

24. Trager, "Political Divorce," p. 322.

25. See Sein Win, *Split Story,* pp. 72–74.

26. Cady, "Swing," p. 18.

27. Sein Win, *Split Story,* pp. 77–81.

28. This source asked not to be identified. Cady has written that the "military police were aligning more and more against Nu's authority" during this period. ("Swing," p. 18.)

29. U Law Yone interview (1959).

30. Htin Fatt, "A Dramatist's Dream," *New Burma Weekly,* IV (Nov. 1, 1958), 336.

31. Speech in *The Nation,* Oct. 27, 1958.

32. See *The Nation,* Oct. 27, 1958.

33. *Ibid.*

34. Maung Maung interview (1960).

35. Ne Win's statement to Parliament, in *The Times* (London), Nov. 1, 1958.

36. *The Times,* Oct. 7, 1958.

37. See Cady, "Swing," p. 18.

38. This source asked not to be identified. For background, see Wolfstone, "The Burmese Army Experiment," pp. 352 and 356–59.

39. Dr. E Maung interview (1960). See also Tinker, "Politics," p. 9, and Cady, "Swing," pp. 18–19. According to Cady, however, the "immediate occasion of the crisis stemmed from a threatened *coup d'état . . .* by several disaffected officers high in the command" of the UMP. I do not agree with this interpretation.

40. *The Nation,* Oct. 3, 1958.

41. A Brigadier at the time, Aung Gyi would not consent to be interviewed. The quotation is from a high Burmese military leader and close friend of Aung Gyi. Other Army officers confirmed that Aung Gyi had stated essentially this on several occasions.

42. For the exchange of letters between U Nu and General Ne Win (as well as the latter's subsequent acceptance speech to the Parliament), see *Government in the Union of Burma, 1958 Nov.–1959 Feb.* (Rangoon: Director of Information, 1959).

43. *The Nation,* Oct. 1, 1958.

44. Thakin Tin interview (1960).

45. This source asked not to be identified.

46. For obvious reasons, this source asked not to be identified.

47. Trager has written that both factions of the AFPFL "agreed in advance to General Ne Win's assumption of power." This was because each believed neither side would obtain a majority in the forthcoming elections. "To both sides, the Army appeared to provide the best assurance of a fair political fight and a stable interregnum." (See "Political Divorce," pp. 322–23.) I uncovered no evidence to support this interpretation nor do I believe that it is consistent with the "Clean" AFPFL's view that the Army was pro-"Stable."

48. *The Nation,* Oct. 1, 1958.

49. Dr. E Maung interview (1960). According to Cady, Nu's acceptance of the Army's demand that he resign the Premiership was "apparently without the full concurrence of his Cabinet." ("Swing," p. 19.)

50. U Kyaw Min interview (1960). Some "Clean" ministers, such as Bo Min Gaung, have said that "the decision to invite Ne Win to be Premier was a Cabinet one." Nu himself has stated that he conferred first with five of his top Cabinet colleagues. *New Burma Weekly,* II (Oct. 4, 1958), 200.

51. *The Nation,* Oct. 15, 1958.

CHAPTER 17

1. The Ne Win government's own account of its efforts against the insurgents can be found in *Is Trust Vindicated?* (Rangoon: Director of Information, 1960), pp. 19–35.

2. *Ibid.,* p. 32.

3. See Walinsky, pp. 257–59.

4. *Ibid.,* pp. 260–61.

5. See Butwell, "Civilians and Soldiers in Burma," p. 80.

6. In teaching international relations and comparative government at Rangoon University in 1959–60, I had both civilian and military students.

7. For a discussion of Ne Win's foreign policy, see J. S. Thomson, "The Ne Win Administration and After," supplement to Furnivall, *Governance,* pp. 138–40.

8. See Maung Maung, "Burma-China Border," pp. 41–42, and Whittam, pp. 179–80.

9. Butwell, "Sino-Burmese Border," p. 16.

10. Clubb, pp. 39–40.

11. This was stated by several Army officers. For the government's public description of the National Solidarity Associations, see *Nine Months after Ten Years,* pp. 17–18.

12. I discussed this subject with Maung Kyaw Thu of the Burmese Chamber of Commerce on August 31, 1959, in Rangoon.

13. Walinsky, pp. 257–58.

14. A resident in Burma at this time, I was personally aware of such abuses.

15. Walinsky, pp. 253–54, is the source of most of the information in this paragraph. See also Haldore Hansen, "Twenty-five Colonels and the Three Evils," *The Reporter,* XXII (June 11, 1959), 28.

16. See K. Rangaswami in *The Hindu* (Madras), Mar. 12, 1959; see also *The Guardian* (magazine), VI (Mar. 1959), 10.

17. Furnivall interview (1959).

18. Thakin Tin interview (1960).

19. See Yangoon Ba Swe. This satirical play (a not even slightly veiled commentary on government under U Nu) was an obvious attempt to discredit Nu, and was distributed with the assistance of the Army.

20. Nu's Mandalay speech and related documents were published under the title *I Want to Bequeath a Legacy of Democracy.*

21. *New Burma Weekly,* IV (Feb. 21, 1959), 261.

22. Nu, *The Government for the People,* pp. 6–7.

23. *Ibid.,* pp. 8–10. 24. *Ibid.,* p. 19.

25. *Ibid.,* p. 27. 26. *Ibid.,* pp. 30–32.

27. *Ibid.,* p. 37.

28. Nu, *Stages of Battle Against Oppression,* p. 4.

29. *The Nation,* May 16, 1959. 30. Nu, *The Pyidaungsu Policy,* p. 64.

31. *The Nation,* Mar. 18, 1960. 32. Nu, *The Pyidaungsu Policy,* p. 50.

33. *Ibid.,* p. 31. 34. *Ibid.,* pp. 56–57.

35. *The Nation,* Jan. 18, 1960.

36. *The Guardian* (daily), Nov. 17, 1959.

37. U Kyaw Min interview (1960).

38. I was told this by persons close to both "Clean" and Army leaders.

39. This was admitted by several military leaders. The National Solidarity Associations are discussed in greater detail in Butwell, "New Political Outlook," pp. 23–24.

40. See *The National Ideology*, p. 14.

41. Lucian W. Pye, "The Army in Burmese Politics," in John J. Johnson (ed.), pp. 232–34.

42. This point is further developed in Butwell, "Wandlungen und Kontinuität in sozialistischen Birma."

43. See *Policy and Program of the "Clean" AFPFL.*

44. U Ohn Khin interview (1960). Other "Clean" politicians have said the same thing.

45. Dr. E Maung interview (1960).

46. *The Nation*, Jan. 13, 1960.

47. *Ibid.*, Jan. 18, 1960.

48. This source asked not to be identified.

49. For an excellent discussion of religion and politics in Burma, see von der Mehden, "Changing Patterns," pp. 63–73.

50. "Hon'ble U Nu's Address of Deep Veneration" (celebrating the conclusion of the Sixth Great Buddhist Synod), in *Burma Weekly Bulletin*, V (June 14, 1956), 68–69.

51. *Burma Weekly Bulletin*, VII (July 31, 1958), 119.

52. *The Nation*, Nov. 22, 1959.

53. The "Stable"-"Clean" interaction during the campaign is described in Butwell and von der Mehden, pp. 144–57. See also Bigelow, pp. 70–74.

54. See Butwell, "U Nu Returns to Power in Burma," pp. 9–10.

CHAPTER 18

1. *Burma Weekly Bulletin*, X (Sept. 7, 1961), 152.

2. Quoted in Maung Maung, "Burma's Constitution Grows Up." *The Guardian*, VII (Sept. 1960), 38.

3. *The Guardian*, VIII (Oct. 1961), 11.

4. See Butwell, "The Four Failures," p. 4.

5. *Burma Weekly Bulletin*, IX (July 7, 1960), 73.

6. The Nu government's own account of its stewardship for the previous year can be found in *Burma: the Fourteenth Anniversary* (Rangoon: Director of Information, 1962).

7. The Constitution (Third Amendment) Act, 1961, appears in *Burma Weekly Bulletin*, X (Aug. 31, 1961), 144.

8. *The Nation*, Aug. 31, 1960.

9. Nu, "Promulgation of Buddhism" (Chamber of Deputies), p. 137.

10. *Burma Weekly Bulletin*, X (Aug. 3, 1961), 105.

11. Wolfstone, "The Phongyis," p. 323.

12. Nu, "Promulgation of Buddhism," (Chamber of Deputies), p. 138.

13. Nu, "Promulgation of Buddhism" (Chamber of Nationalities), pp. 148–49.

14. The text of the Constitution (Fourth Amendment) Act, 1961, appears in *Burma Weekly Bulletin,* X (Oct. 5, 1961), 181.

15. *The Nation,* Sept. 18, 1961.

16. King, p. 157.

17. See *The Nation,* June 15, 1961.

18. For excellent background information, see Josef Silverstein, "The Federal Dilemma in Burma," *Far Eastern Survey,* XXVIII (July 1959), 97–105.

19. See *The Nation,* Apr. 25, 1961.

20. *Far Eastern Economic Review 1962 Yearbook* (Hongkong: Far Eastern Economic Review, 1961), p. 39.

21. Rudolf Sternberg, in *The Guardian* (Manchester), Dec. 2, 1961.

22. *The Nation,* Oct. 6, 1961.

23. *The Guardian* (daily), Mar. 22, 1961. The government's discussions with members of the business community in 1960 suggest, however, that it was tempted to embark on more ambitious projects. See, for example, E. M., "Pipe Dreams," *ibid.,* Sept. 6, 1960.

24. Nu, "Address in the Chamber of Deputies on March 13," p. 440.

25. See "Report of the Public Service Enquiry Commission." See also the account of the subsequent "Public Services Seminar," *Burma Weekly Bulletin,* X (July 27, 1961), 97–104, and X (Aug. 3, 1961), 111.

26. Wolfstone, "The Phongyis," p. 322.

27. Maung Maung, "New Hope," p. 14.

28. *The Nation,* Feb. 26, 1961.

29. See Lelyveld, p. 9.

30. Wolfstone, "The Phongyis," p. 323.

31. See Karnow, p. 33 (as well as p. 31.)

32. See the *New York Times,* Feb. 19, 1961.

33. *Burma Weekly Bulletin,* IX (Apr. 20, 1961), 458.

34. Nu, "Prime Minister's Report to the People," p. 138.

35. This material is drawn from several sources but particularly from the detailed account of Union Party factionalism by U Hla Htway in *The Nation,* Dec. 24, 1960. See also *ibid.,* Nov. 17 and 28, 1961, and *The Guardian* (daily), Dec. 24, 1960, and Nov. 7, 1961.

36. *The Guardian* (daily), Nov. 26, 1960.

37. *The Nation,* Mar. 13 and 14, 1961.

38. *Ibid.,* Mar. 12, 1961.

39. *New York Times,* Mar. 21, 1961.

40. "Prime Minister's Luncheon with Newspapermen," *Burma Weekly Bulletin,* IX (Dec. 14, 1961), 287.

41. See the *New York Times,* Oct. 14, 1961.

42. *New York Times,* Aug. 28, 1961. The text of the Sino-Burmese economic and technical agreement is reproduced in *Burma Weekly Bulletin,* IX (Jan. 19, 1961), 359, and in Wolfstone, "Burma's Honeymoon," p. 353. The major documents concerning the border settlement can be found in *Burma,* IX, No. 4 (Oct. 1960) (Rangoon: Director of Information, 1960), pp. 1–34. See also *Burma Weekly Bulletin,* IX (Oct. 13, 1960), 187–89.

43. *The Nation,* Apr. 18, 1961.

44. *Ibid.,* Apr. 26, 1961.

45. See Rudolf Sternberg, in *The Guardian* (Manchester) Dec. 16, 1961. See also Richard Hughes, in *The Sunday Times* (London), Apr. 2, 1961.

46. See *Observer* Foreign News Service dispatch of Jan. 21, 1961 (by Dennis Bloodworth).

47. See *New York Times,* Jan. 13, 1961.

48. See Wolfstone, "Burma's Honeymoon," p. 353.

49. *The Nation,* Apr. 19, 1961.

50. See A. K. Mukerji, in *The Guardian* (daily), Nov. 24, 1960.

51. *The Nation,* Jan. 17, 1961.

52. U Nu, "Parliament and the Chinese-Burmese Boundary Treaty," *Burma Weekly Bulletin,* IX (Dec. 15, 1960), 312.

53. *The Hindu* (Madras), Feb. 16, 1961.

54. *The Nation,* Jan. 17, 1961.

55. *The Hindu,* Feb. 28, 1961. Although Nu denied seeking to mediate the Sino-Indian dispute during his trip to Delhi, representatives of India and China held three meetings on the subject in neutral Rangoon in 1960. See *The Guardian* (magazine), VII (Dec. 1960), 11.

56. Nu, "Address in the Chamber of Deputies on March 13," p. 441.

57. U Nu, "Address on International Situation," *Burma Weekly Bulletin,* IX (Sept. 29, 1960), 175–76.

58. *Ibid.,* p. 171.

59. Nu, "Address in the Chamber of Deputies on March 13," p. 448.

60. *Burma Weekly Bulletin,* IX (Mar. 30, 1961), 443.

61. See *The Nation,* Dec. 14, 1960.

62. *Ibid.,* Feb. 26, 1961.

63. *Ibid.,* Dec. 21, 1960.

64. Nu, "Address in the Chamber of Deputies on March 13," p. 448.

65. *The Guardian* (daily), Apr. 30, 1961.

66. The Geneva Conference on Laos had not yet concluded at the time of Nu's second ouster as Premier in March 1962. For the texts of the subsequent "Declaration on the Neutrality of Laos" and its protocol, both signed July 23, 1962, see Clubb, pp. 158–66.

67. See "Translation of Joint Communiqué of the Premier of the State Council of the People's Republic of China and the Prime Minister of the Union of Burma" (Apr. 16, 1961), *Burma Weekly Bulletin,* IX (Apr. 27, 1961), 461.

68. See Nu's remarks at his press conference following his return from Belgrade. *The Nation,* Sept. 14, 1961.

69. *The Nation,* Sept. 16, 1961.

70. *The Guardian* (daily), Sept. 3, 1961.

71. This account is based primarily on the reports of M. S. Handler to the *New York Times* and Paul Ghali to the *Chicago Daily News.*

72. *The Nation,* Sept. 15, 1961. For the "Declaration of the Heads of State or Government of Non-Aligned Countries," see *Burma Weekly Bulletin,* X (Sept. 21, 1961), 162–63, and X (Sept. 28, 1961), 174, 176.

73. *New York Times,* Mar. 6, 1962.

74. The speech appears in successive issues of the official *Burma Weekly Bulletin* (Aug. 24–Oct. 5, 1961).

75. *New York Times*, Mar. 6, 1962.

76. *The Guardian* (daily), Mar. 8, 1962.

77. See editorial in *ibid.*, Mar. 3, 1962.

78. *The Guardian* (daily), Mar. 3, 1962.

79. *Ibid.*, Mar. 8, 1962.

CHAPTER 19

1. "Rangoon University Convocation" (Address by Prime Minister U Nu, Chancellor of the University of Rangoon, on December 1), *Burma Weekly Bulletin*, IX (Dec. 8, 1960), 303.

2. Ba Maw, "Military Take-over."   3. See Ba Than, p. 76.

4. *The Nation*, Aug. 23, 1960.   5. *Ibid.*, May 8, 1961.

6. *Burma Weekly Bulletin*, IX (Nov. 10, 1960), 269.

7. *The Nation*, Feb. 12–17, 1961. See also U Nu, *The Wages of Sin*.

8. *The Nation*, Feb. 15, 1961.

9. *Ibid.*, Feb. 17, 1961.

10. *Ibid.*, Nov. 29, 1961.

11. This statement was reported to me in Rangoon in August 1962 by an important Burmese political figure. In order not to embarrass or otherwise inconvenience the persons in question, he and other persons interviewed at that time, who are sources of other information in this section, will not be identified here.

12. Brigadier Aung Gyi's speech to the insurgents, in the government fortnightly *Forward*, I (Oct. 7, 1962), 12–13.

13. See Badgley, "Burma's Military Government," pp. 29–30.

14. *Burmese Way to Socialism*, p. 1.

15. *The Nation*, July 29, 1962.

16. For a sympathetic treatment, see U Maung Maung, "The Revolutionary Government's Approach to Economic Planning—Wise, Humanistic and Socialistic," *Forward*, I (Oct. 22, 1962), 19.

17. See *Constitution of the Burma Socialist Programme Party*.

18. *The Burmese Way to Socialism*, pp. 3–4.

19. Nu, "Asians and Democracy," p. 287.

20. The two most recent surveys of the second Ne Win administration are Fred R. von der Mehden, " 'The Burmese Way to Socialism,' " *Asian Survey*, III (Mar. 1963), 129–35, and Hanna, "Re-revving a Revolution."

21. "A Leaf in the Whirlwind," in Dagon Taya, pp. 57–73.

CHAPTER 20

1. Joseph Lelyveld, in the *New York Times*, October 29, 1968.

2. *Rangoon Daily*, May 5, 1968.

3. *Ibid.*, May 7, 1968.

4. *New York Times,* May 7, 1967.

5. *Botataung* (Rangoon), April 22, 1968.

6. Nu, it should be remembered, pledged several times in the past—even when he was Premier—that he planned a complete retirement from political life.

7. Joseph Lelyveld, in the *New York Times,* October 29, 1968.

8. *Ibid.*

9. Adam Clymer, in the *Baltimore Sun,* August 16, 1968.

10. The author, who visited Burma in 1964 and 1966 (following the publication of his *U Nu of Burma*), particularly looked for the deposed Nu in such exhibitions.

11. On a 1966 visit to Burma the writer was asked repeatedly by both strangers and prior acquaintances how then present circumstances compared with "U Nu's time."

12. *New York Times,* October 29, 1968.

13. Reported by David Van Praagh, in *The Evening Star* (Washington, D.C.), September 15, 1968.

14. *The Guardian* (daily) (Rangoon), June 3, 1969. The serialization—in English—of the recommendations of the National Unity Advisory Board began with this issue, which also included such other materials as General Ne Win's charge to the commission.

15. See Adam Clymer, in the *Baltimore Sun,* April 27, 1969.

16. S. C. Banerji, "Pressing On," in the *Far Eastern Economic Review* (Hongkong), LXIV, No. 3 (January 16, 1969), 92.

17. For an account, see *The Guardian,* June 4, 1969.

18. Nu's memorandum appears in *The Guardian* for June 5, 1969.

19. *Ibid.*

20. Thein Pe Myint, in *Botataung,* June 7, 1969.

21. See "Pilgrim's Progress," in the *Far Eastern Economic Review* (Hongkong), LXIV, No. 21 (May 15, 1969), 374.

22. The *Working People's Daily* is the government-owned successor to the old and vigorous *Nation,* once the chief critic of the government (in the days of Nu's leadership) and one of the most fiercely liberal newspapers in all Asia.

23. *The Guardian,* once the chief English-language competitor of the old *Nation,* differs not at all today in its editorial position from the other major English daily, the *Working People's Daily* (the very name of which is reminiscent of a main Peking paper but was probably not inspired by it).

24. See *The Guardian,* June 4, 1969.

25. *Working People's Daily,* June 3, 1969.

26. *Ibid.*, June 6, 1969.

27. See, for example, the *Mirror* for June 18, 1969, the *Working People's Daily* for June 15 and 17, and *Botataung* for June 15 and 17.

28. See the *Working People's Daily,* June 19, 1969.

29. See the report of Richard Harris ("U Nu says Burmese regime must go") in *The Times* (London) of August 30, 1969.

30. Quoted by Robert Stephens in *The Observer* (London), August 31, 1969.

31. For "U Nu's Challenge to Ne Win" ("Extracts from the declaration made by U Nu in London"), see the *Far Eastern Economic Review*, LXV, No. 36 (September 4, 1969), 605. See also my "A New Dimension" in the same issue, p. 604.

32. For many years the only significant Burmese memoir of the wartime years was Nu's own *Burma under the Japanese*, completed in 1946 and first published in English in 1954. A more comprehensive and impressive volume, however, is *Breakthrough in Burma, Memoirs of a Revolution, 1939–1946*, written by Dr. Ba Maw, Burma's wartime leader during the Japanese occupation. Published by the Yale University Press, Ba Maw's book appeared only in 1968 (having been completed two years earlier and smuggled out of Burma, its author being once again in prison for political reasons).

33. The author was residing in Burma during the 1959–60 electoral campaign and vote and knew only three or four persons who seriously predicted Nu's return to power as late as November 1959.

BIBLIOGRAPHY

The Bibliography is divided into three sections: Selected Works of U Nu, pp. 279–82; Other Books and Articles, pp. 282–90; and Interviews, pp. 290–91.

I. SELECTED WORKS OF U NU

A. Books

An Asian Speaks. Washington: Embassy of the Union of Burma [1955 ?]. Collected speeches of U Nu during his visit to the United States June 29–July 16, 1955.

Burma Looks Ahead. Rangoon: Ministry of Information, 1953. Collected speeches.

Burma under the Japanese. New York: St Martin's Press, 1954.

Forward with the People. Rangoon: Superintendent, Government Printing and Stationery, 1955. Collected speeches.

From Peace to Stability. Rangoon: Superintendent, Government Printing and Stationery, 1951. Collected speeches.

Ganda-layit. Rangoon: Red Dragon Book Club, n.d. In Burmese.

Man, the Wolf of Man. Rangoon: serialized in *The Guardian,* I (June–October 1954), II (November 1954–January 1955).

Modern Plays. Rangoon: Red Dragon Book Club, 1938. In Burmese.

The People Win Through. New York: Taplinger, 1957. This edition of Nu's plays includes a biographical introduction by Edward Hunter. First published by the Society for the Extension of Democratic Ideals, Rangoon, 1952.

"Pyidaungsu Niti, Guide for the People of the Union of Burma" (typescript), Rangoon, 1959. Collected speeches.

Towards Peace and Democracy. Rangoon: Superintendent, Government Printing and Stationery, 1949. Collected speeches.

Towards a Welfare State. Rangoon: Superintendent, Government Printing and Stationery, 1952. Collected speeches.

The Wages of Sin. Rangoon: Dho Ta Wun Press, 1961. Play.

B. Selected Speeches, Articles, Short Stories, and Letters

The official *Burma Weekly Bulletin* contains many other speeches by Nu, and both *The Nation* and *The Guardian* of Rangoon have also published some of Nu's speeches in their entirety. In addition, typescript copies of some of Nu's speeches are on deposit in the Defense Services Historical Research Institute, the Burma Translation Society, and the Social Sciences Library of Rangoon University, all in Rangoon.

"Address by Prime Minister U Nu in the Chamber of Deputies on March 13," *Burma Weekly Bulletin,* IX (March 23, 1961), 429–31, 435–36; IX (March 30, 1961) 440–43; and IX (April 6, 1961), 448–49.

"Address on the International Situation," *Burma Weekly Bulletin,* IX (September 29, 1960), 170–71, 174–76.

"The AFPFL and the Communists: Who Is Right?" (typescript), Rangoon, n.d. This 44-page document includes Nu's speech of November 1, 1946, on the expulsion of the Communists from the AFPFL. In Burmese.

"Asians and Democracy," *Burma Weekly Bulletin,* IX (October 24, 1960), 287, 291.

"Author's Preface," *Man, the Wolf of Man,* in *The Guardian,* I (June 1954), 9–14.

"Broadcast Burma Broadcasting Service September 26," *Burma Weekly Bulletin,* VII (October 2, 1958), 191.

"The Buddha," *The Guardian,* V (February 1958), 9–21.

"Buddhism after Buddha's Death," *The Guardian,* V (May 1958), 13–20.

"Burma's Neutral Foreign Policy," *Burma,* V (January 1955), 1–15.

"The Dhamma," *The Guardian,* V (March 1958), 9–20.

"Do It Now or Don't Do It at All," in *Burmese Affairs.* Edited by Maung Maung Myint. Rangoon: Red Dragon Book Club, n.d. In Burmese.

"Farewell Address in Peking," *Burma Weekly Bulletin,* IX (October 13, 1960), 195.

For World Peace and Progress. Rangoon, 1954.

The Government for the People. Rangoon: "Clean" AFPFL, 1959.

"I Am a Marxist," in *Communism and Dobama.* Edited by Thein Pe. Rangoon: Pyidawsoe Printing Works, 1954.

I Want to Bequeath a Legacy of Democracy. Rangoon: "Clean" AFPFL, 1959. In Burmese.

If You Want to Be a Front-Line Leader. Rangoon: "Clean" AFPFL, 1959. In Burmese.

KMT Aggression. Rangoon, 1953.

"Lecture on the 5 Precepts Delivered by the Hon'ble Prime Minister U Nu at the 6th Synod Great Cave on January 19," *Burma Weekly Bulletin,* VI (January 23, 1958), 346–51.

"On Human Affairs," *The Guardian,* III (September 1956), 25–28.

"On the Pin-Lone Conference," *The Burma Digest,* I (June 15, 1946), 13–14.

"An Open Letter to Principal Mr. D. J. Sloss, University College, Rangoon, from President U Nu," *New Burma,* XVI (February 26, 1936), 11, 14.

"Parliament and the Chinese-Burmese Boundary Treaty," *Burma Weekly Bulletin,* IX (December 15, 1960), 309–12, 316–17.

"P.M.'s Report to Parliament," *Burma Weekly Bulletin,* IX (August 24, 1961), 129–30, 136; IX (August 31, 1961), 141–44; IX (September 7, 1961), 147, 152; IX (September 14, 1961), 160; IX (September 21,

1961), 167; IX (September 28, 1961), 172; and IX (October 5, 1961), 180, 184.

"A Policy for Asia,"*Socialist Asia,* III (August 1954), 3–5.

"Political Ideology of AFPFL," *Burma Weekly Bulletin,* VI (February 6, 1958), 363–84.

Premier Reports to the People. Rangoon: Director of Information, 1957.

"Premier Reports to the People" (on the Sino-Burmese Boundary Treaty), *Burma Weekly Bulletin,* IX (January 12, 1961), 352–53.

"Premier's Address of Veneration (at Opening Ceremony of 6th Great Buddhist Synod)," *Burma Weekly Bulletin,* V (May 3, 1956), 28, 30, 32.

"Premier's Address on Resistance Day" (delivered in Rangoon on March 27, 1956), *Burma Weekly Bulletin,* V (April 5, 1956), 4–5.

Premier U Nu on the 4-Year Plan. Rangoon: Director of Information, 1957.

"Prime Minister's Report to the People," *Burma Weekly Bulletin,* IX (September 1, 1960), 137–44.

"A Program for Asia. Strengthening the Colonial Countries," *Socialist Call,* XXII (October 1954), 14–15.

"Promulgation of Buddhism as the State Religion" (Chamber of Deputies), *Burma Weekly Bulletin,* X (August 31, 1961), 137–40.

"Promulgation of Buddhism as the State Religion" (Chamber of Nationalities), *Burma Weekly Bulletin,* X (September 7, 1961), 148–52.

Pyidaungsu Policy. Rangoon: "Clean" AFPFL, 1960. In Burmese.

The Pyidaungsu Policy. Rangoon: "Clean" AFPFL, 1960. This publication, in English, is a different work from *Pyidaungsu Policy,* above.

Resurgence (Premier U Nu at Bandung). Rangoon: Director of Information, 1955.

"The Sangha," *The Guardian,* V (April 1958), 9–20.

"The Scourge" (Parts 1–3), *The Guardian,* III (January 1956), 9–11; Parts 4–7 (February 1956), 9–13. Short story.

Seven-Point Programme. Rangoon, 1958.

"The Socialist Reconstruction of Burma," *Socialist International Information,* III (1953), 649–52.

"Speech as Chancellor of the University of Rangoon, October 2, 1958," *Burma Weekly Bulletin,* VII (October 9, 1958), 197–99.

"Speech Delivered by the Hon'ble Prime Minister at the Mass Meeting at Bandoola Square on 27 February, 1949" (typescript), Rangoon, 1949.

"Speech Delivered by the Hon'ble Thakin Nu at the Inaugural Meeting of the Regional Autonomy Inquiry Commission: 20 October 1948" (typescript), Rangoon, 1948.

"Speech Delivered by Thakin Nu, President of the AFPFL, at a Mass Meeting BAA Ground on 13/6/48" (typescript), Rangoon, 1948.

"Speech of U Nu to Boycotters, Shwedagon Pagoda, March 3, 1936," *New Burma,* XVI (March 6, 1936), 14.

"Speech of U Nu at Letpadan, March 12, 1936," *New Burma,* XVI (March 18, 1936), 17.

"Speech of U Nu at Paungde, March 13, 1936," *New Burma,* XVII (March 20, 1936), 11.

"Speech of U Nu at Prome, March 13, 1936," *New Burma,* XVII (March 22, 1936), 17.

"Speech to Parliament, June 5, 1956" (Announcing His Decision Not to Stand for Re-election as Prime Minister), *Burma Weekly Bulletin,* V (June 7, 1956), 57–58.

Stages of Battle Against Oppression. Rangoon: "Clean" AFPFL, 1959. In Burmese.

"Statement by the Hon'ble Thakin Nu, President of the AFPFL, on Leftist Unity" (typescript), Rangoon: AFPFL, 1948.

"Statement of Policy, Chamber of Deputies, March 4, 1957," *Burma Weekly Bulletin,* V (March 7, 1957), 387–90.

Summary of the Hon'ble Prime Minister's Speech delivered in Parliament on 3rd October 1950 in Support of "Buddha Sasana Organization Act." Rangoon: Superintendent, Government Printing and Stationery, 1950.

"Summary of Speech by U Nu before the Supreme Council of the AFPFL (Clean) Delivered on September 26, 1959" (typescript), Rangoon: "Clean" AFPFL, 1959.

Towards a Socialist State. Rangoon: Director of Information, 1958.

Translation of the Speech delivered by the Hon'ble U Nu, Prime Minister of the Union of Burma, on "Martyrs' Day," the 19th of July 1958. Rangoon, 1958.

"U Nu's Broadcast on Sino-Burmese Boundary Question," *Burma Weekly Bulletin,* V (November 15, 1956), 255, 260.

"U Nu's Lecture on Buddhism at Peking University," *Burma Weekly Bulletin,* V (November 15, 1956), 256–58.

"U Nu's Letter to General Ne Win," *Burma Weekly Bulletin,* VII (October 2, 1958), 192.

Unite and March. Rangoon, 1955.

War and Its Consequences. Rangoon, 1954.

We Must Defend Democracy. Rangoon: "Clean" AFPFL, 1959. In Burmese.

"What Kind of Independence?," in *Communism and Dobama.* Edited by Thein Pe. Rangoon: Pyidawsoe Printing Works, 1954.

II. OTHER BOOKS AND ARTICLES

Official publications of the British and Burmese governments are listed in the alphabetical sequence by first word of title.

AFPFL Convention Brochure. Rangoon: Students Digest Press, 1947.

AFPFL Rules for Organization and Administration. Rangoon, 1958. In Burmese.

"Agreement between the Government of the Union of Burma and the Government of the People's Republic of China on Economic and Technical Cooperation," *Burma Weekly Bulletin,* IX (January 19, 1961), 359.

Allen, Robert L. "Burma's Clearing Account Agreements," *Pacific Affairs,* XXXI (June 1958), 147–63.

Andrus, J. Russell. *Burmese Economic Life.* Stanford, Calif.: Stanford University Press, 1948.

Anti-Fascist People's Freedom League. *The New Burma in the New World.* Rangoon: Nay Win Kyi Press, n.d.

Attlee, C. R. *As It Happened.* London: Heinemann, 1954.

Aung San. "Burma's Challenge" (mimeographed), Rangoon, 1946.

Badgley, John H. "Burma: the Nexus of Socialism and the Two Political Traditions," *Asian Survey,* III (February 1963), 89–95.

———. "Burma's Military Government: a Political Analysis," *Asian Survey,* II (August 1962), 24–31.

———. "Burma's Political Crisis," *Pacific Affairs,* XXXI (December 1958), 336–51.

———. *Survey of Burma's Foreign Economic Relations 1948–1958.* Rangoon: Rangoon-Hopkins Center for Southeast Asian Studies, Rangoon University, 1959.

Ba Maw. "The Making of a Revolution," *The Nation,* January 4, 1960.

———. "The Military Take-over in Burma," *The Nation,* March 9, 1962.

———. "U Nu Psychoanalyzed," *The Nation,* October 11, 1959.

Ba Swe. *The Burmese Revolution.* 2d ed. Rangoon: Pyidawsoe Printing Works, 1957.

———. "Party Organization," *Socialist Asia,* III (July 1954), 4–9.

Ba Than (Dhammika). *The Roots of the Revolution.* Rangoon: Defense Services Historical Research Institute, 1962.

Ba Tin. *On the Present Political Situation in Burma and Our Tasks* (Communist Party comments on Nu-Attlee Agreement and Party program). Rangoon, 1948.

Battered Burma. Calcutta: The Statesman, 1946.

Ba U. *My Burma.* New York: Taplinger, 1959.

Bigelow, Lee S. "The 1960 Election in Burma," *Far Eastern Survey,* XXIX (May 1960), 70–74.

"Boundary Treaty Between the Union of Burma and the People's Republic of China," *Burma Weekly Bulletin,* IX (October 13, 1960), 187–89.

A Brief Review of the Disturbances in Burma. Rangoon, 1949.

Brimmel, J. H. *Communism in South East Asia.* London: Oxford University Press, 1959.

Burma and the Insurrections. Rangoon, 1949.

Burma During the Japanese Occupation. 2 vols. Simla: Government of Burma, 1943–44.

Burma Gazetteer: "Myaungmya District," Vol. B, No. 13. Rangoon, 1912. *Idem,* 1924.

Burma Speaks. Rangoon, 1950.

Burma: Statement of Policy by His Majesty's Government, May 1945. Cmd. 6635. London: His Majesty's Stationery Office, 1945.

Burma's Fight for Freedom (Independence Commemoration). Rangoon [1948?].

Burma's Freedom: the First Anniversary. Rangoon: Director of Information, 1949.

Burma's Freedom: the Second Anniversary. Rangoon: Director of Information, 1950. From January 1951 this series was issued as the first issue each year of the quarterly *Burma.*

The Burmese Way to Socialism. Rangoon: Information Department, 1962.

Butwell, Richard. "Civilians and Soldiers in Burma," in *Studies on Asia, 1961.* Edited by Robert K. Sakai. Lincoln: University of Nebraska Press, 1961.

———. "The Four Failures of U Nu's Second Premiership," *Asian Survey,* II (March 1962), 3–11.

———. "The New Political Outlook in Burma," *Far Eastern Survey,* XXIX (February 1960), 21–27.

———. "The Sino-Burmese Border Truce," *The New Leader,* XLIII (February 29, 1960), 15–16.

———. "U Nu Returns to Power in Burma," *The New Leader,* XLIII (March 28, 1960), 9–10.

———. "Wandlungen und Kontinuität in sozialistischen Birma," *Europa Archiv,* XVII (September 25, 1962), 645–53.

Butwell, Richard, and Fred von der Mehden. "The 1960 Election in Burma," *Pacific Affairs,* XXXIII (June 1960), 144–57.

Cady, John F. *A History of Modern Burma.* Ithaca, N.Y.: Cornell University Press, 1958.

———. "Religion and Politics in Modern Burma," *Far Eastern Quarterly,* XIV (1953), 149–62.

———. "The Swing of the Pendulum." Supplement to *A History of Modern Burma.* Ithaca, N.Y.: Cornell University Press, 1960.

Christian, John L. *Modern Burma.* Berkeley: University of California Press, 1942.

Clubb, Oliver E., Jr. *The United States and the Sino-Soviet Bloc in Southeast Asia.* Washington: Brookings Institution, 1962.

Collis, Maurice. *Last and First in Burma.* London: Faber and Faber, 1956.

Conference Papers on Current Economic Problems of Burma 1951. Rangoon, 1951.

Constitution (Fourth Amendment) Act, 1961, *Burma Weekly Bulletin,* X (October 5, 1961), 181.

Constitution (Third Amendment) Act, 1961, *Burma Weekly Bulletin,* X (August 31, 1961), 144.

The Constitution of the Burma Socialist Programme Party. Rangoon: Director of Information, 1962.

The Constitution of the Union of Burma. Rangoon, 1948.

Crozier, Brian. *The Rebels: A Study of Post-War Insurrections.* Boston: Beacon Press, 1960.

Cruttwell, Patrick. *A Kind of Fighting.* New York: Macmillan, 1960.

Dagon Taya. *Portraits.* Rangoon: Gyanegyaw Mamale, 1955. In Burmese.

"Declaration of the Heads of State or Government of Non-Aligned Countries," *Burma Weekly Bulletin,* X (September 21, 1961), 162–63, and X (September 28, 1961), 174, 176.

Dhammantaraya. Rangoon, 1959.

Dupuy, Trevor. "Burma and Its Army; a Contrast in Motivations and Characteristics," *Antioch Review,* XX (Winter 1960–61), 428–40.

Education in Burma before Independence and after Independence. Rangoon, 1953.

Elsbree, Willard H. *Japan's Role in Southeast Asian Nationalist Movements 1940 to 1945.* Cambridge, Mass.: Harvard University Press, 1953.

"Extracts Vice-President's Preliminary Report for the Session 1935–36

(July 1935 to January 1936)," *New Burma,* XVI (February 14, 1936), 19–20.

Fifield, Russell H. *The Diplomacy of Southeast Asia: 1945–1958.* New York: Harper, 1958.

Final Report of the Riot Inquiry Committee. Rangoon: Superintendent, Printing and Supplies, 1939.

Foucar, E. C. V. *I Lived in Burma.* London: Dobson, 1956.

Francis, E. V. "Burma's Decade of Independence," *Political Quarterly,* XXIX (July 1958), 251–57.

Frontier Areas Committee of Enquiry. *Report Presented to H. M. Government in the United Kingdom and the Government of Burma.* Rangoon: Government Printing and Stationery Office, 1947.

Furnivall, J. S. *Colonial Policy and Practice.* Cambridge, Eng.: Cambridge University Press, 1957.

———. *The Governance of Modern Burma.* 2d rev. ed. New York: Institute of Pacific Relations, 1960. With supplement on the first Ne Win government by John Seabury Thomson.

———. *Introduction to the Political Economy of Burma.* Rangoon: People's Literature Committee and House, 1957.

———. "Twilight in Burma, Independence and After," *Pacific Affairs,* XXII (June 1949), 155–72.

———. "Twilight in Burma, Reconquest and Crisis," *Pacific Affairs,* XXII (March 1949), 3–20.

"General Ne Win's Letter to U Nu," *Burma Weekly Bulletin,* VII (October 2, 1958), 193.

Government in the Union of Burma, 1958 Nov.–1959 Feb. Rangoon, 1959.

Hagen, Everett E. *The Economic Development of Burma.* Washington, D.C.: National Planning Association, 1956.

Hanna, Willard A. "Re-revving a Revolution," *American Universities Field Staff Reports Service, Southeast Asia Series,* XI (January 24, 1963).

Hinton, Harold C. *China's Relations with Burma and Vietnam.* New York: Institute of Pacific Relations, 1958.

Htin Fatt. "The Consultative Conference," *New Burma Weekly,* I (July 26, 1958), 3–4.

———. "The Psychology of Fear or the Story Behind the AFPFL Split," *New Burma Weekly,* I (May 31, 1958), 2–3.

Interim Report of the Riot Inquiry Committee. Rangoon, 1939.

Is It a People's Liberation?: A Short Survey of the Communist Insurrection in Burma. Rangoon, 1952.

Is Trust Vindicated? Rangoon, 1960.

Johnson, John J., ed. *The Role of the Military in Underdeveloped Countries.* Princeton, N.J.: Princeton University Press, 1962.

Johnstone, William C. *Burma's Foreign Policy: A Study in Neutralism.* Cambridge, Mass.: Harvard University Press, 1963.

Johnstone, William C., and the Staff of the Rangoon-Hopkins Center for Southeast Asian Studies. *A Chronology of Burma's International Relations 1945–58.* Rangoon: Rangoon-Hopkins Center for Southeast Asian Studies, Rangoon University, 1959.

"Joint Press Communiqué (Burma and China)," *Burma Weekly Bulletin,*

V (November 15, 1956), 253. Issued by the Foreign Office in Rangoon on November 10.

Jones, F. C. *Japan's New Order in East Asia: Its Rise and Fall, 1937–1945.* London: Oxford University Press, 1954.

Karen Special Enquiry Commission. Rangoon, 1951.

The Karen Uprising in Burma. Rangoon: Directorate of Information, 1949.

Karnow, Stanley. "A Second Chance for U Nu," *The Reporter,* XXIV (March 30, 1961), 29–33.

King, Winston L. "New Forces in an Old Culture," *Antioch Review,* XXI (Summer 1961), 155–65.

Knappen-Tippetts-Abbett Engineering Co., associated with Pierce Management, Inc., and Robert R. Nathan Associates, Inc. *Preliminary Report on Economic and Engineering Survey of Burma.* Rangoon, 1952.

Knappen-Tippetts-Abbett-McCarthy, Engineers, in association with Pierce Management, Inc., and Robert R. Nathan Associates, Inc. "Comprehensive Report on Economic and Engineering Survey of Burma" (mimeographed), Rangoon, 1953.

Kozicki, Richard J. "The Sino-Burmese Frontier Problem," *Far Eastern Survey,* XXVI (March 1957), 33–38.

Kyaw Min. *The Burma We Love.* 2d ed. Calcutta: India Book House, 1945.

The Land Nationalization Act, 1948. Rangoon, 1948.

Law Yone, "A Hard Look at 'Mr. Tender,' " *The Nation,* March 2, 1957.

Lelyveld, Joseph. "New Calm in Burma," *The New Leader,* XLIII (October 3, 1960), 9–10.

Lockwood, Agnese N. *The Burma Road to Pyidawtha.* New York: Carnegie Endowment for International Peace, 1958.

Lowis, C. C. *Burma.* Rangoon, 1902. Part I: *Report* of *Census of India, 1901,* Vol. XII.

"Manifesto Issued by Publicity Bureau Boycotters' Council," *New Burma,* XVI (March 1 and 4, 1936), 14 and 16–17.

Mansergh, Nicholas. *The Commonwealth and the Nations.* London: Royal Institute of International Affairs, 1948.

Maung Maung, Dr. "The Burma-China Border Settlement," *Asian Survey,* I (March 1961), 38–43.

———. *Burma in the Family of Nations.* Amsterdam: Djambatan, 1956.

———. *Burma's Constitution.* The Hague: Martinus Nijhoff, 1959.

———. "Dr. E Maung," *The Guardian,* IV (March 1957), 25–30.

———. *Grim War Against KMT.* Rangoon: Nu Yin Press, 1953.

———. "M. A. Raschid," *The Guardian,* III (December 1956), 27–34.

———. "New Hope with U Nu," *The Guardian,* VII (August 1960), 13–14.

———. "Portrait of the Burmese Parliament," *Parliamentary Affairs,* X (Spring 1957), 204–9.

———. "Thakin Than Tun," *The Guardian,* III (October 1956), 33–36.

———. "U Ba Swe," *The Guardian,* III (March 1956), 27–31.

———. "U Hla Maung," *The Guardian,* II (July 1955), 9–15.

———. "U Kyaw Nyein," *The Guardian,* II (March 1955), 9–19.

——. "U Thant," *The Guardian,* III (August 1956), 25–29.

Maung Pye. *Burma in the Crucible.* Rangoon: Khittaya Publishing House, 1951.

Mende, Tibor. *South-East Asia between Two Worlds.* London: Turnstile Press, 1955.

Mendelson, E. Michael. "Religion and Authority in Modern Burma," *The World Today,* XVI (March 1960), 110–18.

Morrison, Ian. *Grandfather Longlegs.* London: Faber and Faber, 1947.

Mountbatten, Admiral Lord Louis. *Report to the Combined Chiefs of Staff by the Supreme Allied Commander, South-east Asia, 1943–45.* London: His Majesty's Stationery Office, 1951.

The National Ideology and the Role of the Defence Services. 3d ed. Rangoon: Ministry of Defense, 1960.

The New Burma; a Report from the Government to the People of Burma. Rangoon, 1954.

The Nine Months After the Ten Years. Rangoon: Ministry of Information, 1959.

Panikkar, K. M. *In Two Chinas.* London: Allen and Unwin, 1959.

Parliament (Constituent Assembly) Proceedings. Rangoon. In Burmese.

Parliamentary Proceedings, Chamber of Deputies. Rangoon. In Burmese.

Policy and Program of the "Clean" AFPFL. Rangoon: "Clean" AFPFL [1959?]. In Burmese.

"The Political Evolution of Burma" (mimeographed), London: Empire Information Service, Central Office of Information, 1947.

Pu Galay. *Thakin Nu's Revolution.* Rangoon: Daw Tin Ye, 1949. In Burmese.

Pye, Lucian W. *Politics, Personality, and Nation Building: Burma's Search for Identity.* New Haven, Conn.: Yale University Press, 1962.

The Pyidawtha Conference, August 4–17, 1952: Resolutions and Speeches. Rangoon, 1952.

Pyidawtha, the New Burma. Rangoon: Economic and Social Board, 1954.

"Rangoon University Boycotters' Demands," *New Burma,* XVI (March 1, 1936), 18.

Rau, Santha Rama. "Peace, Rice, Friendship, and the Burma of U Nu," *The Reporter,* XIV (April 19, 1956), 18–22.

Report of the First Asian Socialist Conference (Rangoon, 1953). Rangoon: Burmese Advertising Press, 1953.

Report of the Industrial Development Committee on Industrial Policy. Rangoon, 1949.

"Report of the Public Service Enquiry Commission," *Burma Weekly Bulletin,* X (June 22, 1961), 60–61, and X (June 29, 1961), 70, 72.

Report of the Regional Autonomy Enquiry Commission. Rangoon, 1951.

Report of the Tantabin Incident Enquiry Committee. Rangoon, 1947.

Rose, Jerry A. "Burma and the Balance of Neutralism," *The Reporter,* XXVIII (Jan. 3, 1963), 24–25, 28–29.

Rose, Saul. *Britain and South-East Asia.* Baltimore: The Johns Hopkins Press, 1962.

——. *Socialism in Southern Asia.* London: Oxford University Press, 1959.

Rose, Saul, ed. *Politics in Southern Asia.* New York: St Martin's Press, 1963.

Sarkisyanz, Manuel. "On the Place of U Nu's Buddhist Socialism in Burma's History of Ideas," in *Studies on Asia, 1961.* Edited by Robert K. Sakai. Lincoln: University of Nebraska Press, 1961.

Second Four-Year Plan for the Union of Burma (1961–62 to 1964–65). Rangoon, 1961.

Sein Win. "The Peasant Problem," *Far Eastern Economic Review,* XXVIII (March 17, 1960), 598–600.

———. *The Split Story.* Rangoon: *The Guardian,* 1959.

Silverstein, Josef. "Burma," in *Governments and Politics of Southeast Asia.* Edited by George McT. Kahin. Ithaca, N.Y.: Cornell University Press, 1959.

Singer, Herman. "U Nu on Socialism in Asia, an Interview with Burma's Prime Minister," *Socialist Call,* XXIII (July–August 1955), 16–17.

Soe Maung. *Premier Nu.* Rangoon: Djambatan Ltd. Publishing House, 1956. In Burmese.

Tha Hla. "The 1936 Rangoon University Strike," Part I, *New Burma Weekly,* I (June 21, 1958), 7–10. Part II appears in *ibid.* (June 28, 1958), 12–14; Part III, *ibid.* (July 5, 1958), 12–14; Part IV, *ibid.* (July 19, 1958), 11–14; Part V, *ibid.* (July 26, 1958), 7–10; and conclusion, *ibid.* (August 2, 1958), 11–13.

Than Tun. "Speech Made Before the Second Congress of the Communist Party of India," *People's Age,* VI (March 14, 1948).

———. "Statement on Behalf of the Burma Communist Party," *The Burman,* December 19, 1947.

Thant. "Some Reflections on Burma's Foreign Policy," *The Guardian,* VIII (September 1961), 12–15.

Thein Pe. *Memoirs.* Rangoon: Taing Chit Publishing House, n.d. In Burmese. The author of this book is not to be confused with the younger Thein Pe (Myint).

Thein Pe Myint. *Everything's All Right, Sir, and Other Short Stories.* Rangoon: True Literature Publishing House [1952?]. In Burmese. This reissue of a work first published in 1937 includes two Forewords written by U Nu (in 1937 and 1952).

———. *Political Experiences.* Rangoon: Shwe Pyi Tan Publishing House, 1956. In Burmese.

———. *Student Boycotter.* 2 vols. Rangoon: Red Dragon Book Club, 1938. In Burmese. 2d ed. 1961.

———. *What Happened in Burma.* Allahabad: Kitabistan, 1943.

Thomson, John S. "Burma: A Neutral in China's Shadow," *Review of Politics,* XIX (July 1957), 330–50.

———. "Marxism in Burma," in *Marxism in Southeast Asia.* Edited by Frank N. Trager. Stanford, Calif.: Stanford University Press, 1959.

Time. August 30, 1954, 19–27. Cover story on U Nu.

Tin, Thakin. "New Era for Peasants," *Burma,* III (July 1953), 37–45.

Tin Aung. "Burma's Political Wingaba," *The Guardian,* V (October 1958), 21–26.

Tinker, Hugh. "Burma's Northeast Borderland Problems," *Pacific Affairs,* XXIX (December 1956), 324–46.

———. "Nu, the Serene Statesman," *Pacific Affairs,* XXX (June 1957), 120–37.

———. "The Politics of Burma," in *Politics in Southern Asia.* Edited by Saul Rose. New York: St Martin's Press, 1963.

———. *The Union of Burma.* 3d ed. London: Oxford University Press, 1961.

Tin Tin Shwe. "Barter and All That: Foreign Trade Trends 1947–1960," *Far Eastern Economic Review,* XXVIII (March 17, 1960), 573–79.

"Trade Agreement between the Government of the Union of Burma and the Government of the People's Republic of China," *Burma Weekly Bulletin,* IX (February 9, 1961), 383.

Trager, Frank N. *Building a Welfare State in Burma.* New York: Institute of Pacific Relations, 1958.

———. "Burma: Ten Years of Independence: Retrospect and Prospect," *The Guardian,* V (January 1958), 9–16.

———. "Burma's Foreign Policy, 1948–56: Neutralism, Third Force, and Rice," *Journal of Asian Studies,* XVI (November 1956), 89–102.

———. *Burma's Role in the United Nations, 1948–1955.* New York: Institute of Pacific Relations, 1956.

———. "The New Temper of Burmese Politics," *Foreign Policy Bulletin,* XXXVII (August 15, 1958), 177–79, 182.

———. "Our Visitor from Burma," *The New Leader,* XXXVIII (July 4, 1955), 8–11.

———. "Political Divorce in Burma," *Foreign Affairs,* XXXVII (January 1959), 317–27.

———. "The Political Split in Burma," *Far Eastern Survey,* XXVII (October 1958), 145–55.

Trager, Frank N., and associates. *Burma.* New Haven, Conn.: Human Relations Area Files, 1956.

Trager, Frank N., and Hla Maung. "Burma," *The Guardian,* III (August 1956), 39–41.

"Translation of the Joint Communiqué of the Premier of the State Council of the People's Republic of China and the Prime Minister of the Union of Burma," *Burma Weekly Bulletin,* IX (April 27, 1961), 461–62.

Tun Pe. *Sun Over Burma.* Rangoon: Rasika Ranjani Press, 1949.

———. *Why I Resign from the Cabinet?* Rangoon: the Daily Herald Press, n.d.

Two-Year Plan for Economic Development for Burma. Rangoon, 1948.

"U Nu as a Writer." *Myawaddy,* IV (January 1956), 4–8. In Burmese. The author is Thein Pe Myint, but the article was unsigned.

von der Mehden, Fred R. "Buddhism and Politics in Burma," *Antioch Review,* XXI (Summer 1961), 166–75.

———. " 'The Burmese Way to Socialism,' " *Asian Survey,* III (March 1963), 129–35.

———. "The Changing Pattern of Religion and Politics in Burma," in *Studies on Asia.* Edited by Robert K. Sakai. Lincoln: University of Nebraska Press, 1961.

Walinsky, Louis J. *Economic Development in Burma 1951–1960*. New York: The Twentieth Century Fund, 1962.

Webb, C. Morgan. *Burma, Census of India, 1911,* Vol. IX. Part I: *Report;* Part II: *Tables*. Rangoon, 1912.

Whittam, Daphne E. "The Sino-Burmese Boundary Treaty," *Pacific Affairs,* XXXIV (Summer 1961), 174–83.

Win Pe. "Foreign Investment—a New Climate," *Far Eastern Economic Review,* XXVIII (March 17, 1960), 585–87.

Wolfstone, Daniel. "The Burmese Army Experiment," *Far Eastern Economic Review,* XXVIII (February 18, 1960), 352, 356–59.

———. "Burma's Honeymoon with China," *Far Eastern Economic Review,* XXXIII (August 24, 1961), 353–55.

———. "The Phongyis and the Soldiers," *Far Eastern Economic Review,* XXXIII (August 17, 1961), 322–23.

Woodman, Dorothy. *The Making of Burma*. London: Cresset Press, 1962.

Yangoon Ba Swe. *Actor Ko Gyi Kyaung*. Rangoon: Maung Tun Shwe, 1959. In Burmese.

III. INTERVIEWS

Attlee, Lord. Oxford, May 20, 1960.

Aye Hlaing. Rangoon, January 18, 1960.

Ba Lwin. Rangoon, October 30, 1959.

Ba Maw. Rangoon, August 14, 1959, April 19, 1960, and August 3, 1962.

Ba Nyunt. Rangoon, January 19, 1960, and January 21, 1960.

Barrington, James. Rangoon, March 31, 1960.

Ba Sein. Rangoon, February 23, 1960.

Ba Swe. Rangoon, March 30, 1960.

Ba Thaung. Rangoon, March 30, 1960.

Ba U. Rangoon, February 17, 1960.

Collis, Maurice. Maidenhead, England, May 15, 1960.

Daniels, C. E. W. Rangoon, January 21, 1960.

Das, C. N. Rangoon, July 29, 1959.

E Maung. Rangoon, January 13, 1960.

Furnivall, J. S. Rangoon, July 31, 1959.

Hall, D. G. E. London, May 25, 1960.

Harvey, G. E. Oxford, May 14, 1960.

Hla Gyi. Rangoon, November 2, 1959, and January 6, 1960.

Hla Maung. Rangoon, January 25, 1960.

Hla Pe (University of London). London, May 25, 1960.

Hla Pe (Thakin) (Bo Let Ya). Rangoon, January 5, 1960.

Hmu Aung. Rangoon, March 5, 1960.

Kodaw Hmaing. Rangoon, December 3, 1959.

Kyaw Min. Rangoon, January 26, 1960.

Kyaw Nyein. Rangoon, March 8, 1960.

Kyaw Thet. Rangoon, November 19, 1959.

Kyaw Tun. Rangoon, February 27, 1960.

Kyaw Yin. Rangoon, December 1, 1959.

Law Yone. Rangoon, December 2, 1959, and March 2, 1960.
Let Ya (Bo). Rangoon, January 5, 1960.
Maung Maung (Dr.). Rangoon, February 17, 1960.
Maung Maung (Colonel). Rangoon, April 19, 1960.
Min Gaung. Rangoon, March 30, 1960.
Mya Sein. Rangoon, August 25, 1959.
Myint Thein. Rangoon, February 24, 1960.
Myo Min. Rangoon, September 3, 1959.
Nehru, Jawaharlal. New Delhi, March 23, 1960.
Nyo Mya. Rangoon, September 15, 1959.
Nu. Rangoon, September 29, 1959, and April 19, 1960.
Ohn Khin. Rangoon, January 22, 1960.
Ong Gine. Rangoon, January 21, 1960.
Peacock, D. H. Cambridge, June 3, 1960.
Pearn, B. R. London, May 25, 1960.
Rance, Sir Hubert. Rugby, England, May 23, 1960.
Raschid, M. A. Rangoon, Sept. 16, 1959, and March 31, 1960.
Rose, Saul. Oxford, May 26, 1960.
San Htwa. Rangoon, January 5, 1960.
Saya Hein. Rangoon, January 6, 1960.
Sarkisyanz, Manuel. Rangoon, October 30, 1959.
Sein Win. Rangoon, September 17, 1959.
Sloss, D. J. Oxford, May 13, 1960.
Tha Hla. Rangoon, September 3, 1959.
Thein Han. Rangoon, February 5, 1960.
Thein Maung. Rangoon, February 4, 1960.
Thein Pe Myint. Rangoon, November 13, 1959.
Thin Kyi. Rangoon, January 19, 1960, and February 23, 1960.
Tin (Myanaung). Rangoon, December 15, 1959.
Tin (Thakin). Rangoon, March 2, 1960.
Thant. New York, September 9, 1960.
Tinker, Hugh. London, May 18, 1960; Oxford, December 29, 1961.
Tun Win. Rangoon, November 2, 1959.
Whittam, Daphne E. New York, September 9, 1960.
Win. Rangoon, April 1, 1960.
Win Pe. Rangoon, January 22, 1960.

There were others with whom the author talked in 1959–60 and again in 1962 who asked not to be identified.

IV. SUPPLEMENTARY BIBLIOGRAPHY

This addition to the Bibliography first published in 1963 comprises two parts: new works covering all or part of the period treated in the original text and other works dealing wholly or in part with the subject matter of Chapter 20, which is an addition to the original text.

A. Chapters 1–19

Ba Maw. *Breakthrough in Burma: Memoirs of a Revolution, 1939–1946.* New Haven: Yale University Press, 1968.

Htin Aung. *A History of Burma.* New York: Columbia University Press, 1967.

Guyot, James F. "Bureaucratic Transformation in Burma," in Ralph Braibanti, ed., *Asian Bureaucratic Systems Emergent from the British Imperial Tradition.* Durham, N.C.: Duke University Press, 1966.

Sarkisyanz, E. *Buddhist Backgrounds of the Burmese Revolution.* The Hague: Martinus Nijhoff, 1965.

Smith, Donald E. *Religion and Politics in Burma.* Princeton: Princeton University Press, 1965.

B. Chapter 20

Badgley, John H. "Burma: The Nexus of Socialism and Two Political Traditions," *Asian Survey,* III (February 1963), 89–95.

———. "Burma's China Crisis: The Choices Ahead," *Asian Survey,* VII (November 1967), 753–61.

———. "Burma's Zealot Wingyis: Maoists and St. Simonists," *Asian Survey,* V (January 1965), 55–62.

Banerji, S. C. "Pressing On," *Far Eastern Economic Review,* LXIV (January 16, 1969), 92.

Butwell, Richard. "Burma," in Amry Vandenbosch and Richard Butwell, *The Changing Face of Southeast Asia.* Lexington: University of Kentucky Press, 1966.

———. "Burma Doesn't Want Aid." *The New Republic,* September 3, 1966, pp. 14-15.

———. "Go-It-Alone Burma Is Mending Its U.S. Fences," *The Outlook* section, *The Washington Post,* September 4, 1966.

———. "A New Dimension," *Far Eastern Economic Review,* LXV (September 4, 1969), 604.

———. "Ne Win: Burma's Strong Man," *Christian Science Monitor,* September 2, 1966.

———. "The Tiger's Tail," *Far Eastern Economic Review.* LIII (September 1, 1966), 401–5.

Cady, John F. "Burma's Military Dictatorship," *Asian Studies* (Quezon City, the Philippines), III (December 1965), 409–16.

Davies, Derek. "A Nu Challenge?", *Far Eastern Economic Review,* LXV (August 21, 1969), 444.

———. "What's New, U Nu?", *Far Eastern Economic Review,* LXV (August 28, 1969), 530–32.

Forward (main periodical issued by the Ministry of Information, Government of Burma, Rangoon).

Holmes, Robert A. "Burmese Domestic Policy: Politics of Burmanization," *Asian Survey,* VII (March 1967), 188–97.

Lelyveld, Joseph. "Mandalay Must Not Become Indianapolis," *New York Times Magazine,* January 5, 1969, pp. 30–31, 76, 78–79.

Mya Myaung. "Cultural Values and Economic Change in Burma," *Asian Survey*, IV (March 1964), 757–63.

Nu, U. "Proposal Advising Immediate Formation of a National Government," *The Working People's Daily*, June 5, 1969.

"Pilgrim's Progress," *Far Eastern Economic Review*, LXIV (May 15, 1969), 374.

Polsky, Anthony. "Threatening Command," *Far Eastern Economic Review*, LXIII (September 26, 1968), 605–6.

"Report of the National Unity Advisory Board," *The Guardian* (daily), June 3–8, 1969. This document also appears in *The Working People's Daily* for the same dates.

"Riding the Tiger," *Far Eastern Economic Review*, LXIV (February 20, 1969), 311.

Silverstein, Josef. "First Steps in the Burmese Way to Socialism," *Asian Survey*, IV (February 1964), 716–22.

———. "From Democracy to Dictatorship in Burma," *Current History*, XXXXVI (February 1964), 83–88.

———. "Military Rule in Burma," *Current History*, LII (January 1967), 41–47.

———. "Ne Win's Revolution Reconsidered," *Asian Survey*, VI (February 1966), 85–102.

———. "Problems in Burma: Economic, Political, and Diplomatic," *Asian Survey*, VII (February 1967), 117–25.

The Burmese Way to Socialism. Rangoon: The Revolutionary Council (Government of Burma), April 30, 1962.

The Constitution of the Burma Socialist Programme Party. Rangoon, 1962.

The Guardian (Burma's only English-language monthly magazine).

The System of Correlation of Man and His Environment, The Philosophy of the Burma Socialist Programme Party. Rangoon: Ministry of Information, 1963.

Trager, Frank N. *Burma: From Kingdom to Republic*. New York: Praeger, 1966.

———. "Burma: 1967—A Better Ending Than Beginning," *Asian Survey*, VIII (February 1968), 110–19.

———. "Burma: 1968—A New Beginning," *Asian Survey*. IX (February 1969), 104–14.

———. "The Failure of U Nu and the Return of the Armed Forces in Burma," *Review of Politics*, XXV (July 1963), 309–28.

"U Nu's Challenge to Ne Win" ("Extracts from the declaration made by U Nu in London"), *Far Eastern Economic Review*, LXV (September 4, 1969), 605.

von der Mehden, Fred R. "The Burmese Way to Socialism," *Asian Survey*, III (March 1963), 129–35.

Walinsky, Louis J. "The Rise and Fall of U Nu," *Pacific Affairs*, XXXVIII (1965/66), 269–81.

INDEX

Administration: in efficiency, 119–20, 126, 245; structure, 128–30; aims, 138; Nu's interference with, 141–42, 144; effect of AFPFL split, 166; under Ne Win, 209, 212; during Nu's second Premiership, 229–31, 243

Advisory Committee of Elder Statesmen, 230, 234

Agricultural and Rural Development Corporation, 113, 116

Agriculture: during Nu's first Premiership, 111–14, 118–19; Thakin Tin as minister, 132, 151, 154; during Nu's second Premiership, 228; under the Revolutionary Council, 248

Alaungpaya, King, 67

All-Burma Peasants Organization: founding, 29; within the AFPFL, 49, 147–48; rivalry, 152, 162–63, 166; under Tin's leadership, 154–55, 200, 233; and the "Clean" AFPFL, 217

All-Burma Student Movement, 22

All-Burma Trade Union Congress, 29

All-Burma Youth League, 14–15, 27, 147

Amnesties, 98, 201–3, 228

Anti-Fascist People's Freedom League: early days, 42–43, 45, 94; rise to power, 48–55, 106, 138–39; Executive Council, 50–54, 57, 129–34, 141, 147, 153–54, 157–61 *passim*, 164, 191, 212; Supreme Council, 53, 101, 147, 164, 166; the 1947 assassinations, 57; opposition to, 62, 96, 111; 1958 national congress, 27–28, 74, 116, 149–50, 160–62; Nu's efforts to unify, 87–94 *passim*, 96–101 *passim*, 108, 135–36; organization and administration, 146–

52, 161–62, 166, 212; the 1958 split and after, 149, 156–70, 173, 201, 203, 213, 217, 219, 233, 239

Anti-Fascist Organization, 39, 43–44, 46–48, 150

Anti-Indian riots of 1938, 29

Arab countries, 188, 191, 239, 257

Arakanese, 44, 95, 105, 167–69, 261; statehood, 202, 219, 222, 227, 231

Arakanese National United Organization, 139, 146, 167–69, 207, 229

Army: under British rule, 47, 93; Nu's leftist unity plan, 100, 103; during the rebellions, 106–7; Nu's 1949 government, 136, 163, 183; the 1958 AFPFL split, 167–68; Kuomintang irregulars, 181, 236; during the first *coup*, 202–6; during Ne Win administration, 209–12, 214, 218, 221–23, 228–29, 256; and state religion, 225; attitude toward Nu's government, 231–32, 244–48; the second *coup*, 240–41, 251

Asian Socialist Conference, 151

Asian Socialist Organization, 192

Assassinations of 1947, 55–58

Astrology, 3, 71, 88, 94, 160, 234

Attlee, Clement, 53, 63, 92–93

Aung Bohmu, 252

Aung Gyi, Brigadier, 91, 106, 205–7, 212, 218, 229, 240, 258

Aung San: early political career, 17–18, 27–33 *passim*; 1936 students' strike, 20–25; as Army and AFPFL leader, 36–40, 47–55, 84, 149; assassination, 55–58, 61, 213; political legacy, 89–91, 95–96, 107, 155–56, 244–45

Aung San–Attlee Agreement, 53, 55, 92

Aung Shwe, Brigadier, 232